FOOTBALL
TECHNIQUES IN
PICTURES

Michael Brown

Book Consultant:

Dwight Hollier

Team captain and four-year starter,
University of North Carolina at Chapel Hill
Academic All-Atlantic Coast Conference, 1990 & 1991
Linebacker for the Miami Dolphins

A Perigee Book

Perigee Books
are published by
The Berkley Publishing Group
200 Madison Avenue
New York, NY 10016

Library of Congress Cataloging-in-Publication Data

Brown, Michael, date.
    Football techniques in pictures / by Michael Brown.
        p.   cm.
    ISBN 0-399-51769-3
    1. Football. I. Title.
GV951.B876 1992   92-17124 CIP
796.332—dc20

Cover design by Lisa Amoroso

Front cover photograph © by Brian Drake/Sports/Chrome
East-West

Printed in the United States of America
3 4 5 6 7 8 9 10

CONTENTS

1. Introduction

Football's a great game at any level—the pros, college, high school, or peewee league—and few activities are as challenging and rewarding as a team sport when you practice hard and play to win. You'll have lots of fun, whether you're going out for the team for the first time or have been playing awhile and are making an effort to improve your basic moves.

This book is designed to help young, novice players and youth coaches. Fans and parents should also find our descriptions useful. We've limited our instructions here to the techniques you use as an individual player. For instance, we describe a few elementary techniques for blocking, but don't go into specific tactics used on the offensive line, or overall strategy. The basic building blocks of the game that we describe are used by veteran players in every game they play and have become second nature to them. Your coach can tell you what formations and plays he wants run; this book will tell you what he means when he says, "Pull and block the linebacker."

Mastering the basics will help you play better and enjoy the game more. We hope the time you spend practicing the techniques in this book gives you an advantage on the field and increases your enjoyment of the most popular sport in the United States.

First we cover the proper fit of equipment and stretching and conditioning exercises, and then move on to discuss the techniques used by players in specific positions. We provide an overview of blocking, tackling, ball carrying, throwing, catching, and kicking. Each skill or technique is discussed step by step from starting stance to the finish of the play.

"Know your enemy" is the guiding principle behind the organization of this book. Middle linebackers should be just as interested in the moves and techniques of running backs as they are in their own. The center should learn all he can about the noseguard's bag of tricks. The defensive secondary and the receivers should constantly try to put themselves in each other's shoes.

For this reason, we've grouped skills and techniques together that normally meet head-to-head. Offensive versus defensive line; runnning backs versus linebackers; quarterback right in the middle of the book (where else?); and receivers versus the defensive secondary. The kicking game is discussed at the end, since most drives usually conclude with some form of kick.

When you hit the field, you must be mentally and physically prepared so you can be proud of your own effort and support your teammates' efforts. You must understand the techniques of the game and have the strength and endurance to perform them. If you commit yourself to these goals, you can have a great time playing at any level—from the most elementary to the most sophisticated, no matter what your age or physical ability.

Nevertheless, you'll have to learn and practice the many skills and techniques football involves. Many of these techniques are unique to football and to be executed effectively they must be done in very specific ways. You should work hard to execute them perfectly during practice. Of course, in a real game with a real opponent in your face it is hard to execute anything perfectly. This is all the more reason to practice good habits and proper techniques—so they will become instincts to call on during the game.

Football takes courage, not brutality. You'll probably pick up a few lumps and bruises—that's just the way it is. That prospect might bother you, but if you have to screw up your courage every time you go out there, don't worry about it. Courage is one of those things like strength or coordination—the more you use it, the more of it you develop over time.

Few sports call for more grace, physical power, and timing than football—you needn't be the biggest bruiser out there to succeed. Especially at the beginning level, desire is the most necessary quality in a player. You have to really want to do it. Then learn how to tackle and block; learn the fundamentals and your skill and confidence will grow as your doubts and fears shrink. Good football players are made, not born.

Don't forget, *everyone*, including today's pro stars, began as a young and inexperienced player. You don't have to be Lawrence Taylor. This is a team sport, and you and your teammates are in it together. It's your collective toughness—and smarts—that matters. Be dedicated and work hard; that's the most you can ask of yourself. And remember, your first priority is to have fun.

Naturally, it's more fun to win than to lose, and to win you need aggressiveness and competitiveness. But the most important and productive kind of competition is the kind you wage with yourself to improve your skills. You should always strive to be the best at your position on the team, and unless you are Lawrence Taylor, there's always room for improvement. But set reasonable, obtainable goals for yourself and your team and always keep foremost not winning and losing but the drive to improve, excel, and have fun as an athlete.

What Position Is Right for You?

Try not to worry too much about your natural physical attributes—or lack of them. Your height is your height, your limbs are the length they are, and you can only stretch your physical type so much. But you can build up endurance and strength, which make you tougher by the day. While sports history provides some wild exceptions, your basic physical type may tend to push you toward playing certain positions. It shouldn't, however, box you in! You and your coach should experiment together, as the seasons progress, to find the places that use your talents to their utmost and provide you the most satisfaction. Be open-minded—don't become preoccupied with playing only one position. This isn't pro ball—you'll get to try out various positions without getting locked in for your career! There will be more than one occasion when a team member is injured or ill and you have to fill in for him. This could be your chance to be a hero!

Whatever basic physical and mental abilities you bring to your first practice, remember: The two things that will determine your chance of success are (1) genuine desire and determination, and (2) genuine team spirit. Football also demands incredible amounts of teamwork. Whatever your abilities, this means that in some ways you must be selfless, to put the good of the team above your own desires and ambitions.

2. Fitness and Safety

Equipment

Don't let anyone kid you, football is a rough game. Its "violent" nature, however, is often exaggerated. As a young football player, you are far more likely to be seriously injured in a bicycle mishap or an auto accident than on the football field. Still, caution on any playing field is a must, and this includes safety precautions for every practice or game.

To prevent injuries on the football field, certain equipment—including helmet, shoes, clothing, and pads—is essential. This equipment must fit correctly, be used properly, and be in good repair.

THE HELMET

This is the most important piece of equipment. Make sure your helmet fits snugly at the front, back, and top of your head. It should not be painful to wear, but if it's totally comfortable, it is probably too large, which is dangerous. Just because your helmet is easy to slip on and off doesn't mean it fits right.

The purpose of your helmet is to absorb the impact of a blow or fall before it reaches your skull. If your helmet is too large and your head has room to bounce around inside, it will take a lot of the impact and can easily be injured. A helmet that is too large also can't protect the back of your neck properly or keep your face guard in place: you could end up with a broken nose or cheekbone. Your cheek guards should snugly hold the jaw. Make sure your cheek pads are thick enough and not hardened or worn out. When your chin strap is fastened correctly, your chin should rest in the center of the cup. Your head should contact the crown suspension strap just above your brow.

If your helmet is too tight, you'll find it irritating and it will give you headaches—especially if you get hit. By the way, your helmet should carry the imprint of the National Operating Committee on Standards for Athletic Equipment (N.O.C.S.A.E). That standard insures that it has been tested and found to be sturdy enough to protect your head and face.

PADS

Padding is also important. Like your helmet, all the pads on every part of your body should fit snugly. After enough use, pads wear our. They lost their elasticity and will no longer absorb shock or stay in place. Once they've reached this point, don't try to get one more season out of them.

Check your shoulder pads. If they're too small, your shoulder can be badly bruised, or even separated—a painful injury that can keep you off the field for a good while. If your shoulder pads are too tight around the neck, you could end up with a pinched nerve. Shoulder pads that are too large don't protect your neck and slide around on your shoulders, leaving them vulnerable in places.

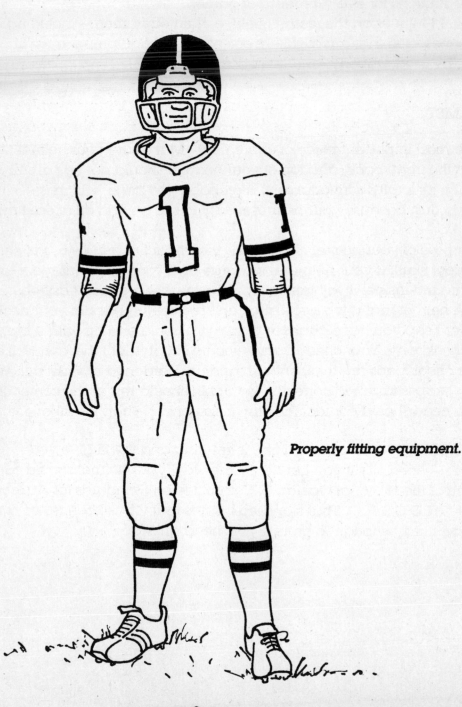

Properly fitting equipment.

Here are a few things to check for:

- make sure your shoulder pads extend just beyond the edge of your shoulders;
- the chest arches on the shoulder pads should not extend too far in front;
- shoulder pads should not ride too high, seeming to swallow up your neck.

Extend your arms over your head and make sure your pads continue to fit snugly at the neck and don't bunch up or dislodge.

Make sure every layer of material in the pad is intact. A cracked, worn-out pad offers little protection.

SHOES

When you're wearing shoes that fit well, your weight will be evenly distributed over the cleated area. Check your shoes from time to time to make sure they're wearing evenly. Signs of uneven wear—for instance, a few cleats wearing down more than all the others—are signs of improper fit and instability. If the upper droops over the sole, the shoes are too narrow for the foot that's been wearing them.

CLOTHING

Don't wear a jersey that's too big and loose. Your jersey should fit close to your body. However, you should have enough loose material to tuck into your pants, which helps hold your shoulder pads down. If your shirt won't stay tucked in, you could end up with exposed skin and a grass burn. Some jerseys are not made to tuck, but should cover the abdomen.

PANTS AND LOWER BODY PADS

Pants should be snug enough to hold the thigh and knee pads in place. If they're either too small or big, they won't hold the pads where they're needed for protection. Don't ever leave out your hip and tail pads "just this once." These pads should always be in place for every play or practice. Make sure the hip pads cover each hipbone and the lower spine and that the knee pads stay in front and cover the knee cap. Be certain that the thigh pads can't slide.

Flexibility

A pulled or torn muscle or ligament can keep you out of more than one game. But you can prevent most pulled muscles by always warming up and stretching before taking to the field for play or practice. Don't injure or tire yourself during the warm-up; just get those muscles warm so they're supple enough to take the hard work ahead. To start off, jog lightly around the field. Immediately afterward, do some muscle stretches. Finally, a few more rigorous calisthenics. After all this, you should be good and warm and ready to go out without damaging your muscles.

STRETCHES

Stretches are for loosening, not conditioning. Keep them simple and start slow. For example, when doing toe touches, don't go all the way to the toe on the first bend. Repeat each stretch a few times until you can make it all the way down. When the stretch has been pushed as far as possible on each rep, you'll feel a slight burning sensation—hold it here a few seconds. Don't take it to the point of searing pain and never use a bouncing motion. Your coach should observe and oversee the stretching to make sure than the right balance is struck. The following stretches cover the important areas. Five to ten reps of each should be plenty.

Hamstring stretch.

Front stretch.

Groin stretch.

Hurdle stretch.

Hamstring stretch

Stand, bend at the waist, keep your legs straight, and reach for your toes or shoe tops. Don't force it on the first go; keep working it up until you can reach your toes easily without strain or pain. If you can't reach your toes, you have something to shoot for as you become more flexible.

Front stretch

Sit on the ground with your toes pointing skyward. Lean forward as far as possible while keeping your legs straight and together.

Groin stretch

You can move from the front stretch into this one quite easily. Still sitting, pull your feet into your groin. Let your knees spread and grasp the ankles as you bend forward.

Hurdle stretch

Start out sitting. Bend your torso down toward one knee. You thighs should be more or less at right angles; after a few repetitions, switch legs.

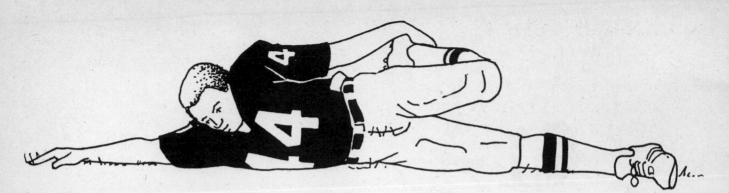

Quadriceps Stretch

Lie on your side with your lower arm extended on the ground over your head; now grab your foot with the other arm and pull it back toward your rear. Do it with each foot. This can also be accomplished while standing.

Trunk stretch

For these you start out lying face down. First extend your arms back and up, then grab the ankles from behind, hold your head up, and gently pull your ankles toward your backside.

Back stretch

You can move right into these after a few trunk stretches; just roll over and lie faceup. Bring your knees to the chest, then your shin above your head, and finally touch your toes to the floor above your head if you can. Return slowly to your original position before doing it again. And don't bounce!

Shoulder stretch

Stand, bring one hand to the upper back from above, the other hand from below until they can clasp fingers, then switch hands. Many people aren't flexible enough to complete this one, so don't hurt yourself.

Conditioning

After warming up, you're ready to take on the strength and conditioning exercises that tone and strengthen your muscles and build stamina. Good conditioning gives you a tremendous competitive edge! It also helps prevent injuries and lessens the severity of any that do occur. With good conditioning, you'll be stronger, have more stamina, and be faster, more agile, and more flexible than you've ever been before. It's also a good way to control your weight, if that's a problem. In general, good conditioning and strengthening exercises will leave you feeling and being healthier, more self-confident, and a better ball player.

But remember, whether you're running sprints or a few miles, or doing your coach's standard regimen of push-ups, pull-ups, sit-ups, etc., always warm up and stretch first.

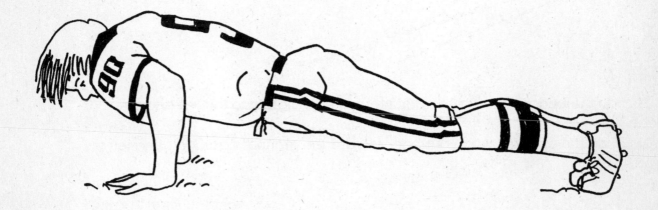

Football is an especially demanding sport that requires a particular kind of strengthening. If you're generally fit from some other sport you'll have a head start, but you still must do the specific exercises and conditioning aimed to satisfy the particular demands of football.

The other sports you've played up till now probably didn't strengthen one set of muscles you really need for football. These are the muscles of your neck, and they help protect your neck, head, and spine. The muscles need to be strong so you can play well, and they also protect some very vulnerable parts of your body that can be the site of disabling injuries.

Head and neck injuries are the most serious sustained by football players, and special care must be taken to prevent them by building up the neck muscles. You want your head and neck muscles to get stronger and stronger as the season progresses. Take your neck-muscle exercises very seriously! Here are some good ones:

Neck bridges

These are excellent neck-strengthening exercises. They're called bridges because you literally make a bridge or arch of your body, with only your helmet and toes contacting the ground, as shown in the illustrations. Always be careful as you do these, and remember the vulnerability of your neck.

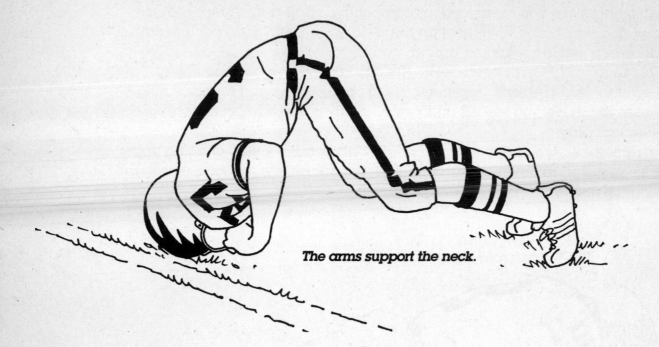

The arms support the neck.

First do the bridge face down, rotating the head slightly to the left and then right.

Next, do the exercise with your back toward the ground, again rotating left and right.

The arms support the neck.

Isometric exercises

These are also very useful for strengthening your neck. Team up with a buddy to do them. One of you gets down on all fours; the other stands with his leg against the side of the kneeling player's helmet. Now the crouching player presses his head sideways against his friend's leg with as much constant force as possible, for a slow count of ten. The standing player presses back with his leg too (obviously he's getting some toning), providing steady resistance and encouraging his buddy to really exert himself.

You can do some simple isometric exercises alone while you're studying or watching television. Try placing your palm against your forehead and pushing, creating enough tension to get your neck muscles tight. Push for a count of ten, then move your hand from your forehead to the back and sides of your head.

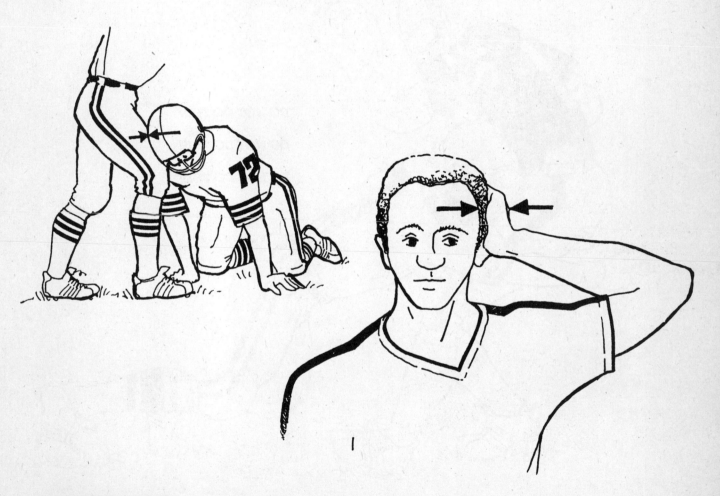

WARMING DOWN

Don't forget that after a vigorous practice, you need to warm down. You should slow down gradually, rather than stopping abruptly. Screech to a halt instead of slowing down gradually, and you'll find yourself very sore the next day. One very easy jog around the field and a few light stretches should do it. Just make sure to keep moving until your heart rate returns to a normal speed.

Safety

Football is a contact sport, and usually the contact gets pretty rough. You and your friends and teammates occasionally can be hurt or injured. It's up to the players and coaches alike to do all they can to keep injuries to a minimum. Getting in shape helps, but it is also very important never to do certain very dangerous things on the field.

DO NOT DO THIS!

DO NOT DO THIS!

DO NOT DO THIS!

SPEARING

Spearing is, simply, hitting your opponent with your head first. Considering that your head is enclosed in a hard helmet, the only reason you'd spear another would player would be to hurt him. It is illegal and you should never do it. It's bad enough to set out to hurt someone else, but know this: the greater danger is to you. A really good spear could land you in the hospital, in a wheelchair for life, or in the morgue. This cannot be overemphasized: DO NOT TACKLE YOUR OPPONENT HEADFIRST.

The worst error a coach or player can commit is to let the helmeted head be used as a battering ram. You're not doing all those neck exercises to create a weapon, but to protect yourself. And your helmet is in place to protect your head, not to spear an opponent. Unless you think having a broken neck would be valuable experience, don't dive, tackle, or fling yourself headfirst at anything or anyone for any reason.

Don't practice or play football if you do not understand how to protect yourself! Your shoulders and trunk should be your main weapons when blocking and tackling. Take a very particular stance and follow a definite procedure: be balanced, bend your knees, keep your back straight, bend your body slightly forward, hold your head up, and brace yourself to take or give the impact mainly with your trunk, but leading with your shoulder.

In addition to not deliberately spearing, take care not to bend your head down when you are tackling or blocking. The individual bones that stack up to form your neck and spine, called the vertebrae, are supposed to stay stacked up straight, or "in alignment." If you bend your head down for a block or tackle, you'll bend the vertebrae out of alignment, and if you are struck at this moment you could be injured slightly or seriously, or even crippled. You are vulnerable in the same way when you curve or bend your back, so keep your back straight.

In the same spirit, never grab or pull an opponent's face mask. This is an illegal move and will result in a penalty. It is also a matter of personal integrity. Players have no right to so dangerously risk each other's health.

In general, players protect themselves and each other by knowing the difference between the aggressiveness needed to play football, and mindless violence and the intent to injure, which have no place on any playing field. Play aggressively, play to win, but do not play dirty and do not play to injure.

HEAT

Football practice might begin as soon as early August, and heat can be a problem. Temperatures that exceed 80 degrees, combined with humidity, exertion, and football equipment, can lead to heat exhaustion and heatstroke. Take precautions:

° drink plenty of fluids at meals and eat a normal amount of salt unless specifically instructed to do otherwise;

° drink plenty of water before practice and during water breaks, whether you feel thirsty or not;

° if the heat is getting to you, take a break in the shade and drink more water. You're not being a wimp—heatstroke is serious, and every good coach knows it.

In addition, the coach should keep an eye on the heat and humidity. If the humidity is greater than 70 percent and the temperature exceeds 80 degrees, you should practice in shorts or indoors. In warmer climates, the first few weeks or even months of practice should probably be confined to the cooler, later hours.

A couple of final safety tips: make sure your field does not contain any hazards such as holes, rocks, glass, or any kind of debris or obstruction. Also, don't chew gum. You could get tackled and inhale it, and no one will even know what's wrong when you start choking.

3. In the Trenches: The Offensive Line Versus The Defensive Line

Offensive Line

Offensive linemen are vital to the success of their teams. Without big, dedicated, competent players on the line to hold off the defense, the running backs and quarterback cannot do their jobs and the team can't score. Linemen battle it out man-to-man in what's probably the hardest work of each and every play. An offensive lineman must work hard in practice to build adequate strength and conditioning for his job, and he must endlessly practice blocking techniques. Unfortunately, a lineman's best moves often go unnoticed, even though his hard work opens up the field so that the "interesting" plays can occur.

The offensive lineman must also contend with the defensive lineman across the way, one of the biggest guys on the field and amazingly quick for his size. If your position is offensive, your job is to neutralize that guy with a good block and preserve the delicate pattern and flow of your offensive play; his job is to disrupt that balance any way he can. He has a huge advantage, too. When the offensive lineman is near the line of scrimmage he is allowed to use his hands to grab you and pull you off balance, turn you around, or literally throw you out of the way. But if you, the offensive lineman, grab the defensive lineman or hook him with an elbow, you'll be called for holding.

This may seem unfair, but you also have some major advantages over your opponent. You and your teammates on offense *know which play you are about to run*, so you know ahead of time exactly what you'll need to do. You also *know what the snap count is,* so you know exactly when to explode into action. When used in conjunction with sound blocking techniques, these advantages should be enough for you to knock your adversary off balance and get some yardage.

However, don't give your advantages away by broadcasting your first move. Always take up a normal balanced stance and don't look, lean, or orient yourself in any way in the direction of the play. Avoid leaning forward on your hand on running plays or back on your heels on pass plays. Before the snap, never obviously look in the direction you'll be moving into for your block. The defensive linemen and linebackers make a habit of watching for clues—don't give your opponents what they need.

BLOCKING

Good blocking requires proper technique. To succeed as a lineman, you need to know the best ways of blocking your opponent—how to stop him from going where he wants, how to move him back or to the left or the right, and how to knock him down. Each of these actions requires a specific kind of block.

Stance

First of all, you need a good stance for balance, which allows you to move quickly. Anyone who must block, whether guard, tackle, or tight end, needs to start with good balance. Come up to the line of scrimmage and take your stance about a yard behind the ball. Stand with your feet parallel and about shoulder width apart. Don't let either foot be more than a half step behind the other. If you're to the right of center, place your left foot slightly back, and vice versa. As time goes on, you'll fine tune this to suit yourself—the most important thing is to find a stance that is comfortable, safe, and works for you.

If you're stationed to the right of center, your right hand should be down on the ground, with your fingertips touching the ground in front of your back foot. If you're left of center, it will will be your left hand that's down. Your lowered elbow should be held about 7 inches in front of your knee. Rest your other arm against the forward thigh to secure your balance. Your knees should stay in line with your feet and hips.

Now, bend forward and raise your hips until your spine is just about parallel to the ground. Don't stress the neck by pulling your head up too far. You only need to see your opponent, not your girlfriend up in the top of the stands.

Make sure to evenly distribute your weight on both feet *and* the hand that's on the ground. Be light enough on your feet to charge quickly forward, or to the left or right. At the same time, it doesn't hurt to think of yourself as a solid object—a human obstacle.

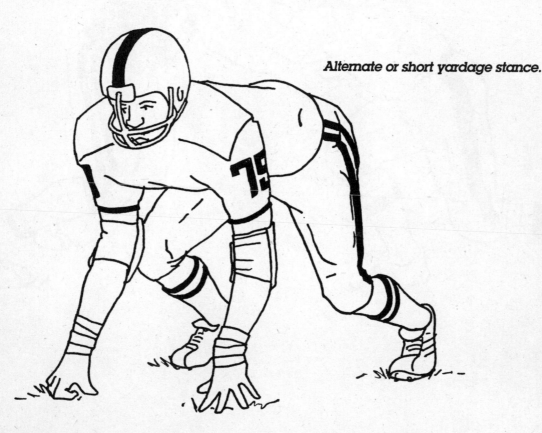

Alternate or short yardage stance.

It's important to work on this stance until it feels very natural to you—and it won't at first. Mastering that solid stance will help you do two things: deliver a steadfast block and maintain contact with your opponent as long as possible (this is your main goal); and to not make preparatory motions that broadcast what you're intending to do.

Listed, the components of the block may seem like individual pieces, but the actual initiation of the block and the first contact happen practically instantaneously, in a firm, fluid motion. Remember, once you've started the block, *carry through*.

Basic block

This one-to-one maneuver ties the defender up during a running play:

- start in the stance described just above;
- lift your hand from the ground, rising up, but keep your weight balanced and your center of gravity low;
- step forward firmly with your front foot, then take a 6-inch-or-so step forward with the back foot;
- aim for the chest area of a standing opponent;
- if your opponent is down in a stance, aim for his chin;

Tie 'em up, then stand 'em up.

- keep your arms and head up, your eyes open, and your hands at about shoulder height;
- your forearms should be the first part of your body to touch your opponent;
- once you're pressing him, keep your weight low with your feet parallel and roughly under your shoulders. Stay lower than your opponent and think in terms of pushing him out of the way of the ball carrier. Use short, choppy steps to keep in balance and maintain firm contact with the ground. Keep at him and keep him blocked and occupied until the whistle blows.

Pivot with short step.

Shoulder block

This variation on the basic block introduces a slant to your motion. Come at your opponent's left or right side rather than straight on. Whatever the direction, be conscious of staying balanced, steady, and stable. Just before you step forward, estimate your distance from and relation to your target. This is so you can plan exactly how you'll make the first contact.

For instance, when executing the shoulder block to your left, gauge your distance and position so that you make first contact with your left shoulder at just under his shoulder pads and your left foot coming down on the ground. This concentrates the main thrust of your strength against the middle of his trunk. The same is true for a block to your right, with your right foot forward and right shoulder at his shoulder. After first contact, push through with shorter steps, shifting your opponent farther and farther to your right and away from the hole you've created for the running back crashing through the line, behind you to your left.

It's *very important* to keep your head up directly over your shoulders, which is often called bulling your neck. Keep your eyes on your man as you charge. Don't tilt your head to the side or look at the ground, or he might give you the slip.

24

The reach or scramble block

This play is tailored for a situation where your opponent is playing outside your position. To use this block to tie up the opponent, you'll start, as before, in the basic stance. As you can see from the illustration, there is some danger to the knees of your opponent. This block should be practiced slowly and carefully until you are absolutely sure you have the ability to execute it without endangering the health and safety of the defensive lineman

The illustration shows a blocker executing a scramble block to his left. His goal is to prevent the defender from moving to the defender's right. First, the blocker steps with his left foot slightly back and out of the line as far as he can. Next he simultaneously sidesteps on the same foot and reaches past his opponent's right foot with his right arm. He doesn't sweep, but punches his arm past that foot. Now the blocker is set to put both hands on the ground and crawl into the defender, turning him back, inside, and to the right.

As you do this technique, you'll feel, with both your hands on the ground, nearly as if you are crawling. Yet in reality you've got to keep your body high enough and solid enough to serve as a real obstacle. Make sure to get your inner arm *beyond* the defensive player. This gives you the leverage you need to prevent him from making *any* progress.

An advanced technique.

Practice only under the coach's supervision.

Pass blocking

This block usually lasts for only a few seconds. It consists of patiently, stolidly holding back the onrushing defensive line. Your goal is to turn the defending player to the outside, until the quarterback has time to get the pass well away. In a sense, you're retreating as you execute this block, because you must make sure you give ground, occupying the defensive line and delaying them as you keep enough space open for the quarterback to do his job.

Controlled retreat.

Here's what to do: Start in the basic stance; at the snap count rise up from your hand-on-ground crouch and extend your arms forward, spread open, at about shoulder height. When your opponent attacks, push your hands forward quickly and step forward with staggered steps. Keep your shoulders and hips behind the toes, and your inside foot slightly forward.

After making contact with your man, keep your head up and your opponent at arm's length so you can tell what he's doing. Use steady, deliberate steps. Don't shuffle—pick up and plant your feet firmly and with short, choppy steps. Your goal is to hold the defender at the point of first contact. Failing that, give ground and hit 'em again. Keep your eyes on the opponent and match him move for move.

Pulling out

Linemen don't need to be as fast as wide receivers, but they certainly can't be slow! When you leave your position to move elsewhere to block, this is called *pulling*. This move is used to trap opponents or block on sweeps or counter-motion plays, but to be effective you've got to move *quickly* without being blatant about your intentions.

Start with the basic stance, but move your weight back a bit, primarily on your back foot, since you will be moving in this direction. Don't be conspicuous about it! At snap count, step back with the other foot. Then swivel your hips in the direction of the back foot, punch your back fist forward, keep your body low, your head up, and run along behind the line, deep enough to avoid getting tangled up, to your next assigned position. Work in practice to do this in one quick, fluid motion. Your teammate the running back is probably a lot faster than you are. He needs you to get to your assigned position and make your block before he hits the line. A quick start is the only way to do this.

Two other commonly used blocks are the double team and fold blocks.

The double team, also called a power block, uses two players to block one defender. One of these players is the *post* player; the other is the *lead*. Both players start in the basic stance and work closely together on this maneuver.

If you're the lead player, you act first. Your job is come up from the basic stance and go at the defender's belt buckle with your shoulder. Hit him hard enough to stop him. The drive man will now come at the defender's side with his other foot and other shoulder. The two of you should be shoulder to shoulder. The drive man swivels on his foot around the defender's hip. Keep your shoulders together and stay low. He won't be able to go between the two of you, and you'll have him trapped. Now, with short firm steps, push him back and away from the play.

Two offensive players also collaborate to carry out the fold block, although here they come up against two defenders. One lineman goes after the linebacker; the other targets the down lineman.

First, the blocker near the linebacker explodes off the line of scrimmage—not directly into the linebacker but diagonally into the defensive lineman. The teammate working with him starts nearer the defensive lineman, but delays an instant until the first blocker moves out of the way, and finally moves diagonally to block the linebacker.

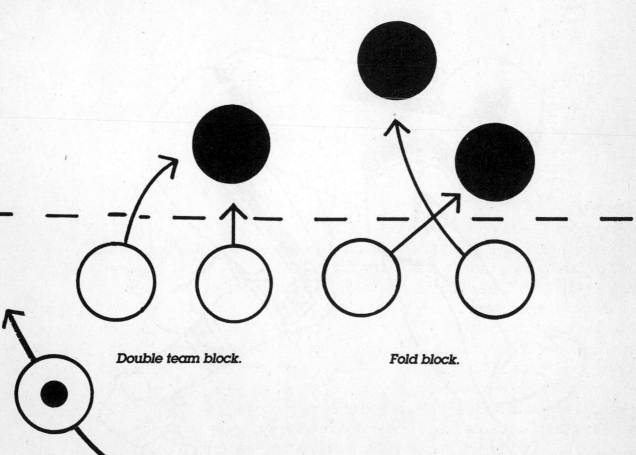

Double team block.   **Fold block.**

THE CENTER

A center must be able to snap the ball to the quarterback *and* block as well as the other defensive players. Sometimes he must do *both* virtually at the same time. The basic stance the center starts with is similar to that of the other offensive players, except the center is not just *touching* the ground with one hand, he's holding the ball. The center might choose to hold the ball in both hands, or he might hold it in just one, cradling his free arm at his knee or holding it on the ground without touching the ball. It's mostly personal preference that determines his style.

His snap-then-block must happen very quickly, but he *must* be sure to snap the ball to the quarterback quickly, cleanly, and with no fumbling.

If you play center, you must:
- keep your back flat;
- hold your head up and not dip it;
- tell the quarterback if you can't feel his hand;
- lift the ball into the quarterback's hands without looping or turning the ball incorrectly;
- let the ball go when the quarterback has it—then block!

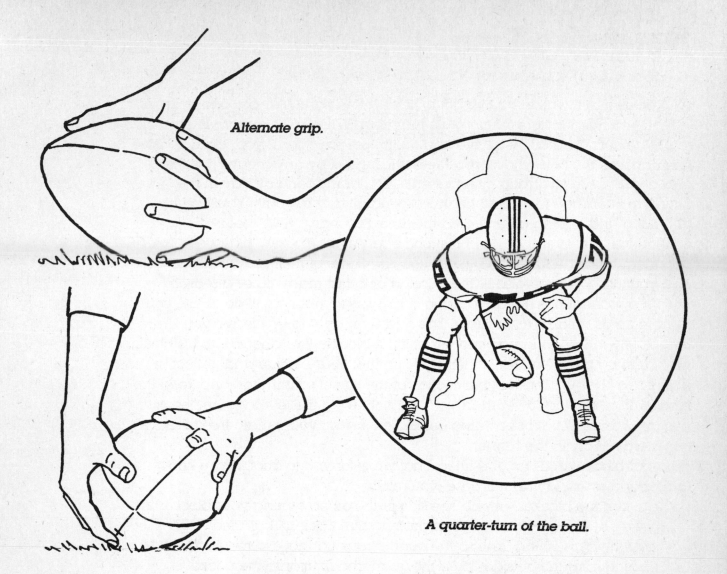

Alternate grip.

A quarter-turn of the ball.

Another part of your job will be to center the ball to the punter or place kicker. This too begins with the basic stance, with your feet wide enough for comfort. In this case, however, you should sacrifice some advantage in blocking by looking back through your legs at the target, which is the kicker's or holder's hands.

For your snap to the punter, use the form that many centers have used to grip and handle the ball: Start by holding its forward half with one hand. With the other hand, press down slightly on the back of the ball. Keep your wrists straight and hold the ball tilted up with the front half slightly off the ground. As you begin the snap, rotate your front hand so that it is on the bottom and your back hand so that it's now on top. Push the ball back between your legs and rotate your hands back so that they reach their original position as the ball reaches your back leg. Release the ball and immediately assume your blocking stance.

You might try a different grip to snap the ball to the holder for a place kick. Place your front hand more to the side of the ball and hold your wrists semi-cocked rather than straight. Release the ball sooner, before it gets to the back leg, to keep the ball lower.

Defensive Line

As a defensive lineman you've got to have a few particular personality traits.

First, you need a taste for absolute mayhem. While the offensive lineman might be described as the brave and dutiful palace guard, you, the defensive lineman, are the one who storms the castle, enters by any means possible, and destroys the civilization it represents. You must spend all day in the offensive lineman's face, and he must spend all day in yours. You'll be attacking and getting attacked all the time. Secondly, you'll need confidence, perseverance, and a strong ego. After all, *every* play your opponent has is designed to bypass you first. Some of their plays will succeed, and you just don't get to sack the quarterback that many times a season.

Your opponent has the advantage of knowing what he will do, while you must react as quickly as possible. This disadvantage doesn't leave you completely in the dark: you know that if the blocker fires ahead into his block, it's a running play. You must then try to control your blocker and deflect or absorb his charge. Control your section of the line of scrimmage and keep the blocker from getting lower than you and achieving the leverage he needs to push you aside. Avoid becoming entangled so that you remain free to move either way to crush the runner.

If your blocker does not fire ahead but waits for you to attack, you know it's probably a pass play. In this case, you must:

- go after the blocker, attack one side or the other, turning your blocker in a way he doesn't want to go or pushing him back off balance;
- stay in your rushing lane so the quarterback cannot escape. If you're rushing from the outside, force the quarterback up into the pocket;
- when you catch the quarterback, wrap up his arms. If you can't catch him before he throws the ball, get your arms up to disrupt his line of vision and/or deflect his throw.

Here are a few of the techniques used to achieve these ends:

Three-point stance
Like offensive linemen, the defensive lineman has a basic stance he takes in preparation for the action of the play. As shown in the illustration, the three-point stance most commonly used requires you to:

- place your hand nearest the ball on the ground;
- have your feet about shoulder-width apart, with your near leg back a bit;
- put most of your weight on your front hand and front leg. This helps you to make
- a fast start and charge powerfully forward;
- keep your back either parallel to the ground or tilted slightly upward;
- keep your head up and your eyes on the blocker's face.

32

A three-point stance.

Four-point stance

The four-point stance is used when the defensive lineman needs a low, powerful charge to block a rushing offensive line. Often, this will be right at the goal line or in short-yardage situations. Starting with the weight low on the hands helps keep the charge low.

As the illustration shows, this stance has its own specific key elements. You must:

- place *both* hands on the ground, with your weight primarily on your spread fingertips;
- have your feet shoulder width apart and even, with neither set back or forward;
- keep your feet parallel and knees bent, ready to charge at the snap; parallel your shoulders to the line of scrimmage;
- tilt your back slightly upward;
- keep your head up and your eyes on the offensive line.

Short yardage stance.

Defensive end's stance.

Defensive-end stance

A defensive end might start erect, or he might start from a three-point stance. The three-point stance lets you make the fastest start, while starting from a more erect stance gives you a better view of the offensive players in the backfield. This better view helps you read the play and react promptly and effectively.

34

Here are some tips for successful play on the defensive line:
- bird-dog your blocker, don't give him time to get balanced and successfully block you—instead, you control him;
- come at your blocker with shoulders square, making your body into the biggest possible obstacle to a running back or to the quarterback's line of sight;
- clog the line, don't let them move you out or pull you to their "other" assignment;
- keep your feet moving, using short, choppy steps.

If you see something—for example, an offensive lineman pulling and moving to your left—that indicates a possible sweep to the left side, you'll want to protect your left side from the block that's probably in store for it. You must attack and neutralize your immediate opponent:
- step into the block with your right foot and drive your right forearm into his number from a low, balanced position, standing him up and pushing him back;
- pivot, shifting more weight onto the left foot, and begin pursuit of the ball carrier.

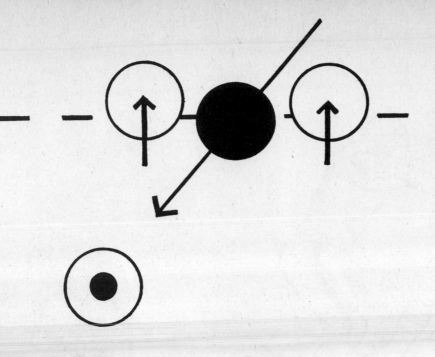

THE SLANT TECHNIQUE

Defensive linemen use this technique to attack basic offensive-line blocks. It is not complicated, although it certainly is not always easy to pull off. Your goal, simply, is to get yourself to the gap in the line between two blockers before the blockers get there. If you make it there first, you can ruin the blocker's plan for the play by just being there, in that gap just behind him. Start looking for the ball! Now the blocker must go much farther out of his way to protect the ball carrier—opening up opportunities for the linebackers.

Slanting has some valuable strategic advantages, too: It can help compensate for a small interior line or it can take the best advantage of a player who has great speed. When well executed, it forces the offensive line to change their strategy in the middle of the play, causing confusion. It can also provide a way for defensive linemen to get at the ball carrier in the backfield, the thing many of them live for.

RUSHING THE PASSER

You don't need to be a defensive lineman very long to know that sacking the quarterback is the high point of this position, but those offensive linemen are just as strong as you are and determined to stop you! The offensive lineman gets a head start, and unless you are awfully quick slanting around him, he's not going to go away. The key to beating him and getting to the quarterback is controlled penetration. Strive to control your blocker and your rushing lane.

Here's how: Quickly make contact. Strike a blow with the hand nearest him, on just one side of the blocker's body, to turn him and establish a new line of scrimmage. Force the blocker into a backpedal and keep him off balance, then move out to the quarterback.

Two techniques often used in clearing the blocker out of the way are known as the "rip" and the "swim."

Dip your shoulder, then rip upward.

The rip
In executing this, use your inside arm to lift up under the blocker's outside shoulder. First try to clear the blocker away from your midline, and if you accomplish that, keep cranking, using your lifting arm as a lever to pry your way to the quarterback.

The swim

This technique gets its name from its obvious resemblance to a swimmer's basic crawl. Using your arms like a windmill, get your arm around back of the blocker and churn, pushing him down, back, and away.

Remember, if you notice the blocker giving you particular pressure from a certain side, that's probably the direction he wants to block you from at all costs. Generally, you must fight *through* that pressure. If you run *around*, you'll be opening up a running lane; at any rate, by the time you shake the blocker, you'll be well out of the play and he'll have done his job.

Once you're clear to the quarterback, elevate! Get your hands up, or he'll find a receiver before you get to him. Even if he does release the ball before you reach him, which happens all too often, it's important to get up and stay up. If you're up, your hands and arms will interfere with his line of vision and you'll be in position to deflect his throw.

If you actually make it to the quarterback and get him, wrap his arms so he can't get the pass off at the last millisecond.

STANCE AT THE GOAL LINE AND FOR SHORT-YARDAGE PLAYS

If you're on the defensive line and the action is taking place fairly close to the goal line, or the offense needs just a few yards to make a first down, be especially careful. Take the regular four-point stance, but bend your knees more and get your body down lower. This is necessary because you're going to have to charge very low and move just a short distance to insert yourself into the offensive line.

Finally, all defensive players must understand the fundamentals of tackling and be able to tackle effectively and efficiently. The specifics of those tackling techniques are covered in the linebacker section.

4. Cat and Mouse: The Backs Versus the Linebackers

The Quarterback

The quarterback leads the offense and holds it together. He introduces each play and sets it in motion. His abilities will make the play work; his inability can doom it to failure. The quarterback creates and carries out offensive strategy. The emphasis here is on leadership. A quarterback needs to be able to offer guidance to his team members in a variety of ways; if that concept makes you uncomfortable, set your sights on another position.

Sometimes the quarterback selects and calls the plays; sometimes the coach does from the sidelines. Either way, as quarterback you must be on top of things at all times. Even if the coach calls the plays, the defenders might shift defenses and catch your team off guard—and you'll have to quickly decide how to react and change the play accordingly, audibly calling out the new signals at the line of scrimmage.

As quarterback, you handle the ball on every play except a few kicking situations. You must always strive to give as fumble-free a performance as humanly possible. There shouldn't be anything choppy about your actions. When you handle the ball, it should be with smooth, seamless motions. To get ready for play, you and the center and the running backs will practice endless ball-carrying and passing drills, repeating every possible ball-handling variation again and again.

THE PLAY

In taking up your position behind the center, scan the defense and survey the area where the play will be carried out—without "telegraphing" to the other team where that area is.

Next, check your own formation to make sure that the receivers and backfield are correctly positioned, that at least seven teammates are in place at the line of scrimmage, and that all the players are on side behind the ball.

If you haven't done so already, plant your feet firmly, shoulder width apart, behind the center, with your weight balanced on both feet. During many practice sessions, you and the center have worked on the exchange. The exact way you do it depends somewhat on the center's size and how you, the quarterback, prefer to receive the ball. For taller centers, quarterbacks usually

40

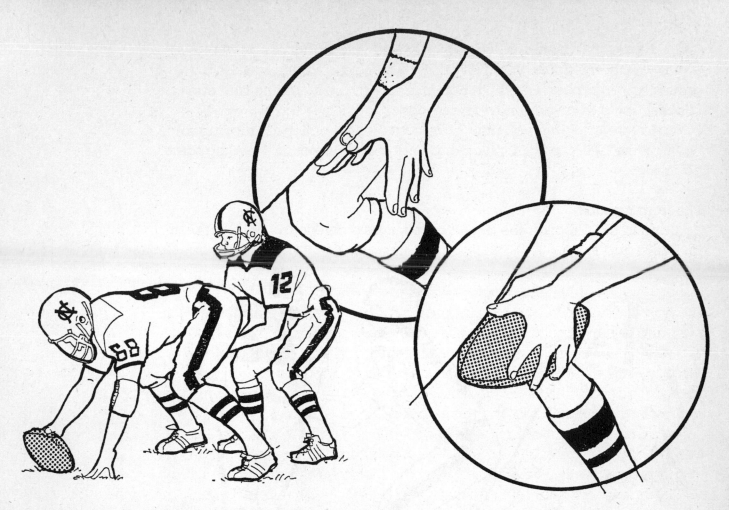

take a more upright stance. Whatever you've worked out between the two of you, you'll now get into that position, ready to receive the ball.

THE SNAP COUNT

The team should think of the play as beginning when the quarterback begins the snap count. You should always deliver the count clearly and loudly so you can be heard at both ends of the line of scrimmage. It's also important to get the rhythm of the count right. Make sure you leave equal pauses between each number you call, and always articulate the call at the same pace. You don't want to catch your own team off guard.

The *snap* is the actual moment when the center presses the ball into the quarterback's hands. Different quarterbacks hold their hands in various ways to take the snap. It will depend on how you and your center are comfortable snapping the ball, which you'll have worked on in practice and drills.

If the center is going to deliver the ball with a quarter turn, you should rest the back of your right hand flush against the curve of the center's backside. Hold your left hand lower than your right and your wrists together, forming a V with your two hands. The center will place the ball into this V. Keeping your thumbs together makes it easier for you to grab the ball and hold it firmly. Press your right hand firmly enough against the center so that he knows where your hand is and doesn't hesitate in placing the ball there. The most important thing, though, is to hold on to that ball.

The snap is complete, you've got the ball in your hands, and the play is under way. Remember, your first priority is to hold on to the ball! Hold it against your stomach with both hands, making sure it's secure and can't be knocked loose during the next few seconds.

If it's a running play, you now have a few simple options in moving to hand off the ball: the front, pivot, and underneath handoffs. Here are some basic ones:

The front handoff
You turn in the direction the play is going; if it's a dive to the right, set off to the right, and so on.

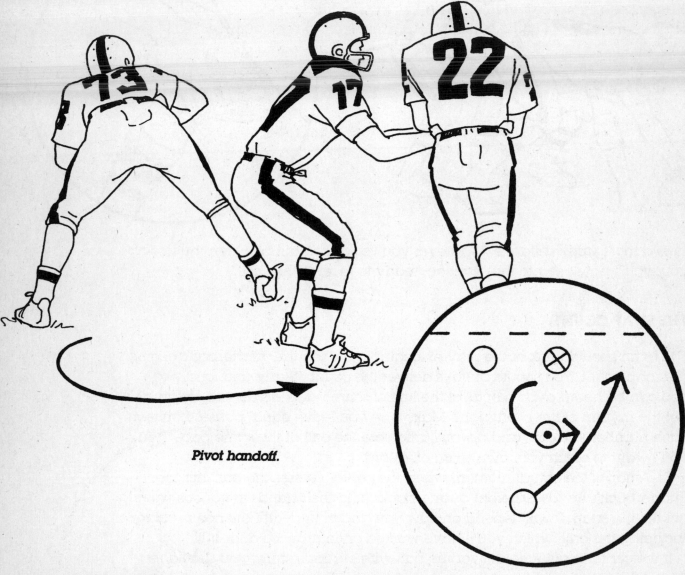

Pivot handoff.

The pivot handoff
First, you head in one direction. Then you abruptly pivot on your foot and turn your back momentarily to the line of scrimmage. While your back's turned, you hand the ball to a back who's heading in the direction opposite to the one in which you initially turned. This is a good way to take advantage of a fast running back.

The Underneath handoff

First you run in the direction opposite that in which the play will go. Then the running back cuts, reversing direction, and passes between you and the line of scrimmage. You hand off the ball at this point.

Whichever of these three courses you take, the key element is the handoff itself. You must get the ball safely into the hands of the running back! There are numerous minor variations in the way running backs create a pocket for the ball: arms apart, arms together, various hand configurations. And while it's nearly always best for you to hand the ball off at belt level, keep in mind that running backs come in different shapes, sizes, and heights. Make sure that you locate the target pocket on the far hip and between his arms; *look* at the pocket as you press the ball firmly into it. Don't hand off on a "broken play." Generally, it's better to lose a few yards than to risk a fumble.

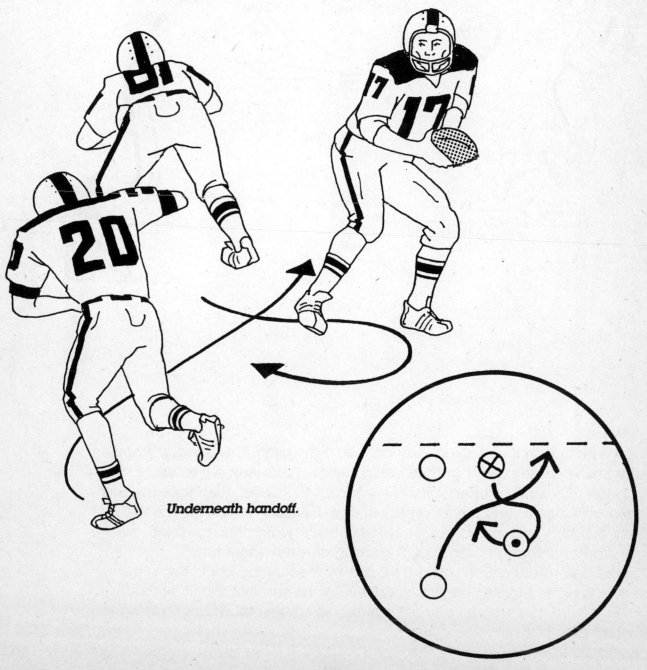

Underneath handoff.

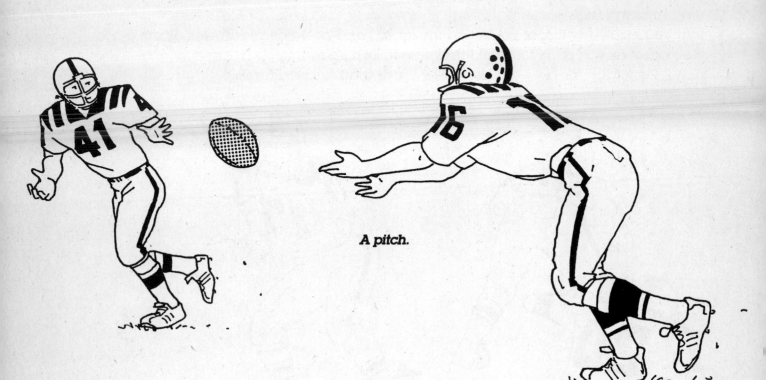

A pitch.

The pitch

One variation on the running-play handoff is the *pitch*. This is useful when your team wants to quickly get the ball out wide. You'll start out as usual by taking the snap and securing it against your body. Roll out, then take the ball in one hand—the right hand for a play in that direction, the left for one to the left—as if to throw a forward pass. Instead of the forward pass, turn and give the ball an underhand toss to a back making an even wider run.

For the best result, and to avoid a fumble by the running back, throw the ball ahead of the running back at chest level so he can "run into it" without breaking stride. This way he can get a firm hold on the ball without having to reach or lunge backward or forward.

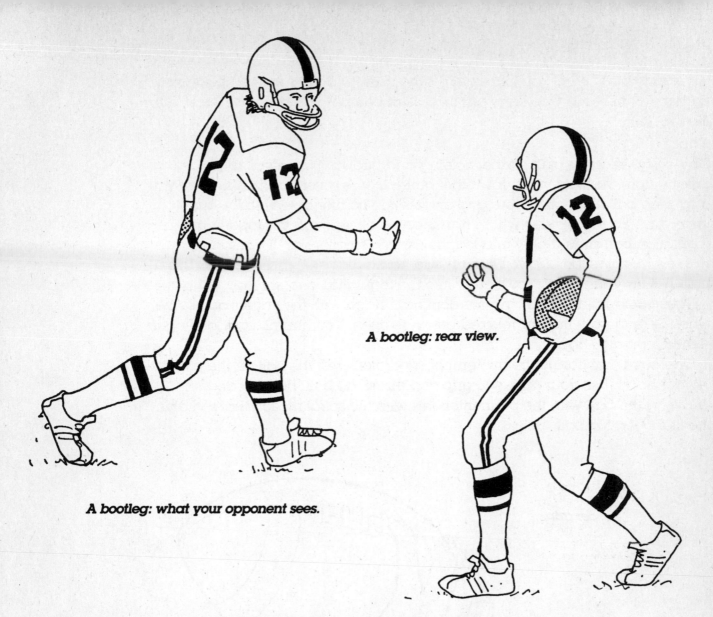

A bootleg: rear view.

A bootleg: what your opponent sees.

If your team is to have any misdirection plays, you must be able to believably fake a handoff. This is a skill worth spending time on. Take special care as you practice that you don't risk fumbling the ball during the actual handoff. Whatever you're faking, the real thing still has to be safe.

To fake, set out with the beginning moves of a real handoff, with the ball secure in both hands. Come just about to the point where you'd leave the ball at the far hip of the first back, pull back, and *immediately* move on to the next part of the play. Carry out both real and fake handoffs at waist height. Make every effort to make it seem that you really did hand it off the first time—you, along with the first faked back, must "sell the play."

Another way to free up the ball carrier is to continue using a faking motion when the ball is already gone—faking a fake. Quarterbacks do this routinely and it can be effective in keeping the defense off balance. Make extra handoff motions after you have actually handed off the ball, or turn your back—anything to avoid communicating that "I don't have the ball anymore." This will create a smoke screen to throw off the defense and buy time for your own ball carrier.

PASSING TECHNIQUE

As quarterback, your most basic tool is the pass, and the most complex pass pattern in the world won't amount to a hill of beans if you don't get the ball to the receiver.

Grip

Obviously, because of its shape, holding and throwing a football differs greatly from the way you throw other balls. There's a very particular way you grip a football. Perfecting your grip and feeling comfortable with it is very important. Young players whose hands aren't big enough to properly grip a regulation ball should play in a league using a smaller size. If you practice with a ball that's too big, you'll learn bad habits that are hard to break. Use a ball that fits your hand. You'll grow into the regulation one.

You should hold the ball in your dominant hand with the fingers across the laces. Spread your fingers, relaxed but wide open. Your thumb and forefinger should form a U shape.

One point that cannot be overemphasized: don't rest the ball on the palm of your hand. Use your *fingers* to grip and throw the ball. Holding and throwing the ball with the palm interferes with the spiral motion that's vital in the flight of a football.

Proper grip.

46

Bring the ball up from your midsection to shoulder height with both hands. When you're ready to throw, step forward, toward your target—on your left foot if you are right-handed, on your right if you're a lefty. Imagine a line that you'll throw the ball along. Step right down on that, your foot pointing in the direction the ball will be traveling. As you throw, release the ball with your thumb, letting it rotate as the laces move from your fingertips. This gives a football its spiral motion.

Make sure you release *through* the ʊ formed by your thumb and index finger. Your index finger is the rudder that guides the ball and should be the last thing that touches the ball, with the other fingers giving it the push.

Here's a helpful checklist to use as you work on your throw:

- start with the ball chest high in both hands, standing sideways and with your head turned to survey the target;
- keep your feet shoulder width apart;
- as you turn and step onto the line to the target, shift your weight and gather power for the throw;
- as you step and shift your weight, raise the ball and pull it back into throwing position;
- face the receiver with the ball cocked;
- lock your wrist and let your elbow lead the ball;
- with your left foot on the ground (if you're right-handed), release the ball just in front of your head and follow through with your hand.

It is important to follow through on a throw the way baseball pitchers do on the mound, letting your throwing hand continue moving down across the body, coming to rest with the palm facing downward.

DROPPING BACK

As a quarterback, you have two basic ways to drop back to pass; turning and running back, or backpedaling.

1)   You can turn around and run back into position, then turn back to face the area of play. The advantage in doing this is that nearly anybody can run more quickly forward than they can backward, so you'll probably be able to get set up more quickly, and are less likely to stumble.

2)   The virtue of backpedaling is that you can continually keep an eye on the whole area where the play is unfolding.

Either way, don't throw the ball while dropping back; wait until you reach the proper spot. You should release the ball as you step forward toward your target.

A third option for quarterbacks is the roll-out pass. To make a pass on the run, you'll roll out either to the right of the line of scrimmage or to the left. Just as with the drop-back pass, a right-handed passer lets go of the ball as he drives off his right foot onto the left. If, as a right-handed player rolling right, you can "turn the corner" around the defensive end, you'll already be heading upfield as you let the ball go—a good position to be in.

If, however, you're rolling out left, you're probably going to have to turn upfield in order to gain the proper position and momentum for an accurate throw. If you can't manage to get turned upfield, both the length and the accuracy of your throw will suffer as you throw because your body's momentum will be in the opposite direction to the throw.

Don't forget, whether you're rolling right or left, stay behind the line of scrimmage as you release the ball.

Dropping back to pass.

48

KINDS OF PASSES

Though there are certainly others, quarterbacks mainly use two passes: the *lofted ball* and a *fast line drive*.

A lofted ball is better for deep cuts, where the receiver is trying to position himself behind all the defensive players. In this case, you'll loft or toss the ball over the defenders to the receiver.

Use a line-drive pass in situations where the receiver is running patterns such as the sideline or the curl. This pass needs to be hit in front of the secondary defenders—don't let the ball stay very long in the air or it might be intercepted by the defense.

FAKING A PASS

To fake a pass, hold the ball securely with both hands and start the normal motions of the pass. Step forward on your front foot. Keep a firm grip on the ball and move your arm confidently forward. Stop the actual release of the ball with your free hand. There's a reason you use your free hand this way instead of just pumping the ball in the air. You need that second hand to help prevent you from accidentally releasing the ball.

After stopping the ball, pull it back toward your body; slide your back foot slightly forward, step toward your target with your leading foot, then immediately carry out the real pass. The possibility that any pass might be a fake keeps the defensive secondary from committing too readily; when you *do* fake, you give the receiver a split-second advantage, and split seconds count for a lot.

A right hander: rolling right.

A right hander: rolling left.

49

The Running Back

Like quarterbacks, players in the running-back position are often standouts. The most talented ones positively amaze the fans and spectators with long, stunning touchdown runs, as well as with the way they can accelerate past or outmaneuver tacklers in the open field and power through the line.

If you play this position, you'll find that in reality a running back's job is complex and generally calls for much more hard work than flash. You must carry the ball, block, catch, and be able to fake carrying the ball. It helps in this job if you're a big guy, but what's more important than size is your skill as an athlete. You have to be in good shape; you need speed, agility, balance, and smarts—because you're a prime target and your opponents are going to be dishing out the punishment to you. The defending team is dedicated to bringing you down. In response, you must remain single-mindedly committed to gaining every yard you possibly can. Against all odds and all tacklers, be determined to keep on your feet and advance toward the goal.

Stance

There are two basic lineups in which running backs spearhead the attack: the I formation and the split backs.

In the *I formation*, the fullback positions himself in front of the tailback in a three-point stance. The tailback stands with his feet parallel and shoulder width apart and his hands resting lightly on his thigh guards. His knees are flexed slightly, his back is straight, and his shoulders are back.

In the *split back* formation, two running backs stand side to side about five yards behind the ball. They crouch in a three- or four-point stance, or stand, mirroring each other. Their feet are parallel, backs flat, knees bent, and heads and eyes forward.

Correct stances: I formation.

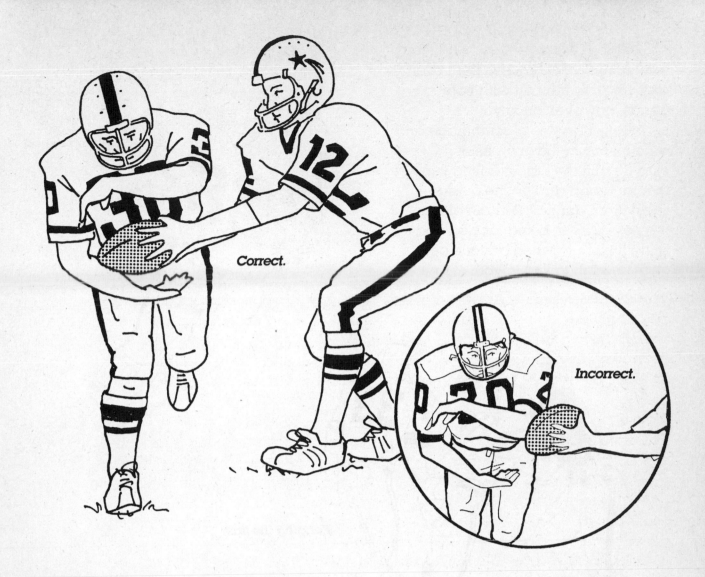

Correct.

Incorrect.

RECEIVING THE BALL

The quarterback will either hand off or toss the ball to the running back, and the back is usually going to be moving *fast* when he receives the ball. No matter how fast the back is going, the quarterback needs to place the ball carefully (not slam it) on the back's hip.

If you're going to be receiving and carrying the ball, it's very important how you position your arms and hands, especially your ball-side elbow. If you hold your elbow too low it will almost inevitably prevent the quarterback from placing the ball correctly and you might fumble.

As the quarterback begins the handoff, your elbow should be up. When you feel the light pressure of the ball on your hip, immediately lower your quarterback-side elbow over the ball and bring it around. Once you've actually got the ball, cradle it firmly in *both* hands and *both* arms. This helps you protect the ball if you get hit. When you take the ball, you'll have to depend on feel. You're not going to be able and you shouldn't try to keep your eyes on the ball while you're actually receiving it. That's right—*don't watch the ball*. Instead, watch the line of scrimmage for the hole your teammate is opening for you.

It can be awkward and not all that
easy to run quickly when bent over
and cradling the ball with both
hands. However, once you've
penetrated the line of scrimmage and
are running in the open field, it's
okay to shift the ball, cradling it in
the hand and arm on the outside,
away from danger. Remain alert to
the possibility of being tackled and
bring it back in when anyone gets
close enough to tackle you.

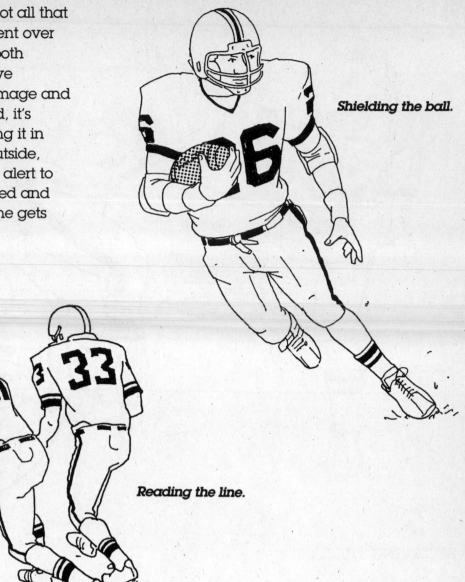

Shielding the ball.

Reading the line.

When you're in the position of running back, individual circumstances will
determine whether you should keep your eye on the defensive line or your
own blockers. Usually it's better to watch the defensive line. For instance, if
you see which side the defenders are going to protect, then you'll have the
information you need to break the other way when you receive the ball. Of
course, blocks aren't always successful; when they fail, you'll need to
improvise and find your own hole in the line.

Cradling the ball with both arms and hands also provides a key ingredient
in a fundamental technique you must learn as a running back: to skillfully
fake carrying the ball. You want to draw the linebackers to you while they're

Acting ability.

having a hard time seeing the *real* runner through the battle at the line of scrimmage. Good running backs pull this off frequently.

The downside, of course, is that if you convince the defense you have the ball, they'll go after you. The longer you keep up the fake, the more you help the offense; but it also means the defense will be after you longer and you'll take a few extra hits. You just have to take the hits when you fake carrying the ball.

In the illustration, a runner makes a convincing fake by curling forward and grasping his elbows. Using the same body posture and acting as elusively as if he had the ball, he'll run until he's tackled.

Dip left.

Drive right.

There's also a role for faking in the open field. While you can't fake having the ball, you can mislead any onrushing tacklers about the direction you're going to take it. Usually, a runner dips his head and shoulder to one side, giving the impression that this is the direction he'll go, but then, as the tackler approaches, the runner accelerates in the opposite direction. You might even be able to rebound off the tackler's body. This is probably the easiest feint to pull off while carrying the ball.

A quick change in your pace can also be an effective fake. When approaching a potential tackler, run at not quite top speed. Hold back just a little, but try to appear to be running as fast as you possibly can. Only release that extra burst of speed when the tackler lunges at you. He'll have paced himself for what he thought was your top speed, and if you accelerate quickly enough, you might be able to elude him.

Linebackers

The linebacker plays a major role, if not *the* major role, for the defense. The linebacker calls the defensive plays and makes sure that the coach's defensive game plan is carried out. If any sudden changes occur in midgame, the linebacker must make sure his teammates pick up on it and shift defenses accordingly. He is the quarterback of the defense.

Although any player may shift roles in a given play, a defensive lineman concentrates mainly on stopping the run and pressuring the passer, and a defensive back mainly on preventing pass receptions. A defensive linebacker does it all. This is a big job, and to do it well, you need the strength to stop the ball carrier and the speed to prevent pass plays. Like the quarterback, you must have an instinct for the game as a whole. A good linebacker either senses or very quickly figures out, once the ball is snapped, what kind of play is coming down. He must react quickly, too.

If you're a linebacker, it helps to be able to see over the offensive line as they're blocking, but don't worry if you're not particularly tall. Your job is to take your position (usually behind and in a gap between two offensive linemen) and read and react to the play. Far more important than height are your football smarts, strength, and speed. The offensive line and blocking backs will continually strive to keep you away from the place you need to be.

Obviously, when you asked to play linebacker, you took on one of football's most difficult assignments. The list of what you must do and must endure is awesome:

- cover several different holes or running lanes;
- move quickly not just forward but sideways, too;
- be an outstanding tackler;
- be able to read keys and follow the ball and the offense accurately.

In short, you must be able to do everything and must know everything that can be known about football, about your teammates, and about your opponents. The particulars below give you a good place to start.

Stance

You don't get as low as the line does in their three-point stance. Your crouch is more a semi-crouch; bring your hands, hanging loosely, only about halfway down between your knees and feet. Keep your feet parallel and your head up. Your weight should be forward and on the balls of your feet.

THE TACKLE

As a linebacker (or in any other defensive position), you need to do more than just lunge at the ball carrier. Once you are in position to tackle, you assume a very specific hitting position. Bend your knees and balance your body with your feet about shoulder width apart and your eyes on your target. Your target is not the *carrier*, but his *belt buckle*.

The reason you target the running back's belt buckle is that running backs are known for their good sense of balance and their ability to recover and change direction quickly. A running back can fake with every part of his body—except with that area of the body where the belt buckle rests. Wherever his belt buckle goes, he will go.

Once you are in the position, move in. On contact, use your helmet to push back the arm that's holding the ball, which might dislodge it. Encircle the hips of the carrier with your arms, and use your legs, back, and arms to raise the ball carrier up and drive him back. Don't let him fall forward for extra yardage. Keep your legs driving.

It's a reflex action to close your eyes when you tackle, but don't do it. Once you're this close to the ball carrier, he'll be his most elusive. He's going to try to pull a directional fake on you, or do anything he can to change direction and ricochet away. If you close your eyes just before you hit, you may find yourself with an armful of air.

A solid hit.

Good tackling with the body.

*Weak tackling with
the arms only.*

Think about your angle of tackle. Although the straight-ahead tackle provides a textbook example of proper tackler's technique, most tackles occur at an angle. When the ball carrier is traveling toward the outside, you can't meet him head-on. You'll have to come at him with a side-body tackle, still targeting his belt buckle. From the hitting position, push your head and shoulders in front of the ball carrier and encircle him with your arms. Hang on and roll with him as he falls.

Make sure to drive both shoulders across the front of the ball carrier. If you use only an arm to block his forward motion, he's going to break away and keep going. Your arms alone are no match for his pumping legs.

Driving your head across the front of the ball carrier doesn't mean spearing him in the chest or gut with it. By now you know better than to use your helmeted head as a battering ram.

Here's a check list to help you perfect your tackle:
- keep your head up, bulled;
- watch his buckle;
- target the ball;
- keep your eyes open before and at contact;
- time the hit so the power of it comes from fully extended legs;
- assume a 45-degree angle from the ground at impact;
- use short, choppy steps as you make the hit;
- lock your arms around him and hold on;
- don't stop driving with your feet until the whistle blows.

RECOVERING A FUMBLE

You must forever be alert when you play football, but you must be especially vigilant for a chance to recover a fumble. When an opportunity comes, know how to use this special technique of recovery: Dive for the ball and create a cavity for it with the top of your thighs and your trunk. With one hand pull the ball up into the space you have fashioned for it, then secure it with both arms and curl around it.

5. Football in the Air: The Receivers Versus The Defensive Secondary

Receivers

As the name implies, a receiver exists mainly to receive passes that are thrown to him. You must be able to catch the ball well, consistently, confidently, and hold on to it as you run, or while you are being hit. Believe it or not, you need something that a pianist needs: great sensitivity in your hands—without it you won't ever succeed in this position. Of course, you need to be pretty fast to be a receiver, but being able to outrun a horse won't matter if you can't hold on to the ball. Decent speed and great catching ability will always be preferred to great speed and average catching.

You also need to be a good blocker when a running back breaks a play. You'll often find yourself in a very useful blocking position, but because you're far from the ball carrier, timing your block will be crucial. Resist the temptation to block too early, before the ball carrier is close enough. If you do, your man will have enough time to get up and go again. If you wait to block until the carrier is just five or six steps away, your block probably will be much more effective.

Stance

Your work begins with the stance you take before the ball is snapped. Like that of players in all other positions, your starting stance is important. You—and any other receiver posted on the outside—should start from a two-point stance. Get yourself comfortable. You can hold your inside leg back a bit, flex your knees, and lean your weight slightly forward. Your head should be raised as you listen to the quarterback's signals. Hold your hands loose at your sides, and keep yourself well-balanced so you're ready to burst forward.

Before the snap, survey the defensive line and, without being obvious about it, check out the area where you are expecting to make your run. Take a few seconds to sum up in your mind the plan, your pattern, and how you intend to beat the coverage.

Listen and look.

Avoid the bump.

Keep your eye on the ball until it snaps, since it may be hard to hear, and when it is snapped, you should drive forcefully forward, practically falling forward to muster every possible ounce of momentum. Simultaneous with this burst of speed, keep an eye on your defensive back, so you can avoid him in case his plan is to give you a bump and delay, or disrupt your pattern or the timing of the play.

Once the ball is snapped, receivers employ various kinds of patterns, depending on which route their run will take. Whatever the route, you'll need all the speed, agility, and determination you can muster to break free from the defenders at the line of scrimmage and the defensive secondary.

61

BREAK AND RUN

If the route you are set on demands a 90-degree angle cut, you must make a crisp, well-ordered break. Use choppy steps to fake a run past the defender; moderate your speed, though, to stay in control. The pivot itself takes practice: bend your knees, lower your backside, and turn on the foot of your intended direction of cut while pushing off on the far-side foot.

Carry out your pass pattern and be prepared to use good catching technique when and if the ball comes to you. Although you are running a pattern and will be expected to be in a certain place at a certain time, all receivers improvise on the way—this is a skill that separates the good from the great. Dip your shoulder, change speed, stutter your steps, employ anything in your bag of tricks to get the work done. *When play breaks down*, good receivers run back toward the quarterback, away from coverage, to help him to find someone to "dump the ball to."

No matter how the ball comes, high or low, fast or lobbed, the first rule of good catching is to catch with your hands, not trap the ball against your body. Here are some further techniques to work on:

Basic high catch

When the ball's coming at or above your head and shoulders, the best technique is to catch it with your hands and your hands alone.

A mental alarm should sound off—not to mention your coach—if you find yourself catching with hands and chest or hands and shoulder pads. Not only do footballs bounce off pads, but when you use any of these surfaces to help you catch you lose a great deal of control. Once the ball is caught and secured in both hands, take it down and hold it against your ribs. Remember, though, that the actual act of catching during a high catch must be a hands-only enterprise. Coach and player alike should insist on this.

A good technique for this kind of catch is to bend both arms slightly and extend them out from your body. Your palms will face out, with your hands only a bit farther apart than the size of the ball, with thumbs just inches apart and fingers spread and pointed upward, with your thumbs and index fingers forming a w.

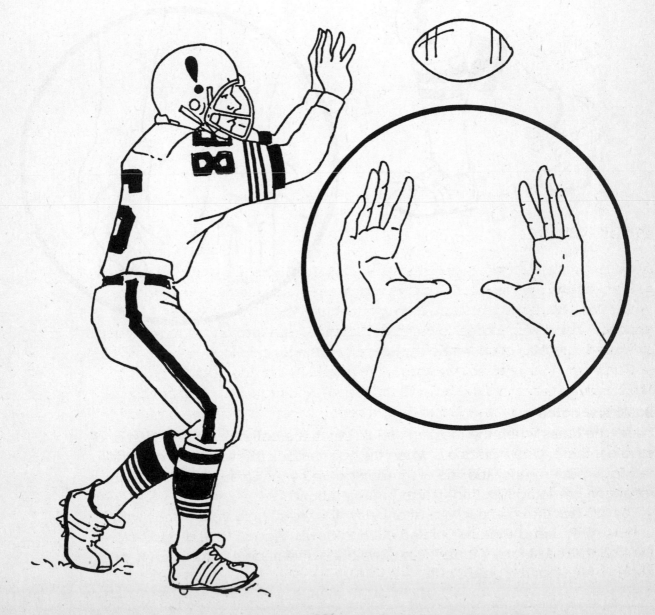

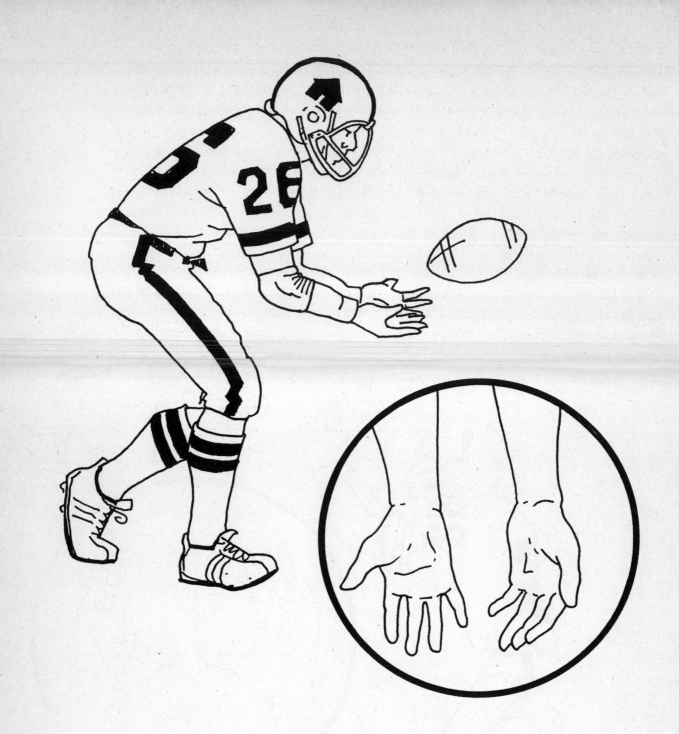

Basic low catch

There are times when the receiver *should* catch the ball at his midsection and cradle it there. One instance is when the quarterback throws low in a short-yardage pattern near the line of scrimmage and you can make a first-down reception by doing little more than turning around.

For catches that come lower, at or below the waist, hold your hands with fingers spread and thumbs pointed out and down. Again, form a pocket for the ball that's just larger than the ball, with the little fingers forming an M and nearly touching, the palms out.

When a ball is thrown over all the defenders and a receiver needs to run under it, he might be tempted to extend his hands too soon, which will slow him down and prevent him from reaching the right spot. Work on your timing on lofted balls so you take them in full stride, waiting to extend the hands until a step or two before the ball arrives.

It's important for wide receivers to remember two things: a ball high in the air is anybody's ball; and don't wait for a ball thrown deep, but instead come back to catch it and always try to catch it at the highest point you can.

Perfect timing.

The Defensive Secondary

The defensive secondary usually is made up of four players, occupying the safety and cornerback positions. These guys are vital for blocking passes and tackling the ball carrier when he escapes the linemen and linebackers. They are some of the fastest men on the team, and they're fast whether they're going forward or backward. They've got to be able to backpedal with good speed in order to cover the receivers.

While their primary job is to prevent passes, looking out for running plays is also important. They must be good tacklers and be tough enough to stop any back who breaks out. Most of all, these players need the alertness to react quickly and the speed to get where they're needed in an instant.

Stance

The stance is a semi-crouch; you won't bend over very far at all. With your inside foot slightly back, keep your eyes on the ball and your arms hanging loosely.

66

As a member of the secondary, you'll have the job of covering the receiver, generally in either a "one-on-one" or a "zone" coverage. In zone coverage, you'll cover any receivers who come into your area and back up any fellow defensive backs. In one-on-one coverage, you'll follow the receiver along his route and mirror his movements—while running backward. You'll stay in your backpedal until the wideout closes the gap. It will be nearly impossible for you to do this and continue to look for the ball at the same time. It's better to watch the receiver. Learn to read his body and face; they will tell you when the ball is coming your way. When he looks at it, that's the time to make your move.

Of course, no matter how well you mark them, receivers do get the ball a good portion of the time. However, an unwary receiver, after he's started his pattern, can be thrown off by a defensive back who gives him a little bump just as he starts his run. If you can manage that, you can slow him down and throw him off his timing and out of his intended pattern.

As we've mentioned earlier, running backward is a skill that must be developed and practiced. As the illustration shows, you begin the backward movement by bending your body forward and taking a short step back with your feet low to the ground and close together. Keep your arms close to your sides with your elbows pumping up in back.

Try to go as fast as you can while staying low and taking short steps. Be aware of head and shoulder fakes, and be ready to switch quickly from a backpedal into a sidestep if the receiver changes direction.

Mirroring the receiver's moves works best if you keep inside of his inside shoulder. This puts you in the best position to learn from him where the ball is and to know the right moment to take your eyes off him and look at the ball. Remember, copy his motions, but try not to anticipate *too* much, or you'll help him fake you out.

In a position to strike.

Defensive backs should make sure to practice "stripping the ball." As the defender in this tackle, when you see you are too late to knock the receiver down or prevent a possible catch, you should come up behind the receiver and raise your arms above the receiver's shoulders.

As the ball arrives, come down in a bear hug outside his arms with your hands curled inside on the ball, and pull his arms apart, forcing the receiver to release the ball.

THE INTERCEPTION

The midair interception provides some of the most thrilling action of football. If you have managed during the play to do a respectable job of covering the receiver, and if you're prepared to take advantage of the interception opportunity, this may be your moment to earn some glory. Be ready to carry out the interception. This means that the moment you realize the ball is yours, be confident, committed, and *go*. It won't be easy—after all, you're in the midst of backpedaling or sidestepping. Just make sure you go hard and *at least get a hand on it*. By trying for the ball, you will probably be taking yourself out of position to tackle the receiver, and the last thing you want to do is allow him a chance to catch the ball and break a big play.

Don't wait for the ball to come to you—drive to the ball and try to catch it at its highest point. Think the ball into your hands with your eyes. Yell "ball" to stop any possible hindrance from your own teammates and alert your other secondary defenders to back you up and the rest of your team to get busy blocking.

At the highest possible point.

6. The <u>Foot</u> Ball Game: Punting, Kicking, Kick Returning

Punting

The punt can be a powerful weapon. When a punter kicks, his defensive team depends on him to move the ball deep inside their opponents' territory. The offense has a very tough time pushing out of their end of the field, since they must play very carefully to avoid giving up the ball near their goal line. With a well-placed kick, the defense will have room to gamble on a little blitz or try to strip the ball, which will help them to intimidate the offense.

Punting is a special kind of kicking and requires a particular technique. Young athletes usually first learn the three-step punting technique: right foot step, left foot step, then kick with the right foot.

As you wait for the center's pass, stand with your left foot in front of you (if you're right-handed and therefore a right-footed kicker). Keep your body relaxed, with your knees slightly bent. It's important to stay balanced, relaxed, and alert—the snap might be a little high or low. You must be ready to move to a miscentered ball with your whole body, whether that means jumping, bending, or sidestepping.

You should give the center a target, using your hands and spreading your fingers. Stretch your arms out with your elbows slightly bent and catch the ball with both hands. That way, you've already got the ball out in front of your body, ready to drop, not held against your chest. This will save crucial seconds.

Once you have the ball in your hands, rotate it to make sure the laces are up—if your foot strikes the laces you could send the ball haywire.

With the laces up and the ball held firmly in two hands, take the first step with your right foot. You should now be balanced and set up for the kick; you shouldn't need to take a full stride or cover a lot of distance.

Next, take a step with your left foot. As you do, draw your right foot back for the kick and release the ball. Make sure that the ball is parallel to the ground as it falls and that you bend your kicking leg back at the knee.

As you bring your kicking leg forward, straighten your knee. Many punters don't straighten their kicking legs completely, but leave the knee slightly bent as they strike the ball. Letting your knee straighten out completely just at impact might give you an extra snap of power. Once they've released the ball, most punters extend their arms at an angle and raise them up to shoulder height as they lift their bodies up. Through all this, the left foot stays on the ground. The right leg keeps on moving for the follow through and keeps going up to head level.

In a more abbreviated punt, the two-step punt, you start with your feet planted together, then take a short step by the left and the big kick.

A big "boot" can be an offensive weapon.

Placekicking

The placekick is a joint effort among three players: the center who snaps the ball, the holder who receives it, and the placekicker who sends it aloft.

Everything the kicker does on a placekick applies also when he's kicking from a tee, as is done during a kickoff. The kicker's motions are identical, but there is no center or holder. He just sets up the ball on the tee as he wants it.

THE CENTER'S ROLE

The center and holder together must place the ball in the right spot for the kicker quickly. The center's job is simple: He lifts the ball from the ground with two hands and hurls it to the holder. This isn't as easy as it sounds, though, because he must accomplish this move from an upside-down position. Practice and more practice is the only thing that gets a center up to speed on this.

Some tips: Lift the ball off the ground and a bit forward before aiming at the holder's hands; then snap it back. Also, hold your power hand more to the side of the ball and release it *before* it reaches your back leg.

Center's correct stance, kicking situation.

72

The holder is the back-up quarterback.

It could be a fake.

THE HOLDER

The player who holds the ball for the kicker is more than a piece of equipment. His is an important job. He must be in the right position to catch the ball and then place the ball exactly as the kicker wants it.

To get in proper position to receive the ball, he should bend down on the knee that's near the kicker and support himself with the other leg. He holds both hands open in a pocket for the ball, arms straight out from his trunk. As soon as he receives the ball, he puts it down about six inches in front of the foot closest to the kicker.

With the ball planted tip down, he rotates it quickly so the laces are toward the goalpost and secures it with his index finger.

The center and the holder train and practice placekick snaps together. Practice will also help them make sure they get the ball in the right position.

73

THE KICKER

A style of placekick originating from soccer, which became popular in football during the 1970s, is the instep kick. It is widely used now, although some kickers still use the old toe kick.

Like the punt, the soccer-style kick requires three steps. Rather than getting set directly behind the ball, the kicker sets up diagonally behind it, at about a 45-degree angle to the left.

Some kickers like to keep their eyes on the place where the ball will be planted and set off as soon as it appears there. Others eye the ball from the moment the center snaps it. In either case, while approaching the ball a kicker should always keep his head down and his eyes on the ball once he has focused on it.

If you've assumed the kicking responsibility, you and your coach together will work to develop a style that suits you. Here are some tips that should help:

- during the set up, stay loose and lean your weight slightly forward;
- immediately before the approach, hold your left foot slightly forward (if you're right-footed), then take one short step on your right foot with the knee slightly bent;

Plant.

Cock.

- next, take one step on your left foot, placing it 8 to 10 inches behind and to the left of the ball. This is the pivot position, from which you'll pivot on your left foot until it points at the target;
- you'll usually want to come down into this pivot on the heel of the left foot. If the field is very wet or slippery, flatten your foot out a bit for stability;
- while planting your pivot foot, you'll have pulled the kicking leg back so that the calf and thigh more or less form a 45-degree angle, with the calf parallel to the ground;
- step three is the kick itself. Let loose with a powerful but controlled sweep, using the front part of the ankle/shoelace area to strike the ball just below its center. While kicking, bring your full body—trunk, hips, shoulders—around to face the goalposts;
- finally, straighten your knee completely as the ball leaves your foot. Concentrate on a follow-through that leaves the kicking foot *and* the plant foot pointed between the goalposts.

Snap.

Follow.

Concentrate!

Kick Returning

The guy who returns the kick is as brave as anyone on the field. Barring a fair catch, he's got to concentrate on catching the ball with steady hands while looking forward to an immediate onslaught of big tacklers. There's also the chance that he'll have to capture a loose ball bouncing crazily about in his own territory.

A punt returner also needs a special instinct about when to catch the punt, when to let it roll, and the right time for a fair catch. Whether a fair catch or not, once you have decided to return a punt or kickoff, your first job is to make sure you catch the ball cleanly.

Don't try to catch a punt as you run; it's too chancy. Concentrate, watch the ball in the air, then move under the ball to catch. Keep your body balanced, and open your hands up with the palms turned to your chest. Firmly grip the ball with both hands before you put it away. Then and only then begin to run.

You need to be fast enough on your feet to elude at least the first tacklers to come at you, fearless enough not to let the idea of them rattle you, and tough enough to take it when they do.

A clear signal.

If you're going to call a fair catch, you will again watch the ball in the air and then move under the ball to complete the catch. In this case, however, you'll have determined that you cannot return it. As you get into position to catch, raise your right arm and give a clear wave. That's the signal for a fair catch. Continue to wave long enough to make the signal clear, then move both hands down and catch it just as described above.

7. Conclusion

For the football novice, the material we've presented here represents a lot of new information. It's up to you to develop strength and endurance, but no matter what your age or natural physical ability, if you're mentally and physically prepared to perform the many skills and techniques of the game, you can have a great time practicing and playing.

Someday when you're a veteran player, these elementary techniques for blocking, tackling, ball carrying, throwing, catching, and kicking will be second nature to you. For now, we hope you're better prepared for the challenges and rewards of this popular team sport, and ready to practice hard and play to win.

Remember, great football players are made, not born.

Have fun!

Sports Rules in Pictures and *Sports Techniques in Pictures* are available at your bookstore or wherever books are sold, or for your convenience, we'll send them directly to you. Just call 1-800-788-6262 or fill out the coupon below and send it to:

The Putnam Publishing Group
390 Murray Hill Parkway, Dept. B
East Rutherford, NJ 07073

			US	CANADA
_____	Baseball Rules in Pictures	399-51597-6	$7.95	$10.50
_____	Basketball Rules in Pictures	399-51590-9	$7.95	$10.50
_____	Football Rules in Pictures	399-51689-1	$7.95	$10.50
_____	Football Techniques in Pictures	399-51769-3	$7.95	$10.50
_____	Golf Rules in Pictures	399-51438-4	$7.95	$10.50
_____	Golf Techniques in Pictures	399-51664-6	$7.95	$10.50
_____	Hockey Rules in Pictures	399-51772-3	$7.95	$10.50
_____	Official Little League Baseball® Rules in Pictures	399-51531-3	$7.95	$10.50
_____	Soccer Rules in Pictures	399-51647-6	$7.95	$10.50
_____	Soccer Techniques in Pictures	399-51701-4	$7.95	$10.50
_____	Softball Rules in Pictures	399-51728-6	$7.95	$10.50
_____	Tennis Rules and Techniques in Pictures	399-51674-3	$7.95	$10.50
_____	Volleyball Rules in Pictures	399-51537-2	$7.95	$10.50

Subtotal $ _____
*Postage & handling $ _____
Sales tax $ _____
(CA, NJ, NY, PA)
Total amount due $ _____
Payable in U.S. funds
(no cash orders accepted)
$15.00 minimum for credit card orders.

*Postage & Handling: $2.50 for 1 book, 75¢ for each additional book up to a maximum of $6.25.

Please send me the titles checked above. Enclosed is my:

❑ check   ❑ money order

Please charge my:

❑ Visa   ❑ MasterCard   ❑ American Express

Card # _____ Expiration date _____

Signature as on charge card _____

Name _____

Address _____

City _____ State _____ Zip _____

Please allow six weeks for delivery. Prices subject to change without notice.

Source key #15

Writer's Choice

Teacher's Annotated Edition

GRAMMAR
WORKBOOK

7

McGraw-Hill

New York, New York Columbus, Ohio Mission Hills, California Peoria, Illinois

Glencoe/McGraw-Hill

A Division of The McGraw·Hill Companies

Printed in the United States of America.

Send all inquiries to:
Glencoe/McGraw-Hill
936 Eastwind Drive
Westerville, Ohio 43081

ISBN 0-02-635148-X (Teacher Edition)
Writer's Choice Grammar Workbook 7

3 4 5 6 7 8 9 10–DBH–00 99 98 97 96

Contents

*H*andbook of Definitions and Rules

SUBJECTS AND PREDICATES

1. The **simple subject** is the key noun or pronoun that tells what the sentence is about. A **compound subject** is made up of two or more simple subjects that are joined by a conjunction and have the same verb.
   The **lantern** glows.   **Moths** and **bugs** fly nearby.

2. The **simple predicate** is the verb or verb phrase that expresses the essential thought about the subject of the sentence. A **compound predicate** is made up of two or more verbs or verb phrases that are joined by a conjunction and have the same subject.
   Rachel **jogged** down the hill.
   Pete **stretched** and **exercised** for an hour.

3. The **complete subject** consists of the simple subject and all the words that modify it.
   Golden curly hair framed the child's face.
   The soft glow of sunset made her happy.

4. The **complete predicate** consists of the simple predicate and all the words that modify it or complete its meaning.
   Lindy **ate a delicious muffin for breakfast.**
   The apple muffin **also contained raisins.**

5. Usually the subject comes before the predicate in a sentence. In inverted sentences, all or part of the predicate precedes the subject.
   (You) Wait for me at the corner. (request)
   Through the toys **raced** the **children.** (inverted)
   Is the **teacher** feeling better? (question)
   There **are seats** in the first row.

PARTS OF SPEECH

Nouns

1. A **singular noun** is a word that names one person, place, thing, or idea.
   aunt   meadow   pencil   friendship

   A **plural noun** names more than one person, place, thing, or idea.
   aunts   meadows   pencils   friendships

2. To help you determine whether a word in a sentence is a noun, try adding it to the following sentences. Nouns will fit in at least one of these sentences:
   He said something about _____.   I know something about a(n) _____.
   He said something about **aunts.**   I know something about a **meadow.**

3. A **common noun** names a general class of people, places, things, or ideas.
   sailor   city   holiday   music

   A **proper noun** specifies a particular person, place, thing, event, or idea. Proper nouns are always capitalized.
   Captain Ahab   **Rome**   **Memorial Day**   *Treasure Island*

4. A **concrete noun** names an object that occupies space or that can be recognized by any of the senses.

   leaf   melody   desk   aroma

   An **abstract noun** names an idea, a quality, or a characteristic.
   peace   health   strength   contentment

5. A **collective noun** names a group. When the collective noun refers to the group as a whole, it is singular. When it refers to the individual group members, the collective noun is plural.
   The **family** eats dinner together every night. (singular)
   The **council** vote as they wish on the pay increase. (plural)

6. A **possessive noun** shows possession, ownership, or the relationship between two nouns.
   Monica's book   the **rabbit's** ears   the **hamster's** cage

Verbs

1. A **verb** is a word that expresses action or a state of being and is necessary to make a statement. A verb will fit one or more of these sentences:
   He _____.   We _____.   She _____ it.
   He **knows**.   We **walk**.   She **sees** it.

2. An **action verb** tells what someone or something does. The two types of action verbs are transitive and intransitive. A **transitive verb** is followed by a word or words—called the direct object—that answer the question *what?* or *whom?* An **intransitive verb** is not followed by a word that answers *what?* or *whom?*
   Transitive: The tourists **saw** the ruins.   The janitor **washed** the window.
   Intransitive: Owls **hooted** during the night.   The children **played** noisily.

3. An indirect object receives what the direct object names.
   Marcy sent **her brother** a present.

4. A **linking verb** links, or joins, the subject of a sentence with an adjective or nominative.
   The trucks **were** red. (adjective)
   She **became** an excellent swimmer. (nominative)

5. A **verb phrase** consists of a main verb and all its auxiliary, or helping, verbs.
   We **had been told** of his arrival.
   They **are listening** to a symphony.

6. Verbs have four **principle parts** or forms: base, past, present participle, and past participle.
   Base: I **talk**.   Present Participle: I am **talking**.
   Past: I **talked**.   Past Participle: I have **talked**.

7. **Irregular verbs** form their past form and past participle without adding *-ed* to the base form.

PRINCIPAL PARTS OF IRREGULAR VERBS

Base Form	Past Form	Past Participle	Base Form	Past Form	Past Participle
be	was, were	been	lead	led	led
beat	beat	beaten	lend	lent	lent
become	became	become	lie	lay	lain
begin	began	begun	lose	lost	lost
bite	bit	bitten *or* bit	put	put	put
blow	blew	blown	ride	rode	ridden
break	broke	broken	ring	rang	rung
bring	brought	brought	rise	rose	risen
catch	caught	caught	run	ran	run
choose	chose	chosen	say	said	said
come	came	come	see	saw	seen
do	did	done	set	set	set
draw	drew	drawn	shrink	shrank *or* shrunk	shrunk *or* shrunken
drink	drank	drunk			
drive	drove	driven	sing	sang	sung
eat	ate	eaten	sit	sat	sat
fall	fell	fallen	speak	spoke	spoken
feel	felt	felt	spring	sprang *or* sprung	sprung
find	found	found			
fly	flew	flown	steal	stole	stolen
freeze	froze	frozen	swim	swam	swum
get	got	got *or* gotten	take	took	taken
give	gave	given	tear	tore	torn
go	went	gone	tell	told	told
grow	grew	grown	think	thought	thought
hang	hung *or* hanged	hung *or* hanged	throw	threw	thrown
			wear	wore	worn
have	had	had	win	won	won
know	knew	known	write	wrote	written
lay	laid	laid			

8. The principle parts are used to form six verb tenses. The **tense** of a verb expresses time.

Simple Tenses
Present Tense: She **speaks.** (present or habitual action)
Past Tense: She **spoke.** (action completed in the past)
Future Tense: She **will speak.** (action to be done in the future)

Perfect Tenses
Present Perfect Tense: She **has spoken.** (action just done or still in effect)
Past Perfect Tense: She **had spoken.** (action completed before some other past action)
Future Perfect Tense: She **will have spoken.** (action to be completed before some future time)

9. **Progressive forms** of verbs are made up of a form of *be* and a present participle and express a continuing action. **Emphatic forms** are made up of a form of *do* and a base form and add emphasis or ask questions.

   Progressive: Marla **is babysitting.**   The toddlers **have been napping** for an hour.
   Emphatic: They **do prefer** beef to pork.
              We **did ask** for a quiet table.

10. The **voice** of a verb shows whether the subject performs the action or receives the action of the verb. A sentence is in the **active voice** when the subject performs the action. A sentence is in the **passive voice** when the subject receives the action of the verb.

    The robin **ate** the worm. (active)
    The worm **was eaten** by the robin. (passive)

Pronouns

1. A **pronoun** takes the place of a noun, a group of words acting as a noun, or another pronoun.

2. A **personal pronoun** refers to a specific person or thing. **First-person** personal pronouns refer to the speaker, **second-person** pronouns refer to the one spoken to, and **third-person** pronouns refer to the one spoken about.

	Singular	Plural
First Person	I, me, my, mine	we, us, our, ours
Second Person	you, your, yours	you, your, yours
Third Person	he, she, it, him, her, his, hers, its	they, them, their, theirs

3. A **reflexive pronoun** refers to the subject of the sentence. An **intensive pronoun** adds emphasis to a noun or another pronoun. A **demonstrative pronoun** points out specific persons, places, things, or ideas.

   Reflexive: **Nikki** prepares **himself** for the day-long hike.
   Intensive: **Nikki himself** prepares for the day-long hike.
   Demonstrative: **That** was a good movie! **These** are the files you wanted.

4. An **interrogative pronoun** is used to form questions. A **relative pronoun** is used to introduce a subordinate clause. An **indefinite pronoun** refers to persons, places, or things in a more general way than a personal pronoun does.

   Interrogative: **Whose** are these?   **Which** did you prefer?
   Relative: The bread **that** we tasted was whole wheat.
   Indefinite: **Someone** has already told them. **Everyone** agrees on the answer.

5. Use the subject form of a personal pronoun when it is used as a subject or when it follows a linking verb.

   He writes stories.   Are **they** ready?   It is **I.** (after linking verb)

6. Use the object form of a personal pronoun when it is an object.

   Mrs. Cleary called **us.** (direct object)   Stephen offered **us** a ride. (indirect object)
   Sara will go with **us.** (object of preposition)

7. Use a **possessive pronoun** to replace a possessive noun. Never use an apostrophe in a possessive personal pronoun.

   Their science experiment is just like **ours.**

8. When a pronoun is followed by an appositive, use the subject pronoun if the appositive is the subject. Use the object pronoun if the appositive is an object. To test whether the pronoun is correct, read the sentence without the appositive.
We eighth-graders would like to thank you.
The success of **us** geometry students is due to Ms. Marcia.

9. In incomplete comparisons, choose the pronoun that you would use if the missing words were fully expressed.
Harris can play scales faster than **I** (can).
It is worth more to you than (it is to) **me**.

10. In questions use *who* for subjects and *whom* for objects.
Who wants another story?
Whom will the class choose as treasurer?

In subordinate clauses use *who* and *whoever* as subjects and after linking verbs, and use *whom* and *whomever* as objects.
These souvenirs are for **whoever** wants to pay the price.
The manager will train **whomever** the president hires.

11. An **antecedent** is the word or group of words to which a pronoun refers or that a pronoun replaces. All pronouns must agree with their antecedents in number, gender, and person.
Marco's **sister** spent **her** vacation in San Diego.
The huge old **trees** held **their** own against the storm.

12. Make sure that the antecedent of a pronoun is clearly stated.
UNCLEAR: Mrs. Cardonal baked cookies with her daughters, hoping to sell **them** at the bake sale.
CLEAR: Mrs. Cardonal baked cookies with her daughters, hoping to sell **the cookies** at the bake sale.
UNCLEAR: If you don't tie the balloon to the stroller, **it** will blow away.
CLEAR: If you don't tie the balloon to the stroller, **the balloon** will blow away.

Adjectives

1. An **adjective** modifies, or describes, a noun or pronoun by providing more information or giving a specific detail.
The **smooth** surface of the lake gleamed.
Frosty trees glistened in the sun.

2. Most adjectives will fit this sentence:
The _____ one seems very _____.
The **handmade** one seems very **colorful.**

3. **Articles** are the adjectives *a, an,* and *the.* Articles do not meet the preceding test for adjectives.

4. A **proper adjective** is formed from a proper noun and begins with a capital letter.
Tricia admired the **Scottish** sweaters.
Our **Mexican** vacation was memorable.

5. The comparative form of an adjective compares two things or people. The superlative form compares more than two things or people. Form the comparative by adding *-er* or combining with *more* or *less.* Form the superlative by adding *-est* or combining with *most* or *least.*

POSITIVE	COMPARATIVE	SUPERLATIVE
slow	slower	slowest
charming	more charming	most charming

6. Some adjectives have irregular comparative forms.

POSITIVE:	good, well	bad	far	many, much	little
COMPARATIVE:	better	worse	farther	more	less
SUPERLATIVE:	best	worst	farthest	most	least

Adverbs

1. An **adverb** modifies a verb, an adjective, or another adverb. Adverbs tell *how, where, when,* or *to what extent.*
   The cat walked **quietly.** (how)
   She **seldom** misses a deadline. (when)
   The player moved **forward.** (where)
   The band was **almost** late. (to what extent)

2. Many adverbs fit these sentences:

She thinks _____.	She thinks _____ fast.	She _____ thinks fast.
She thinks **quickly.**	She thinks **unusually** fast.	She **seldom** thinks fast.

3. The comparative form of an adverb compares two actions. The superlative form compares more than two actions. For shorter adverbs add *-er* or *-est* to form the comparative or superlative. For most adverbs, add *more* or *most* or *less* or *least* to form the comparative or superlative.
   We walked **faster** than before.
   They listened **most carefully** to the final speaker.

4. Avoid **double negatives,** which are two negative words in the same clause.
   INCORRECT: I have not seen no stray cats.
   CORRECT: I have not seen any stray cats.

Prepositions, Conjunctions, and Interjections

1. A **preposition** shows the relationship of a noun or a pronoun to some other word. A **compound preposition** is made up of more than one word.
   The trees **near** our house provide plenty **of** shade.
   The schools were closed **because of** snow.

2. Common prepositions include these: *about, above, according to, across, after, against, along, among, around, as, at, because of, before, behind, below, beneath, beside, besides, between, beyond, but, by, concerning, down, during, except, for, from, in, inside, in spite of, into, like, near, of, off, on, out, outside, over, past, round, since, through, till, to, toward, under, underneath, until, up, upon, with, within, without.*

3. A **conjunction** is a word that joins single words or groups of words. A **coordinating conjunction** joins words or groups of words that have equal grammatical weight. **Correlative conjunctions** work in pairs to join words and groups of words of equal weight. A **subordinating conjunction** joins two clauses in such a way as to make one grammatically dependent on the other.

I want to visit the art gallery **and** the museum. (coordinating)

Both left **and** right turns were impossible in the traffic. (correlative)

We go to the park **whenever** Mom lets us. (subordinating)

COMMON CONJUCTIONS

Coordinating:	and	but	for	nor	or	so	yet

Correlative:	both...and	neither...nor	whether...or
	either...or	not only...but also	

Subordinating:	after	as though	since	when
	although	because	so that	whenever
	as	before	than	where
	as if	even though	though	wherever
	as long as	if	unless	whether
	as soon as	in order that	until	while

4. A **conjunctive adverb** clarifies a relationship.

Frank loved the old maple tree; **nevertheless,** he disliked raking its leaves.

5. An **interjection** is an unrelated word or phrase that expresses emotion or strong feeling.

Look, there are two cardinals at the feeder.   **Good grief!** Are you kidding?

CLAUSES AND COMPLEX SENTENCES

1. A **clause** is a group of words that has a subject and a predicate and is used as a sentence or a part of a sentence. There are two types of clauses: main and subordinate. A **main clause** has a subject and a predicate and can stand alone as a sentence. A **subordinate clause** has a subject and a predicate, but it cannot stand alone as a sentence.

     main   sub.

She became a veterinarian because she loves animals.

2. There are three types of subordinate clauses: adjective, adverb, and noun.

   a. An **adjective clause** is a subordinate clause that modifies a noun or pronoun.
   The wrens **that built a nest in the backyard** are now raising their young.

   b. An **adverb clause** is a subordinate clause that often modifies the verb in the main clause of the sentence. It tells *when, where, how, why,* or *under what conditions.*
   Before they got out, the goats broke the fence in several places.

   c. A **noun clause** is a subordinate clause used as a noun.
   Whatever we do will have to please everyone. (subject)
   The prize goes to **whoever can keep the squirrels away from the feeder.** (object of preposition)

3. Main and subordinate clauses can form several types of sentences. A **simple sentence** has only one main clause and no subordinate clauses. A **compound sentence** has two or more main clauses. A **complex sentence** has at least one main clause and one or more subordinate clauses.

                            main
Simple: The apples fell off the tree.

                   main   main
Compound: The dancers bowed, and the audience clapped.

                       sub.   main
Complex: Because they turn to face the sun, these flowers are called sunflowers.

4. A sentence that makes a statement is classified as a **declarative sentence**.
My dad's favorite horses are buckskins.

An **imperative sentence** gives a command or makes a request.
Please close the door on your way out.

An **interrogative sentence** asks a question.
When will the mail carrier arrive?

An **exclamatory sentence** expresses strong emotion.
Watch out!
What a view that is!

Phrases

1. A **phrase** is a group of words that acts in a sentence as a single part of speech.

2. A **prepositional phrase** is a group of words that begins with a preposition and ends with a noun or pronoun, which is called the **object of the preposition**. A prepositional phrase can act as an adjective or an adverb.
The house **on the hill** is white. (modifies the noun *house*)
Everyone **in the house** heard the storm. (modifies the pronoun *everyone*)
The geese flew **toward warmer weather**. (modifies the verb *flew*)

3. An **appositive** is a noun or pronoun that is placed next to another noun or pronoun to identify it or give more information about it. An **appositive phrase** is an appositive plus its modifiers.
Our sister **Myra** is home from college. Her college, **Purdue University**, is in Indiana.

4. A **verbal** is a verb form that functions in a sentence as a noun, an adjective, or an adverb. A **verbal phrase** is a verbal and other words that complete its meaning.

  a. A **participle** is a verbal that functions as an adjective. Present participles end in *-ing*. Past participles usually end in *-ed*.
    The **squeaking** floor board gave me away.   The **twisted** tree was ancient.

  b. A **participial phrase** contains a participle and other words that complete its meaning.
    Moving quickly across the room, the baby crawled toward her mother.

c. A **gerund** is a verbal that ends in *-ing.* It is used in the same way a noun is used.
Sailing is a traditional vacation activity for the Andersons.

d. A **gerund phrase** is a gerund plus any complements or modifiers.
Walking to school is common for many school children.

e. An **infinitive** is a verbal formed from the word *to* and the base form of a verb. It is often used as a noun. Because an infinitive acts as a noun, it may be the subject of a sentence or the direct object of an action verb.
To sing can be uplifting. (infinitive as subject)
Babies first learn **to babble**. (infinitive as direct object)

f. An **infinitive phrase** contains an infinitive plus any complements or modifiers.
The flight attendants prepared **to feed the hungry passengers**.

SUBJECT-VERB AGREEMENT

1. A verb must agree with its subject in person and number.
   The kangaroo **jumps.** (singular)   The kangaroos **jump.** (plural)
   She **is leaping.** (singular)   They **are leaping.** (plural)

2. In **inverted sentences** the subject follows the verb. The sentence may begin with a prepositional phrase, the word *there* or *here,* or a form of *do.*
   Into the pond **dove** the *children.*
   Does a *bird* **have** a sense of smell?
   There **is** a *squeak* in that third stair.

3. Do not mistake a word in a prepositional phrase for the subject.
   The **glass** in the window **is** streaked. (The singular verb *is* agrees with the subject, *glass.*)

4. A title is always singular, even if nouns in the title are plural.
   Instant World Facts **is** a helpful reference book.

5. Subjects combined with *and* or *both* need a plural verb unless the parts are of a whole unit. When compound subjects are joined with *or* or *nor,* the verb agrees with the subject listed last.
   Canterbury and Coventry have famous cathedrals.
   A **bagel and cream cheese is** a filling snack.
   Either two short **stories or** a **novel is** acceptable for your book report.

6. A verb must agree in number with an indefinite pronoun subject. Indefinite pronouns that are always singular: *anybody, anyone, anything, each, either, everybody, everyone, everything, neither, nobody, no one, nothing, one, somebody, someone,* and *something*
   Always plural: *both, few, many, others,* and *several*
   Either singular or plural: *all, any, most, none,* and *some*

   Most of the snow **has** melted.   **All** of the children **have** eaten.

USAGE GLOSSARY

a lot, alot Always write this expression, meaning "very much" or "a large amount," as two words.
The neighbors pitched in, and the job went **a lot** faster.

accept, except *Accept,* a verb, means "to receive" or "to agree to." *Except* may be a preposition or a verb. As a preposition it means "other than." As a verb it means "to leave out, to make an exception."
I **accept** your plan.   We ate everything **except** the crust.

all ready, already *All ready* means "completely prepared." *Already* means "before" or "by this time."
They were **all ready** to leave, but the bus had **already** departed.

all together, altogether The two words *all together* mean "in a group." The single word *altogether* is an adverb meaning "completely" or "on the whole."
The teachers met **all together** after school.
They were **altogether** prepared for a heated discussion.

beside, besides *Beside* means "next to." *Besides* means "in addition to."
The sink is **beside** the refrigerator.
Besides the kitchen, the den is my favorite room.

between, among Use *between* to refer to or to compare two separate nouns. Use *among* to show a relationship in a group.
The joke was **between** Hilary and Megan.
The conversation **among** the teacher, the principal, and the janitor was friendly.

bring, take Use *bring* to show movement from a distant place to a closer one. Use *take* to show movement from a nearby place to a more distant one.
You may **bring** your model here.
Please **take** a brochure with you when you go.

can, may *Can* indicates the ability to do something. *May* indicates permission to do something.
Constance **can** walk to school.
She **may** ride the bus if she wishes.

choose, chose *Choose* means "to select." *Chose* is the past participle form, meaning "selected."
I **choose** the blue folder.
Celia **chose** the purple folder.

fewer, less Use *fewer* with nouns that can be counted. Use *less* with nouns that cannot be counted.
There were **fewer** sunny days this year.
I see **less** fog today than I expected.

formally, formerly *Formally* is the adverb form of formal. *Formerly* is an adverb meaning "in times past."
They **formally** agreed to the exchange.
Lydia **formerly** lived in Spain, but now she lives in New York City.

in, into Use *in* to mean "inside" or "within" and *into* to indicate movement or direction from outside to a point within.
The birds nest **in** the trees.
A bird flew **into** our window yesterday.

its, it's *Its* is the possessive form of the pronoun *it*. Possessive pronouns never have apostrophes. *It's* is the contraction of *it is*.
The dog lives in **its** own house.   Who is to say whether **it's** happy or not.

lay, lie *Lay* means "to put" or "to place," and it takes a direct object. *Lie* means "to recline" or "to be positioned," and it never takes an object.
We **lay** the uniforms on the shelves each day.
The players **lie** on the floor to do their sit-ups.

learn, teach *Learn* means "to receive knowledge." *Teach* means "to give knowledge."
Children can **learn** foreign languages at an early age.
Mr. Minton will **teach** French to us next year.

leave, let *Leave* means "to go away." *Let* means "to allow" or "to permit."
I will **leave** after fourth period.
Dad will **let** me go swimming today.

loose, lose Use *loose* to mean "not firmly attached" and *lose* to mean "to misplace" or "to fail to win."
The bike chain was very **loose**.
I did not want to **lose** my balance.

many, much Use *many* with nouns that can be counted. Use *much* with nouns that cannot be counted.
Many ants were crawling near the anthill.
There was **much** discussion about what to do.

precede, proceed *Precede* means "to go or come before." *Proceed* means "to continue."
Lunch will **precede** the afternoon session.
Marly can **proceed** with her travel plans.

quiet, quite *Quiet* means "calm" or "motionless." *Quite* means "completely" or "entirely."
The sleeping kitten was **quiet**.
The other kittens were **quite** playful.

raise, rise *Raise* means "to cause to move upward," and it always takes an object. *Rise* means "to get up"; it is intransitive and never takes an object.
Please **raise** your hand if you would like to help.
I left the bread in a warm spot to **rise**.

sit, set *Sit* means "to place oneself in a sitting position." It rarely takes an object. *Set* means "to place" or "to put" and usually takes an object. *Set* can also be used to describe the sun going down.
Please **sit** in your assigned seats.   **Set** those dishes down.
The sun **set** at 6:14.

than, then *Than* is a conjunction that is used to introduce the second element in a comparison; it also shows exception. *Then* is an adverb meaning "at that time."
Wisconsin produces more milk **than** any other state.
First get comfortable, **then** look the pitcher right in the eye.

their, they're *Their* is the possessive form of the personal pronoun *they*. *They're* is the contraction of *they are*.
The Westons returned to **their** favorite vacation spot.
They're determined to go next year as well.

theirs, there's *Theirs* means "that or those belonging to them." *There's* is the contraction of *there is.*
Theirs is one of the latest models.
There's another pitcher of lemonade in the refrigerator.

to, too, two *To* is a preposition meaning "in the direction of." *Too* means "also" or "excessively." *Two* is the number that falls between one and three.
You may go **to** the library.
It is **too** cold for skating.
There are only **two** days of vacation left.

where at Do not use *at* in a sentence after *where.*
Where were you yesterday afternoon? (*not* Where were you at yesterday afternoon?)

who's, whose *Who's* is the contraction of *who is. Whose* is the possessive form of *who.*
Who's willing to help me clean up?
Do you know **whose** books these are?

your, you're *Your* is the possessive form of *you. You're* is the contraction of *you are.*
Please arrange **your** schedule so that you can be on time.
If **you're** late, you may miss something important.

CAPITALIZATION

1. Capitalize the first word of every sentence, including direct quotations and sentences in parentheses unless they are contained within another sentence.
   In *Poor Richard's Almanack,* Benjamin Franklin advises, "**W**ish not so much to live long as to live well." (**T**his appeared in the almanac published in 1738.)

2. Capitalize the first word in the salutation and closing of a letter. Capitalize the title and name of the person addressed.
   Dear **P**rofessor **N**ichols:
   Sincerely yours,

3. Always capitalize the pronoun *I* no matter where it appears in the sentence.
   Since **I** knew you were coming, **I** baked a cake.

4. Capitalize the following proper nouns:

   a. Names of individuals, the initials that stand for their names, and titles preceding a name or used instead of a name

Governor **C**ordoba	**A. C. S**hen
Aunt **M**argaret	**D**r. **H. C. H**arada
General **D**iaz	

   b. Names and abbreviations of academic degrees, and *Jr.* and *Sr.*
   Richard **B**oe, **Ph.D.**
   Sammy **D**avis **Jr.**

   c. Names of cities, countries, states, continents, bodies of water, sections of the United States, and compass points when they refer to a specific section of the United States

Boston	**D**ade **C**ounty	**N**orth **C**arolina	**A**ustralia
Amazon **R**iver	the **S**outh		

   d. Names of streets, highways, organizations, institutions, firms, monuments, bridges, buildings, other structures, and celestial bodies

Route 51	**C**ircle **K S**ociety	**T**omb of the **U**nknown **S**oldier
Golden **G**ate **B**ridge	**C**oventry **C**athedral	**N**orth **S**tar

   e. Trade names and names of documents, awards, and laws

No-**S**neez tissues	the **F**ourteenth **A**mendment
Golden **G**lobe **A**ward	the **M**onroe **D**octrine

   f. Names of most historical events, eras, holidays, days of the week, and months

Boston **T**ea **P**arty	**B**ronze **A**ge	**L**abor **D**ay	**F**riday **J**uly

   g. First, last, and all important words in titles of literary works, works of art, and musical compositions

"**I A**sk **M**y **M**other to **S**ing" (poem)	*Giants in the Earth* (book)
Venus de **M**ilo (statue)	"**A**merica, the **B**eautiful" (composition)

   h. Names of ethnic groups, national groups, political parties and their members, and languages

Hispanics	**C**hinese	**I**rish	**I**talian	**R**epublican party

5. Capitalize proper adjectives (adjectives formed from proper nouns).

English saddle horse	**T**hai restaurant	**M**idwestern plains

PUNCTUATION, ABBREVIATIONS, AND NUMBERS

1. Use a period at the end of a declarative sentence and at the end of a polite command.
   Mrs. Miranda plays tennis every Tuesday.
   Write your name in the space provided.

2. Use a question mark at the end of an interrogative sentence.
   When will the new books arrive?

3. Use an exclamation point to show strong feeling and indicate a forceful command.

   Oh, no!   It was a terrific concert!   Don't go outside without your gloves on!

4. Use a comma in the following situations:

   a. To separate three or more words, phrases, or clauses in a series
   A tent, sleeping bag, and sturdy shoes are essential wilderness camping equipment.

   b. To set off two or more prepositional phrases
   After the sound of the bell, we realized it was a false alarm.

   c. After an introductory participle and an introductory participial phrase
   Marveling at the sight, we waited to see another shooting star.

   d. After conjunctive adverbs
   Snow is falling; however, it is turning to sleet.

   e. To set off an appositive if it is not essential to the meaning of the sentence
   Mr. Yoshino, the head of the department, resigned yesterday.

   f. To set off words or phrases of direct address
   Micha, have you called your brother yet?
   It's good to see you, Mrs. Han.

   g. Between the main clauses of compound sentences
   Whiskers liked to watch the goldfish, and she sometimes dipped her paw in the bowl.

   h. After an introductory adverb clause and to set off a nonessential adjective clause
   Whenever we get careless, we always make mistakes.
   Spelling errors, which are common, can now be corrected by computer.

   i. To separate parts of an address or a date
   1601 Burma Drive, Waterbury, Connecticut
   She was born on February 2, 1985, and she now lives in Bangor, Maine.

   j. After the salutation and close of a friendly letter and after the close of a business letter
   Dear Dad,   Cordially,   Yours,

5. Use a semicolon in the following situations:

   a. To join main clauses not joined by a coordinating conjunction
   The house looks dark; perhaps we should have called first.

   b. To separate two main clauses joined by a coordinating conjunction when such clauses already contain several commas
   After a week of rain, the farmers around Ames, Iowa, waited hopefully; but the rain, unfortunately, had come too late.

   c. To separate main clauses joined by a conjunctive adverb or by *for example* or *that is*
   Jen was determined to win the race; nonetheless, she knew that it took more than determination to succeed.

6. Use a colon to introduce a list of items that ends a sentence.
   Bring the following tools: hammer, speed square, and drill.

7. Use a colon to separate the hour and the minute in time measurements and after business letter salutations.
   12:42 A.M.   Dear Sir: Dear Ms. O'Connor:

8. Use quotation marks to enclose a direct quotation. When a quotation is interrupted, use two sets of quotation marks. Use single quotation marks for a quotation within a quotation.
   "Are you sure," asked my mother, "that you had your keys when you left home?"
   "Chief Seattle's speech begins, 'My words are like the stars that never change,'" stated the history teacher.

9. Always place commas and periods inside closing quotations marks. Place colons and semicolons outside closing quotation marks. Place question marks and exclamation points inside closing quotation marks only when those marks are part of the quotation.
   "Giraffes," said Ms. Wharton, "spend long hours each day foraging."
   You must read "The Story of an Hour"; it is a wonderful short story.
   He called out, "Is anyone home?"
   Are you sure she said, "Go home without me"?

10. Use quotation marks to indicate titles of short stories, poems, essays, songs, and magazine or newspaper articles.
    "The Thrill of the Grass" (short story)
    "My Country 'Tis of Thee" (song)

11. Italicize (underline) titles of books, plays, films, television series, paintings and sculptures, and names of newspapers and magazines.
    Up from Slavery (book)
    Free Willy (film)
    The Spirit of '76 (painting)
    Chicago Tribune (newspaper)
    Weekend Woodworker (magazine)

12. Add an apostrophe and -*s* to form the possessive of singular indefinite pronouns, singular nouns, and plural nouns not ending in -*s*. Add only an apostrophe to plural nouns ending in -*s* to make them possessive.
    everyone's best friend
    the rabbit's ears
    the children's toys
    the farmers' fields

13. Use an apostrophe in place of omitted letters or numerals. Use an apostrophe and -*s* to form the plural of letters, numerals, and symbols.
    is + not = isn't
    will + not = won't
    1776 is '76
    Cross your *t*'s and dot your *i*'s.

14. Use a hyphen to divide words at the end of a line.
    esti-mate   mone-tary   experi-mentation

15. Use a hyphen in a compound adjective that precedes a noun. Use a hyphen in compound numbers and fractions used as adjectives.
    a blue-green parrot
    a salt-and-pepper beard
    twenty-nine
    one-third cup of flour

16. Use a hyphen after any prefix joined to a proper noun or a proper adjective. Use a hyphen after the prefixes *all-*, *ex-*, and *self-* joined to a noun or adjective, the prefix *anti-* joined to a word beginning with *i-*, and the prefix *vice-* except in the case of *vice president*.
    all-knowing   ex-spouse   self-confidence
    anti-inflammatory   vice-principal

17. Use dashes to signal a break or change in thought.
    I received a letter from Aunt Carla—you have never met her—saying she is coming to visit.

18. Use parentheses to set off supplemental material. Punctuate within the parentheses only if the punctuation is part of the parenthetical expression.
    Place one gallon (3.8 liters) of water in a plastic container.

19. Abbreviate a person's title and professional or academic degrees.
    Ms. K. Soga, **Ph.D.**
    Dr. Quentin

20. Use the abbreviations *A.M.* and *P.M.* and *B.C.* and *A.D.*
    9:45 **A.M.**   1000 **B.C.**   **A.D.** 1455

21. Abbreviate numerical measurements in scientific writing but not in ordinary prose.
    The newborn snakes measured 3.4 **in.** long.
    Pour 45 **ml** warm water into the beaker.

22. Spell out cardinal and ordinal numbers that can be written in one or two words or that appear at the beginning of a sentence.
    Two hundred twenty runners crossed the finish line.
    Observers counted **forty-nine** sandhill cranes.

23. Express all related numbers in a sentence as numerals if any one should be expressed as a numeral.
    There were **127** volunteers, but only **9** showed up because of the bad weather.

24. Spell out ordinal numbers.
Nina won **third** place in the spelling bee.

25. Use words for decades, for amounts of money that can be written in one or two words, and for the approximate time of day or when A.M. or P.M. is not used.

the **nineties**   **ten** dollars   **sixty** cents   half past **five**

26. Use numerals for dates; for decimals; for house, apartment, and room numbers; for street or avenue numbers; for telephone numbers; for page numbers; for percentages; for sums of money involving both dollars and cents; and to emphasize the exact time of day or when A.M. or P.M. is used.

June **5, 1971**   Apartment **4G**   **$207.89**
0.0045   **1520 14**th Street   **8:20** A.M.

VOCABULARY AND SPELLING

1. Clues to the meaning of an unfamiliar word can be found in its context. Context clues include definitions, the meaning stated; example, the meaning explained through one familiar case; comparison, similarity to a familiar word; contrast, opposite of a familiar word; and cause and effect, a reason and its results.

2. The meaning of a word can be obtained from its base word, its prefix, or its suffix.
telegram **tele** = distant   dentate **dent** = tooth
subarctic **sub** = below   marvelous **-ous** = full of

3. The *i* comes before the *e*, except when both letters follow a *c* or when both letters are pronounced together as an $\bar{a}$ sound. However, many exceptions exist to this rule.
yield (*i* before *e*)   rec**ei**ve (*ei* after *c*)   weigh ($\bar{a}$ sound)   **height** (exception)

4. An unstressed vowel is a vowel sound that is not emphasized when the word is pronounced. Determine how to spell this sound by comparing it to a known word.
inform**a**nt (compare to *information*)   hospit**a**l (*compare to hospitality*)

5. When joining a prefix that ends in the same letter as the word, keep both consonants.
illegible   **diss**ervice

6. When adding a suffix to a word ending in a consonant + *y*, change the *y* to *i* unless the prefix begins with an *i*. If the word ends in a vowel + *y*, keep the *y*.
tr**ied**   play**ed**   spra**ying**

7. Double the final consonant before adding a suffix that begins with a vowel to a word that ends in a single consonant preceded by a single vowel if the accent is on the root's last syllable.
pop**ping**   transfer**red**   unforget**table**

8. When adding a suffix that begins with a consonant to a word that ends in silent *e*, generally keep the *e*. If the suffix begins with a vowel or *y*, generally drop the *e*. If the suffix begins with *a* or *o* and the word ends in *ce* or *ge*, keep the *e*. If the suffix begins with a vowel and the word ends in *ee* or *oe*, keep the *e*.
state**ly**   noisy   courag**eous**   agree**able**

9. When adding -*ly* to a word that ends in a single *l*, keep the *l*. If it ends in a double *l*, drop one *l*. If it ends in a consonant + *le*, drop the *le*.
   meal, mea**lly**   full, ful**ly**   incredible, incredi**bly**

10. When forming compound words, maintain the spelling of both words.
   backpack   honeybee

11. Most nouns form their plurals by adding -*s*. However, nouns that end in -*ch*, -*s*, -*sh*, -*x*, or -*z* form plurals by adding -*es*. If the noun ends in a consonant + *y*, change *y* to *i* and add -*es*. If the noun ends in -*lf*, change *f* to *v* and add -*es*. If the noun ends in -*fe*, change *f* to *v* and add -*s*.
   mark**s**   leach**es**   rash**es**   fox**es**
   fl**ies**   el**ves**   li**ves**

12. To form the plural of proper names and one-word compound nouns, follow the general rules for plurals. To form the plural of hyphenated compound nouns or compound nouns of more than one word, make the most important word plural.
   Wilson**s**   Diaz**es**   housekeeper**s**
   sister**s**-in-law   editor**s**-in-chief

13. Some nouns have the same singular and plural forms.
   deer   moose

Composition

Writing Themes and Paragraphs

1. Use **prewriting**to find ideas to write about. One form of prewriting, **freewriting**, starts with a subject or topic and branches off into related ideas. Another way to find a topic is to ask and answer questions about your starting subject, helping you to gain a deeper understanding of your chosen topic. Also part of the prewriting stage is determining who your readers or **audience**will be and deciding your **purpose**for writing. Your purpose—writing to persuade, to explain, to describe something, or to narrate—is partially shaped by who your audience will be.

2. To complete your first **draft** organize your prewriting into an introduction, body, and conclusion. Concentrate on unity and coherence of the overall piece. Experiment with different paragraph orders: **chronological order**places events in the order in which they happened; **spatial order**places objects in the order in which they appear; and **compare/contrast order**shows similarities and differences in objects or events.

3. **Revise**your composition if necessary. Read through your draft, looking for places to improve content and structure. Remember that varying your sentence patterns and lengths will make your writing easier and more enjoyable to read.

4. In the **editing** stage, check your grammar, spelling, and punctuation. Focus on expressing your ideas clearly and concisely.

5. Finally, prepare your writing for **presentation**. Sharing your composition, or ideas, with others may take many forms: printed, oral, or graphic.

Outlining

1. The two common forms of outlines are **sentence outlines** and **topic outlines**. Choose one type of outline and keep it uniform throughout.

2. A period follows the number or letter of each division. Each point in a sentence outline ends with a period; the points in a topic outline do not.

3. Each point begins with a capital letter.

4. A point may have no fewer than two subpoints.

SENTENCE OUTLINE
I. This is the main point.
    A. This is a subpoint of *I*.
      1. This is a detail of *A*.
        a. This is a detail of *1*.
        b. This is a detail of *1*.
      2. This is a detail of *A*.
    B. This is a subpoint of *I*.
II. This is another main point.

TOPIC OUTLINE
I. Main point
    A. Subpoint of *I*
      1. Detail of *A*
        a. Detail of *1*
        b. Detail of *1*
      2. Detail of *A*
    B. Subpoint of *I*
II. Main point

Writing Letters

1. **Personal letters** are usually handwritten in indented form (first line of paragraphs, each line of the heading and inside address, and the signature are indented). **Business letters** are usually typewritten in block or semiblock form. Block form contains no indents; semiblock form indents only the first line of each paragraph.

2. The five parts of a personal letter are the heading (the writer's address and the date), salutation (greeting), body (message), complimentary close (such as "Yours truly,"), and signature (the writer's name). Business letters have the same parts and also include an inside address (the recipient's address).

PERSONAL LETTER

Heading	_____
_____ Salutation	
Body	
Complimentary Close _____	
Signature _____	

BUSINESS LETTER

Heading	_____
_____ Inside Address	
_____ Salutation	
_____ Body	
Complimentary Close	
Signature _____	

3. Reveal your personality and imagination in colorful personal letters. Keep business letters brief, clear, and courteous.

4. **Personal letters** include letters to friends and family members. **Thank-you notes** and **invitations** are personal letters that may be either formal or informal in style.

5. Use a **letter of request**, a type of business letter, to ask for information or to place an order. Be concise, yet give all the details necessary for your request to be fulfilled. Keep the tone of your letter courteous, and be generous in allotting time for a response.

6. Use an **opinion letter** to take a firm stand on an issue. Make the letter clear, firm, rational, and purposeful. Be aware of your audience, their attitude, how informed they are, and their possible reactions to your opinion. Support your statements of opinion with facts.

*T*roubleshooter

· ·

Sentence Fragment

PROBLEM 1

Fragment that lacks a subject

frag	Martha asked about dinner. (Hoped it was lasagna.)
frag	I jogged around the park twice. (Was hot and tired afterward.)
frag	Li Cheng raced to the bus stop. (Arrived just in the nick of time.)

SOLUTION

Martha asked about dinner. She hoped it was lasagna.

I jogged around the park twice. I was hot and tired afterward.

Li Cheng raced to the bus stop. He arrived just in the nick of time.

Make a complete sentence by adding a subject to the fragment.

PROBLEM 2

Fragment that lacks a predicate

frag	The carpenter worked hard all morning. (His assistant after lunch.)
frag	Ant farms are fascinating. (The ants around in constant motion.)
frag	Our class went on a field trip. (Mammoth Cave.)

SOLUTION

The carpenter worked hard all morning. His assistant helped after lunch.

Ant farms are fascinating. The ants crawl around in constant motion.

Our class went on a field trip. Mammoth Cave was our destination.

Make a complete sentence by adding a predicate.

PROBLEM 3

Fragment that lacks both a subject and a predicate

frag   I heard the laughter of the children. In the nursery.

frag   After the spring rain. The whole house smelled fresh and clean.

frag   The noisy chatter of the squirrels awakened us early. In the morning.

SOLUTION

I heard the laughter of the children in the nursery.

After the spring rain, the whole house smelled fresh and clean.

The noisy chatter of the squirrels awakened us early in the morning.

Combine the fragment with another sentence.

More help in avoiding sentence fragments is available in Lesson 5.

Run-on Sentence

PROBLEM 1

Two main clauses separated only by a comma

run-on (Extra crackers are available, they are next to the salad bar.)

run-on (Hurdles are Sam's specialty, he likes them best.)

SOLUTION A

Extra crackers are available. They are next to the salad bar.

Make two sentences by separating the first clause from the second with end punctuation, such as a period or a question mark, and starting the second sentence with a capital letter.

SOLUTION B

Hurdles are Sam's specialty; he likes them best.

Place a semicolon between the main clauses of the sentence.

PROBLEM 2

Two main clauses with no punctuation between them

run-on (The law student studied hard she passed her exam.)

run-on (Kamil looked for the leash he found it in the closet.)

SOLUTION A

The law student studied hard. She passed her exam.

Make two sentences out of the run-on sentence.

SOLUTION B

Kamil looked for the leash, and he found it in the closet.

Add a comma and a coordinating conjunction between the main clauses.

PROBLEM 3

Two main clauses without a comma before the coordinating conjunction

run-on	You can rollerskate like a pro but you cannot ice skate.
run-on	Julian gazed at the moon and he marveled at its brightness.

SOLUTION

You can rollerskate like a pro, but you cannot ice skate.
Julian gazed at the moon, and he marveled at its brightness.

Add a comma before the coordinating conjunction.

More help in avoiding run-on sentences is available in Lesson 6.

Lack of Subject-Verb Agreement

PROBLEM 1

A subject separated from the verb by an intervening prepositional phrase

agr	The stories in the newspaper (was) well written.
agr	The house in the suburbs (were) just what she wanted.

SOLUTION

The stories in the newspaper were well written.

The house in the suburbs was just what she wanted.

Make sure that the verb agrees with the subject of the sentence, not with the object of a preposition. The object of a preposition is never the subject.

PROBLEM 2

A sentence that begins with here or there

agr	Here (go) the duck with her ducklings.
agr	There (is) the pencils you were looking for.
agr	Here (is) the snapshots from our vacation to the Grand Canyon.

SOLUTION

Here goes the duck with her ducklings.

There are the pencils you were looking for.

Here are the snapshots from our vacation to the Grand Canyon.

In sentences that begin with *here* or *there,* look for the subject after the verb. Make sure that the verb agrees with the subject.

PROBLEM 3

An indefinite pronoun as the subject

agr   Each of the animals (have) a unique way of walking.

agr   Many of the movies (was) black and white.

agr   None of the leaves (is) turning colors yet.

SOLUTION

Each of the animals has a unique way of walking.

Many of the movies were black and white.

None of the leaves are turning colors yet.

Some indefinite pronouns are singular, some are plural, and some can be either singular or plural. Determine whether the indefinite pronoun is singular or plural, and make the verb agree.

PROBLEM 4

A compound subject that is joined by and

agr	The students and the teacher (adores) the classroom hamster.
agr	The expert and best source of information (are) Dr. Marlin.

SOLUTION A

The students and the teacher adore the classroom hamster.

Use a plural verb if the parts of the compound subject do not belong to one unit or if they refer to different people or things.

SOLUTION B

The expert and best source of information is Dr. Marlin.

Use a singular verb if the parts of the compound subject belong to one unit or if they refer to the same person or thing.

PROBLEM 5

A compound subject that is joined by or or nor

agr	Either Hester or Sue (are) supposed to pick us up.
agr	Neither pepper nor spices (improves) the flavor of this sauce.
agr	Either Caroline or Robin (volunteer) at the local food pantry.
agr	Neither the coach nor the screaming fans (agrees) with the referee's call.

SOLUTION

Either Hester or Sue is supposed to pick us up.

Neither pepper nor spices improve the flavor of this sauce.

Either Caroline or Robin volunteers at the local food pantry.

Neither the coach nor the screaming fans agree with the referee's call.

Make the verb agree with the subject that is closer to it.

More help with subject-verb agreement is available in Lessons 50–54.

Incorrect Verb Tense or Form

PROBLEM 1

An incorrect or missing verb ending

tense	We (talk) yesterday for more than an hour.
tense	They (sail) last month for Barbados.
tense	Sally and James (land) at the airport yesterday.

SOLUTION

We talked yesterday for more than an hour.
They sailed last month for Barbados.
Sally and James landed at the airport yesterday.

To form the past tense and the past participle, add *-ed* to a regular verb.

PROBLEM 2

An improperly formed irregular verb

tense	Our hair (clinged) to us in the humid weather.
tense	Trent (drinked) all the orange juice.
tense	The evening breeze (blowed) the clouds away.

Troubleshooter

Copyright © by Glencoe/McGraw-Hill

32 *Writer's Choice Grammar Workbook 7,* Troubleshooter

SOLUTION

Our hair clung to us in the humid weather.

Trent drank all the orange juice.

The evening breeze blew the clouds away.

Irregular verbs vary in their past and past participle forms. Look up the ones you are not sure of. Consider memorizing them if you feel it is necessary.

PROBLEM 3

Confusion between a verb's past form and its past participle

tense   Helen (has took) first place in the marathon.

SOLUTION

Helen has taken first place in the marathon.

Use the past participle form of an irregular verb, and not its past form, when you use the auxiliary verb *have*.

More help with correct verb forms is available in Lessons 16–21.

Incorrect Use of Pronouns

PROBLEM 1

A pronoun that refers to more than one antecedent

pro	The wind and the rain came suddenly, but (it) did not last.
pro	Henry ran with Philip, but (he) was faster.
pro	When Sarah visits Corinne, (she) is glad for the company.

SOLUTION

The wind and the rain came suddenly, but the rain did not last.
Henry ran with Philip, but Philip was faster.
When Sarah visits Corinne, Corinne is glad for the company.

Substitute a noun for the pronoun to make your sentence clearer.

PROBLEM 2

Personal pronouns as subjects

pro	(Him) and Mary unfurled the tall, white sail.
pro	Nina and (them) bought theater tickets yesterday.
pro	Karen and (me) heard the good news on the television.

SOLUTION

He and Mary unfurled the tall, white sail.

Nina and they bought theater tickets yesterday.

Karen and I heard the good news on the television.

Use a subject pronoun as the subject part of a sentence.

PROBLEM 3

Personal pronouns as objects

pro	The horse galloped across the field to Anne and ⓘ.
pro	The new signs confused Clark and ⓣhey.
pro	Grant wrote ⓢhe a letter of apology.

SOLUTION

The horse galloped across the field to Anne and me.

The new signs confused Clark and them.

Grant wrote her a letter of apology.

An object pronoun is the object of a verb or preposition.

More help with correct use of pronouns is available in Lessons 22–27.

Incorrect Use of Adjectives

PROBLEM 1

Incorrect use of good, better, best

adj   Is a horse (more good) than a pony?

adj   Literature is my (most good) subject.

SOLUTION

Is a horse better than a pony?

Literature is my best subject.

The words *better* and *best* are the comparative and superlative forms of the word *good*. Do not use the words *more* or *most* before the irregular forms of comparative and superlative adjectives.

PROBLEM 2

Incorrect use of bad, worse, worst

adj   That game was the (baddest) game our team ever played.

SOLUTION

That game was the worst game our team ever played.

Do not use the suffixes *-er* or *-est* after the irregular forms of comparative and superlative adjectives. Do not use the words *more* or *most* before the irregular forms of comparative and superlative adjectives.

PROBLEM 3

Incorrect use of comparative adjectives

adj	This bike is (more faster) than my old bike.

SOLUTION

This bike is faster than my old bike.

Do not use *-er* and *more* together.

PROBLEM 4

Incorrect use of superlative adjectives

adj	Kara said it was the (most biggest) lawn she ever had to mow.

SOLUTION

Kara said it was the biggest lawn she ever had to mow.

Do not use *-est* and *most* together.

**More help with the correct use
of adjectives is available in
Lessons 28–32.**

Incorrect Use of Commas

PROBLEM 1

Missing commas in a series of three or more items

com	We saw ducks geese and seagulls at the park.
com	Jake ate dinner watched a movie and visited friends.

SOLUTION

We saw ducks, geese, and seagulls at the park.

Jake ate dinner, watched a movie, and visited friends.

If there are three or more items in a series, use a comma after each item except the last one.

PROBLEM 2

Missing commas with direct quotations

com	"The party" said José "starts at seven o'clock."
com	"My new book" Roger exclaimed "is still on the bus!"

SOLUTION

"The party," said José, "starts at seven o'clock."
"My new book," Roger exclaimed, "is still on the bus!"

If a quotation is interrupted, the first part ends with a comma followed by quotation marks. The interrupting words are also followed by a comma.

PROBLEM 3

Missing commas with nonessential appositives

com   Maria our new friend is from Chicago.

com   The old lane a tree-lined gravel path is a great place to walk on a hot afternoon.

SOLUTION

Maria, our new friend, is from Chicago.
The old lane, a tree-lined gravel path, is a great place to walk on a hot afternoon.

Decide whether the appositive is truly essential to the meaning of the sentence. If it is not essential, set it off with commas.

PROBLEM 4

Missing commas with nonessential adjective clauses

com	Karen who started early finished with her work before noon.

SOLUTION

Karen, who started early, finished with her work before noon.

Decide whether the clause is truly essential to the meaning of the sentence. If it is not essential, then set it off with commas.

PROBLEM 5

Missing commas with introductory adverb clauses

com	When the wind rises too high the boats lower their sails.

SOLUTION

When the wind rises too high, the boats lower their sails.

Place a comma after an introductory adverbial clause.

More help with commas is available in Lessons 73–77.

PROBLEM 1

Singular possessive nouns

apos	(Pablos) new bicycle is in (Charles) yard.
apos	(Bills) video collection is really great.
apos	That (horses) saddle has real silver on it.

SOLUTION

Pablo's new bicycle is in Charles's yard.

Bill's video collection is really great.

That horse's saddle has real silver on it.

Place an apostrophe before a final -*s* to form the possessive of a singular noun, even one that ends in -*s*.

PROBLEM 2

Plural possessive nouns that end in -s

apos	The (girls) team won the tournament.
apos	The (boats) sails are very colorful against the blue sky.
apos	The model (cars) boxes are in my room.

Troubleshooter

SOLUTION

The girls' team won the tournament.

The boats' sails are very colorful against the blue sky.

The model cars' boxes are in my room.

Use an apostrophe by itself to form the possessive of a plural noun that ends in -*s*.

PROBLEM 3

Plural possessive nouns that do not end in -s

apos	The (deers) best habitat is a deep, unpopulated woodland.
apos	The (childrens) clothes are on the third floor.

SOLUTION

The deer's best habitat is a deep, unpopulated woodland.

The children's clothes are on the third floor.

When a plural noun does not end in -*s*, use an apostrophe and an -*s* to form the possessive of the noun.

PROBLEM 4

Possessive personal pronouns

apos	The poster is (her's) but the magazine is (their's.)

SOLUTION

The poster is hers, but the magazine is theirs.

Do not use apostrophes with possessive personal pronouns.

PROBLEM 5

Confusion between its *and* it's

apos   The old tree was the last to lose (it's) leaves.

apos   (Its) the best CD I have ever heard them put out.

SOLUTION

The old tree was the last to lose its leaves.
It's the best CD I have ever heard them put out.

Use an apostrophe to form the contraction of *it is.* The possessive of the personal pronoun *it* does not take an apostrophe.

More help with apostrophes and possessives is available in Lessons 10 and 82.

Incorrect Capitalization

PROBLEM 1

Words that refer to ethnic groups, nationalities, and languages

> *cap*   Many (irish) citizens speak both (english) and (gaelic.)

SOLUTION

Many Irish citizens speak both English and Gaelic.

Capitalize proper nouns and adjectives referring to ethnic groups, nationalities, and languages.

PROBLEM 2

The first word of a direct quotation

> *cap*   Yuri said, "(the) rain off the bay always blows this way."

SOLUTION

Yuri said, "The rain off the bay always blows this way."

Capitalize the first word of a direct quotation if it is a complete sentence. A direct quotation is the speaker's exact words.

More help with capitalization is available in Lessons 68–71.

Grammar

Unit 1: Subjects, Predicates, and Sentences

Lesson 1

Kinds of Sentences: Declarative and Interrogative

A **sentence** is a group of words that expresses a complete thought. Different kinds of sentences have different purposes. A **declarative sentence** makes a statement. It begins with a capital letter and ends with a period. An **interrogative sentence** asks a question. It begins with a capital letter and ends with a question mark.

My hobby is reading mystery books. (declarative)
Have you read the latest Nancy Drew book? (interrogative)

▶ **Exercise 1** Write in the blank *dec.* before each declarative sentence and *int.* before each interrogative sentence.

int.   Have you ever played a mandolin?

dec.   **1.** Sleet and ice kept us housebound last weekend.

int.   **2.** Do you know how to word process?

int.   **3.** How much do these sweaters cost?

dec.   **4.** Those shelves smell like lemon oil.

int.   **5.** Do you think my hair is too long?

dec.   **6.** Tamara worked long hours to finish her painting.

int.   **7.** Are you going to Richard's party?

int.   **8.** Was the English test difficult?

dec.   **9.** Da-chun and his dad won the sack race.

dec.   **10.** I think blue is my favorite color.

dec.   **11.** The rusty hinges creaked as Grant opened the old door.

int.   **12.** Were you born in Montana, or did you move here?

int.   **13.** Could you help me with my homework tonight?

dec.   **14.** Jane wiped her hand across her forehead.

dec.   **15.** Clear expression is an art.

___dec.___ **16.** Grandma is the computer games champion in our family.

___int.___ **17.** Have you ever seen purple cotton candy?

___dec.___ **18.** This year's starting quarterback is a math genius.

___int.___ **19.** Who's going to bring the noisemakers?

___int.___ **20.** Did the squirrels eat all the tulip bulbs?

▶ **Exercise 2** Write *dec.* before each declarative sentence and *int.* before each interrogative sentence. Add correct punctuation and capitalization where needed.

___dec.___ the library has several good books on the subject.

___int.___ **1.** Have you met Nadine?

___int.___ **2.** will you help me with my home economics project?

___dec.___ **3.** Polly perched briefly on Aunt Kara's shoulder.

___dec.___ **4.** all the leaves had fallen from the tree within a day or two.

___int.___ **5.** Can you name that tune?

___dec.___ **6.** Zahara is visiting with her aunt this week.

___dec.___ **7.** Ricardo makes dinner on Tuesdays while his mom studies.

___int.___ **8.** have you looked it up in the encyclopedia?

___dec.___ **9.** we can't leave until I finish my chores.

___dec.___ **10.** Mirna lives in the apartment above Mrs. Ting.

___int.___ **11.** Have you taken any classes at the art museum?

___int.___ **12.** Will you make a copy of that photograph for me?

___int.___ **13.** how did Katherine tear the cartilage in her knee?

___dec.___ **14.** Kenny walked across the floor on his hands.

___int.___ **15.** Have you heard Amelia sing her solo?

___int.___ **16.** Did you see that boy in the plumed hat?

___int.___ **17.** would you like to go to the park with us?

___dec.___ **18.** the refrigerator is almost empty.

___dec.___ **19.** this spider web wasn't here yesterday.

___dec.___ **20.** A strand of ivy was painted around Marcia's room.

Lesson 2
Kinds of Sentences: Exclamatory and Imperative

The purpose of an exclamatory sentence is to express strong feeling. It begins with a capital letter and ends with an exclamation point.

I aced the test! (exclamation)

An imperative sentence gives a command or makes a request. Its subject is not stated directly, but is understood to be *you*. Imperative sentences also begin with a capital letter and usually end with a period. A strong command may end with an exclamation point.

(You) Put your essay on my desk when you are finished. (imperative)
(You) Give me a break! (strong imperative)

▶ **Exercise 1** Write in the blank *exc.* before each exclamatory sentence and *imp.* before each imperative sentence. If a sentence is neither exclamatory nor imperative, write *neither.*

exc. *or* imp.	Let's get out of here!
imp.	**1.** Choose one and then pass the rest along.
exc.	**2.** It's a touchdown!
imp.	**3.** Please keep this to yourself.
exc.	**4.** I can do it myself!
imp.	**5.** Run away from trouble.
imp.	**6.** Leave the dance before midnight.
neither	**7.** Have you ever ridden in a hot-air balloon?
imp.	**8.** Call 911 in an emergency.
exc.	**9.** This really makes me angry!
imp.	**10.** Be particularly careful with this antique clock.
exc.	**11.** We won!
imp. *or* exc.	**12.** Be careful!
exc.	**13.** Rhoda just set a record for the broad jump!

neither _____ **14.** The dense grass felt like smooth carpet.

imp. *or* exc. _____ **15.** Let me try!

imp. *or* exc. _____ **16.** Listen to me!

imp. _____ **17.** Wear protective clothing.

imp. _____ **18.** Kiss the Blarney Stone before you leave Ireland.

exc. _____ **19.** That's a great idea!

imp. _____ **20.** Remember to stand when Dr. Chou enters the room.

exc. _____ **21.** I can't believe it!

imp. _____ **22.** Please pass the honey.

neither _____ **23.** Joachim dressed as a chocolate bar for the costume party.

neither _____ **24.** Are you interested in going to a movie?

imp. _____ **25.** Move the picnic table to the shade.

neither _____ **26.** Apricot jam is a good glaze for baked ham.

exc. _____ **27.** How clever you are!

imp. _____ **28.** Be alert to rapidly changing weather conditions.

imp. *or* exc. _____ **29.** Give me a chance!

exc. _____ **30.** I don't believe it!

imp. _____ **31.** Be careful.

imp. _____ **32.** Never disturb nesting birds.

imp. _____ **33.** Tuck your pants inside your socks when hiking.

neither _____ **34.** Our new neighbors moved in yesterday.

imp. _____ **35.** Define the word *monsoon*.

neither _____ **36.** Did you notice the price of that saddle?

neither _____ **37.** There is a Thai restaurant around the corner from us.

imp. _____ **38.** Hold that pose while I adjust the camera lens.

exc. _____ **39.** What a mess your room is!

imp. _____ **40.** Raise the flag at sunrise.

Lesson 3
Subjects and Predicates

Every sentence has a subject and a predicate, which together express a complete thought. The **subject** of a sentence tells whom or what the sentence is about. The **predicate** of the sentence tells what the subject does or has. It can also tell what the subject is or is like.

SUBJECT   PREDICATE
Sunlight   shone through the cracks in the old shed.

The **simple subject**, usually a noun or a pronoun, is the main word or group of words in the complete subject. The **complete subject** is the simple subject with all of its modifiers. The **simple predicate**, which is always a verb, is the main word or group of words in the complete predicate. The **complete predicate** is the simple predicate with all of its modifiers.

	SUBJECT	PREDICATE
SIMPLE	The **noise** of the thunder	**scared** the children.
COMPLETE	**The noise of the thunder**	**scared the children.**

▶ **Exercise 1** Draw a line between the complete subject and the complete predicate. Underline each simple subject once and each simple predicate twice.

Ireland | is known as the Emerald Isle.

1. The rolling, green landscape | glows against its blue backdrop.

2. Mild temperatures | keep the lush vegetation deep green.

3. Regular rainfall | keeps the soil dark and moist.

4. Trees | once added greatly to the greenness.

5. Little woodland | remains in Ireland today, however.

6. Farmlands | cover most of central Ireland.

7. Many mountain ranges | rise near the coasts.

8. Ireland's highest peak | is in the Mountains of Kerry.

9. Kerry | is one of Ireland's twenty-six counties.

10. Kerry | is a beautiful area of lakes and mountains.

11. Ireland's beautiful landscape | inspired her many writers and artists.

12. <u>Dramatists</u> from the Emerald Isle | <u>include</u> Padraic Colum, Sean O'Casey, and John Synge.

13. These playwrights' <u>works</u> | <u>appear</u> at the Abbey Theater in Dublin.

14. <u>William Butler Yeats</u> | <u>started</u> this theater.

15. <u>Yeats</u> | <u>was</u> a memorable Irish poet and dramatist.

16. <u>He</u> | <u>lived</u> during the time of the Irish Literary Revival.

17. Other <u>writers</u> of this age | <u>were</u> James Joyce, George Augustus Moore, and George Russell.

18. <u>Joyce</u> | <u>is</u> the most famous of the three.

19. <u>He</u> | often <u>wrote</u> about Dublin and about the Irish people.

20. The <u>influence</u> of Irish writers | <u>extended</u> beyond their native country.

21. <u>George Bernard Shaw</u> | <u>was</u> popular in English and American theaters.

22. Shaw's <u>works</u> | <u>include</u> *Arms and the Man, Man and Superman,* and *Pygmalion.*

23. <u>Oscar Wilde</u> | also <u>found</u> fame in England and the United States.

24. <u>Wilde</u> | <u>is</u> the author of *A Woman of No Importance* and *The Importance of Being Earnest* as well as the novel *The Picture of Dorian Gray.*

25. Several Irish <u>painters</u> | <u>perfected</u> their craft with the help of the Royal Hibernian Academy.

26. Two Irish <u>artists</u> | <u>are</u> Maurice MacGonigal and Estella Solomon.

27. <u>Artists</u> from Ireland | <u>produced</u> great treasures over the years.

28. <u>Each</u> | <u>captured</u> the beauty of the Emerald Isle.

Lesson 4
Compound Subjects and Predicates

A sentence may have more than one simple subject or simple predicate. Two or more simple subjects that have the same predicate form a **compound subject**. The subjects are joined by *and, or,* or *but.*

Keisha or **Alex** can fix that bike for you.

A **compound predicate** has two or more simple predicates, or verbs, that have the same subject. The simple predicates are connected by *and, or,* or *but.*

Wasps **drink** nectar and **eat** other insects.

► **Exercise 1** Draw one line under each part of a compound subject. Draw two lines under each part of a compound predicate.

Furniture and knickknacks were available at the craft show.

1. Sally and Mike will lead the parade.

2. Spaghetti and manicotti were the restaurant's specialties.

3. The people in the village first resisted but then accepted the new factory.

4. New carpet or wallpaper would brighten this old kitchen.

5. Before the show, Simon and Ashley practiced their dialogue.

6. The lucky quarter rolled and bounced down the steps.

7. Pink or peach will be the color of the bridesmaids' gowns.

8. A clown with shoes the size of clipper ships sang and danced at Carley's birthday party.

9. Lindsay and Neil filled food baskets for the homeless in their community.

10. The speaker hesitated but soon began his presentation.

11. Sleet or rain is predicted for the tri-state area tonight.

12. Jake baked brownies and cooked pasta for the surprise party.

13. Mr. Lawson wrote, directed, and produced this musical.

14. The old car's engine sputtered but eventually roared to life.

15. The crowd <u>called</u> and <u>waved</u> to the three astronauts.

16. <u>Leave</u> your jacket on the coat rack or <u>hang</u> it in the closet.

17. In the program, <u>Claire</u> and <u>Sue</u> were listed before Scott.

18. <u>Crocuses</u> or <u>daylilies</u> would grow well there.

19. <u>Basil</u>, olive <u>oil</u>, and <u>spinach</u> are used in that recipe.

20. The tailback <u>slashed</u>, <u>spun</u>, and <u>pounded</u> his way through the opposing team's

defense.

21. The <u>Spanish Club</u> and <u>field hockey</u> are Dora's favorite extracurricular activities.

22. Our soccer team <u>played</u> hard but <u>lost</u> the game in the last minute.

23. <u>Joan</u>, <u>Tom</u>, or <u>Wing</u> will head the decorations committee.

24. On election day, the levy <u>will pass</u> or <u>fail</u>.

25. <u>Cake</u> and <u>ice cream</u> were served to all the guests.

26. <u>Alligators</u> or <u>sea lions</u> will be the topic of her report.

27. <u>Books</u>, <u>clothes</u>, and other <u>items</u> <u>had been collected</u> and <u>sold</u> at the fundraiser.

28. Sven <u>hurried</u> but <u>missed</u> his plane.

29. Dr. Tarini <u>writes</u> or <u>phones</u> every participant in the study once a week.

30. <u>Cards</u> and <u>letters</u> on behalf of the popular television program poured into the

network's corporate offices.

31. The pinch hitter <u>swung</u> at every pitch but <u>missed</u> the ball each time.

32. <u>Pizza</u> or cherry <u>pie</u> is Arthur's favorite snack.

33. The <u>Thomases</u> and the <u>Jordans</u> are planning a trip to Costa Rica.

34. <u>Suits</u> and <u>ties</u> are worn daily at that all-boys school.

35. The <u>rings</u> of Saturn and the <u>moons</u> of Jupiter have been seen through this telescope.

Lesson 5
Sentence Fragments

A sentence must have a subject and a predicate and must express a complete thought. A group of words that does not have both a subject and a predicate is an incomplete sentence, or sentence fragment

The truck, an old red one. (lacks a predicate)
Slowly climbed the steep hill. (lacks a subject)
On the country road outside of town. (lacks a subject and a predicate)

▶ **Exercise 1** Write *sent.* in the blank if the group of words is a sentence and write *frag.* if it is a fragment.

frag.   Learned about bees.

sent.   **1.** Geneticist Warwick Kerr studied honeybees.

frag.   **2.** At the University of São Paulo in Brazil.

sent.   **3.** In 1956 he imported some African queen bees.

sent.   **4.** These bees had a savage reputation.

frag.   **5.** Attacked animals and people without warning.

sent.   **6.** However, African bees sting only to defend their nest.

sent.   **7.** Most stinging incidents occur during the swarming season.

frag.   **8.** The hot summer months.

sent.   **9.** Stinging attacks by large numbers of bees are uncommon.

sent. **10.** Dr. Kerr carefully kept the bees in enclosures.

frag. **11.** Not another beekeeper.

frag. **12.** Allowed twenty-six queens and their swarms to escape.

sent. **13.** The African bees readily nested in the wilds of Brazil.

frag. **14.** Reproducing quickly and swarming frequently.

sent. **15.** The African honeybees began to spread.

frag. **16.** In all directions.

Grammar

▶ **Exercise 2** Write *S* in the blank if the fragment lacks a subject and *P* if it lacks a predicate. If the sentence is complete, write *sent.*

___P___   Honey bees, digger wasps, and red ants.

___S___   **1.** Live together in colonies.

__sent.__ **2.** Did you know that a colony may contain thousands of insects?

___P___   **3.** One queen.

___S___   **4.** Produce all the eggs.

___P___   **5.** A special room or cell for the queen.

__sent.__ **6.** Bees, wasps, and ants undergo a complete metamorphosis.

___P___   **7.** The four stages of these insects.

___P___   **8.** The egg, the larva, the pupa, and the adult.

___P___   **9.** The female workers.

__sent.__ **10.** Workers have many jobs.

___S___ **11.** Collect food and take care of the nest, the queen, and her offspring.

__sent.__ **12.** Some workers protect the nest from enemies.

___S___ **13.** Search for food to bring back to the colony.

___P___ **14.** Insects' various ways of communication.

▶ **Writing Link** **Write four complete sentences containing both a subject and a predicate.**

_____

_____

_____

_____

_____

_____

_____

_____

_____

_____

Lesson 6
Simple and Compound Sentences

A **simple sentence** has one subject and one predicate. However, a simple sentence may have a compound subject, a compound predicate, or both.

Saturn and **Jupiter** are the two largest planets in our solar system. (compound subject)

Queen bees **survive** the winter and **lay** eggs in the spring. (compound predicate)

Juan and **Luis throw** and **catch** the softball. (compound subject and compound predicate)

A **compound sentence** contains two or more simple sentences joined by a comma and a coordinating conjunction or by a semicolon. (*and, but, or, nor* or *for*)

Priscilla enjoys reading about technology, **but** she doesn't care for science fiction.

Paramecium are very small; a microscope is needed to examine them.

A **run-on sentence** is two or more sentences incorrectly written as one sentence. To correct a run-on sentence, divide it into separate sentences or add the necessary words or punctuation to form one complete sentence.

Run-on: The movie was long I got restless.
Corrected: The movie was long. I got restless.
Corrected: The movie was long, and I got restless.

▶ **Exercise 1** Write *S* in the blank before each simple sentence, *C* before each compound sentence, and *R* before each run-on sentence.

___S___ The directions are simple and straight-forward.

___C___ 1. Florida and Georgia are the only southern states I've visited, but I've been in every state in New England.

___S___ 2. Skating and skiing are Aaron's favorite cold weather sports.

___R___ 3. Turn right at the stop sign go left at the next corner.

___R___ 4. Six inches of snow are predicted, I'd better find my boots.

___S___ 5. Both Kuma and Angie enjoy hiking and backpacking.

___R___ 6. Try it, you'll like it.

___C___ 7. Liam had a solo in last year's concert; he hopes to have one this year, too.

Grammar

_____S_____ **8.** Niabi plays both the oboe and the piano and plays them very well.

_____C_____ **9.** George and Helene can't agree on a country for their report, but they want to choose one in Eastern Europe.

_____S_____ **10.** Lately, all of my clothes seem too small.

_____S_____ **11.** The meal ended with carrot cake and tea.

_____S_____ **12.** Why do I have to clean my room and the bathroom?

_____R_____ **13.** I have too many clothes, my closet is stuffed.

_____C_____ **14.** We went to the reptile house, and later we saw the pachyderms.

_____C_____ **15.** I always agree with Marta, and Marta always agrees with me.

_____C_____ **16.** The shelves are filled with books, but I can't find one I want.

_____R_____ **17.** Tia can't come she has to baby-sit.

_____R_____ **18.** Conserve resources, use them wisely.

_____C_____ **19.** Please be kind to Amy; she needs a friend right now.

_____C_____ **20.** Should I take the bus to school, or should I walk?

_____R_____ **21.** Rain forced cancellation of the game, it is rescheduled for next week.

_____S_____ **22.** Beth and Ricardo need a ride to the pep rally tomorrow.

_____C_____ **23.** The storm blew down a tree on our street, but there was no other damage.

_____S_____ **24.** We have a new system for recycling at home.

_____R_____ **25.** Don't use a stapler, use paper clips.

_____S_____ **26.** Look for Jeff and Dominic in the crowd.

_____C_____ **27.** Yoko's aunt lives in California, and her uncle lives in Arizona.

_____R_____ **28.** A canoe is not as stable as a rowboat, be careful not to tip it.

_____C_____ **29.** Terry has just moved here, and she doesn't know very many people.

_____R_____ **30.** The accident ruined the car, fortunately no one was seriously injured.

Grammar

✓ Unit 1 **Review**

▶ **Exercise 1** Write *dec.* before each declarative sentence, *int.* before each interrogative sentence, *imp.* before each imperative sentence, and *exc.* before each exclamatory sentence.

<u>imp.</u>　　　Button your sweater.

<u>int.</u>　**1.** How much memory does that computer have?

<u>exc.</u>　**2.** Tricia, your hair's on fire!

<u>dec.</u>　**3.** The Lopez family enjoys watching old movies together.

<u>int.</u>　**4.** How can I get this project done on time?

<u>dec.</u>　**5.** Georgia knows that author.

<u>imp.</u>　**6.** Try to have supper ready at six o'clock.

<u>exc.</u>　**7.** You look elegant!

<u>dec.</u>　**8.** That combination of colors is quite striking.

<u>imp.</u>　**9.** Put out the trash on Wednesday morning.

<u>dec.</u>　**10.** Both soccer and tennis have great teams this year.

<u>exc.</u>　**11.** Get the fire extinguisher!

<u>int.</u>　**12.** Will you turn out the lights before you go to bed?

<u>imp.</u>　**13.** Turn out the lights before you go to bed.

<u>imp.</u>　**14.** Pull the thorn out before your finger blisters.

▶ **Exercise 2** Draw one line under the complete subject and two lines under the complete predicate.

1. Marla's pet monkey chatters all day long.

2. Enrico's mom has photos of her trip to South America.

3. The population of the United States is increasing.

4. Do you know how to make snickerdoodles?

5. I am so excited!

6. Larry hid Easter eggs in his neighbor's backyard.

Cumulative Review: Unit 1

▶ **Exercise 1** Write *S* next to each simple sentence, *C* next to each compound sentence, *frag.* next to each sentence fragment, and *R* next to each run-on sentence. Draw one line under each simple subject and two lines under each simple predicate in the simple and compound sentences.

frag.		Too sweet to be forgotten.
_S_	**1.**	Lucy practices jai alai four hours a day.
frag.	**2.**	Mount Fuji, one of the most famous volcanoes in Japan.
_C_	**3.**	I played the marimba, and George played guitar.
_S_	**4.**	The musty cave housed ancient Mayan carvings.
_C_	**5.**	The judge banged the gavel, and a hush fell instantly over the courtroom.
_R_	**6.**	The candle cast a dim glow upon the curtain, the scene looked eerie.
frag.	**7.**	The success of the demonstration.
_S_	**8.**	Max rode Lightning through the stream and up the hill.
frag.	**9.**	Shot a few hoops with Jim yesterday.
_S_	**10.**	Shovel the walks, please.
_S_	**11.**	Díaz and Benny coach a little league team.
_S_	**12.**	Josh washed and polished the car.
frag.	**13.**	Enlisted in the Coast Guard at eighteen.
frag.	**14.**	The sleepy lion with the orange mane.
_R_	**15.**	Rain fell for hours the basement flooded.
_C_	**16.**	Ivan the Great was the first czar of Russia; however, Ivan the Terrible was more powerful.
_S_	**17.**	Sergei's family is from Moscow.
_S_	**18.**	The wolf huffed and puffed.
frag.	**19.**	Moved round the cove and next to the cliffs.
_C_	**20.**	The job was easy, but the pay was low.

Grammar

Unit 2: Nouns

Lesson 7
Nouns: Proper and Common

A **noun** names a person, place, thing, or idea. A **singular noun** names one person, place, thing, or idea. A **plural noun** names more than one. Plural nouns are usually formed by adding *-s* or *-es* to the singular noun.

SINGULAR: student   bench   hotel   truth
PLURAL: students   benches   hotels   truths

A **proper noun** names a specific person, place, thing, or idea. A **common noun** names any person, place, thing, or idea.

PROPER: Thomas Alvarez   Canada   Sears Tower   the Bronze Age
COMMON: man   country   building   age

▶ **Exercise 1** Write *sing.* in the blank if the italicized word is a singular noun. Write *pl.* if it is plural.

__pl.__   Juanita suggested that my *boys* visit the circus.

__sing.__   **1.** Circus Royale was the name of the circus that came to *town* last week.

__sing.__   **2.** The opening *parade* was a great introduction to the event.

__pl.__   **3.** The nine *elephants* were trained by a man named Zingarelli.

__pl.__   **4.** One of the best acts was a family of *acrobats* from Paris.

__sing.__   **5.** A *juggler* managed to juggle eight saucers at once.

__pl.__   **6.** A band played *marches* by Sousa and rags by Joplin.

__sing.__   **7.** The ringmaster's voice was loud enough to be heard without a *microphone.*

__sing.__   **8.** When the wildcat *act* appeared, the audience applauded with glee.

__pl.__   **9.** Besides lions and *tigers,* a cheetah and a panther were in the act.

__pl.__   **10.** After the wildcat act, fourteen *clowns* emerged from a tiny car.

__sing.__   **11.** Do you have any idea how all of them could fit into that tiny *car?*

__sing.__   **12.** Although they used a *net,* the Flying Greiners were thrilling on the trapeze.

__sing.__   **13.** My little *sister,* Nina, wants to learn to perform on the high wire.

__sing.__ **14.** However, my favorite act was the *magician*.

__pl.__ **15.** I would go to *circuses* every week if I had the chance.

▶ **Exercise 2** Draw one line under each common noun and two lines under each proper noun.

P.T. Barnum has a name that reminds many people of the circus.

1. He was born in Bethel, Connecticut, as Phineas Taylor Barnum.

2. In 1841, Barnum began to work in New York City, managing the American Museum.

3. Charles Dickens and Edward VII were among those who came to the museum.

4. Charles S. Stratton probably brought in the most money.

5. Only 25 inches tall, Stratton called himself "General Tom Thumb."

6. In 1871, William Cameron Coup joined Barnum to take the circus on the road.

7. They called it "The Greatest Show on Earth."

8. The two showmen amazed many government leaders, including Abraham Lincoln and Queen Victoria.

9. During the run of the circus, Barnum served a term as mayor of Bridgeport, Connecticut.

10. After some time in politics, Barnum visited the London Zoo.

11. There, he acquired a large African elephant.

12. The elephant, named Jumbo, weighed over six tons!

13. James A. Bailey, a later partner of Barnum, helped to improve the circus.

14. Before his death in 1891, Barnum hosted many famous people, including Mark Twain.

15. In 1907, after Bailey died, the Ringling Brothers bought the show.

▶ **Writing Link** Write two or three sentences about what job you would like to have in a circus. Include both common and proper nouns.

_____

_____

_____

_____

Lesson 8
Nouns: Concrete, Abstract, and Collective

Concrete nouns name things that you can recognize with your senses.

Abstract nouns name ideas, qualities, or feelings.

A **collective noun** gives a single name to a group of individuals. When referring to a group as a unit, the noun is singular. When referring to the individual members of the group, the noun is plural.

The **mob** was waiting at the door for the store to open. (a unit, singular)
The **panel** are discussing the issues with each other. (individual members, plural)

CONCRETE:	ABSTRACT:	COLLECTIVE:
inventor	idea	crowd
city	progress	committee
calendar	time	family
jazz	culture	team

▶ **Exercise 1** Write in the blank *concrete* or *abstract* to identify the type of noun in italics.

_____abstract_____ The boys had great *sympathy* for Juan's situation.

_____concrete_____ 1. Why did Sharon begin playing the *tuba?*

_____abstract_____ 2. The entire house was decorated with excellent *taste.*

_____abstract_____ 3. Barry's adoration for his grandmother brought her much *joy.*

_____concrete_____ 4. The hissing of the *radiator* distracted him.

_____concrete_____ 5. The barbershop quartet rehearsed in the *cafeteria.*

_____concrete_____ 6. The spectators saw the entire production on a huge *monitor.*

_____abstract_____ 7. *Cleanliness* is important to my mother.

_____abstract_____ 8. If anyone has a better *idea,* I'll support it.

_____concrete_____ 9. Dad enjoyed listening to *music* on his new car CD player.

_____concrete_____ 10. My friend brought some *oranges* back from Florida.

_____abstract_____ 11. The *success* of the recycling program depended on everyone's cooperation.

_____concrete_____ **12.** Margit's new *bedspread* is very colorful.

_____abstract_____ **13.** It took *courage* to sing the solo in front of so many people.

_____concrete_____ **14.** Aside from one *baby,* the audience was extremely quiet.

_____abstract_____ **15.** Bella showed great *ability* for solving logic problems.

▶ **Exercise 2 Draw two lines under the verb that agrees with the collective noun subject.**

The band (is, are) polishing their instruments before the competition.

1. A new committee (has been, have been) formed to plan the field trip.

2. The team (selects, select) their officers by secret ballot.

3. The Audubon Society (promote, promotes) the conservation of wild birds.

4. The audience (is, are) aware that they were lucky to get tickets.

5. Because it is fed only once daily, the flock (eats, eat) very fast.

6. The trio (performs, perform) at many local festivities.

7. My family (begin, begins) the holiday at six o'clock.

8. The jury (is, are) all members of the community.

9. The team (has, have) an awards banquet at the end of the regular season.

10. A panel of judges (presides, preside) over the Supreme Court.

11. Although it is small, our orchestra (is, are) well rehearsed.

12. The school club (provides, provide) assistance to local charities.

13. The committee (disagrees, disagree) with each other about proper procedure.

14. Outside my bedroom window, the swarm of bees (buzzes, buzz) loudly.

15. The matinee audience (is, are) usually smaller than the evening crowd.

▶ **Writing Link Write a short paragraph about selecting officers for a club to which you belong. Use examples of concrete, abstract, and collective nouns.**

_____

_____

_____

_____

Lesson 9
Nouns: Compound and Possessive

Compound nouns are nouns that are made up of two or more words. To form a plural of a compound noun written as one word, add *-s* or *-es*. Add *-es* to words ending in *ch, sh, s, x,* and *z*. When the compound noun is hyphenated or written as more than one word, make the most important part of the noun plural.

doorknob**s**   mailbox**es**   great-grandmother**s**   dining room**s**   sister**s**-in-law

A **possessive** noun names who or what owns or has something. To form the possessive for all singular nouns and for plural nouns not ending in *-s*, add an apostrophe and an *-s.* To form the possessive of all plural nouns already ending in *-s*, add only an apostrophe.

a girl**'s** coat   Hans**'s** job   children**'s** voices   boy**s'** shoes   bakerie**s'** cakes

▶ **Exercise 1** Write in the blank the correct plural form of the compound noun in parentheses.

_____**grandmothers**_____   During the holidays, we visit both of my (grandmother).

_____**teardrops**_____   **1.** The (teardrop) fell from her cheek as she sobbed.

_____**Moonbeams**_____   **2.** (Moonbeam) cut through the trees of the forest.

_____**snowballs**_____   **3.** After school, we hurled (snowball) at our friends.

_____**Earthworms**_____   **4.** (Earthworm) improve the soil in our garden.

_____**runners-up**_____   **5.** At the end of the contest, the (runner-up) collected their awards.

_____**record holders**_____   **6.** This Olympics is filled with (record holder).

_____**nutcrackers**_____   **7.** My Aunt Minya collects (nutcracker).

_____**nursery rhymes**_____   **8.** Before bedtime, Carla's father reads her two (nursery rhyme).

_____**mothers-in-law**_____   **9.** Our family tradition calls for all (mother-in-law) to bake a pie at Thanksgiving.

_____**morning stars**_____   **10.** Just before sunrise, the (morning star) twinkle beautifully.

_____**Lighthouses**_____   **11.** (Lighthouse) protect the coastline of Maine.

_____**lifeguards**_____   **12.** The (lifeguard) at the amusement park do a noble job.

_____overpasses_____ **13.** The city is repairing several (overpass).

_____keyholes_____ **14.** Old houses have (keyhole) that you can look through.

_____music boxes_____ **15.** My little sister has a whole collection of (music box).

▶ **Exercise 2** Write in the blank the possessive form of the noun in italics.

_____Ann's_____ *Ann* calculator was missing from her bookbag.

_____Washington's_____ **1.** George *Washington* troops crossed the Delaware River.

_____son's_____ **2.** Sonja was surprised by her *son* interests.

_____Charles's_____ **3.** *Charles* new bike sparkled in the sun.

_____class's_____ **4.** The *class* projects exceeded the teacher's expectations.

_____students'_____ **5.** My part-time job fits most *students* needs.

_____project's_____ **6.** Her science *project* name was "Food Production Without Soil."

_____mother's_____ **7.** For the poster, we clipped words and pictures from my *mother* magazines.

_____vegetables'_____ **8.** Fresh *vegetables* flavor often exceeds that of canned ones.

_____countries'_____ **9.** Many *countries* goals include less crime.

_____animals'_____ **10.** The *animals* habitats are quickly being destroyed.

_____crop's_____ **11.** A *crop* yield can supply hundreds with food.

_____Marta Evans's_____ **12.** *Marta Evans* hobbies include skiing and dancing.

_____atmosphere's_____ **13.** Some believe that the *atmosphere* ozone layer is disappearing.

_____teachers'_____ **14.** The two *teachers* classes all followed the same theme.

_____team's_____ **15.** The football *team* hopes were dashed in the playoffs.

▶ **Writing Link** Write a short paragraph about a favorite leisure activity. Be sure to include compound and possessive nouns (both singular and plural).

_____

_____

_____

_____

_____

Lesson 10

Nouns: Distinguishing Plurals, Possessives, and Contractions

Grammar

Some plural nouns and possessive nouns sound alike, but their spellings and meanings differ.

The **farmers** harvested the corn. (plural noun)
The **farmers'** harvests were plentiful. (plural possessive noun)
The **farmer's** harvest is finished. (singular possessive noun)

A **contraction** is a word made by combining two words into one by leaving out one or more letters and adding an apostrophe.

Katarina's homework is perfect. (possessive)
Katarina's preparing for the test. (contraction of *Katarina is*)

▶ **Exercise 1** Write *possessive, contraction,* or *plural* to identify the type of noun in italics.

possessive		The Old *West's* method of delivering mail was the Pony Express.
possessive	1.	The Pony *Express's* name comes from the mail carriers riding ponies.
possessive	2.	The *service's* route stretched between St. Joseph, Missouri, and Sacramento, California.
plural	3.	The Pony Express was around in the early *1860s.*
possessive	4.	*Senator William H. Russell's* freighting firm funded the Pony Express.
contraction	5.	*Russell's* better known than Senator William Gwin, the man who helped him.
plural	6.	The mail *prices* once cost five dollars for a one-half-ounce letter.
plural	7.	However, the *costs* soon dropped to only one dollar.
possessive	8.	The *rider's* equipment included a special mailbag and sometimes a weapon.
plural	9.	Some famous Pony Express *riders* included historical figures like "Buffalo Bill" Cody.
possessive	10.	Another of the *Express's* famous riders was "Pony Bob" Haslam.
plural	11.	It was amazing the way the *riders* could change horses so quickly.

Grammar

**possessive** **12.** As a result, the Pony *Express's* average speed was two hundred miles per day.

**plural** **13.** Although they faced many *troubles,* few riders were seriously hurt.

**plural** **14.** After the transcontinental telegraph opened, the Pony Express shut down in two *days.*

**contraction** **15.** The Pony Express—*that's* the basis for the modern American postal system.

▶ **Exercise 2 Underline the noun in parentheses that best completes each sentence.**

(Telephones, telephone's) have changed greatly over the past few years.

1. Speaker (phones, phone's) are already commonplace in some American homes.

2. The cellular (phones, phone's) mobility is very convenient.

3. Many (satellites, satellite's) have replaced familiar phone lines.

4. Satellite communication eliminates many (delays, delay's).

5. New (horizons, horizon's) are upon us as we enter the twenty-first century.

6. Telephones that include video (images, image's) are already being perfected.

7. These (videophones, videophone's) may soon become standard communication.

8. Many (computers, computer's) regulate the phone lines.

9. Business (executives, executives') travels are simplified with this technology.

10. Can you imagine the (problems, problem's) people used to have with the old phones?

11. Now salespeople can show their (products, products') on television.

12. Then, (payments, payment's) can be completed over the phone.

13. A regular telephone (visits, visit's) a good cure for loneliness.

14. Taking place over phone lines, online data (services, service's) connect people across the world.

15. Soon, most people will have access to all (types, type's) of communication.

16. A (persons, person's) going to be amazed at all the new possibilities.

Copyright © by Glencoe/McGraw-Hill

Grammar

Lesson 11
Appositives

An **appositive** is a noun placed next to another noun to identify it or add information about it.

My brother, **Jean,** will accompany me to the boat.

An **appositive phrase** is a group of words that includes an appositive and other words that describe the appositive. Many appositives are set off by commas.

Raji Pabijan, **a distinguished geologist,** will speak at the Science Club meeting.

▶ **Exercise 1** Underline each appositive or appositive phrase.

Connie, <u>my neighbor</u>, waters her yard every day.

1. Trucks, <u>large and small cargo carriers</u>, come in all colors.

2. A toy poodle, <u>the smallest house dog</u>, makes an excellent pet.

3. Jerry, <u>my uncle from Wisconsin</u>, took me to the Packers' game.

4. Macy's, <u>a large department store</u>, is centered in New York.

5. In that movie I had a job as an extra, <u>an actor in a group scene</u>.

6. The bald eagle, <u>our national bird</u>, soared above the trees.

7. Flying a Spitfire, <u>a plane used in World War II</u>, was once my grandfather's job.

8. Benito Grasselli, <u>a friend of mine</u>, is a professional artist.

9. Ken and Joyce, <u>Ken's wife</u>, are business partners.

10. Min, <u>the leader of our club</u>, had the final decision.

11. I finished the hole with a birdie, <u>only two strokes</u>.

12. Michelle, <u>the more experienced of the two</u>, was promoted over Janil.

13. I would love a bright red Porsche, <u>a sports car</u>.

14. The car, <u>a battered green sedan</u>, was parked in the driveway.

15. I invited Dale, <u>my friend from Washington</u>, to have breakfast.

16. Camelot was defended by King Arthur's court, <u>the knights of the Round Table</u>.

17. The pyramid of Khufu, <u>the Great Pyramid</u>, loomed over the explorers.

18. Carla and Ramón, <u>the writers of the school play</u>, came on stage to take a bow.

19. The Special Olympics, <u>an international program</u>, supports physical fitness for mentally or physically challenged athletes.

20. <u>An excellent librarian</u>, my grandma worked in a library all her life.

▶ **Exercise 2** **Underline each appositive or appositive phrase. Add commas.**

Kayley, <u>my dog</u>, is a mixture of German shepherd and collie.

1. Alice visited Dave, <u>her second cousin</u>.

2. That car, <u>the green Ford</u>, belongs to my grandmother.

3. The oak, <u>a slow-growing tree</u>, is highly prized for lumber.

4. The nylon tent, <u>a new model</u>, sleeps six.

5. She drives a foreign car, <u>a Japanese model</u>.

6. He saw Jack Miller, <u>the well-known painter</u>, before he came home.

7. Mrs. Hernandez, <u>our principal</u>, is new to our school.

8. Jogging, <u>a vigorous exercise</u>, is good for one's circulation.

9. Carl's son, <u>Tomás</u>, is nine years old.

10. Penicillin, <u>an antibiotic</u>, is used to treat bacterial infections.

11. Annette, <u>the tallest girl in school</u>, plays center on the basketball team.

12. The chainsaw, <u>an old one</u>, broke.

13. Have you met Mrs. Fernandez, <u>our substitute teacher</u>?

14. Kareem, <u>the new boy at school</u>, sings very well.

15. We always look forward to Thanksgiving dinner, <u>a wonderful meal</u>.

16. The house, <u>a log cabin</u>, had a green door.

17. Vegetables, <u>the leafy kind</u>, make excellent contributions to the diet.

18. Trigger, <u>a palomino</u>, was Roy Rogers's horse.

19. Bill Peschak, <u>my trumpet teacher</u>, plays with the symphony.

20. <u>A talented man</u>, my father is often asked to play the piano at parties.

✓ Unit 2 **Review**

▶ **Exercise 1** Write in the blank *plural, possessive, contraction,* or *appositive* to identify the word in italics.

appositive		Herve, the *server,* deserved a large tip.
plural	**1.**	The children laughed at the *monkeys* in the cage.
possessive	**2.**	The *Newmans'* vacation was last month.
contraction	**3.**	*Sheila's* on her way to the skating rink.
appositive	**4.**	Molly, my *friend,* wants to borrow my bicycle.
contraction	**5.**	After the dance, *Helmut's* leaving for Rome.
contraction	**6.**	Do you know if the *cat's* come back?
plural	**7.**	*Conestogas* were the famous wagons of the western trails.
appositive	**8.**	Give it to Jake, the *butler.*
possessive	**9.**	All the *mechanic's* tools were missing.
appositive	**10.**	John lost his baseball, a *souvenir.*
appositive	**11.**	Rosita married my cousin *Harry.*
contraction	**12.**	*Jimmy's* not home.
plural	**13.**	The scene was crowded with *ambulances* and workers.
contraction	**14.**	*Rover's* not the smartest dog who ever lived.
plural	**15.**	The bright *lights* of the midway attracted every child in town.
possessive	**16.**	Is there a *beginner's* position available?
possessive	**17.**	His *father's* name is Amahl.
appositive	**18.**	Marta, a petite *woman,* could wear her daughter's clothes.
plural	**19.**	The waves from the large *boats* disturbed the swimmers.
possessive	**20.**	Can you see this from a *teacher's* point of view?

Cumulative Review: Units 1–2

▶ **Exercise 1** Draw a vertical line between the complete subject and the complete predicate. Underline the nouns in the complete subject and circle the nouns in the complete predicate.

Jason and his friend | ran to the theater.

1. Kim | liked John's picture of the Vietnam Veterans Memorial.

2. The class | toured the new factory.

3. The kitchen, filled with pots and pans, | sparkled.

4. At the campground, | the counselors | split the children into four groups.

5. The computer in my father's office | can do some amazing tricks.

6. My boss | asked the employees to work extra hours.

7. The writer of the play | is a complete genius.

8. The uncomfortable family | waited patiently in the lobby.

9. Who | is going to the theater with us?

10. Andy | removed the magazine from the office.

11. The Lin family | enjoyed a holiday at the Grand Canyon.

12. The history test | is on Thursday.

13. Grandma | was shocked to be in the Queen's ceremony.

14. Honda | has plants all over the world.

15. Uncle Miller's prize pig | won the contest at the fair.

16. The store | is on the corner of Pearl Street and Maple Lane.

17. *Air Force One* | is reserved for the president.

18. Those radishes | are as large as turnips!

19. The actors | argued with the director over the scene.

20. Luis | bought a new set of paintbrushes from the hobby shop.

Unit 3: Verbs

Lesson 12
Action Verbs

An **action verb** is a word that names an action and tells what a subject does. It may contain more than one word. Action verbs can express physical actions or mental actions.

She **kicks** the ball. (physical action)   She **likes** piano lessons. (mental action)

Have, has, and *had* are often used before verbs. They can also be used by themselves as action verbs when they name what the subject owns or holds.

The sports arena **has** 20,000 seats.   Our coaches **had** a new playbook.
The opponents **have** blue uniforms.   We **have played** this team before.

▶ **Exercise 1 Draw two lines under each action verb. Write *physical* or *mental* in the blank to indicate whether the verb expresses physical action or mental action.**

_____physical_____ Many athletes successfully represented the United States in the

modern Olympics.

_____physical_____ **1.** African American Jesse Owens broke world records in track and field

events.

_____physical_____ **2.** Owens attended The Ohio State University.

_____physical_____ **3.** At a 1935 event in Ann Arbor, Michigan, Owens broke three world records.

_____mental_____ **4.** Many people consider Owens the greatest track-and-field athlete ever.

_____physical_____ **5.** Owens won four gold medals at the 1936 Summer Olympics in Berlin,

Germany.

_____mental_____ **6.** Owens's strong performance angered Adolf Hitler.

_____physical_____ **7.** Owens wore the victor's oak leaf crown during the presentation ceremony.

_____physical_____ **8.** Owens later gave many speeches about values and moral principles.

_____mental_____ **9.** Another African American athlete captured the world's attention in the

1960 Italy games.

physical **10.** Cassius Clay <u>boxed</u> his way to the light heavyweight gold medal.

physical **11.** Clay later <u>changed</u> his name to Muhammad Ali.

physical **12.** Ali <u>gained</u> the title of heavyweight champion of the world four years later.

physical **13.** Other Americans in the 1960 Olympics <u>challenged</u> their opponents, too.

physical **14.** Wilma Rudolph <u>dazzled</u> the crowds in the track-and-field competition.

physical **15.** Rudolph <u>ran</u> for gold medals in the 100- and 200-meter track events.

physical **16.** Al Oerter, an American discus thrower, <u>dominated</u> his event from 1956 to 1968.

physical **17.** Oerter <u>claimed</u> four gold medals for his accomplishments.

physical **18.** During practice in 1964, Oerter <u>ripped</u> the cartilage from his rib cage.

physical **19.** In bandages and ice packs, he <u>competed</u> despite his injury.

physical **20.** He <u>threw</u> for another Olympic record and his third straight gold medal.

physical **21.** That same year, American swimmer Dawn Fraser <u>clocked</u> an Olympic record in the 100-meter event.

physical **22.** Eight years later, American swimmer Mark Spitz <u>achieved</u> additional recognition for the United States.

mental **23.** In Mexico City four years earlier, Spitz <u>had promised</u> himself six gold medals.

physical **24.** However, he <u>won</u> only two medals.

physical **25.** For the next four years, Spitz <u>pushed</u> himself to the limit.

physical **26.** In Munich in 1972, Spitz <u>competed</u> again.

mental **27.** This time he <u>promised</u> nothing.

mental **28.** He <u>remembered</u> the disappointment of the Mexico City games.

physical **29.** In Munich, he <u>beat</u> all previous times in four individual events.

physical **30.** Spitz also <u>teamed</u> with three other Americans in three relay races.

physical **31.** They all <u>earned</u> gold medals.

physical **32.** In total, Spitz <u>won</u> seven gold medals in a single Olympics.

Lesson 13
Verbs: Transitive and Intransitive

Grammar

Depending on its use in a particular sentence, an action verb can be either transitive or intransitive. A **transitive verb** is followed by a word or words called the **direct object** that answers the question *what?* or *whom?* An **intransitive verb** is an action verb that does not have a direct object.

TRANSITIVE: Shawn **painted** landscapes and portraits. (*Landscapes* and *portraits* make up the compound direct object that answers the question *what?* Shawn painted.)

INTRANSITIVE: Shawn **painted** beautifully. (There is no direct object answering the question *what?* or *whom?* Shawn painted.)

▶ **Exercise 1** Draw two lines under each action verb. Draw one line under each direct object. In the blank, write *T* if the verb is transitive or *I* if the verb is intransitive.

___T___   Aaron painted his house white.

___T___   **1.** Hiroko plays softball and tennis every summer.

___T___   **2.** The pigeon drank water from the muddy puddle.

___I___   **3.** The eagle soared higher and higher in the sky.

___T___   **4.** The stern judge gave a harsh sentence to the defendant.

___T___   **5.** The happy baby wore a toothless grin.

___I___   **6.** New Zealand lies about 1,000 miles (1,600 kilometers) southeast of Australia.

___I___   **7.** City council meets once a week.

___T___   **8.** Maria prepares dinner for the family.

___T___   **9.** The artist paints colorful, geometric designs.

___T___ **10.** The news reporter lifted her eyebrows in disbelief.

___T___ **11.** The news of war shocked the nation and the world.

___I___ **12.** The timid man muttered under his breath.

___T___ **13.** Most dinosaurs resembled birds in their leg and foot structure.

___T___ **14.** The assistant coach made a suggestion.

___I___ **15.** The buffalo herd stampeded across the prairie.

I ___ **16.** Mr. Armstrong <u>bragged</u> about his five children.

T ___ **17.** The magician <u>pulled</u> a <u>bird</u> out of his sleeve.

T ___ **18.** The proud peacock <u>displayed</u> its <u>feathers</u>.

T ___ **19.** The dental technician <u>cleaned</u> <u>teeth</u> with expertise.

T ___ **20.** The sad clown <u>wiped</u> his <u>eyes</u> with an oversized handkerchief.

I ___ **21.** The small airplane <u>landed</u> safely in the snowstorm.

T ___ **22.** Alma <u>poured</u> <u>syrup</u> over her waffle.

T ___ **23.** Bette Davis <u>won</u> two <u>Academy Awards</u> for best actress in the 1930s.

T ___ **24.** Most diamond crystals <u>have</u> eight <u>sides</u>.

I ___ **25.** The giant octopus <u>lives</u> in the Pacific Ocean.

T ___ **26.** Candy Lightner <u>founded</u> <u>Mothers Against Drunk Driving (MADD)</u> in 1980.

T ___ **27.** The skillful waitress <u>carried</u> four <u>plates</u> of food to the table.

T ___ **28.** Latoya <u>lit</u> a <u>candle</u> after the power outage.

I ___ **29.** The ball <u>dropped</u> in Times Square on New Year's Eve.

I ___ **30.** The rugged trail <u>wound</u> over hills and through a thick forest.

T ___ **31.** The comedian <u>amused</u> <u>everyone</u> in the audience.

I ___ **32.** The elevator <u>stopped</u> on the tenth floor.

I ___ **33.** The friendly dog <u>barked</u> happily.

T ___ **34.** The chess champion <u>challenged</u> her <u>rival</u> to another match.

T ___ **35.** The choir <u>sang</u> holiday <u>songs</u>.

I ___ **36.** In 1980, Mount St. Helens <u>erupted</u> in a huge blast.

T ___ **37.** The drummer <u>played</u> a drum <u>solo</u>.

T ___ **38.** Fred <u>studied</u> <u>science</u> and <u>history</u> in study hall.

T ___ **39.** Water <u>flooded</u> the <u>basement</u> after the downpour.

I ___ **40.** The boy <u>grumbled</u> about his responsibility to take out the garbage.

T ___ **41.** To Neal's dismay, the teacher <u>assigned</u> <u>homework</u> over the weekend.

I ___ **42.** The canoe <u>floated</u> peacefully in the large pond.

Grammar

Lesson 14
Verbs with Indirect Objects

In addition to a direct object, an indirect object may follow an action verb. An **indirect object** answers the question *to whom?* or *for whom?* an action is done.

The doctor gives the **patient** some medicine. (*To whom* did the doctor give medicine?)

Mario reserved **us** a seat. (*For whom* did Mario reserve a seat?)

The indirect object always comes between the verb and the direct object. To determine if a word is an indirect object, put the preposition *to* or *for* in front of it, and change its position in the sentence. If it is an indirect object, the sentence will still make sense.

I gave **Jo** a game. (*Jo* is the indirect object before the direct object, *game.*)
I gave a game **to Jo**. (To determine whether it is an indirect object, *Jo* can be placed behind the preposition *to* and the sentence still makes sense.)

▶ **Exercise 1** Write in the blank whether the word in italics is a *DO* (direct object) or an *IO* (indirect object).

___IO___ Mrs. Cruz made her *children* lunch.

___DO___ **1.** The electrician installed the light *fixture*.

___IO___ **2.** The eager student showed the *teacher* her latest poem.

___DO___ **3.** The game show host asked the contestants difficult *questions*.

___DO___ **4.** Alice explained the movie *plot* to Troy.

___DO___ **5.** The young girl could not describe her *feelings*.

___DO___ **6.** Fluffy white clouds covered the *sky*.

___IO___ **7.** Alex sent his *teacher* a get-well card.

___IO___ **8.** The roller coaster gave *me* an upset stomach.

___DO___ **9.** The voters elected a *newcomer* to office.

___DO___ **10.** The seamstress carefully stitched the *hem* of the dress.

___IO___ **11.** The coach brought the *team* a healthful snack.

___IO___ **12.** The assistant gave his *boss* some phone messages.

_____IO_____ **13.** Jason bought his *grandmother* stationery for her birthday.

_____DO_____ **14.** Albert Schweitzer won the *Nobel Peace Prize* in 1952.

_____IO_____ **15.** We fed our *cat* leftover turkey.

_____DO_____ **16.** The junior high teacher graded *papers* at night.

_____DO_____ **17.** The gourmet chef tasted her new *entree.*

_____IO_____ **18.** Mitsuyo's father saved *us* seats at the baseball game.

_____DO_____ **19.** Eric took his brother's *advice.*

_____DO_____ **20.** The slugger hit the *ball* out of the park.

▶ **Exercise 2 Draw two lines under each action verb and one line under each indirect object.**

Jason <u><u>brought</u></u> his <u>mother</u> his report card.

1. The catcher <u><u>threw</u></u> the <u>pitcher</u> a new ball.

2. The football punter <u><u>kicked</u></u> the ball to the other team.

3. The Book Club president <u><u>brewed</u></u> coffee for the members.

4. The company <u><u>sent</u></u> its <u>employees</u> holiday bonuses.

5. The curious toddler <u><u>pulled</u></u> the puppy's ears.

6. The clerk <u><u>sold</u></u> the <u>customers</u> three computers.

7. The noisy dog <u><u>disturbed</u></u> the quiet neighborhood.

8. The conductor <u><u>praised</u></u> the violin players.

9. The firefighters <u><u>showed</u></u> the <u>students</u> the procedure for putting out a fire.

10. Jamaal <u><u>showed</u></u> his <u>friends</u> his baseball card collection.

11. The school board president <u><u>presented</u></u> <u>Superintendent Stover</u> a plaque at his

    retirement banquet.

12. The pediatrician <u><u>gave</u></u> the <u>boy</u> a flu shot.

13. Raul's mother <u><u>made</u></u> <u>him</u> a chocolate milkshake.

14. The earthquake <u><u>shook</u></u> our house.

15. Jeff <u><u>threw</u></u> his <u>dog</u> the Frisbee.

16. Jessica's friends <u><u>gave</u></u> <u>her</u> a bridal shower before her wedding.

Lesson 15
Linking Verbs and Predicate Words

A **linking verb** connects the subject of a sentence with a word in the predicate that identifies or describes the subject. *To be* in all its forms is the most common linking verb.

George Washington **was** a general. (The linking verb *was* links *general* to the subject, *George Washington*.)

The computer **will be** useful. (The linking verb *will be* links *useful* to the subject, *computer*.)

COMMON LINKING VERBS

appear	feel	look	seem	sound	taste
become	grow	remain	smell	stay	turn

▶ **Exercise 1** Draw two lines under each verb. Place a check (✔) in the blank next to each sentence that contains a linking verb.

✔ _____ Niagara Falls <u>looks</u> breathtaking.

✔ _____ **1.** Niagara Falls <u>is</u> a most spectacular natural wonder!

_____ **2.** The water <u>plunges</u> over a cliff in two separate waterfalls.

_____ **3.** The American Falls <u>lies</u> within the United States.

✔ _____ **4.** Its home state <u>is</u> New York.

_____ **5.** The Horseshoe Falls <u>lies</u> within Canada.

✔ _____ **6.** Ontario <u>is</u> its home province.

✔ _____ **7.** The Niagara River <u>is</u> the source of both of these waterfalls.

✔ _____ **8.** This river <u>becomes</u> part of the border between the United States and Canada.

_____ **9.** It <u>carries</u> the overflow from four of the Great Lakes.

_____ **10.** Niagara Falls <u>is</u> about halfway between Lake Erie and Lake Ontario.

_____ **11.** Goat Island <u>separates</u> the Horseshoe Falls and the American Falls.

_____ **12.** A huge amount of water <u>roars</u> over the cliffs every second.

_____ **13.** Eighty-five percent of the water <u>flows</u> over the Horseshoe Falls.

✔ _____ **14.** The water supply <u>seems</u> unending.

_____✔_____ **15.** Niagara Falls <u>is</u> a great source of power.

_____ **16.** The water <u>moves</u> through hydroelectric power plants downstream.

_____✔_____ **17.** The Robert Moses power plant <u>is</u> a facility on the American side of the river.

_____✔_____ **18.** Two Sir Adam Beck power plants <u>are</u> Canadian.

_____ **19.** The falls <u>provide</u> electricity for many nearby industries.

_____✔_____ **20.** The name *Niagara* <u>is</u> an old Iroquois word.

_____✔_____ **21.** The actual word <u>was</u> *onguiaahra,* "the strait."

_____ **22.** The waterfalls <u>formed</u> about twelve thousand years ago.

_____ **23.** Lake Erie <u>overflowed</u> with water from a great ice sheet.

_____✔_____ **24.** This overflow <u>became</u> the Niagara River.

_____ **25.** The river <u>flowed</u> over a high cliff.

_____ **26.** The water <u>gouged</u> a deep gorge at the bottom of the cliffs.

_____✔_____ **27.** The gorge <u>remains</u> deep.

_____✔_____ **28.** The gorge <u>grows</u> larger and larger over time.

_____ **29.** In fact, it <u>reaches</u> about seven miles beyond Niagara Falls.

_____ **30.** Nearly three miles below Niagara Falls, the Whirlpool Rapids <u>begin</u>.

_____ **31.** The rushing water <u>erodes</u> the underlying rock layers.

_____ **32.** Over time, the violent current <u>carved</u> a round basin out of the rock.

_____ **33.** The Cave of the Winds <u>exists</u> behind the American Falls.

_____ **34.** It <u>formed</u> under a shelf of hard limestone.

_____✔_____ **35.** The formation of such a cave <u>seems</u> very interesting.

_____ **36.** Hard, thick limestone layers <u>cover</u> softer layers of limestone, sandstone, and shale.

_____ **37.** Water <u>erodes</u> the softer under layers first.

_____ **38.** Because of this, the hard top layers soon <u>extend</u> beyond the other layers in certain places.

A linking verb connects the subject of a sentence with a noun or an adjective in the predicate. A **predicate noun** follows a linking verb and tells what the subject is. A **predicate adjective** follows a linking verb and describes what the subject is like. Predicate nouns or predicate adjectives may be compound.

Lance is my **brother** and my best **friend**. (compound predicate noun)
He is **loyal** and **trustworthy**. (compound predicate adjective)

▶ **Exercise 2** Draw two lines under each verb. Write *PN* above each predicate noun and *PA* above each predicate adjective. Not all sentences contain a PN or PA.

PN
A trip to Niagara Falls is a treat.

PA
1. The air grows misty near the waterfalls.

2. You feel the mist on your face.

3. A thunderous noise greets visitors upon their arrival.

PA
4. The never-ending din is horrific.

PA
5. Tourists seem awestruck by the environment.

PA
6. At night, wide beams of colorful lights look beautiful on the cascades of water.

7. Each year about ten million people visit Niagara Falls.

PN
8. Recreational parks remain areas of enjoyment near the falls.

PA
9. Visitors seldom grow weary of the beautiful sights of the area.

PA
10. Many hotels and gift shops look successful.

PN
11. Tourism is big business at Niagara Falls.

12. Many industries also operate close by.

PA
13. Some people feel angry about the nearby businesses and industries.

14. To them, businesses ruin the area's scenic beauty.

PN
15. Steamers are the transportation for the tourists.

Grammar

16. The steamers, all called *The Maid of the Mist,* <u>stay</u> close to the base of the falls. **PA**

17. Some people on the steamers <u>become</u> wet from the falls' foam and mist. **PA**

18. The water <u>smells</u> extremely musty. **PA**

19. The thunderous water <u>sounds</u> especially loud. **PA**

20. However, the view from the steamers <u>is</u> spectacular. **PA**

21. Some people <u>are</u> afraid of the fierce water. **PA**

22. Such sites as Prospect Point, Table Rock, and Terrapin Point <u>seem</u> safer. **PA**

23. From these areas, rainbows <u>are</u> arches of beauty in the mist. **PN**

24. Rainbow Bridge <u>spans</u> the gorge below Niagara Falls.

▶ **Writing Link** Write a paragraph using linking verbs, predicate nouns, and predicate adjectives to describe a tour you might lead as a guide for a travel agency.

_____

_____

_____

_____

_____

_____

_____

_____

_____

_____

_____

_____

_____

Grammar

Lesson 16
Verb Tenses: Present, Past, and Future

The **tense** of a verb tells when an action takes place.

The **present tense** of a verb names an action that is happening now or happens regularly. It can also express a general truth.

In the present tense of a verb, the base form of the verb is used with all subjects except singular nouns and *he, she,* or *it.* When the subject is a singular noun or *he, she,* or *it, -s* or *-es* is added to the verb.

Lou **hears** the airplane overhead. (happening now)
I **speak** to my uncle once a week. (happens regularly)
The president **serves** a four-year term. (expresses a general truth)

The **past tense** of a verb names an action that already happened. The past tense of many verbs is formed by adding *-ed* to the base form of the verb.

The teacher **graded** papers yesterday.

The **future tense** of a verb names an action that will take place in the future. In the future tense the word *will* is used before the verb. Sometimes *shall* is used when the pronoun *I* or *we* is the subject.

They **will see** the play tomorrow night.   We **shall be** late.

▶ **Exercise 1 Draw two lines under each verb. Write its tense, *present, past,* or *future,* in the blank.**

___present___   Winter officially <u>starts</u> in December.

___past___   **1.** John Steinbeck <u>earned</u> the 1962 Nobel Prize in literature.

___present___   **2.** Squirrels <u>gather</u> nuts every autumn in preparation for winter.

___future___   **3.** Carlos <u>will play</u> second base in tomorrow's game.

___past___   **4.** Wilma <u>fielded</u> the ball very well in yesterday's game.

___present___   **5.** Polar bears often <u>wander</u> into populated areas in Canada.

___present___   **6.** Great brown bears <u>weigh</u> up to 1,540 pounds (700 kilograms).

___present___   **7.** Canada <u>contains</u> one third of the world's supply of fresh water.

___past___   **8.** Mai <u>visited</u> her relatives in Vietnam two years ago.

___future___   **9.** Na and his uncle <u>will travel</u> to the United States next year.

__present__   **10.** During the holidays, people <u>enjoy</u> family traditions.

__past__   **11.** Jared <u>carved</u> the turkey last Thanksgiving.

__present__   **12.** Sally <u>lists</u> her resolutions every New Year's Day.

__future__   **13.** The choir <u>will visit</u> the retirement home next week.

__past__   **14.** The plant-eating stegosaurus <u>lived</u> many years ago.

__future__   **15.** Mrs. Johnson <u>will test</u> her students tomorrow.

__past__   **16.** The pilot carefully <u>landed</u> the airplane during the storm last night.

__present__   **17.** The craters on the moon <u>look</u> like dark spots.

__past__   **18.** The running back <u>scored</u> four touchdowns in our last game.

__future__   **19.** Aunt Rosa <u>will walk</u> at least one mile a day.

__present__   **20.** The bus <u>stops</u> at Lincoln and Reed once every hour.

__present__   **21.** Lawanda <u>plays</u> with her baby brother every night before bedtime.

__past__   **22.** The stock market <u>crashed</u> in October of 1929.

__past__   **23.** The puppy <u>followed</u> its master everywhere.

__future__   **24.** Our country <u>will elect</u> a new leader.

__present__   **25.** My grandparents <u>remember</u> the old radio dramas.

__past__   **26.** Laura's great-grandmother <u>lived</u> in Europe during World War II.

__present__   **27.** Alkas often <u>talks</u> about her after-school job.

__past__   **28.** President Nixon <u>resigned</u> in August of 1974.

__past__   **29.** Last night our dog <u>destroyed</u> the throw pillows on our couch.

__present__   **30.** Americans <u>vote</u> for a president every four years.

▶ **Exercise 2 Write in the blank the tense of the verb as indicated in parentheses.**

Kurt ___will absorb___ himself in each new project. (*absorb,* future)

1. The student council ___helps___ communication between teachers and students. (*help,* present)

2. Who ___will live___ in your home in ten years? (*live,* future)

3. The president ___will travel___ to Europe in one month. (*travel,* future)

4. The continent of Europe _____ **borders** _____ Asia. (*border*, present)

5. Mrs. Samuels _____ **attends** _____ a Book Club meeting every Tuesday. (*attend*, present)

6. Bruno _____ **will help** _____ his brother with his homework. (*help*, future)

7. The frisky puppy _____ **chased** _____ the ball when I threw it. (*chase*, past)

8. The sick baby _____ **coughs** _____ a lot at night. (*cough*, present)

9. The school newspaper always _____ **lists** _____ the students on the honor roll. (*list*, present)

10. When she was a child, Mrs. Nguyen _____ **wanted** _____ to go to college. (*want*, past)

11. The letter _____ **triggered** _____ fond memories of last summer. (*trigger*, past)

12. The garden _____ **will flourish** _____ in Grandpa's capable hands. (*flourish*, future)

13. Every day after school, Lindsay _____ **gulps** _____ down a glass of milk. (*gulp*, present)

14. Barney _____ **fetches** _____ sticks only for his master. (*fetch*, present)

15. We _____ **jiggled** _____ the lock, but it still would not work. (*jiggle*, past)

16. The leaves _____ **swirl** _____ busily in the fall breeze. (*swirl*, present)

17. Bryce _____ **will imitate** _____ various politicians in the variety show. (*imitate*, future)

18. The old cloth quickly _____ **absorbed** _____ the child's spilled milk. (*absorb*, past)

19. They _____ **wedge** _____ the door open with this piece of wood. (*wedge*, present)

20. The tiny spring _____ **trickles** _____ merrily. (*trickle*, present)

21. The crowd _____ **gasped** _____ in surprise. (*gasp*, past)

22. On Sunday they _____ **will dedicate** _____ the new organ. (*dedicate*, future)

23. The committee _____ **will vary** _____ the evening's music. (*vary*, future)

24. Anna _____ **accomplishes** _____ most of her work in the morning. (*accomplish*, present)

25. The young pianist _____ **trembled** _____ as he began his performance. (*tremble*, past)

26. The couple _____ **strolls** _____ through the mall each evening. (*stroll*, present)

27. Storms often _____ **delay** _____ one's travel plans. (*delay*, present)

28. The strong clap of thunder _____ **jolted** _____ the campers awake. (*jolt*, past)

Grammar

29. The kindergartner _____fastened_____ his coat by himself. (*fasten*, past)

30. The two sides _____will unite_____ to accomplish the task. (*unite*, future)

31. Kelly _____goes_____ to the senior citizen center every Monday after school. (*go*, present)

32. The Broadway singer _____remembered_____ her first solo. (*remember*, past)

33. Tomorrow we _____will watch *or* shall watch_____ the solar eclipse. (*watch*, future)

34. Bears _____hibernate_____ in the winter. (*hibernate*, present)

35. Our cat Taboo _____stalked_____ a mourning dove in our backyard. (*stalk*, past)

36. The computer _____needed_____ repair. (*need*, past)

37. We _____walk_____ around the block every evening after dinner. (*walk*, present)

38. Margo _____will take_____ the test when she returns to school. (*take*, future)

39. Emilio _____does_____ the dishes whenever his parents work late. (*do*, present)

40. I _____learned_____ to knit from my grandmother. (*learn*, past)

▶ **Writing Link** Write a paragraph sharing something about your past, your present, and your hopes for the future. Use the past, present, and future tenses of verbs.

_____

_____

_____

_____

_____

_____

_____

_____

_____

_____

_____

Lesson 17
Main Verbs and Helping Verbs

Verbs have four principal parts that are used to form all tenses.

PRINCIPAL PARTS OF THE VERB *CALL*

Base Form	Present Participle	Past Form	Past Participle
call	*calling*	*called*	*called*

A **helping verb** helps the **main verb** tell about an action or make a statement. A **verb phrase** consists of one or more helping verbs followed by a main verb.

The girl is **calling** her parents. (*Is* is the helping verb, and the present participle *calling* is the main verb. Together they form a verb phrase.)

The most common helping verbs are *be, have,* and *do.* Forms of the helping verb *be* include *am, is,* and *are* in the present and *was* and *were* in the past. They combine with the present participle of the main verb. Forms of the helping verb *have* include *have* and *has* in the present and *had* in the past. They combine with the past participle form of a verb.

We have **explored** this cave. (*Have* is the helping verb, and the past participle *explored* is the main verb. Together they form a verb phrase.)

▶ **Exercise 1** Draw two lines under each participle. Write in the blank whether it is a *pres. part.* (present participle) or a *past part.* (past participle).

_____pres. part._____ The sailor is <u><u>anchoring</u></u> the sailboat.

_____past part._____ 1. Every year my aunts have <u><u>shopped</u></u> together on the day after Thanksgiving.

_____past part._____ 2. Wars have <u><u>claimed</u></u> countless lives throughout history.

_____pres. part._____ 3. Advancements in telecommunication technology are <u><u>enhancing</u></u> our daily lives.

_____past part._____ 4. Has your father <u><u>called</u></u> the bank about your savings account?

_____past part._____ 5. Usually by April, the winter's snow has <u><u>melted</u></u>.

_____pres. part._____ 6. On the far side of the lake, the two are <u><u>fishing</u></u> at their favorite spot.

_____pres. part._____ 7. The set of instructions with the kit was <u><u>confusing</u></u> to everyone.

_____past part._____ 8. The sculptor has <u><u>molded</u></u> the clay into a bud vase.

Grammar

___past part.___   **9.** The special weather report had <u>advised</u> viewers against unnecessary

               travel.

___pres. part.___ **10.** As a special project for school, I am <u>interviewing</u> our state representative.

___pres. part.___ **11.** The carpenters were <u>altering</u> our house plans unnecessarily.

___pres. part.___ **12.** The Quick Lunch Deli is <u>catering</u> the dinner next Saturday.

___past part.___ **13.** Fran had <u>apologized</u> for her tardiness.

___past part.___ **14.** The car's fan belt has <u>squealed</u> several times before.

___pres. part.___ **15.** The special invitation was <u>requesting</u> our presence at the gala affair.

___past part.___ **16.** Because of bad weather, the program has been <u>postponed</u> indefinitely.

___pres. part.___ **17.** Our close family friends are <u>inviting</u> us to their lakeside cabin.

___pres. part.___ **18.** In the final scene of the film, the horse and rider were <u>fading</u> into the

               sunset.

___past part.___ **19.** While in Florida, we had <u>plucked</u> grapefruit right from the tree.

___pres. part.___ **20.** I am currently <u>residing</u> in an apartment in New York City.

___pres. part.___ **21.** Feng Ying was <u>preparing</u> the food for the banquet.

___past part.___ **22.** We have <u>looked</u> everywhere for the missing pen.

___past part.___ **23.** They had already <u>discovered</u> the rust spot on the car.

___pres. part.___ **24.** I am <u>looking</u> forward to my grandma's visit.

___pres. part.___ **25.** The fish were <u>becoming</u> ill from the dirty water.

▶ **Exercise 2 Draw two lines under the correct form of the helping verb in parentheses.**

   The children (was, <u>were</u>) playing on the swingset.

1. The school (<u>had</u>, have) changed very little over the years.

2. Sue (<u>was</u>, were) looking at the beautiful rainbow.

3. The bird (<u>is</u>, are) soaring over the purple mountains.

4. The determined team (<u>was</u>, had) practicing for two hours each night.

5. Environmentalists (were, <u>have</u>) urged people to recycle.

6. The owl (were, <u>was</u>) looking for a place to nest in the abandoned barn.

7. The cat (was, <u>had</u>) spied a plump mouse scurrying across the floor.

8. The home owner (<u>was</u>, were) thinking about tearing down the old garage.

9. The cattle (had, <u>were</u>) grazing contentedly in the field.

10. The excited children (were, <u>had</u>) watched their favorite movie.

11. The snow (is, <u>has</u>) stopped coming down.

12. The colorful fruit salad (were, <u>was</u>) chilling in the refrigerator.

13. The whole school (has, <u>is</u>) depending on us.

14. The heat wave (had, <u>was</u>) making people miserable.

15. The funny clown (<u>is</u>, were) performing with the touring circus.

16. Last year Hilda (is, <u>had</u>) wished for a new gerbil.

17. The crab (<u>was</u>, have) crawling across the hot sand.

18. The starfish (is, <u>had</u>) washed up on the seashore.

19. The lifeguard (<u>was</u>, has) shielding her eyes from the sun.

20. The children (<u>had</u>, were) picked up seashells in the morning.

21. My dad (<u>was</u>, had) finishing the spaghetti when Mom asked for more.

22. The city council member (was, <u>had</u>) advocated new lights for our streets.

23. The Drama Club (<u>was</u>, had) meeting in the auditorium.

24. We (<u>are</u>, have) waiting for the pep rally to begin.

25. Our best soccer player (was, <u>has</u>) wounded his knee.

▶ **Exercise 3 Draw two lines under the correct form of the helping verb in parentheses and two lines under each participle to complete each verb phrase. Write in the blank whether the participle is a *pres. part.* (present participle) or a *past part.* (past participle).**

<u>pres. part.</u>   The soft music (<u>was</u>, had) <u>relaxing</u> to me.

<u>pres. part.</u> 1. Surfers (<u>are</u>, was) <u>riding</u> the waves with abandon.

<u>pres. part.</u> 2. Vincent (<u>was</u>, has) <u>putting</u> on his new shoes for the first time.

<u>past part.</u> 3. The train (have, <u>had</u>) <u>derailed</u> late last night.

<u>pres. part.</u> 4. The helicopter (were, <u>is</u>) <u>hovering</u> over the accident.

<u>past part.</u> 5. The movie (were, <u>has</u>) <u>played</u> for eight weeks.

pres. part.   **6.** The car (has, <u>was</u>) <u>moving</u> very slowly up the hill.

pres. part.   **7.** The grasshopper (has, <u>is</u>) <u>hopping</u> energetically through the field.

pres. part.   **8.** After lunch, the chef (<u>was</u>, are) <u>preparing</u> for dinner.

past part.   **9.** The actress (<u>has</u>, is) <u>learned</u> all her lines for the play.

pres. part.   **10.** The nervous speaker (are, <u>was</u>) <u>stumbling</u> over his words.

pres. part.   **11.** The lion (has, <u>is</u>) <u>pacing</u> back and forth in his cage.

past part.   **12.** The truck's headlights (were, <u>had</u>) <u>scared</u> the deer.

past part.   **13.** The elevator (are, <u>has</u>) <u>stopped</u> at the tenth floor.

past part.   **14.** Industrial pollution (<u>has</u>, is) <u>caused</u> acid rain in some areas.

past part.   **15.** Oil spills (<u>have</u>, are) <u>happened</u> all around the world.

past part.   **16.** Scientists (are, <u>have</u>) <u>studied</u> dinosaurs for more than 160 years.

past part.   **17.** My dad (<u>had</u>, was) <u>disguised</u> himself well.

past part.   **18.** The early American settlers (were, <u>had</u>) <u>struggled</u> to survive.

past part.   **19.** The Vikings (is, <u>had</u>) <u>landed</u> on American shores hundreds of years before other Europeans.

pres. part.   **20.** During the basketball game, some parents (<u>were</u>, have) <u>selling</u> popcorn.

▶ **Writing Link** Write a paragraph about going to a music store with a friend. Use main verbs and helping verbs with both present and past participles.

_____

_____

_____

_____

_____

_____

_____

_____

_____

_____

Lesson 18
Progressive Forms: Present and Past

The **present progressive form** of a verb names an action or condition that is continuing in the present. The present progressive form of a verb consists of the present form of the helping verb *be* and the present participle of the main verb.

PRESENT PROGRESSIVE FORM

SINGULAR
I **am watching**.
You **are watching**.
He, she, *or* it **is watching**.

PLURAL
We **are watching**.
You **are watching**.
They **are watching**.

The **past progressive form** of a verb names an action or condition that was continuing for some time in the past. The past progressive form of a verb consists of the past form of the helping verb *be* and the present participle of the main verb.

PAST PROGRESSIVE FORM

SINGULAR
I **was hoping**.
You **were hoping**.
He, she, *or* it **was hoping**.

PLURAL
We **were hoping**.
You **were hoping**.
They **were hoping**.

▶ **Exercise 1** Write the present progressive (pres. prog.) form or past progressive (past prog.) form of the verb given in parentheses.

Historians _____**are discovering**_____ more about the exploration of the New World. (*discover,* pres. prog.)

1. Native Americans _____**were living**_____ in the Americas for many years before Christopher Columbus arrived. (*live,* past prog.)

2. They _____**were dwelling**_____ in well-established civilizations. (*dwell,* past prog.)

3. Native Americans _____**were migrating**_____ from Asia. (*migrate,* past prog.)

4. Many Native Americans _____**were dying**_____ from diseases brought from Europe. (*die,* past prog.)

5. Columbus _____**was sailing**_____ on behalf of the Spanish rulers. (*sail,* past prog.)

6. He _____**was hoping**_____ to chart a new course to Asia. (*hope,* past prog.)

7. Researchers _____**are studying**_____ Columbus's early voyages. (*study,* pres. prog.)

8. Other countries _____ were making _____ voyages to the New World. (*make*, past prog.)

9. The English _____ were traveling _____ to the mid-Atlantic coast. (*travel*, past prog.)

10. The French _____ were settling _____ in the Northeast. (*settle*, past prog.)

11. In the late 1400s, rulers and merchants _____ were financing _____ more and more

traveling expeditions. (*finance*, past prog.)

12. They _____ were hoping _____ for increased trade and riches. (*hope*, past prog.)

13. The spice trade in Asia _____ was becoming _____ profitable. (*become*, past prog.)

14. Columbus's ships _____ were carrying _____ gold, spices, birds, and plants. (*carry*, past

prog.)

15. These early explorers _____ are receiving _____ some attention. (*receive*, present prog.)

▶ **Exercise 2** If the verb in parentheses is in the present tense, write its present progressive form in the blank. If the verb is in the past tense, write its past progressive form.

_____ were claiming _____ Spanish explorers (claimed) lands in North, Central, and South America in the early 1500s.

_____ was claiming _____ **1.** Amerigo Vespucci (claimed) he arrived in mainland America before Columbus.

_____ was deciding _____ **2.** A German mapmaker (decided) to name America after this Italian explorer.

_____ are dismissing _____ **3.** Most historians (dismiss) Amerigo Vespucci's claim.

_____ was exploring _____ **4.** Juan Ponce de León, a Spaniard, also (explored) the New World.

_____ was sailing _____ **5.** In 1493, he (sailed) on Christopher Columbus's second voyage.

_____ was founding _____ **6.** Ponce de León (founded) a Spanish settlement in Puerto Rico in 1508.

_____ was governing _____ **7.** He (governed) the island for three years.

_____ was learning _____ **8.** He (learned) about the legendary Fountain of Youth from the Native Americans.

_____ was searching _____ **9.** The explorer, with an expedition, (searched) for it.

_____ was discovering _____ **10.** He (discovered) other lands, including present-day Florida, during his search.

●

Lesson 19
Perfect Tenses: Present and Past

The **present perfect tense** of a verb names an action that happened some time in the past. It also names an action that happened in the past and is still happening now. The present perfect tense consists of the helping verb *have* or *has* and the past participle of the main verb.

PRESENT PERFECT TENSE

SINGULAR	PLURAL
I **have traveled.**	We **have traveled.**
You **have traveled.**	You **have traveled.**
He, she *or* it **has traveled.**	They **have traveled.**

The **past perfect tense** of a verb names an action that happened before another event or action in the past. The past perfect tense of a verb consists of the helping verb *had* and the past participle of the main verb.

I had traveled.   You **had traveled.**   They **had traveled.**

▶ **Exercise 1** Write in the blank the present perfect tense of the verb in parentheses.

Some students _____**have missed**_____ school because of the weather. (miss)

1. The townspeople _____**have prepared**_____ for the cold winter. (prepare)

2. Thousands _____**have purchased**_____ new snow shovels. (purchase)

3. E & Z Salting _____**has checked**_____ all of its salt trucks. (check)

4. Many families _____**have installed**_____ their storm windows. (install)

5. Some car owners _____**have acquired**_____ chains for their tires. (acquire)

6. Parents _____**have retrieved**_____ boxes of warm winter clothing from storage. (retrieve)

7. Children _____**have asked**_____ for new snow sleds. (ask)

8. The weather reporter _____**has warned**_____ people about frostbite. (warn)

9. Many people _____**have wished**_____ for a mild winter. (wish)

10. Even the squirrels _____**have prepared**_____ for winter. (prepare)

11. They _____**have gathered**_____ an assortment of nuts. (gather)

12. Many animals' coats _____**have thickened**_____ in preparation for a cold winter. (thicken)

13. Many of the birds _____**have traveled**_____ south already. (travel)

14. Some, such as cardinals, _____**have remained**_____ for the winter. (remain)

15. My dog _____**has liked**_____ to stay inside more than usual. (like)

16. My brother always _____**has enjoyed**_____ the cold weather. (enjoy)

17. He _____**has constructed**_____ big forts out of snow. (construct)

18. He _____**has rolled**_____ snow into big balls to make snowmen. (roll)

19. My parents _____**have provided**_____ an old hat for the snowman. (provide)

20. My father _____**has collected**_____ wood for my grandmother's fireplace. (collect)

▶ **Exercise 2** **Write in the blank the past perfect tense of the verb in parentheses.**

My baby sister _____**had experienced**_____ her first winter. (experience)

1. Everyone _____**had hoped**_____ for an early spring. (hope)

2. The frigid winter _____**had caused**_____ people to stay indoors. (cause)

3. The snowstorms _____**had stopped**_____ the bus service for a few days. (stop)

4. Driving in so much snow _____**had resulted**_____ in many accidents. (result)

5. Only a small amount of the ice below the snow _____**had melted**_____. (melt)

6. The snowplows _____**had reached**_____ only the main streets. (reach)

7. By the time we shoveled our walk, six inches of new snow _____**had arrived**_____.

   (arrive)

8. Authorities _____**had canceled**_____ school for two days in a row. (cancel)

9. Ice and extremely cold temperatures _____**had caused**_____ power lines to snap. (cause)

10. At one point, the mayor _____**had called**_____ an emergency town meeting. (call)

11. Some families _____**had moved**_____ in with relatives. (move)

12. I _____**had noticed**_____ very few people exercising outside. (notice)

13. People were worried because the snow _____**had continued**_____ for three days.

    (continue)

14. Truck drivers _____**had altered**_____ their routes because they could not travel

    through the snow-filled city streets. (alter)

15. People _____**had realized**_____ that they needed to stock up on supplies. (realize)

Lesson 20
Irregular Verbs I

The irregular verbs below are grouped according to the way their past form and past participle are formed.

IRREGULAR VERBS

PATTERN	BASE FORM	PAST FORM	PAST PARTICIPLE
One vowel changes to form the past and the past participle.	begin	began	begun
	sing	sang	sung
	spring	sprang or sprung	sprung
	swim	swam	swum
The past form and the past participle are the same.	bring	brought	brought
	catch	caught	caught
	feel	felt	felt
	get	got	got *or* gotten
	keep	kept	kept
	lead	led	led
	leave	left	left
	lose	lost	lost
	make	made	made
	pay	paid	paid
	say	said	said
	seek	sought	sought
	sit	sat	sat
	think	thought	thought
	win	won	won

▶ **Exercise 1** **Write in the blank the past tense or the past participle of the verb in parentheses.**

Several recent presidents have _____**made**_____ a lasting impression on the American public. (make)

1. Before his presidency, John F. Kennedy had _____**got *or* gotten**_____ involved in World War II as an officer in the United States Navy. (get)

2. He _____**won**_____ recognition for saving a disabled sailor after their PT boat was destroyed. (win)

3. Despite an injured back, he _____**swam**_____ safely to shore towing the crewman. (swim)

4. As president, Kennedy _____sought_____ to put the first man on the moon. (seek)

5. He _____felt_____ that it was important to accomplish this before the Soviet Union did. (feel)

6. Kennedy _____said_____ that the goal was to reach the moon before the end of the 1960s. (say)

7. The United States _____lost_____ Kennedy to an assassin's bullet in 1963. (lose)

8. The Soviet Union _____kept_____ ahead of the United States space program. (keep)

9. However, the Americans finally _____caught_____ up with the Soviet Union in the "space race." (catch)

10. In 1969, the United States astronauts _____made_____ it to the moon. (make)

11. Neil Armstrong was the first person who _____left_____ his footprints on the moon. (leave)

12. Many Americans have _____sung_____ praises of Kennedy for inspiring this event. (sing)

13. After Kennedy's death, Lyndon Johnson _____led_____ the country. (lead)

14. Johnson _____won_____ the 1964 election with 61 percent of the popular vote. (win)

15. President Johnson _____began_____ a "War on Poverty." (begin)

16. He _____sought_____ increased U.S. involvement in Vietnam. (seek)

17. Some Americans have _____thought_____ that Johnson was wrong to send so many troops. (think)

18. Many think we _____paid_____ a dear price in Vietnam. (pay)

19. The war also _____brought_____ unhappiness and unrest at home. (bring)

20. Partially provoked by the Vietnam war, public demonstrations _____sprang_____ up during the 1960s. (spring)

21. Johnson _____left_____ office in 1968. (leave)

22. After Johnson, Richard M. Nixon _____sat_____ in the Oval Office. (sit)

23. Nixon _____kept_____ his campaign focused on traditional values. (keep)

24. He _____sought_____ to make diplomatic trips to China. (seek)

Lesson 21
Irregular Verbs II

The following irregular verbs are grouped according to the way their past form and past participle are formed.

IRREGULAR VERBS

PATTERN	BASE FORM	PAST FORM	PAST PARTICIPLE
The base form and the past participle are the same.	become	became	become
	come	came	come
	run	ran	run
The past form ends in *-ew* and the past participle ends in *-wn.*	blow	blew	blown
	draw	drew	drawn
	fly	flew	flown
	grow	grew	grown
	know	knew	known
	throw	threw	thrown
The past participle ends in *-en.*	bite	bit	bitten *or* bit
	break	broke	broken
	choose	chose	chosen
	drive	drove	driven
	eat	ate	eaten
	fall	fell	fallen
	give	gave	given
	ride	rode	ridden
	rise	rose	risen
	see	saw	seen
	speak	spoke	spoken
	steal	stole	stolen
	take	took	taken
	write	wrote	written
The past form and the past participle do not follow any pattern.	am, are, is	was, were	been
	do	did	done
	go	went	gone
	tear	tore	torn
	wear	wore	worn
The base form, past form, and past participle are all the same.	cut	cut	cut
	let	let	let

Grammar

▶ **Exercise 1** Write in the blank the past tense or the past participle of the verb in parentheses.

Have you ____worn____ your new skirt yet? (wear)

1. I have ____seen____ the same movie seven times. (see)

2. Yoko has ____run____ in several cross-country races. (run)

3. Steven ____grew____ three inches in only one year! (grow)

4. The Adams have ____driven____ to the state park four times this summer. (drive)

5. The little girl ____chose____ the black licorice. (choose)

6. Chris has ____given____ his red remote-controlled car to his best friend. (give)

7. The gold and red leaves have ____fallen____ from the tree. (fall)

8. The autumn wind ____blew____ the newspaper across the lawn. (blow)

9. The foul ball ____broke____ the window of a nearby car. (break)

10. The woman had never ____known____ such happiness. (know)

11. The pitcher has ____thrown____ too many slow pitches. (throw)

12. The geese ____flew____ in an orderly V-shaped formation. (fly)

13. The spider has ____gone____ into the corner. (go)

14. Then she ____stole____ home plate. (steal)

15. Ms. Mazurik ____became____ upset during her phone call. (become)

16. My goldfish has ____bit *or* bitten____ the plastic plant in its bowl. (bite)

17. Have you ____eaten____? (eat)

18. I have ____been____ happy with my grades these last few weeks. (am)

19. What has she ____done____ to earn that award? (do)

20. The experienced pilot has ____flown____ many different kinds of planes. (fly)

21. The catcher ____threw____ the ball to second base. (throw)

22. I already ____ate____ lunch. (eat)

23. The neighbor's dog ____bit____ the tail of a stray cat. (bite)

24. The presidential candidate has ____chosen____ a running mate. (choose)

25. Diana's parents have _____spoken_____ to the principal. (speak)

26. Omar _____came_____ in second in the spelling bee. (come)

27. The sun _____rose_____ slowly above the horizon. (rise)

28. Have you _____ridden_____ on the biggest roller coaster in the park? (ride)

29. The puppy _____let_____ the toddlers pet him. (let)

30. This is the second pair of jeans I have _____torn_____ in a month. (tear)

31. Our class has _____written_____ to members of Congress. (write)

32. Leonardo da Vinci has _____drawn_____ many scientific illustrations. (draw)

33. I _____cut_____ through the green and white frosting of the birthday cake. (cut)

34. President Harry S Truman _____grew_____ up in Independence, Missouri. (grow)

35. Esteban _____wore_____ gloves when he shoveled the sidewalk. (wear)

36. Helen's family _____went_____ to Washington, D.C. (go)

37. The baserunner had already _____stolen_____ third base. (steal)

38. I have not _____seen_____ that new comedy. (see)

39. Michael has _____taken_____ five books out of the library. (take)

40. I _____saw_____ the constellation Orion in last night's sky. (see)

▶ **Exercise 2** **Underline the verb in parentheses that best completes each sentence.**

I (falled, <u>fell</u>) from my bicycle yesterday.

1. My English teacher has (spoked, <u>spoken</u>) to me about revising my paper.

2. I have (did, <u>done</u>) that puzzle before!

3. I have never (saw, <u>seen</u>) such lovely flowers!

4. Has your shoelace (tore, <u>torn</u>)?

5. Tina's mom (<u>drove</u>, drived) her to tennis practice.

6. The Bexley Lions have (were, <u>been</u>) on a winning streak.

7. Judy (come, <u>came</u>) to the conclusion that she needed a part-time job.

8. The robins have (flew, <u>flown</u>) south for the winter.

9. My dad (<u>cut</u>, cutted) the apple pie into eight pieces.

10. My brother has (grew, <u>grown</u>) two inches in the last year.

11. Rosita (<u>rose</u>, risen) this morning at 7:00 A.M.

12. The squirrels have (ate, <u>eaten</u>) the birds' food.

13. Carlos and Dimitri have (went, <u>gone</u>) to the museum every weekend this month.

14. My thoughtful aunt has (brung, <u>brought</u>) us the sports page.

15. Isaiah (<u>threw</u>, throwed) the dirty towel into the hamper.

16. Dave (breaked, <u>broke</u>) his tooth when he fell off his bike.

17. My mother has (chose, <u>chosen</u>) a new career.

18. Kirsten and I (blowed, <u>blew</u>) up balloons.

19. Why has she (<u>let</u>, letted) him borrow so many CDs?

20. The coach (<u>gave</u>, given) her players a pep talk at halftime.

▶ **Writing Link** Write a paragraph about what you did after school one day this week. Use at least four past forms and four past participles from the list on page 97.

_____

_____

_____

_____

_____

_____

_____

_____

_____

_____

_____

_____

_____

Grammar

✓ Unit 3 **Review**

▶ **Exercise 1** Draw two lines under each verb. In the blank, write *transitive*, *intransitive*, or *linking* to identify the kind of verb. Write *PN* above each predicate noun and *PA* above each predicate adjective.

_____linking_____ The principal appeared calm. [PA above "calm"]

_____intransitive_____ **1.** Several mice lived behind the wall.

_____linking_____ **2.** All of the jackets were brown. [PA above "brown"]

_____transitive_____ **3.** I discovered a box of macaroni and cheese in the pantry.

_____transitive_____ **4.** The largest dog gave the others the food.

_____linking_____ **5.** The people seemed very grateful for the help. [PA above "grateful"]

_____transitive_____ **6.** My cat chased some mice away.

_____linking_____ **7.** The painting was an orange and white watercolor. [PN above "watercolor"]

_____intransitive_____ **8.** The goose hissed loudly.

_____transitive_____ **9.** The skater lost her skates.

_____transitive_____ **10.** The singer gave the guitar to her manager.

▶ **Exercise 2** Draw two lines under each verb or verb phrase. In the blank, write the tense or form of the verb: *present, past, future, present perfect, past perfect, present progressive,* or *past progressive.*

_____past_____ My father gave me my allowance.

_____future_____ **1.** We will attend the city council meeting tonight.

present progressive **2.** Congress is suggesting a new tax.

_____past_____ **3.** We played volleyball in gym class.

past progressive **4.** Students were complaining about the football team's defeat.

_____past perfect_____ **5.** The teacher had asked for more work.

present perfect **6.** This has become the best event of the summer.

Grammar

Cumulative Review: Units 1–3

▶ **Exercise 1** Draw one line under each complete subject and two lines under each complete predicate. Above each noun, write *prop.* for proper or *com.* for common.

com. **prop.**
My family has toured Europe.

prop. **com.** **prop.** **com.**
1. Dr. Drew, famous for his work during World War II, organized blood banks for the

prop.
Red Cross.

com. **com.** **prop.**
2. My uncle was a soldier in Vietnam.

com. **com.** **com.**
3. Her collection of baseball cards is in the closet.

com. **prop.**
4. We attended a band concert at Roosevelt Junior High.

prop. **com.** **com.**
5. Riverview Hospital employs students as aides.

prop. **com.** **prop.**
6. Vivian and I listen to the radio every Sunday.

prop. **com.** **prop.** **prop.** **prop.**
7. Hiroshi and his family visited Mount Rushmore, near Rapid City, South Dakota.

prop. **com.** **prop.** **prop.**
8. Mario drove with his dad in their old Toyota to the Kenwood Mall.

com. **com.** **prop.** **com.** **prop.**
9. Our class, with the help of Mrs. Bluth, an outside specialist, studied Shakespeare and

com.
put on skits.

▶ **Exercise 2** Draw two lines under each verb or verb phrase. In the blank, write the tense or form of the verb: *present, past, future, present perfect, past perfect, present progressive,* or *past progressive.*

_____**present perfect**_____ Who has given food items to the needy?

_____**present progressive**_____ 1. We are celebrating the last day of school.

_____**present**_____ 2. Scientists use highly technical equipment.

_____**future**_____ 3. I will read more about world history.

_____**past progressive**_____ 4. I was waiting for a spot on the team.

_____**past perfect**_____ 5. Dale had given the teacher his homework assignment.

_____**past**_____ 6. Ahmik played tennis in a summer league.

Unit 4: Pronouns

Lesson 22
Pronouns: Personal

A **pronoun** is a word that takes the place of a noun or a group of nouns.

A **personal pronoun** replaces the subject or object in a sentence. It refers to a specific person or thing and can be singular or plural. A **subject pronoun** is used as the subject of a sentence. An **object pronoun** is used as the object of a verb or of a preposition.

He enjoys the movie.   **They** enjoy the movie. (used as the subject)
Tara opened the book and read **it**. (used as the object of a verb)
David gave the tickets to **us**. (used as the object of a preposition)

SINGULAR SUBJECT	PLURAL SUBJECT	SINGULAR OBJECT	PLURAL OBJECT
I	we	me	us
you	you	you	you
he, she, it	they	him, her, it	them

▶ **Exercise 1** **Write in the blank the personal pronoun that replaces the word or phrase in parentheses.**

_____He_____ (Walt Disney) was one of the most famous motion picture producers in history.

_____He_____ 1. (Walt Disney) may be best known for creating Mickey Mouse.

_____he_____ 2. However, (Disney) had many other achievements during his lifetime.

_____them_____ 3. Some of (the achievements) include creating the first cartoon with sound.

_____They_____ 4. (Cartoon characters) made Disney famous around the world.

_____he_____ 5. Along with his partner, (Disney) brought to life characters such as Donald Duck, Goofy, and Pluto.

_____It_____ 6. (The Disney studio) also makes feature-length animated movies.

_____He_____ 7. (Disney) is credited with the first feature-length animated movie.

_____It_____ 8. (That animated film) was called *Snow White and the Seven Dwarfs*.

Grammar

_____it_____ 9. Many other successful movies followed (that one).

_____They_____ 10. (Some of the successful films) were *Dumbo, Pinocchio, Fantasia,* and *Bambi.*

_____they_____ 11. In the 1950s, (Disney and his partners) began to make films with live actors, too.

_____them_____ 12. *Treasure Island* and *20,000 Leagues Under the Sea* were some of (the films).

_____them_____ 13. Disney also brought (the audience) the musical *Mary Poppins* in 1964.

_____She_____ 14. (Mary Poppins) was a nanny who could fly.

_____her_____ 15. All children seem to love (Mary Poppins).

_____it_____ 16. However, (Disney's work) was not limited to films.

_____He_____ 17. (Disney) also developed programs for television.

_____It_____ 18. (*The Mickey Mouse Club*) entertained many children who watched it on television.

_____him_____ 19. *The Mickey Mouse Club* was also a success for (Disney).

_____They_____ 20. (Two large amusement parks) also bear Disney's name.

▶ **Exercise 2** Write in the blank the personal pronoun that replaces the italicized word or phrase. Also, write *subj.* (subject) or *obj.* (object) to identify its usage.

_____They, subj._____ *Filmmakers* found that animals were easier to draw than people.

_____It, subj._____ 1. *The dictionary* defines animation as "to bring to life."

_____They, subj._____ 2. *Animators* give the illusion of life and movement to drawings, cartoons, and other objects.

_____it, obj._____ 3. Hand-drawn pictures are only a small part of *animating.*

_____them, obj._____ 4. Most of *today's animated movies* include sound and many special effects.

_____them, obj._____ 5. Computers help animators give life to *cartoons and other objects.*

_____them, obj._____ 6. Animated characters' movements should look smooth to *the people watching.*

_____they, subj._____ 7. To achieve smoothness, *animators* create one drawing for each frame of film.

_____her, obj._____ 8. A single word said by *a little girl in a cartoon* may take as many as eight drawings.

Lesson 23
Pronouns and Antecedents

The noun or group of words to which a pronoun refers is called its **antecedent**. A pronoun must agree in number and gender with its antecedent.

Sue went to the store. **She** bought some fruits and vegetables. (*Sue* is the antecedent of *she*.)

The antecedent must be clear.

Todd looks like his father. He is an optometrist. (unclear)
Todd looks like his father. His father is an optometrist. (clear)
They sell many used cars at the dealership. (unclear)
The dealership sells many used cars. (clear)

▶ **Exercise 1** Write the correct pronoun in each blank. Then, draw an arrow to its antecedent. Be sure the pronoun agrees in number and gender with the antecedent.

Jane and Carla went to the store. _____**They**_____ left soon after I did.

1. Kim looked as though she had seen a ghost. _____**She**_____ must have been very scared.

2. We ran into Tim at the mall. _____**He**_____ was in a hurry.

3. I saw the car accident. _____**It**_____ seemed to happen in slow motion.

4. Our tour guide showed us his favorite sights. _____**He**_____ took us to many great places.

5. The potholes in the road made our trip a bumpy ride. _____**They**_____ made the car shake.

6. Olivia gave the book to Steve. _____**She**_____ gave _____**It**_____ to _____**him**_____ as a present.

7. The wrestlers are on a winning streak. Fans love to watch _____**them**_____.

8. The mud was thick everywhere. _____**It**_____ made football practice hazardous.

9. Sumi, Richard, and I reached the top quickly. _____**We**_____ were out of breath.

10. We read Aesop's fable "The Lion and the Mouse." _____**It**_____ was amusing.

11. My little brother left when he saw the spiders. _____**He**_____ is afraid of _____**them**_____.

12. Antonio ran for class treasurer. _____**He**_____ won easily.

13. We walked carefully to avoid the broken glass. Pieces of _____**It**_____ were

everywhere.

14. I looked everywhere for Sarah. _____**She**_____ was nowhere to be found.

15. Frank and I rode our bikes after school. _____**We**_____ were home before dark.

16. Jerod knocked over the paint cans. Then _____**he**_____ picked _____**them**_____ up.

17. We had lima beans for dinner. I didn't eat any because I don't like _____**them**_____.

18. Ahmed mowed lawns last summer. _____**He**_____ earned enough money to buy a bike.

19. Pat and Mariko walked to the movie. _____**They**_____ were tired when they got home.

20. Dad spoke to James and me about the mess. He told _____**us**_____ to clean it up.

21. The choir recital lasted more than three hours. _____**It**_____ had two intermissions.

22. Kangaroos are interesting. _____**They**_____ nourish their young in pouches.

23. Ben and Scott joined Benito and me for a set of tennis. _____**They**_____ beat _____**us**_____ by

two games.

24. Melanie was injured in a bicycle accident. _____**She**_____ broke her wrist.

25. Our campground was hidden behind many trees. _____**It**_____ was difficult to find.

26. Alberto and I joined the science club. _____**We**_____ go every Friday after school.

27. The noises outside bothered Jill. _____**They**_____ made sleep difficult for _____**her**_____.

28. Graham moved here from New Zealand. _____**He**_____ and his family adjusted well.

29. Claire plays the piano and the trumpet. _____**She**_____ plays _____**them**_____ equally well.

30. Yvonne is interested in medicine. _____**She**_____ wants to be a doctor someday.

Lesson 24
Using Pronouns Correctly

Subject pronouns (*I, you, he, she, it, we, you, they*) are used in compound subjects.

She and Larry planned to sing a duet.

In formal writing and speech, use a subject pronoun after a linking verb.

The owner of that jacket is **she.**

Object pronouns (*me, you, him, her, it, us, you, them*) are used in compound objects.

Mother told Carmen and **me** to wear our jackets.

An object pronoun should also be used as the object of a preposition.

Eric asked someone to ride with **him.**

▶ **Exercise 1 Underline the pronoun in parentheses that best completes each sentence.**

He and (I, me) played checkers.

1. Inali lent his skateboard to (I, me).

2. Should Erica and (I, me) meet you and (her, she)?

3. Stacy and (her, she) are making the scenery for the play.

4. The teacher told Nancy and (I, me) to work together.

5. I used to baby-sit for Jane and (he, him).

6. Brad and (I, me) packed our suitcases for vacation.

7. I met Joel and (he, him) in the library.

8. Uncle Jack brought gifts for Katrina and (I, me).

9. The winner of the poetry contest was (her, she).

10. Daniel's pen pal sent a letter to (he, him).

11. Would you like a photograph of (her, she)?

12. We spoke to (he, him) after class.

13. After we became peer counselors, anyone with a problem came to (we, us).

Grammar

14. Jordan lent his bike helmets to Marty and (I, <u>me</u>).

15. Chad and (<u>I</u>, me) were not invited to the party.

16. Let's keep this just between you and (I, <u>me</u>).

17. The little boy is named after (he, <u>him</u>).

18. Phil and (me, <u>I</u>) tried to climb over the fence.

19. My cuts felt better after my dad put bandages on (<u>them</u>, they).

20. Math interests (<u>us</u>, we) more than science.

▶ **Exercise 2** Underline the pronoun in parentheses that best completes each sentence. In the blank, write *O* for object or *S* for subject to identify the correct form.

_____0_____ The magician performed for the sixth graders and (<u>us</u>, we).

_____S_____ **1.** Max and (<u>he</u>, him) shared a chocolate malt.

_____0_____ **2.** Mr. Baird showed Kari and (<u>her</u>, she) how to do the experiment.

_____0_____ **3.** The music was too loud for Erin and (I, <u>me</u>).

_____S_____ **4.** Meagan and (<u>I</u>, me) usually rode the bus.

_____0_____ **5.** The team complained that the opponents didn't shake hands with (they, <u>them</u>).

_____S_____ **6.** (Us, <u>We</u>) and Hiroko did a report on the Civil War.

_____0_____ **7.** My brother helped Joe and (I, <u>me</u>) with our homework.

_____0_____ **8.** Jessie was grateful for the help I gave (<u>her</u>, she).

_____0_____ **9.** I trust my brother Tim, and I often confide in (he, <u>him</u>).

_____0_____ **10.** The biggest roller coaster in the park was the favorite one for (<u>us</u>, we).

_____S_____ **11.** Both he and (<u>I</u>, me) are eligible for the prize.

_____0_____ **12.** The day was too rainy for (<u>us</u>, we) to go outside.

_____0_____ **13.** Dad told David and (I, <u>me</u>) that he would take us fishing Saturday.

_____S_____ **14.** (<u>He</u>, him) and Tom went to the swim meet together.

_____0_____ **15.** The computer class is easy for Andy and (<u>her</u>, she).

_____S_____ **16.** (Them, <u>They</u>) and Yoko roasted marshmallows over the fire.

Lesson 25
Pronouns: Possessive and Indefinite

A **possessive pronoun** shows who or what has something. Possessive pronouns replace possessive nouns. They may come before a noun or may be used alone.

	USED BEFORE NOUNS	USED ALONE
Singular:	my, your, his, her, its	mine, yours, his, hers, its
Plural:	our, your, their	ours, yours, theirs

Tara's teacher was Mrs. Rodriguez. **Her** teacher was Mrs. Rodriguez.
The book was Sara's. The book was **hers**.

▶ **Exercise 1** Underline each possessive pronoun.

Tell them not to wear <u>their</u> hats inside.

1. <u>Her</u> diary was ruined when she dropped it in the mud.

2. Chad wants a video game like <u>hers</u>.

3. Are these <u>our</u> baseballs or <u>theirs</u>?

4. <u>My</u> drawing won an award in the contest.

5. The keys on the table are <u>yours</u>.

6. <u>Our</u> favorite place to drive is in the country.

7. The dog wagged <u>its</u> tail at dinnertime.

8. Here is <u>your</u> hockey stick.

9. <u>My</u> brother lost <u>his</u> wallet at the football game.

10. <u>Our</u> goal was to help the children learn to ice skate.

11. <u>Your</u> sweater looks just like <u>mine</u>.

12. Because <u>their</u> match was in another city, the soccer players took a bus.

13. The orthodontist put braces on <u>my</u> teeth.

14. Did you bring <u>your</u> radio along?

15. Miguel has been <u>my</u> friend since <u>his</u> family moved here three years ago.

An **indefinite pronoun** does not refer to a particular person, place, or thing. Some indefinite pronouns are singular, some are plural, and some can be either singular or plural. The indefinite pronouns *all, any, most, none,* and *some* can be singular or plural, depending on the sentence.

Is **anyone** coming to the party? A **few** of the boys are coming.
All of the sheet music is here. **All** are attending the show.

	SINGULAR		PLURAL
another	everybody	no one	both
anybody	everyone	nothing	few
anyone	everything	one	many
anything	much	somebody	others
each	neither	someone	several
either	nobody	something	

▶ **Exercise 2** Draw one line under the indefinite pronoun in each sentence. Draw two lines under the correct verb in parentheses.

All of the computers in the lab (are, is) working.

1. Some of the students (make, makes) no effort to pay attention.

2. Everyone (run, runs) when the coach blows her whistle.

3. Both (worry, worries) that the levy won't pass.

4. Most of the students (pass, passes) the tests easily.

5. Nothing (change, changes) their minds.

6. One (get, gets) goose bumps thinking about that scary movie.

7. Someone (turn, turns) off the television at bedtime.

8. All of the archaeologist's discoveries (are, is) fascinating.

9. Many (know, knows) about the ride of Paul Revere.

10. Each of the picture frames (were, was) cracked.

11. Both of the girls (talk, talks) about careers in pharmacy.

12. If others (were, was) as helpful as Pedro, there would be no problem.

13. Everybody (agree, agrees) that Margo did the right thing.

14. No one (are, is) as dedicated as Sandra.

15. Several of the teachers (are, is) planning a field trip.

Lesson 26
Pronouns: Reflexive and Intensive

A **reflexive pronoun** refers to a noun or another pronoun and indicates that the same person or thing is involved. A reflexive pronoun is formed by adding -*self* or -*selves* to certain personal and possessive pronouns.

REFLEXIVE PRONOUNS

Singular: myself   yourself   himself   herself   itself
Plural: ourselves   yourselves   themselves

George bought **himself** a birthday present.

An **intensive pronoun** adds emphasis to a noun or pronoun that has already been named.

You **yourself** can understand how I feel.

▶ **Exercise 1** Underline the reflexive or intensive pronoun in each sentence. Draw an arrow to the noun or pronoun it refers to.

Deep-sea divers dive to observe sea life, which <u>itself</u> can be fascinating.

1. Deep-sea divers must take measures to protect <u>themselves</u> under water.

2. Divers wear wet suits to protect <u>themselves</u> from the cold of the deep water.

3. If you were a diver, you would buy <u>yourself</u> a JIM suit or a helmet.

4. The JIM suit <u>itself</u> contains a breathing apparatus to help divers breathe.

5. This type of suit allows divers to lower <u>themselves</u> to a depth of 2,000 feet.

6. Helmets are needed for extra weight when divers <u>themselves</u> do not need to move

   around much.

7. If swimming in strong ocean currents, you would need weight to keep <u>yourself</u> down.

8. You would also need help to keep <u>yourself</u> breathing.

9. Divers use external air supplies to enable <u>themselves</u> to breathe under water.

Grammar

10. A diver must supply <u>himself</u> or <u>herself</u> with a mixture of oxygen and different gases.

11. Divers must also protect <u>themselves</u> against decompression sickness, or "the bends."

12. This illness manifests <u>itself</u> with joint pain, and it can be fatal.

13. The bends occurs when divers raise <u>themselves</u> to the top too quickly.

14. Divers must time <u>themselves</u> to be sure they rise at the right speed.

▶ **Exercise 2 Fill in the blank with the correct intensive or reflexive pronoun.**

One book that Rachel Carson ____herself____ wrote was called *Silent Spring.*

1. One person who made ____herself____ a career based on the sea was Rachel Carson.

2. Carson didn't see the ocean for ____herself____ until after college.

3. However, the sea ____itself____ fascinated Carson at a young age.

4. She earned a degree for ____herself____ in marine zoology from Johns Hopkins University in 1932.

5. In that era, there were few jobs for scientists ____themselves____ and even fewer for women scientists.

6. Carson found work for ____herself____ as a writer for a radio show about the sea.

7. Later she became an aquatic biologist with the U.S. Bureau of Fisheries, no small feat in ____itself____.

8. A conflict between science and writing resolved ____itself____ when she realized she could do both.

9. Her first book, *Under the Sea-Wind,* described struggles sea creatures find ____themselves____ facing.

10. In 1949 Carson ____herself____ was finally able to visit the deep.

11. Carson put on a diver's helmet and explored the reefs of the Florida Keys for ____herself____.

12. Her later life was marked with conservation efforts that we ____ourselves____ can learn from.

Lesson 27
Pronouns: Interrogative

An **interrogative pronoun** is used to introduce an interrogative sentence.

Who and *whom* refer to people. *Which* and *what* refer to things.
Whose shows possession.

Who will bring Andreas to the dance?   To **whom** should the check be made payable?

Which of the poems is your favorite?   **What** is the best way to study for the test?
Whose is that?

(Do not confuse *whose* with *who's*, the contraction for *who is*.)

▶ **Exercise 1** Underline the word in parentheses that best completes each sentence.

(<u>Which</u>, What) of these medicines is the best remedy for a cold?

1. (<u>Who</u>, Whom) is the girl in the blue dress?

2. (<u>Whose</u>, Who's) is this?

3. (<u>What</u>, Which) is the name of the team in red?

4. (<u>Who</u>, Whom) likes to play pinball at the arcade?

5. For (who, <u>whom</u>) does Sheila make those cookies?

6. (<u>Which</u>, Who) is the story about the future of the planet?

7. With (who, <u>whom</u>) does your brother work?

8. To (who, <u>whom</u>) does Marcus send letters?

9. (What, <u>Which</u>) of the names did you choose for the puppy?

10. (<u>What</u>, Which) does your mom like to play on the guitar?

11. (<u>Who</u>, Whom) has completed the assignment?

12. (<u>Which</u>, What) of the cars is in the driveway?

13. (Who's, <u>Whom</u>) can you see on the stage?

14. (<u>Who</u>, Whom) is the highest ranking official in the United States?

15. To (who, <u>whom</u>) did Jay lend his video game?

16. (Which, <u>What</u>) are you doing after school today?

17. (<u>What</u>, Who) is the answer to his question?

18. (Who, <u>Whom</u>) do you trust?

19. (<u>Which</u>, What) of the recipes did your mom use?

20. (<u>What</u>, Which) did you think of his speech?

▶ **Exercise 2 Fill in the blank with the correct interrogative pronoun.**

_____Who_____ is your favorite musical performer?

1. _____What_____ should we do about the broken vase?

2. To _____whom_____ were you talking when I saw you in the hall?

3. _____Which_____ of those instruments is yours?

4. _____Who_____ is playing football after school?

5. _____What_____ can I help you do?

6. _____Whom_____ do you call when you need advice?

7. _____What_____ are his chances of winning the race?

8. _____Which_____ of those snakes is poisonous?

9. _What or Which_ is the language that the people of Borneo speak?

10. _____Which_____ of your new shirts will you wear to the recital?

11. _____Who_____ wrote the novel *Little Women*?

12. _____What_____ did you decide to do for the science project?

13. _____Who_____ is going to make the brownies for the bake sale?

14. _____What_____ does an archaeologist do?

15. To _____whom_____ did you deliver the messages?

16. _____Which_____ of the computers did you use in the lab?

17. _____Who_____ remembered to pick up the pizza?

18. _Whom or What_ did Winona photograph for the school paper?

19. _What or Which_ is the most difficult subject for you?

20. From _____whom_____ did you get that bracelet?

✓ Unit 4 **Review**

▶ **Exercise 1** Underline the pronoun in each sentence. Write *poss.* (possessive), *per.* (personal), *ref.* (reflexive), *int.* (intensive), *ind.* (indefinite), or *inter.* (interrogative) to indicate the type of pronoun.

inter. _____ <u>Whom</u> did Cristina ask to the dance?

per. _____ 1. <u>She</u> and Jason finished the race at the same time.

ref. _____ 2. Jerry was proud of <u>himself</u> for achieving the goal.

inter. _____ 3. To <u>whom</u> is the letter addressed?

poss. _____ 4. Ellen fastened <u>her</u> seat belt before Gordon left.

ind. _____ 5. <u>Anyone</u> interested in the stars can be in the Astronomy Club.

per. _____ 6. The speech was interesting to Ahmed and <u>me</u>.

ref. _____ 7. The members of the rescue team did not consider <u>themselves</u> heroes after finding the lost girl.

inter. _____ 8. <u>Which</u> is the song Beth chose to sing?

int. _____ 9. Only Congress <u>itself</u> can declare war.

ref. _____ 10. The doctor told Aunt Carol to take better care of <u>herself</u>.

ind. _____ 11. <u>Each</u> of the students has done a report on the book.

poss. _____ 12. Jeanette often does errands for <u>her</u> grandmother.

inter. _____ 13. <u>Whose</u> is that CD?

per. _____ 14. Wendy and <u>I</u> played in the soccer tournament.

ind. _____ 15. <u>Most</u> of the students rode in the parade.

inter. _____ 16. <u>Who</u> found the stray dog?

ind. _____ 17. <u>Everyone</u> knows the story "Little Red Riding Hood."

per. _____ 18. The argument was between Kevin and <u>him</u>.

poss. _____ 19. <u>Your</u> part in the play is a large role.

ref. _____ 20. Akia bought <u>himself</u> the book to celebrate.

Grammar

Name _____ Class _____ Date _____

Cumulative Review: Units 1–4

▶ **Exercise 1** Draw a vertical line between the subject and predicate in each sentence. In the blank, write whether the verb is in the present, past, future, present perfect, or past perfect.

__present perfect__   William|has written many letters to me.

__future__   **1.** Kim|will go to the bus stop in a few minutes.

__past__   **2.** The dogs|barked loudly at the stranger.

__past__   **3.** The young girl in the front booth|ate cole slaw and two

hamburgers.

__present perfect__   **4.** I|have seen that movie several times.

__present__   **5.** Ray|presents the awards at the banquet.

__past perfect__   **6.** I|had waited for Ty for two hours.

__future__   **7.** Zach|will join the Debate Club when he is old enough.

__present__   **8.** The pencils and notebooks|are in my backpack.

__past perfect__   **9.** Fred and Joan|had been good friends in fifth grade.

__present perfect__   **10.** They|have gone away for the weekend.

▶ **Exercise 2** Underline the word in parentheses that best completes each sentence.

(Saturdays, <u>Saturday's</u>) game was his best ever.

1. (Keats, <u>Keats's</u>) poetry inspired him.

2. The army is engaged in the (nations, <u>nation's</u>) defense.

3. The (childrens, <u>children's</u>) favorite sport was soccer.

4. The portrait looked nothing like Dan and (he, <u>him</u>).

5. I made dinner for Jake and (<u>them</u>, they).

6. The (choirs, <u>choir's</u>) performance got a standing ovation.

7. (<u>Who's</u>, Whose) going to play this video game?

8. (Us, <u>We</u>) and Aunt Lydia will stay for the entire show.

Unit 5: Adjectives and Adverbs

Lesson 28
Adjectives

An **adjective** is a word that provides information about the size, shape, color, texture, feeling, sound, smell, number, or condition of a noun or a pronoun. Most adjectives come before the words they modify.

Bright sunlight bathed the **sandy** beach.

A **predicate adjective** always follows a linking verb. It modifies the subject of the sentence.

Movies are **popular** throughout Europe and America.

The present participle and past participle forms of verbs are often used as adjectives and predicate adjectives. A **present participle** is formed by adding *-ing* to a verb. A **past participle** is usually formed by adding *-ed* to a verb.

The sound of a thunderstorm is **frightening**. (present participle)
The **varied** shapes of pasta do not alter its taste. (past participle)

▶ **Exercise 1** Underline each adjective.

The beautiful city of St. Petersburg was founded in 1703.

1. St. Petersburg is famous for its architecture.

2. Architects were brought from the West to design elegant palaces.

3. Peter the Great wanted a magnificent city.

4. Impressive St. Petersburg has lush parks and lovely streets.

5. Several leaders after Peter added more features to the city.

6. Elizabeth, the daughter of Peter, built two palaces.

7. Catherine, wife of Peter III, obtained many outstanding pieces of art for the palaces.

8. After the death of Vladimir Lenin in 1924, the fascinating city was renamed Leningrad, but in 1991 the name was changed back to St. Petersburg.

9. Today, it still contains two major museums.

Grammar

10. <u>Ornate</u> details of the <u>original</u> city grace <u>every</u> corner.

11. <u>Gilded</u> statues decorate the bridges and <u>spacious</u> squares.

12. In the center of <u>one</u> square stands a <u>bronze</u> statue of Peter the Great.

13. Now a museum, St. Isaac's Cathedral has one of the <u>largest</u> domes in the world.

14. The dome is covered with a <u>hundred</u> kilograms of <u>pure</u> gold.

15. It is one of the <u>many</u> sights that make St. Petersburg a <u>glorious</u> city.

▶ **Exercise 2 Write *PA* above each predicate adjective and *part.* above each participle.**

                                                      part.

The first Russian ballet school was opened in thriving St. Petersburg in 1738.

                   part.

1. Nearly 150 years later, a talented ballet dancer appeared in the same city.

                   PA

2. Anna Pavlova's family was poor.

                   part.

3. Nevertheless, she joined the famed Imperial School of Ballet in St. Petersburg.

                   PA

4. Anna's teachers were famous themselves.

                   part.

5. In 1899 Anna Pavlova became a respected member of the Imperial Ballet.

                   PA

6. She seemed eager to improve in her art.

                   PA

7. She was successful in the lead role in *Giselle.*

                   part.

8. After several years Pavlova received the desired title of prima ballerina.

                   part.

9. Her dancing style was classical.

                   PA

10. While others tried new approaches, she remained faithful to the traditional methods.

                   part.

11. Pavlova achieved great success in several celebrated tours.

                   part.

12. Her controlled yet artful movements won her many fans.

                   PA

13. Her performances were magical to those who had never seen ballet before.

                   part.

14. A few of Pavlova's breathtaking performances are still available.

                   part.

15. You can see them in the enchanting film *The Immortal Swan.*

Lesson 29
Articles and Proper Adjectives

The words *a, an,* and *the* make up a special group of adjectives called **articles**. *A* and *an* are called **indefinite articles** because they refer to one of a general group of people, places, things, or ideas. *A* is used before words beginning with a consonant sound. *An* is used before words beginning with a vowel sound.

a fountain   **a** carnival   **a** union   **an** orchard   **an** envelope

The is called a **definite article** because it identifies specific people, places, things, or ideas.

The pot of gold was discovered at **the** end of **the** rainbow.

Proper adjectives are formed from proper nouns. A proper adjective always begins with a capital letter.

Maria practiced **Irish** step dancing on Mondays and **Italian** cooking on Thursdays.

Some proper adjectives are the same as the related proper nouns. Most proper adjectives are formed from proper nouns by adding an ending such as *-an* (German, Moroccan, American, African), *-ian* (Belgian, Indian, Egyptian, Russian), *-ese* (Japanese, Portuguese, Sudanese, Chinese), or *-ish* (Scottish, British, Swedish, English). Some are irregular and should be checked in a dictionary.

▶ **Exercise 1** Write the correct indefinite article for each word or group of words.

___a___   pair of gloves

___a___ 1. Native American folktale   ___a___ 11. signature

___an___ 2. organ   ___a___ 12. newspaper

___a___ 3. wind tunnel   ___an___ 13. umbrella

___a___ 4. suitcase   ___a___ 14. factory

___an___ 5. ostrich   ___an___ 15. icicle

___an___ 6. electric car   ___a___ 16. railroad

___a___ 7. surfboard   ___a___ 17. duchess

___a___ 8. butterfly   ___an___ 18. airport

___an___ 9. encyclopedia   ___a___ 19. university

___a___ 10. schedule   ___an___ 20. African spiritual

Name _____ Class _____ Date _____

▶ **Exercise 2** Rewrite the phrase, changing the italicized words to a proper adjective. Consult a dictionary if necessary.

the economist *from Germany* ___the German economist_____

1. a rock group *from Britain* ___a British rock group_____
2. the painting *from America* ___the American painting_____
3. a program *from Sweden* ___a Swedish program_____
4. a novel *from England* ___an English novel_____
5. a radio *from Japan* ___a Japanese radio_____
6. the language *from Portugal* ___the Portuguese language_____
7. the song *from Ireland* ___the Irish song_____
8. ivory statue *from Egypt* ___Egyptian ivory statue_____
9. the leather *from Morocco* ___the Moroccan leather_____
10. the coat *from Russia* ___the Russian coat_____
11. dance *from South America* ___South American dance_____
12. a gourd whistle *from the Sudan* ___a Sudanese gourd whistle_____
13. the flower *from China* ___the Chinese flower_____
14. the wood *from Africa* ___the African wood_____
15. the inventor *from Belgium* ___the Belgian inventor_____
16. the fabric *from India* ___the Indian fabric_____
17. the dessert *from Greece* ___the Greek dessert_____
18. the horn *from East Africa* ___the East African horn_____
19. the skater *from Norway* ___the Norwegian skater_____
20. the suit *from Italy* ___the Italian suit_____

▶ **Writing Link** Write three sentences about your favorite kind of food. Underline each article. Use at least one proper adjective.

_____

_____

_____

Lesson 30
Comparative and Superlative Adjectives

Grammar

Adjectives can compare two or more nouns or pronouns. The **comparative form** of an adjective compares two things or people. The **superlative form** of an adjective compares more than two things or people. For most one-syllable and some two-syllable adjectives, -er and -est are added to form the comparative and superlative.

The blue car is **larger** than the red one. (comparative)
The green truck is the **largest** vehicle in the parking lot. (superlative)

Some adjectives form irregular comparatives and superlatives.

ADJECTIVE	COMPARATIVE	SUPERLATIVE
good	better	best
bad	worse	worst
many	more	most
much	more	most
little (amount)	less	least

▶ **Exercise 1**   **Write in the blank the correct form of the adjective in parentheses.**

Mount Everest is the world's _____highest_____ mountain peak. (high)

1. The parrots were _____louder_____ this morning than yesterday. (loud)

2. That is the _____smallest_____ monkey I've ever seen. (small)

3. The tree in my front yard is the _____tallest_____ in the neighborhood. (tall)

4. The new well has to be _____deeper_____ than the old one. (deep)

5. The _____largest_____ bell of that kind is in New York City. (large)

6. I think my packages are _____heavier_____ than yours. (heavy)

7. Twyla is taking lessons so that she can be an even _____better_____ actress. (good)

8. That is the _____strangest_____ book in the library. (strange)

9. Don't open the door any _____wider_____. (wide)

10. This ceiling is the _____lowest_____ in the entire building. (low)

11. My brother grew six inches last year, so now he looks even _____thinner_____. (thin)

12. We'll just have to get a much _____longer_____ ladder. (long)

13. Jillian is the _____**best**_____ writer in the class. (good)

14. The _____**oldest**_____ person in our family is Great-Aunt Tillie. (old)

15. Mrs. Bourke said this puzzle is _____**easier**_____ than the last one. (easy)

16. Look for the _____**freshest**_____ fruit you can find. (fresh)

17. The team's record is _____**worse**_____ this year than last. (bad)

18. Krista's ring cost _____**less**_____ than Carol's bracelet. (little)

19. Julia is three years _____**younger**_____ than I am. (young)

20. Try to sand this wood so it is a little bit _____**smoother**_____. (smooth)

21. Haven't we had the _____**oddest**_____ weather recently? (odd)

22. Your card expresses _____**more**_____ sympathy than the others. (much)

23. I've grown much _____**wiser**_____ in the last few years. (wise)

24. Last week I had the _____**most**_____ fun ever. (much)

25. Get the _____**coldest**_____ water you can. (cold)

26. Next time we will buy _____**fewer**_____ supplies. (few)

27. This basement is _____**damper**_____ than I'd like it to be. (damp)

28. I have many baseball cards, but Jake has _____**more**_____. (many)

29. Have you seen Amanda's _____**newest**_____ haircut of all? (new)

30. Make the lights _____**dimmer**_____ than this, please. (dim)

31. Don't you think it is _____**hotter**_____ this summer than last? (hot)

32. Rámon has the _____**brownest**_____ eyes I've ever seen. (brown)

33. Bring me the _____**sharpest**_____ pencil you have. (sharp)

34. Tonight will be even _____**foggier**_____ than last night. (foggy)

35. The very _____**busiest**_____ people accomplish the most. (busy)

36. Leonard was _____**angrier**_____ than ever after he read the letter. (angry)

37. Ellie's new dress is the _____**palest**_____ blue I've ever seen. (pale)

38. The sidewalk is _____**icier**_____ than when you arrived. (icy)

39. Jim has the _____**keenest**_____ sense of humor of anyone I know. (keen)

40. That was the _____**worst**_____ dream I've ever had. (bad)

Lesson 31
More Comparative and Superlative Adjectives

The comparative and superlative forms of most one-syllable and some two-syllable adjectives are formed by adding *-er* and *-est* to the adjective. However, for most adjectives with two or more syllables the comparative and superlative are formed by adding *more* and *most* before the adjective.

Tennis is **more popular** at my school than field hockey. (comparative)
Computer games are the **most popular** form of entertainment. (superlative)

An adjective of three or more syllables uses *less* and *least* to form the negative comparative and superlative.

Do you have any styles that are **less traditional?** (negative comparative)
Eileen is the **least traditional** member of the family. (negative superlative)

Do not use *more, most, less,* or *least* before adjectives that already end with *-er* or *-est.* This is called a double comparison and is incorrect.

The **smaller** instruments have **higher** pitches. (not *more smaller* or *more higher*)

▶ **Exercise 1** Write the indicated form of each adjective.

beautiful *comparative* __more beautiful__

1. likable *comparative* __more likable__

2. careful *superlative* __most careful__

3. numerous *superlative* __most numerous__

4. familiar *negative comparative* __less familiar__

5. wonderful *comparative* __more wonderful__

6. modern *superlative* __most modern__

7. dramatic *negative superlative* __least dramatic__

8. surprised *comparative* __more surprised__

9. profitable *negative superlative* __least profitable__

10. efficient *superlative* __most efficient__

11. reluctant *negative comparative* __less reluctant__

12. helpful *comparative* __more helpful__

13. gracious *comparative* __more gracious_____

14. elaborate *superlative* __most elaborate_____

15. difficult *negative superlative* __least difficult_____

▶ **Exercise 2 Write in the blank the correct form of the adjective in parentheses.**

Zookeeping sounds like the _____most enjoyable_____ job a person could have. (enjoyable)

1. I want to be the _____most dedicated_____ zookeeper at the city zoo. (dedicated)

2. What could be _____more rewarding_____ than taking care of animals? (rewarding)

3. Of course, I will need _____more reliable_____ experience with animals than I have had in the past. (reliable)

4. So far, my _____most impressive_____ accomplishment has been to hold my dog Pepper long enough to give him a bath. (impressive)

5. I can gain _____more useful_____ experience than I get with Pepper by caring for my neighbors' pets. (useful)

6. When I am older, I hope to become the _____most hard-working_____ assistant Pepper's veterinarian has ever had. (hard-working)

7. Then I will go to college and become even _____more knowledgeable_____. (knowledgeable)

8. Aunt Sara is the _____most respected_____ zookeeper I know. (respected)

9. She says some animals are _____more cooperative_____ than others. (cooperative)

10. Some are _____more playful_____ than others, too. (playful)

11. Her pets at home seem _____more friendly_____ than the zoo animals. (friendly)

12. They appear to be _____more comfortable_____ with humans than zoo animals ever can be. (comfortable)

13. My aunt thinks I am _____more skilled_____ with animals than most students my age. (skilled)

14. She is giving only the _____more *or* most promising_____ students a tour of the zoo. (promising)

15. I don't know which of us is _____more excited_____ than the other. (excited)

Lesson 32
Demonstratives

The words *this, that, these,* and *those* are called **demonstratives.** They demonstrate, or point out, people, places, or things. *This* and *these* point out people or things close by, and *that* and *those* point out people or things at a distance. *This* and *that* are singular; *these* and *those* are plural.

When *this, that, these,* and *those* describe nouns, they are **demonstrative adjectives.** Demonstrative adjectives point out something and describe nouns by answering the questions *which one?* or *which ones?* When *this, that, these,* and *those* point out something and take the place of nouns, they are **demonstrative pronouns.**

DEMONSTRATIVE ADJECTIVES
That piano is too heavy to move.
Consider buying **this** bicycle.
Those mountains are enormous.
Who can play **these** games?

DEMONSTRATIVE PRONOUNS
That is a beautiful piano.
This is the world's best bicycle.
Those are the Alps.
Who can play **these?**

The words *here* and *there* should not be used with demonstrative adjectives. The words *this, these, that,* and *those* already point out the locations *here* and *there*. The object pronoun *them* should not be used in place of the demonstrative adjective *those*.

This ancient rattle is called a sistrum. (not *This here ancient rattle*)
Those finger cymbals are the smallest cymbals. (not *Them finger cymbals*)

▶ **Exercise 1 Underline the word in parentheses that best completes each sentence.**

(This, <u>These</u>) packages need to be delivered today.

1. (Them, <u>Those</u>) shells from Fiji certainly make an interesting collection.

2. Tools like the ones in (<u>this</u>, these) exhibit have been used by people for thousands of years.

3. (Those, <u>These</u>) coins in my hand are Spanish money.

4. (<u>These</u>, These here) speakers provide a clearer sound than the others.

5. (This, <u>That</u>) dessert Akili has in the back of the room is baklava.

6. (Them, <u>Those</u>) seeds will produce lettuce and carrots.

7. Statues like (this here, <u>this</u>) one are made from brass or bronze.

7. Statues like (this here, <u>this</u>) one are made from brass or bronze.

8. (<u>That</u>, This) large gong at the back of the stage makes a deep, rich sound.

9. Flowers like (<u>that</u>, that there) grow in tropical climates.

10. Celebrations like the one in (<u>this</u>, <u>that</u>)* picture I am framing are held in Indonesia.

11. (<u>Those</u>, Those there) are bamboo sticks used to make baskets.

12. (<u>That</u>, Those) discovery Ben Franklin made was electricity.

13. (This, <u>These</u>) stores sell sporting goods.

14. (That, <u>Those</u>) instruments will be used in the science experiment.

15. (<u>That</u>, That there) tape contains my favorite music.

*Accept either word.

▶ **Exercise 2** Write *adj.* in the blank if the demonstrative is an adjective and *pro.* if the demonstrative is a pronoun.

<u>pro.</u>   These belong to the girl who lives next door.

<u>pro.</u> **1.** This appears to be the best seat available.

<u>pro.</u> **2.** Please send me those in the mail.

<u>adj.</u> **3.** Does anyone know how to bake this cake?

<u>adj.</u> **4.** You can check that book out of the library tomorrow.

<u>adj.</u> **5.** That singer is quite talented.

<u>pro.</u> **6.** Those do not heat as well as some.

<u>pro.</u> **7.** Take these to the room down the hall.

<u>adj.</u> **8.** This aisle contains what Susan wants.

<u>adj.</u> **9.** These tickets are for the concert Tuesday night.

<u>pro.</u> **10.** Dave hopes that will help us.

<u>adj.</u> **11.** George and Ivan painted those posters for the athletic banquet.

<u>pro.</u> **12.** This will surely amuse Hannah's guest.

<u>adj.</u> **13.** Those tangerines taste delicious after a spicy meal.

<u>pro.</u> **14.** Give these to the gentleman in the gray suit.

<u>adj.</u> **15.** That ship has been docked for three days now.

Lesson 33
Adverbs

An **adverb** is a word that modifies, or describes, a verb, an adjective, or another adverb.

Jennifer smiled **broadly** at the audience. (modifies verb)
The first-place medal went to a **very** worthy contestant. (modifies adjective)
The conversation ended **rather** abruptly. (modifies adverb)

When modifying a verb, an adverb may describe *how, when,* or *where* the action is done.

Erin approached Mrs. Binder **cautiously**. (describes *how*)
Try to get to school **early**. (describes *when*)
Ron and I have looked **there**. (describes *where*)

Many adverbs are formed by adding *-ly* to adjectives. However, not all words that end in *-ly* are adverbs. The words *friendly, lively, kindly,* and *lonely* are usually adjectives. Similarly, not all adverbs end in *-ly*. The following words are all adverbs that do not end in *-ly: afterward, sometimes, later, often, soon, here, there, everywhere, not, fast, hard, long,* and *straight.*

▶ **Exercise 1 Underline each adverb.**

I went to bed <u>too</u> <u>late</u> last night so <u>now</u> I'm tired.

1. Pedro <u>enthusiastically</u> supported Zach's bid for student council president.

2. Spend your money <u>wisely</u>.

3. Marissa waited <u>quietly</u> for the play to begin.

4. <u>Lightly</u> underline the words you want to emphasize.

5. <u>Now</u> I want everyone to turn to page 36.

6. <u>After</u> surgery Lu Chan stretched his muscles <u>slowly</u> and <u>painfully</u>.

7. Ada whispered <u>softly</u> so she would <u>not</u> disturb the other people.

8. Will you sit <u>close</u> to me?

9. I am <u>terribly</u> confused about the schedule.

10. This project is <u>finally</u> and <u>completely</u> finished.

Grammar

11. The sun shone <u>brightly</u> through the thin haze.

12. Look <u>around</u> and see what is different.

13. Sarah was <u>extremely</u> disappointed when she realized she could <u>not</u> go.

14. My horse Buttercup trotted <u>gingerly</u> along the bridle path.

15. It <u>often</u> seems like hard work, but I guess it's worth it.

▶ **Exercise 2 Draw an arrow from each adverb to the word it modifies.**

Do you think we will be received graciously?

1. Mac looked everywhere for his jacket but could not find it.

2. Tom threw the ball fast and hard.

3. Soon it will be time to go to sleep.

4. Dorothy asked her questions firmly but politely.

5. Mimi was extremely exhausted after the mile run on a hot day.

6. The goalie defended forcefully but gracefully.

7. Matt's parents briefly spoke to his teacher.

8. Though the path was marked for beginning backpackers, it seemed rather steep to us.

9. Rosemarie is very conscientious about everything she does.

10. Who is on the phone now?

11. Stacey was somewhat hesitant at first, but now she is enthusiastic.

12. The president's press conference seemed unusually short.

13. What did you do next?

14. The volunteer coordinator at the library greeted us cheerfully.

15. Please carry the tray carefully.

Grammar

Lesson 34
Intensifiers

When modifying a verb, an adverb may give information about *when, where,* or *how* the action of a sentence takes place. When describing an adjective or another adverb, an adverb often emphasizes or intensifies the word it modifies. An adverb that emphasizes or intensifies an adjective or adverb is called an **intensifier**.

This information is **rather** new, so it won't be in the encyclopedia.
Jeff finished **just** slightly behind Audrey in the two-mile race.

Common intensifiers used to describe adjectives and other adverbs include *almost, extremely, just, nearly, practically, quite, rather, really, so, somewhat, such, too,* and *very.*

▶ **Exercise 1** Draw an arrow from each intensifier to the word it modifies.

Barry and Pat were extremely anxious to get the results.

1. I am somewhat unclear about the details.

2. Jorge's score on that test was nearly perfect.

3. Although I was quite nervous, I appeared calm and collected.

4. The dinner was really delicious.

5. Chico almost always comes to school with Mr. Fernandez.

6. Mrs. Phillips is a very dedicated teacher.

7. That serving is just enough for me.

8. Grandma was rather annoyed with Jason.

9. This crossword puzzle seems too easy.

10. These flowers are so beautiful.

11. Anita is an extremely sound sleeper.

12. Both my parents have to work quite late tonight so I have to watch Tommy.

13. This model airplane takes too much time to put together.

14. I am so proud of you!

15. Those watches are practically indestructible.

16. These directions are very confusing.

17. I think this sweatshirt is too large so I would like to exchange it.

18. My mom is rather tense about her speech, though she has practiced it several times.

19. Can you hear me over such loud noise?

20. Andy grew nearly four inches over the summer.

▶ **Exercise 2** Underline the word that the italicized intensifier modifies. In the blank, identify the underlined word as an *adj.* (adjective) or *adv.* (adverb).

**adv.** I would prefer to proceed *rather* slowly.

**adj.** **1.** Manuel is an *extremely* careful worker.

**adj.** **2.** Katherine's room is always *somewhat* messy.

**adj.** **3.** Grandpa is *such* a good swimmer.

**adv.** **4.** Perhaps you are being *just* too cautious.

**adj.** **5.** Guitar music can be *very* soothing.

**adj.** **6.** Waverly is a *quite* accomplished chess player.

**adv.** **7.** The disease spread *very* rapidly throughout the school.

**adv.** **8.** The reunion took place *rather* recently.

**adv.** **9.** Mrs. Leal *quite* proudly introduced her family.

**adv.** **10.** Denise *practically* always finishes her homework before dinner.

**adj.** **11.** That's *just* enough salt; do not add any more.

**adj.** **12.** Pam got a *really* different haircut last week.

**adv.** **13.** Nick and Steve both play tennis *rather* effortlessly.

**adj.** **14.** Hula hoops were *enormously* popular in the 1950s.

Lesson 35
Adverbs: Comparative and Superlative

The **comparative form** of an adverb compares two actions. The **superlative form** of an adverb compares more than two actions. Short adverbs use *-er* as the comparative ending and *-est* as the superlative ending. Long adverbs require the use of *more* or *most*.

The bus is running **later** than usual this morning.
This is the **latest** I have ever arrived at school.
I will try to wait **more patiently,** but it won't be easy.
Abram attends the club meetings **most frequently.**

Some adverbs form comparatives and superlatives in an irregular manner.

ADVERB	COMPARATIVE	SUPERLATIVE
well	better	best
badly	worse	worst
little (amount)	less	least
far (distance)	farther	farthest
far (degree)	further	furthest

The words *less* and *least* are used before both short and long adverbs to form the negative comparative and superlative.

Which one is used **less frequently?**
The back room is in use the **least often.**

Do not use *more, most, less,* or *least* before adverbs that already end in *-er* or *-est.*

▶ **Exercise 1** Rewrite the sentence or phrase using the indicated form of the italicized adverb.

Work *swiftly.*	comparative	Work more swiftly.
1. Approach *slowly.*	comparative	Approach more slowly.
2. Get *well.*	comparative	Get better.
3. *far* from my mind	superlative	furthest from my mind
4. *finely* carved	superlative	most finely carved
5. Come *quickly.*	comparative	Come more quickly.
6. *favorably* received	comparative	more favorably received
7. ran *fast*	superlative	ran fastest

8. *far* away	comparative	**farther away**
9. came *soon*	comparative	**came sooner**
10. went *smoothly*	superlative	**went most smoothly**
11. worked *industriously*	neg. comparative	**worked less industriously**
12. reacted *affectionately*	neg. superlative	**reacted least affectionately**
13. answered *intelligently*	neg. superlative	**answered least intelligently**
14. settled *comfortably*	neg. comparative	**settled less comfortably**
15. listened *calmly*	comparative	**listened more calmly**

▶ **Exercise 2 Write in the blank the correct form of the adverb in parentheses.**

Of the three students Sondra always arrives _____ **latest** _____ . (late)

1. Jacob traveled _____ **farther** _____ than Rachel to attend the reunion. (far)

2. Pasqual reacted _____ **more *or* less eagerly** _____ than Scott. (eagerly)

3. Samantha accepted the criticism _____ **more *or* less graciously** _____ than Jack. (graciously)

4. Our principal reacted _____ **most *or* least favorably** _____ of all. (favorably)

5. Which of the five employees has progressed _____ **furthest** _____ toward her goals? (far)

6. Jenny performed _____ **better *or* less well** _____ today than yesterday. (well)

7. Of Miami, Orlando, and Tallahassee, Miami is located _____ **farthest** _____ south. (far)

8. Mr. Aravjo follows the stock market _____ **more *or* less closely** _____ than my dad does. (closely)

9. Jonathan finished his homework _____ **earlier** _____ than usual yesterday. (early)

10. Which of these four low-priced cars performed _____ **worst** _____ in the tests? (badly)

▶ **Writing Link Write a paragraph comparing two sports. Use comparative adverbs.**

_____

_____

_____

_____

_____

Lesson 36
Using Adverbs and Adjectives

Grammar

Adverbs and adjectives are often confused, especially when they are used after verbs. Use a **predicate adjective** after a linking verb (such as *be, seem, appear,* or *become*) to describe the subject of the sentence. Use an **adverb** to describe an action verb.

The winner seemed **breathless** as she crossed the finish line. (predicate adjective)
She collapsed **breathlessly** when the race was over. (adverb)

Good, bad, well, and *badly* are often used incorrectly. *Good* and *bad* are adjectives; use them after linking verbs. *Well* and *badly* are adverbs; use them to describe action verbs. *Well* may also be used as an adjective when describing someone's health.

Sean and Lila should be **good** after so much practice. (predicate adjective)
The weather was **bad** when we left. (predicate adjective)
Katie sang **well** today even though she has a cold. (adverb)
The number of absentees **badly** affected the band's performance. (adverb)

▶ **Exercise 1** Underline the word in parentheses that best completes each sentence.

Philo Taylor Farnsworth was an (unusual, unusually) high school student.

1. He worked (careful, carefully) on an idea for a new invention.

2. He thought pictures could be sent (easy, easily) through the air like sound.

3. Philo was (eager, eagerly) to learn more, so he attended the University of Utah.

4. However, after his father died, he dropped out of school and searched (quick, quickly) for a job.

5. One of his interviewers, George Everson, seemed (great, greatly) impressed with his invention.

6. Everson and a partner were (possible, possibly) able to help.

7. In fact, they were (happy, happily) to provide the money for Philo to develop a working model of his system.

8. This system, known as television, was developed (slow, slowly) in a rented house in Los Angeles.

9. Neighbors were (suspicious, suspiciously) and called the police.

10. The police toured the house but remained (complete, completely) confused about what Philo was trying to make.

11. A new investor, W.W. Crocker, insisted (sudden, suddenly) that Philo move his laboratory to San Francisco.

12. (Simple, Simply) pictures painted on a piece of glass were the first images to appear on television.

13. Philo's efforts to improve his invention went (bad, badly), but he persisted.

14. In 1930 Philo's invention was (good, well) enough to receive patents.

15. Then Philo was (glad, gladly) to share his ideas with the companies that were interested in it.

▶ **Exercise 2 Write _adv._ (adverb) or _PA_ (predicate adjective) in the blank to identify the word in italics.**

___PA___ Many television programs are _entertaining._

___adv.___ **1.** From the early days of television, entertainment was _frequently_ found on the small screen.

___adv.___ **2.** Singers, actors, and comedians performed _well_ on the new medium.

___adv.___ **3.** Programs varied _slightly_ in length, with many as short as fifteen minutes.

___adv.___ **4.** Famous radio personalities were _soon_ familiar faces on television.

___adv.___ **5.** New stars were born _swiftly_ as well.

___PA___ **6.** Before long, evenings in front of the television became _common._

___PA___ **7.** Everyone was _fascinated_ by the live images broadcast into each home.

___adv.___ **8.** News could _immediately_ show important world events.

___PA___ **9.** Sports fans seemed _pleased_ that they could watch many games in their living rooms.

___adv.___ **10.** As the years went by, more and more uses were _certainly_ discovered for television.

Grammar

Lesson 37
Avoiding Double Negatives

Negative words express the idea of "no." The negative word *not* often appears in shortened form as part of a contraction.

is + not = isn't   can + not = can't   will + not = won't

Other words besides *not* may be used to express the negative. Each negative word has several opposites. These are **affirmative words**, or words that show the idea of "yes."

NEGATIVE	AFFIRMATIVE
never	ever, always
nobody	anybody, somebody
none	one, all
no one	everyone, someone
nothing	something, anything
nowhere	somewhere, anywhere
scarcely, hardly	some, any

Two negative words used together in the same sentence create an error called a **double negative**. Avoid using double negatives. Only one negative word is necessary to convey a negative meaning. Correct a sentence that has a double negative by removing one of the negative words or by replacing one of the negative words with an affirmative word.

▶ **Exercise 1 Underline the word or words in parentheses that best complete each sentence.**

Doesn't (nobody, <u>anybody</u>) understand the question?

1. They didn't do (<u>anything</u>, nothing) to solve the problem.

2. No one (<u>ever</u>, never) succeeds all the time.

3. Don't use (no, <u>any</u>) sugar in that recipe.

4. Sometimes it seems I can't (never, <u>ever</u>) win, but then I do.

5. No one (<u>can</u>, can't) play basketball in this weather.

6. The car didn't go (<u>anywhere</u>, nowhere); it just went in circles.

7. She looked inside the box, but there (was, <u>wasn't</u>) anything in it.

8. He hardly (<u>ever</u>, never) makes a mistake.

9. They hoped for some help, but they didn't get (none, <u>any</u>).

10. Nobody did (nothing, <u>anything</u>) wrong, but they still got into trouble.

11. No one (wouldn't, <u>would</u>) forget to study for the test.

12. They had brought (<u>nothing</u>, anything) with them.

13. Nobody (<u>can</u>, can't) swim better than Melissa.

14. The homework is lost; I can't find it (<u>anywhere</u>, nowhere).

15. No one (<u>should</u>, shouldn't) break traffic laws.

16. (<u>Anybody</u>, Nobody) in the back of the stadium could scarcely see the game.

17. Nothing bad (<u>ever</u>, never) happens to me.

18. You won't (never, <u>ever</u>) succeed in school unless you study.

19. We (<u>shouldn't</u>, should) ever turn in arithmetic work without checking it.

20. Lek tried to find an easy way to learn math, but he couldn't find (none, <u>any</u>).

▶ **Exercise 2** Write in the blank the contraction for the word in italics.

_____hadn't_____ Isra *had not* ever seen snow until today.

_____isn't_____ **1.** We can start now because Jacob *is not* coming today.

_____Weren't_____ **2.** *Were not* Jane and Abay scheduled to perform?

_____won't_____ **3.** You *will not* believe what just happened to me!

_____don't_____ **4.** I *do not* think I have met you before.

_____didn't_____ **5.** Tony *did not* get to the bus stop on time this morning.

_____wouldn't_____ **6.** Mom just *would not* change her mind.

_____wasn't_____ **7.** Brad *was not* planning on joining the choir, but he changed his mind.

_____can't_____ **8.** Alison and Karen still *cannot* agree on a topic.

_____shouldn't_____ **9.** You *should not* tell secrets when other people are around.

_____couldn't_____ **10.** Jamie wanted to play softball, but she *could not*.

✓ Unit 5 **Review**

▶ **Exercise 1** Draw an arrow from the word in italics to the word it modifies. Write *adj.* in the blank if the word in italics is an adjective and *adv.* if it is an adverb.

adj.   Ivan's accomplishment is the *best* news I have heard this week.

adv.   **1.** After missing the rebound the first time, Marion jumped *again.*

adj.   **2.** All *the* trees in the orchard were filled with ripe fruit.

adv.   **3.** We could tell from the beginning that the play was about something *very* silly.

adv.   **4.** Chris and Ahmed are taking their boat out on a *fairly* large river.

adv.   **5.** The politician *somewhat* reluctantly answered the reporter's question.

adj.   **6.** Betsy Ross designed the first *American* flag in 1776.

adj.   **7.** Uncle Giovanni has a unique walk and a great *bellowing* voice.

adj.   **8.** The story I am about to tell you is absolutely *true.*

adj.   **9.** The diplomat handled the *delicate* situation quite well.

adv.   **10.** The Toshio family *rarely* play tennis for more than three hours at a time.

adj.   **11.** *Those* members gave away the location of our secret clubhouse.

adv.   **12.** Everything seems to come *fully* alive in the spring.

adj.   **13.** Holly brought an *overdue* book back to the library.

adj.   **14.** Please take *this* film to the shop on the corner.

adv.   **15.** The soccer team worked *swiftly* to score another goal.

adj.   **16.** Lila was fascinated by the *stone* statue in the center of the courtyard.

adj.   **17.** *These* muffins are the best I have ever tasted.

adj.   **18.** The advertisement states that other games are *available.*

Grammar

Name _____ Class _____ Date _____

Cumulative Review: Units 1–5

▶ **Exercise 1** Write the part of speech above each word in italics: *N* (noun), *V* (verb), *pro.* (pronoun), *adj.* (adjective), or *adv.* (adverb).

     N   adj.
    Ben gave a *short* speech after dinner.

  adj.   V
 1. *The* Watsons *are going* fishing in Montana.

  pro.   N
 2. *She* will plan the meeting with the committee *members*.

              adv.   pro.
 3. Chef Ramirez *often* makes *us* delicious meals.

       adj.   adj.
 4. The *pretty* quilt had a design of *red* and blue rings.

             adv.   V
 5. A porch swing *gently moved* back and forth in the breeze.

    adj.   N
 6. A *bright* moon glowed against the midnight *sky*.

            pro.   adj.
 7. We will meet *them* near the *sparkling* fountain.

  pro.   adj.
 8. *That* began a friendship which continues to *this* day.

             V   N
 9. Miranda *is hosting* a birthday *party* Friday night.

      pro.   V
10. Samdi *himself taught* Rick how to ski.

        adj.   N
11. Laura was *a* junior *bridesmaid* in her cousin Tina's wedding.

    adj.   adv.
12. A *small* bird fluttered *quietly* from one tree to another.

  pro.   V
13. *They* could *hear* some musicians rehearsing in the next room.

                    V   adj.
14. The grandfather clock *chimed* the *new* hour.

                adj.   adv.
15. I have never tried *this* sport *before*.

       V   N
16. Tanya *helps* her father in the *greenhouse* each day after school.

        adj.   adv.
17. The *whimpering* dog *slowly* curled up in a corner of the kitchen.

  pro.   pro.
18. *It* rolled across the highway until *someone* picked it up.

              N   V
19. Janice and *Saul will enter* the pie-eating contest.

    N   adj.
20. *Wildflowers* grow in the *green* meadow next to the pond.

Grammar

▶ **Exercise 2** Draw two lines under each verb or verb phrase. Write in the blank whether the verb is *T* (transitive), *I* (intransitive), or a *LV* (linking verb).

__T__ Lena brought two friends to the picnic.

__I__ 1. Many boxes were piled up inside the house.

__T__ 2. Through the telescope, Michelle could see several constellations.

__T__ 3. Our class took a field trip to the Art Institute of Chicago.

__LV__ 4. Samantha became treasurer of the garden association.

__T__ 5. Tim made the shirt himself.

__LV__ 6. The night air seemed chilly to the guests at the outdoor reception.

__I__ 7. Julian climbed up the mountain to the abandoned cottage.

__I__ 8. A glistening sailboat was docked next to a small yacht.

__T__ 9. Aunt Nadine sent Missy a beautiful necklace with her birthstone in it.

__T__ 10. Kendra studies geography each day after lunch.

__LV__ 11. The bread in the oven smells wonderful.

__LV__ 12. Mrs. Callahan is the chairperson of the social committee.

__T__ 13. Dad and I are building new shelves for the basement.

__T__ 14. We explored the new shop on the corner Sunday afternoon.

__I__ 15. Bill experimented with his new computer the entire evening.

__T__ 16. Bridget plays the piano quite well for a beginner.

__LV__ 17. The sky appeared gray and cloudy in spite of the sunny forecast.

__T__ 18. Jason paints incredibly accurate portraits.

__LV__ 19. The song on the radio is one of my favorites.

__I__ 20. They walked through the Park of Roses.

__LV__ 21. The bird's song was truly melodic.

__T__ 22. Jasmine sent me a postcard from Greece.

▶ **Exercise 3** Write in the blank the correct form (comparative or superlative) of the adjective or adverb in parentheses.

My uncle makes the _____**best**_____ burritos imaginable. (good)

Name _____ Class _____ Date _____

1. The book I am reading for this book report is _____**longer**_____ than the book I read for the last one. (long)

2. Barbara must be the _____**fastest**_____ sprinter on the team. (fast)

3. Diane's speech was _____**more *or* less calmly**_____ delivered than Catherine's. (calmly)

4. Jeremy's house is the _____**farthest**_____ from the ballpark, so he may be a little late. (far)

5. The campaign produced results _____**sooner**_____ than we expected. (soon)

6. That movie has been _____**more *or* less eagerly**_____ awaited than the other one. (eagerly)

7. The person with the _____**most creative**_____ slogan wins the contest. (creative)

8. Juan chose the _____**smallest *or* smaller**_____ apple and the largest dessert. (small)

9. Of everyone in the play, Yolanda learned her lines _____**most *or* least quickly**_____. (quickly)

10. The temperature today is _____**colder**_____ than it was yesterday. (cold)

11. Raymond seems _____**happier**_____ now that his family has moved to their new home. (happy)

12. The _____**strangest**_____ thing happened to Christy on her way to school. (strange)

13. Denny's brother is four years _____**younger**_____ than he is. (young)

14. We crossed the river at its _____**widest**_____ point. (wide)

15. This cereal costs much _____**less**_____ than that one. (little)

16. Though she couldn't arrive by the time the concert started, Keisha promised to come _____**later**_____. (late)

17. Mom said the homemade vase was the _____**greatest**_____ gift she could have received. (great)

18. Ms. Hadley welcomed the guests _____**more *or* less graciously**_____ than Ms. Tilford did. (graciously)

19. This week's football game was much _____**shorter**_____ than last week's game. (short)

20. That is the _____**most beautiful**_____ shade of purple I've ever seen! (beautiful)

Grammar

Unit 6: Prepositions, Conjunctions, and Interjections

Lesson 38
Prepositions and Prepositional Phrases

Grammar

A **preposition** is a word that connects a noun or a pronoun to another word in a sentence. A **compound preposition** consists of more than one word.

I can meet you **at** the library.   Eat vegetables **instead of** junk food.

A **prepositional phrase** is a group of words that begins with a preposition and ends with a noun or pronoun called the **object of the preposition**

We walked **along the beach.**   They stood **beside us.**

COMMONLY USED PREPOSITIONS

about	before	during	off	to
above	behind	for	on	toward
across	below	from	onto	under
after	beneath	in	out	until
against	beside	inside	outside	up
along	between	into	over	upon
among	beyond	like	since	with
around	by	near	through	within
at	down	of	throughout	without

COMMONLY USED COMPOUND PREPOSITIONS

according to	aside from	in front of	instead of
across from	because of	in place of	on account of
along with	far from	in spite of	on top of

▶ **Exercise 1** Underline each prepositional phrase. Draw a second line under the preposition or compound preposition and circle the object of the preposition.

Food contains nutrients that we need for good health.

1. There are six groups of nutrients: carbohydrates, fats, proteins, water, minerals, and vitamins.

2. We could not live without carbohydrates.

Grammar

3. Energy stored in carbohydrates is released quickly.

4. Among the carbohydrates are sugars, starch, and fiber.

5. Some foods with sugar have few nutrients.

6. Sugar, however, is found in all fruits.

7. Our bodies also get sugar from young vegetables.

8. Refined sugar is found in products like candy and soft drinks.

9. Along with bread, pasta and potatoes provide us with starch.

10. Our bodies change starch into glucose.

11. Glucose then releases energy throughout our bodies.

12. We get our fiber through foods like vegetables and grains.

13. Fiber does not release energy within our bodies.

14. However, because of fiber, our digestive tract is kept healthy.

15. Many doctors believe in a high-fiber diet to guard against cancer.

16. Like carbohydrates, fats also provide energy.

17. Fats release energy slowly, instead of the quick release from carbohydrates.

18. We also have healthy skin and hair because of fats.

19. However, too much saturated fat from food turns into excess body fat.

20. Saturated fats come from animal products.

21. Unsaturated fats are found in vegetables and nuts.

22. Because of proteins children can develop into healthy adults.

23. Proteins supply material for the production of new cells.

24. Fish, poultry, and milk supply protein to our bodies.

25. Combinations of other foods, like nuts and grains, also provide protein.

26. Perhaps you never thought about water for nourishment.

27. Yet, no one can live without water in his or her body.

28. Water helps control the temperature inside the body.

29. Blood, which contains water, carries oxygen to the cells.

30. Minerals are important for bone strength.

Lesson 39
Pronouns as Objects of Prepositions

When a pronoun is the object of a preposition, use an object pronoun, not a subject pronoun.

Sherilyn threw the ball to Cindy. Sherilyn threw the ball to **her**.

If a preposition has a compound object with both a noun and a pronoun, use an object pronoun.

LaToya entered the race with Carmen and **me**.

Use the object pronoun *whom* after a preposition.

To **whom** did you give the folder?   The person with **whom** I'm going is Tad.

▶ **Exercise 1 Draw two lines under each preposition or compound preposition. Underline the correct form of the pronoun in parentheses.**

The dog likes to run <u>with</u> Tammy and (he, <u>him</u>).

1. Give the books <u>to</u> Eduardo and (I, <u>me</u>).

2. I never heard <u>of</u> either Mr. Cameron or (<u>him</u>, he).

3. There is some difference <u>of</u> opinion <u>between</u> Juana and (they, <u>them</u>).

4. Is that the teacher <u>of</u> (<u>whom</u>, who) you speak so highly?

5. Oh, you got here <u>in front of</u> (I, <u>me</u>).

6. I'll go later because I don't want to run <u>into</u> (<u>him</u>, he).

7. I like to sit <u>near</u> Keshia and (<u>her</u>, she).

8. Don't get caught <u>between</u> the bear cub and (she, <u>her</u>).

9. If you hurry, you can go <u>to</u> the concert <u>with</u> (we, <u>us</u>).

10. Hakeem stood <u>behind</u> Tracy and (<u>me</u>, I) and yelled "Boo!"

11. This present is <u>from</u> Martha and (he, <u>him</u>).

12. <u>To</u> (who, <u>whom</u>) should I address this package?

13. <u>Aside from</u> Zina and (<u>them</u>, they), who else was there?

14. I don't think the nurse appreciated the jokes <u>by</u> Jim and (<u>me</u>, I).

15. I don't want to leave <u>without</u> (<u>her</u>, she).

16. Food <u>of</u> any kind looks delicious <u>to</u> (we, <u>us</u>) starving hikers.

17. I don't want to sit <u>in front of</u> (<u>him</u>, he).

18. We came <u>to</u> the party <u>without</u> the Joneses or (<u>them</u>, they).

19. The balloons floated <u>above</u> (we, <u>us</u>).

20. The speech was given <u>by</u> (she, <u>her</u>).

21. Yoko will give her book report <u>for</u> the teacher and (they, <u>them</u>).

22. Mother sat <u>between</u> Jim and (I, <u>me</u>).

23. When the halfback went down, the whole opposing team piled <u>on top of</u> (he, <u>him</u>).

24. They lost their home <u>in</u> the flood, and I feel sorry <u>for</u> (they, <u>them</u>).

25. Is that the person <u>behind</u> (<u>whom</u>, who) you sat <u>at</u> the movie?

26. Because she knows so much <u>about</u> the outdoors, I like camping <u>with</u> (<u>her</u>, she).

27. Why don't you come <u>to</u> the parade <u>along with</u> Sam and (<u>us</u>, we)?

28. I threw the ball <u>beyond</u> (<u>them</u>, they).

29. The baby took her first steps <u>toward</u> Dad and (we, <u>us</u>).

30. The king had been fighting <u>against</u> (they, <u>them</u>) <u>for</u> years.

31. The broken lamp <u>in</u> our den fell <u>on top of</u> (she, <u>her</u>).

32. I met the explorer <u>about</u> (who, <u>whom</u>) you wrote <u>in</u> your letter.

33. Joe wants to go <u>to</u> the spelling bee <u>in place of</u> (I, <u>me</u>).

34. They want to paint a portrait <u>of</u> Toshi and (<u>him</u>, he).

35. The painter shouted <u>at</u> the worker <u>on</u> the ladder <u>above</u> (she, <u>her</u>).

36. I think Pravat looks quite a bit <u>like</u> (he, <u>him</u>).

37. The new students feel accepted <u>by</u> the teacher and (we, <u>us</u>).

38. Lara stood <u>in awe of</u> the beautiful valley <u>below</u> (<u>her</u>, she).

39. I always feel uncomfortable <u>around</u> Diana and (<u>her</u>, she).

40. The victim <u>of</u> the robbery pointed <u>to</u> the suspect and (he, <u>him</u>).

Lesson 40

Prepositional Phrases as Adjectives and Adverbs

A prepositional phrase sometimes functions as an **adjective phrase** that tells about a noun or a pronoun.

The land **around the lake** was rocky. (The prepositional phrase *around the lake* describes the noun *land.)*

An **adverb phrase** is a prepositional phrase that tells about a verb, an adjective, or another adverb. An adverb phrase tells *when, where,* or *how* the action in the verb takes place.

The mice hid **from the owl**. (describes the verb *hid*)
The horse is tired **after his workout**. (describes the adjective *tired*)
The cat slept late **in the morning**. (describes the adverb *late*)

▶ **Exercise 1** Underline each prepositional phrase. Write *adj.* or *adv.* in the blank to identify the type of phrase.

___adj.___   Translators of Spanish work here.

___adj.___ **1.** Do you know the name of that monument?

___adv.___ **2.** In a strong voice, the actor delivered his speech.

___adv.___ **3.** The cat jumped off the fence.

___adj.___ **4.** I can't understand the label on the package.

___adj.___ **5.** My relatives from Phoenix are coming next week.

___adv.___ **6.** The Bonillas have a new deck in their backyard.

___adv.___ **7.** After classes, the scientist gave a lecture.

___adv.___ **8.** A pep rally was held in the gym.

___adj.___ **9.** I'd love a piece of that pie!

___adj.___ **10.** I bought you a new book about astronomy.

___adv.___ **11.** A loud crash came from the darkened house.

___adj.___ **12.** We spent all of our allowance.

___adv.___ **13.** Did I leave my keys in your car?

___adv.___ **14.** <u>Because of the broken ski lift</u>, we had to climb the mountain.

___adv.___ **15.** The percussion section is practicing <u>on their drums</u>.

___adv.___ **16.** <u>Between halves</u>, the band performed a splendid show.

___adv.___ **17.** I dreamed I traveled <u>to Paris</u>.

___adj.___ **18.** The cat <u>with the long fur</u> is ours.

___adv.___ **19.** She is going to vote <u>in the mid-year election</u>.

___adj.___ **20.** We'll get there sooner if we take the road <u>through the hills</u>.

▶ **Exercise 2 Underline each prepositional phrase. Circle the word it describes.**

    Raul (works) <u>in a busy office</u>.

1. Jorge (wrote) a piece <u>for the school band</u>.

2. We (waited) <u>for at least a half hour</u>!

3. We plan to (meet) Fernando <u>at the video store</u>.

4. Della got a flat (tire) <u>on her bicycle</u>.

5. The art museum has marble (lions) <u>with huge paws</u>.

6. Don likes to work the crossword (puzzles) <u>in the newspaper</u>.

7. The mountain goats (climbed) <u>up the rocky hillside</u>.

8. The lion (groomed) her cubs <u>with her tongue</u>.

9. The coach (left) suddenly <u>during the rally</u>.

10. Enrique took (photographs) <u>of the stained glass windows</u>.

11. The audience (focused) <u>on the lead singer</u>.

12. Aurelia adjusted the (eyepiece) <u>on her telescope</u>.

13. The wind (blew) <u>with frightening suddenness</u>.

14. The winning runner (crossed) the finish line <u>in a flash</u>.

15. The prospector (stored) his gold <u>in a safe</u>.

16. The Academy Awards show (is broadcast) <u>to a worldwide audience</u>.

17. The (elms) <u>along our street</u> have all died.

18. The (house) <u>near the waste dump</u> had to be evacuated.

Lesson 41
Conjunctions and Interjections

A **coordinating conjunction** connects words or phrases in a sentence. The words *and, but, or, for,* and *nor* are coordinating conjunctions. Such conjunctions can be used in several ways.

Rain **or** snow is expected tomorrow. (compound subject)
Floodwaters reached the levee **and** flowed over it. (compound predicate)
Angel called to Carla **and** Olivia. (compound object of a preposition)
I can't run fast, **but** I can run long distances. (compound sentence)

Correlative conjunctions are pairs of conjunctions. They include *both/and, either/or, neither/nor,* and *not only/but also.*

Madeline **not only** plays hockey **but also** teaches it to younger students. (compound predicate)

An **interjection** is a word or phrase that expresses feelings but has no grammatical connection to the sentence. Separate interjections from the sentence with a comma or an exclamation point, depending on the strength of feeling.

Oh, you don't need to worry.   **Ouch!** I really am sunburned.

COMMON INTERJECTIONS

aha	come on	ha	oh, no	ouch	whoops
alas	gee	hey	oh, well	phew	wow
awesome	good grief	hooray	oops	what	yes

▶ **Exercise 1** Underline each conjunction. Write whether it joins a compound subject (*subj.*), a compound predicate (*pred.*), a compound object of a preposition (*obj.*), or a compound sentence (*sent.*).

<u>obj.</u>   I really miss the humor of Angie <u>and</u> Gwen.

<u>subj.</u> **1.** Hiroshi <u>and</u> Takeo competed in the finals.

<u>pred.</u> **2.** The audience booed <u>and</u> hissed at the villain.

<u>obj.</u> **3.** I will study with <u>either</u> Mom <u>or</u> Dad.

<u>pred.</u> **4.** The tornado picked up the empty car <u>and</u> threw it against the barn.

<u>subj.</u> **5.** Botany <u>and</u> astronomy are Jake's main interests.

<u>sent.</u> **6.** We asked Belle to dinner, <u>but</u> she had other plans.

obj.   **7.** Mr. Lee gave grades to the seventh- <u>and</u> eighth-grade classes.

pred.   **8.** The runner jumped the gun <u>and</u> was disqualified from the race.

subj.   **9.** Manny <u>and</u> I have to write a report.

pred. **10.** Georgia <u>not only</u> has a paper route <u>but also</u> works at a craft shop.

sent. **11.** I think Mr. Wilson will recover, <u>but</u> his family is not hopeful.

sent. **12.** Grandma thinks it will rain tomorrow, <u>for</u> her joints are aching.

subj. **13.** <u>Both</u> Mini <u>and</u> Poloma are good at the shot put.

obj. **14.** Chocolate is good for <u>neither</u> dogs <u>nor</u> cats.

pred. **15.** The cat pounced at the bird <u>but</u> missed it.

obj. **16.** We will travel to <u>either</u> Yellowstone <u>or</u> Yosemite next summer.

sent. **17.** I can't roller skate, <u>but</u> I'm a whiz on a skateboard.

obj. **18.** The dog comes to <u>neither</u> my call <u>nor</u> the whistle.

subj. **19.** Aunt Renee <u>or</u> Uncle Johnny will call us tonight.

pred. **20.** Tatanka cared for the orphaned baby raccoon <u>and</u> then released it.

▶ **Exercise 2 Circle the interjection in each sentence.**

(Wow)! I see the parade coming!

1. We're going to be late. (Oh, no)!

2. (Hooray) the teacher decided not to give us a test today!

3. (Whoops) I guess I misjudged the distance from the couch to the floor.

4. (Alas), someone else got my favorite parking space.

5. I thought there was no rainbow, but, (wow), there it is!

6. (Yes), I'd love to go to the car show with you.

7. (Aha)! I thought I saw you creeping up on me.

8. (Hey), aren't you Marcy's brother?

9. I forgot these boots have holes in them. (Good grief)!

10. (Oh, no), the squirrel is in the birdfeeder again.

✓ Unit 6 **Review**

▶ **Exercise 1** Draw one line under each preposition and two lines under each conjunction. Circle each interjection.

(Yes) Tyrone <u>and</u> I get to go <u>to</u> the pool.

1. The neighbor's dog <u>and</u> our cat like to chase each other.

2. (Wow), did you see my photograph <u>in</u> the paper?

3. <u>Neither</u> Mae <u>nor</u> Mason entered the contest.

4. I don't know whether to wear my shorts <u>or</u> my jeans <u>to</u> the rally.

5. (Oops), I dropped my ring <u>into</u> the garbage disposal.

6. (Hey)! Don't throw the ball <u>or</u> swing that bat <u>in</u> the house!

7. Do I like to swim <u>in</u> the pool? (Yes)!

8. Dad <u>not only</u> built much <u>of</u> our house <u>but also</u> painted it.

9. Monica <u>and</u> Rachel are identical twins, <u>but</u> they have very different interests.

10. (Oh, no), the raccoons have dragged the garbage <u>out of</u> the can again.

11. Dad bought tickets <u>for</u> Mom <u>and</u> her.

12. Jed will study <u>either</u> painting <u>or</u> sculpture <u>in</u> college.

13. It's almost time <u>for</u> the game. (Hooray)!

14. Our school won the band competition <u>and</u> got a trophy. (Awesome)!

15. (Wow), Adita shot <u>from</u> center court <u>and</u> scored three points.

16. Janine liked the movie a lot, <u>but</u> I thought it was silly.

17. Have you ever heard <u>of</u> <u>either</u> Florence Nightingale <u>or</u> Clara Barton?

18. (Good grief)! That was a difficult test!

19. Sally delivered holiday cards <u>to</u> her paper route customers.

20. Koko gave his dog a bath <u>and</u> then cleaned himself <u>with</u> a big towel.

Cumulative Review: Units 1–6

▶ **Exercise 1** Label each noun, verb, adjective, and adverb by writing *N, V, adj.,* or *adv.* above the correct word or words.

      adj.   N   V   V   adj.   N   adv.
     The scientists will announce their new discovery tomorrow.

      adj. adj.   N   V   adv.   adj. adj.   adj.   N
1. The ancient train crept slowly up the steep, dangerous hill.

      adj. adj.   N   adv.   V   adj. adj.   N
2. The faster runners quickly tackled the slower quarterback.

      adj. adj.   N   adv.   V   adj.   N
3. The small gymnast gracefully performed her final exercise.

          adj. adj.   N   V   V   V   adj. N   V   adj.
4. After the accident victims had been treated, the room became quiet.

          adj.   N   V   V   adj. N   V   adj.   N
5. When the movie was completed, the VCR rewound the videotape.

      N   N   V   V   adj. N   adj.   N   adv.
6. Reggie and Yana will compete in the finals of the contest tomorrow.

      adj. N V   adv.   adj. N V   adv.
7. The rain fell heavily, and the river rose steadily.

      adj.   adj.   N   V   adv.   adj. adj.   N
8. The professional skiers sped smoothly down the steep slope.

      adj. adj.   N   V   adv.   adj.
9. The long movie was awfully boring.

          adj.   N   N   V   adj. N   adj.   N   V
10. When the squirrel and my cat met in the garage, both animals fled.

          adj.   N   V   adj.   N
11. On our summer vacation, we drove through twelve states.

      adj.   N   adj. N   N   V   adj.
12. The performance by the band at halftime was spectacular.

      adj. N V   V   V   adj.   N
13. The baby has been crying for several hours.

        V   adv. V   N   N   adv.
14. I have not seen Jason or Terry lately.

                     N   adj. N   V   N   adj.   N
15. After his encounter with a skunk, we washed our dog in tomato juice.

            adj. adj.   N   adj. adj.   N   V   N   adv.
16. On the wild pitch, the quick runner stole home easily.

      adj. N   N   V   adj.   adj.   N   adj. N   adj.   N
17. A flock of gulls lands in the parking lot of the mall each morning.

        V   N   adj. N
18. Take your feet off the table!

        N   V   adv.
19. Ellen writes to me regularly.

        N   V adv.   adj.   adj.   N
20. Buffalo were very numerous in the West.

        V   adv. V adj.   adj.   N
21. Have you ever held a long-haired rabbit?

        V   adj. adj.   N
22. Sign me up for the Music Club.

▶ **Exercise 2** Draw one line under each simple subject and two lines under each simple predicate. Then draw a vertical line between the complete subject and complete predicate.

The singing <u>birds</u>|<u><u>wake</u></u> us early each morning.

1. The hot <u>sand</u>|<u><u>scorched</u></u> my bare feet.

2. That long-legged wading <u>bird</u>|<u><u>is</u></u> either a heron or an egret.

3. The <u>players</u> in the red jerseys|<u><u>are</u></u> the Midtowners.

4. The <u>videotape</u>|<u><u>goes</u></u> into this opening.

5. Our <u>neighbors</u> across the street|<u><u>collect</u></u> old records.

6. That <u>girl</u> in the yellow raincoat|<u><u>looks</u></u> like my cousin.

7. <u>I</u>|<u><u>will tell</u></u> you the plot of the movie.

8. Several <u>students</u> from our school |<u><u>qualified</u></u> for the finals.

9. The hungry <u>alligator</u>|<u><u>slid</u></u> off the bank and into the water.

10. <u>We</u>|<u><u>will see</u></u> the dinosaur exhibit tomorrow.

11. The <u>carrier</u>|always <u><u>throws</u></u> the paper right in front of our door.

12. The <u>townspeople</u>|<u><u>collected</u></u> food for the victims of the flood.

13. Our <u>class</u>|<u><u>recycles</u></u> its paper and plastic.

14. The <u>sound</u> of approaching thunder|<u><u>echoed</u></u> through the hills.

15. The <u>lifeguard</u>|<u><u>called</u></u> people out of the pool.

16. Jacob's <u>skateboard</u>|easily <u><u>avoided</u></u> the cracks in the sidewalk.

17. Greg's <u>sister</u>|<u><u>wants</u></u> to be a scientist.

18. The <u>skaters</u>|<u><u>circled</u></u> the arena to the strains of ballet music.

19. Our guidance <u>counselor</u>|<u><u>gave</u></u> me good advice about college.

20. Several <u>limbs</u> from the tree|<u><u>fell</u></u> during the violent windstorm.

21. Your <u>paintings</u>|<u><u>are</u></u> so original!

22. Our first <u>experiment</u>|<u><u>flowed</u></u> smoothly.

23. <u>Mariette</u>|<u><u>visits</u></u> the residents at Autumn Years Nursing Home.

24. My <u>dog</u>|shamelessly <u><u>begs</u></u> food from everybody.

▶ **Exercise 3** Draw one line under each preposition or compound preposition and two lines under each conjunction. Circle each interjection.

(Phew), this blister on my foot not only hurts but also slows me down.

1. (Hey), should I read the book or see the movie first?

2. Put the produce into the crisper and the dry goods on top of the counter.

3. Jack sits across from me and between Lila and Betty.

4. According to our teacher, the universe is older and larger than imaginable.

5. Ogima studies after school, but I wait until evening.

6. (Yes), Hano will climb Mount Baldy in the spring.

7. Sonia not only identifies plants but also gives their Latin names. (Wow)!

8. Either Molly or her sister will represent our school in the contest.

9. (Oh, no), that video is at the other store.

10. Namid volunteers at the recycling center during the weekend.

11. I met Marsha and her brother, Joshua, outside the art museum.

12. Across from the park are railroad tracks and a patch of rare flowers.

13. (Alas), someone is sitting in my favorite seat.

14. The lion crept toward the grazing zebras, but they sensed his presence and fled.

15. (Hey), didn't we do this page of problems already?

16. Neither Tonia nor Sophie remembers where she lived during her childhood.

17. I got an A on my report. (Hooray)

18. (Good grief)! Sam taped his family and sent the video to that TV show.

19. Would I play with that band? (Yes!)

20. Where in the world did you find that bicycle, and how old is it?

21. Do you use one capful of ammonia or one cup of bleach?

22. John, covered with sticky cobwebs, emerged from the attic.

23. Light the electric candles displayed in the window.

24. (Ha!) I don't believe a word of that story about the monster under your bed.

Unit 7: Clauses and Complex Sentences

Lesson 42

Simple and Compound Sentences and Main Clauses

A **simple sentence** has one complete subject and one complete predicate.

COMPLETE SUBJECT	COMPLETE PREDICATE
A pretty flower	grows in the garden.
Roses and tulips	grow and bloom in the garden.

A **compound sentence** contains two or more simple sentences. Each simple sentence within a compound sentence is called a **main clause**. Main clauses are joined either by a comma followed by a conjunction or by a semicolon. The comma may be omitted if the main clauses are very short.

I watch **and** I learn.
Flowers are delicate, **and** they need tender care.
Flowers are delicate; they need tender care.

▶ **Exercise 1** Write in the blank *simple* or *compound* to identify the type of sentence.

compound   Mexican food is very unique, and it has a spicy flavor.

simple   1. People across America have developed an appreciation for Mexican food.

compound   2. We enjoy going to a Mexican restaurant, but sometimes we must wait in line for over an hour.

compound   3. The taco is a popular item, and it is easy to prepare.

simple   4. A taco usually consists of a folded corn tortilla, ground beef, cheese, lettuce, and tomato.

compound   5. Tacos come in two varieties; their shells can be either hard or soft.

compound   6. Some cooks buy taco shells already made; others fry and form the shells themselves.

simple   7. Browning ground beef in a shallow skillet is the first step.

compound   8. Drain the grease frequently; too much grease makes tacos unhealthful.

simple   9. Spices and chopped onions can be added to the cooked ground beef.

simple   10. A layer of ground beef is then spooned into the taco shell.

__compound__ 11. I like cheese on top of the beef; some add lettuce.

__simple__ 12. Chunks of red tomatoes give the taco a colorful appearance.

__simple__ 13. Toppings such as black olives and sour cream can also be added.

__simple__ 14. Some people add hot sauce or salsa.

__compound__ 15. Tacos are nutritious, and they are also delicious.

▶ **Exercise 2 Underline each main clause. Add a comma or a semicolon as needed.**

Food from specific countries is known as ethnic food; a large variety exists.

1. Ethnic foods come from around the world, and they can be found all over the United States.

2. World foods add diversity to American cuisine; they provide a flavorful change of pace.

3. Many ethnic foods use common ingredients, but they taste different because of the spices.

4. Chinese soft noodles are long, thin strips of pasta, and some pasta dumplings contain cheese or meat.

5. Regional foods normally use local ingredients; these are fresh and economical.

6. The different flavors come from special ingredients; some may not be available in your area.

7. Different styles of Chinese cooking include Szechwan, Mandarin, and Cantonese; Szechwan is spicier than the others.

8. Chinese food is popular, and fortune cookies are always fun!

9. Thai dishes often include rice, but sometimes rice noodles are used instead.

10. The names of some Thai dishes begin with the words *kin khao*; this expression means "come eat."

Lesson 43

Complex Sentences and Subordinate Clauses

A **complex sentence** has a main clause and one or more subordinate clauses. A **main clause** has a subject and a predicate, and it can stand alone as a sentence. A **subordinate clause** also has a subject and a predicate, but it cannot stand alone as a sentence. It depends on the main clause to complete its meaning. It can act as an adjective, an adverb, or a noun.

MAIN CLAUSE	SUBORDINATE CLAUSE
They are playing music	that I like to hear. (adjective)
We must stop skating	when the music stops. (adverb)
I will tell you	what happened at the rink. (noun)

▶ **Exercise 1** Write in the blank *simple* or *complex* to identify the type of sentence.

_____complex_____ February 2, which is the midpoint of winter, is an unusual day.

_____simple_____ 1. It is Groundhog Day and is celebrated all over the country.

_____complex_____ 2. The groundhog, which is actually a woodchuck, emerges from hibernation on that day.

_____complex_____ 3. If the groundhog sees its shadow, there will be six more weeks of winter weather.

_____complex_____ 4. After the groundhog sees its shadow, it returns to its burrow until spring.

_____complex_____ 5. If the day is cloudy and the groundhog does not see its shadow, spring will come early.

_____complex_____ 6. The groundhog stays outside because it expects spring.

_____complex_____ 7. People enjoy this custom although most do not believe in it.

_____simple_____ 8. Statistical evidence does not support this popular superstition.

_____complex_____ 9. The groundhog that most people watch for is in Punxsutawney, Pennsylvania.

_____complex_____ 10. Its name is Phil, probably from the word *fillip*, which means "anything that stirs or livens up."

_____simple_____ 11. About seven thousand townspeople gather on February 2 and watch for the famous groundhog.

complex   12. Since the tradition began in 1887, the furry forecaster has seen its shadow all but eleven times.

simple   13. Our Groundhog Day tradition is based on an old German fable.

complex   14. This fable says that if an animal casts a shadow on February 2, there will be bad weather.

complex   15. This fun tradition inspired the 1993 movie *Groundhog Day,* which takes place in Punxsutawney.

▶ **Exercise 2 Underline each main clause. Write in the blank *simple* or *complex* to identify the type of sentence.**

complex   The groundhog, which is also called a woodchuck, is a kind of marmot.

simple   1. This makes it a member of the squirrel family.

complex   2. Adult groundhogs are usually two feet long, including their bushy tails, which are about five inches long.

simple   3. They have coarse brownish-gray fur with hints of red.

complex   4. Groundhogs live in the eastern and central United States where there are open fields.

complex   5. They feed on grasses and whatever vegetation they can find.

simple   6. They particularly like plants such as clover and alfalfa.

complex   7. When groundhogs come out of their holes to look for food, they stop to listen for signs of danger.

complex   8. Because groundhogs often sit still on their haunches, they can be easy targets for hunters.

simple   9. Groundhogs hibernate in burrows during the winter months.

complex   10. Before they hibernate, they eat large amounts of food.

complex   11. Groundhogs are able to sleep for most of the winter because the food they ate turns to fat.

complex   12. Groundhogs are fun and fascinating animals to observe, especially since there is an annual holiday named after them!

Copyright © by Glencoe/McGraw-Hill

Lesson 44
Adjective Clauses

An **adjective clause** is a subordinate clause that modifies a noun or pronoun in the main clause. An adjective clause follows the word it modifies. As with any subordinate clause, an adjective clause has a subject and a verb, but is not a complete sentence and cannot stand by itself. Generally, an adjective clause begins with a **relative pronoun** such as *that, which, who, whom, whose, whoever,* or *whomever*. It can also begin with *where* or *when*. A relative pronoun that begins an adjective clause can be the subject of the clause.

This book, **which was written in 1915,** is very interesting.
A railroad flare produces a bright flame **that can be seen hundreds of yards away.**

▶ **Exercise 1** Draw one line under each adjective clause. Draw a second line under each word that introduces an adjective clause.

Cartoon characters that were introduced in the 1930s are still popular today.

1. A university is a college where many subjects are studied.

2. Cable television, which was originally used to bring in distant stations, provides many types of specialized programming.

3. Juke boxes that used to play a song for a dime now cost much more.

4. Help came at a time when Stan needed it most.

5. John Chapman, who was nicknamed Johnny Appleseed, planted apple seeds in Ohio, Indiana, and Illinois.

6. Hummingbirds are tiny birds that are less than three inches long.

7. The Irish wolfhound, which is a hunting dog, is the tallest breed of the species.

8. The diver whose turn it was waved to the crowd.

9. Hurricanes are tropical cyclones that have wind speeds of up to 150 miles per hour.

10. Abraham Lincoln, who moved from Illinois to Washington, grew up in Kentucky.

11. The *Arabian Nights* is a collection of stories that have been passed down from one generation to the next.

12. Is Natalie the keyboard player <u>whom you asked to join the band</u>?

13. I need to edit this report <u>that I am writing</u>.

14. Many students <u>who bring their lunches to school</u> buy milk in the cafeteria.

15. Athens, <u>which is the capital of Greece</u>, is believed to have been named after Athena.

16. Moshe, <u>who has written music for other schools</u>, wrote the music for our class play.

17. The cook on duty this evening, <u>whoever that may be</u>, will prepare an excellent meal.

18. He <u>who laughs last</u> laughs best.

19. The giant armadillo, <u>which can grow to more than three feet long</u>, lives in South

    America.

20. Susan B. Anthony, <u>who was a schoolteacher</u>, was active in the antislavery movement.

▶ **Exercise 2** Draw one line under each adjective clause. Draw an arrow to the noun that it modifies.

The woman <u>who received the award</u> gave a fine speech.

1. Jacques, <u>whom we haven't met until now</u>, just enrolled at our school.

2. The clock <u>that I just bought</u> has a digital readout.

3. Acrobats perform complicated feats <u>that seem to defy gravity</u>.

4. Maria is the student <u>whose poetry won a prize</u>.

5. Many people in Belgium speak Flemish, <u>which is similar to Dutch</u>.

6. The *Katzenjammer Kids,* <u>which was one of the first comic strips to appear in a</u>

   <u>periodical</u>, appeared in *American Humorist* in 1897.

7. Mr. Griffin is a teacher <u>whom you will like</u>.

8. Can you see the mountain <u>that lies just beyond the tree line</u>?

9. Thuong likes to walk on trails <u>where he can see wildlife</u>.

10. Most people have days <u>when they cannot get organized</u>.

Lesson 45
Adverb Clauses

An **adverb clause** is a subordinate clause that often modifies a verb in the main clause of a complex sentence. It can also modify an adjective or an adverb. An adverb clause tells *how, when, where, why,* or *under what conditions* the action occurs. When an adverb clause introduces a sentence, it is usually separated from the main clause by a comma. When an adverb clause comes at the end of a sentence, it usually does not take a comma.

Before she signs up for next year's classes, Deena will talk with her counselor. Calvin passed the ball **because his teammate had an open shot**.

The first word of an adverb clause is a **subordinating conjunction**.

COMMON SUBORDINATING CONJUNCTIONS

after	before	than	when	whereas
although	if	though	whenever	wherever
as	since	unless	where	while
because	so that	until		

▶ **Exercise 1** Underline each adverb clause. Circle the subordinating conjunction.

You should count your pages (before) you begin.

1. Builders use plywood in the construction of small boats (because) it is easy to shape.

2. I haven't spoken with Jane (since) she moved.

3. Airplanes sometimes fly to unscheduled cities (when) the weather is bad.

4. I'll wear my sandals (if) the weather is warm.

5. (Whenever) I walk to school, my cat follows me down the street.

6. Please read the book (while) it's still available from the library.

7. (Since) it was just painted, don't lean against the wall.

8. Tomatoes taste best (when) they're fully ripened.

9. Everybody ate dessert (after) they finished eating the main course.

10. (Although) it was written in 1814, "The Star-Spangled Banner" did not become the

official national anthem until 1931.

11. Soldiers must stand at attention (when) they speak to an officer.

12. I'll cut the grass today (if) it doesn't rain.

13. (When) they feel threatened, dogs sometimes display aggressive behavior.

14. Incandescent and fluorescent bulbs produce light differently (although) they both serve

the same purpose.

15. The concert will end at 10:30 P.M. (unless) the audience insists on several encores.

16. You will receive extra credit (if) you turn in your project early.

17. Grace swims better (than) she dives.

18. The pep rally won't begin (until) the last class of the day has ended.

19. Keiko wrote her name on the chalkboard (after) she finished the problem.

20. Elena will groom the horse in the morning (so that) she can ride it in the afternoon.

▶ **Exercise 2 Underline each adverb clause. Draw an arrow to the verb that it modifies.**

Dad painted the fence because he didn't want it to rust.

1. When the principal called her name, Rosa stepped up to the podium.

2. Binoculars and telescopes magnify images because they have special lenses.

3. Whenever I hear the words of Dr. Martin Luther King Jr., I feel inspired.

4. Always check the expiration date before you buy perishable food.

5. Sprinters run at their limit during their races whereas distance runners pace themselves.

6. After the winter sports season ends, the athletes attend a banquet.

Grammar

Lesson 46
Noun Clauses

A **noun clause** is a subordinate clause used as a noun. It may serve as a subject, direct object, predicate noun, or object of a preposition.

Whoever rides in a car should wear seat belts. (subject)
Claude said **that he is watching television.** (direct object)
Listening to tapes is **how I learned Spanish.** (predicate noun)
Please listen to **what the director says.** (object of a preposition)

WORDS THAT INTRODUCE NOUN CLAUSES

how	what	where	who	whomever
however	whatever	which	whom	whose
that	when	whichever	whoever	why

▶ **Exercise 1** Draw one line under each noun clause. Draw a second line under each word that introduces a noun clause.

You can read <u><u>whichever</u> book you like.</u>

1. City Hall is <u><u>where</u> the parade begins.</u>

2. I don't know <u><u>which</u> one I should choose.</u>

3. Jamaal's little sister likes to do <u><u>whatever</u> he does.</u>

4. <u><u>When</u> you reach the next grade level</u> depends on <u><u>how</u> well you study.</u>

5. <u><u>Whoever</u> needs a new locker</u> should sign the sheet outside the office.

6. Our science teacher explained <u><u>why</u> the sun turns shades of pink and red at sunset.</u>

7. The clerk said <u><u>that</u> this was the last sweatshirt in stock.</u>

8. Can you please demonstrate <u><u>how</u> this computer works?</u>

9. New York is <u><u>where</u> people of many nationalities live.</u>

10. José couldn't add any facts to <u><u>what</u> had already been said.</u>

11. <u><u>However</u> you want to arrange the living room furniture</u> is okay with me.

12. He told me <u><u>what</u> he wanted for his birthday.</u>

13. <u><u>Whatever</u> you want to eat</u> is fine with me.

14. Do you remember <u><u>when</u> you tried to throw the ball all the way to home plate?</u>

15. The test question asked <u>whose ancestors lived in Egypt and Syria</u>.

16. The field trip was different from <u>what they had expected</u>.

17. Joel said <u>that he will visit his cousin this summer</u>.

18. Friday evening is <u>when I watch comedies</u>.

19. For your party, you can invite <u>whomever you want</u>.

20. <u>Why he dropped that pass</u> is a mystery.

► **Exercise 2** Underline each noun clause. In the blank, identify the clause as *subj.* (subject), *DO* (direct object), *OP* (object of a preposition), or *PN* (predicate noun).

_**PN**_   A steep hill and plenty of snow are <u>what we need for sledding</u>.

_**OP**_   **1.** Your athletic skills will be valuable in <u>whichever sport you choose</u>.

**subj.**   **2.** <u>Whoever is waiting for the governor</u> should stand in line.

**subj.**   **3.** <u>When Canadian geese head south</u> is the time of winter's approach.

_**DO**_   **4.** The coach said <u>that this will be the best team in several years</u>.

_**DO**_   **5.** Choir directors seek <u>whoever has a good voice</u>.

_**PN**_   **6.** His problem is <u>that he doesn't write down his assignments</u>.

_**PN**_   **7.** This is <u>how students select their major</u>.

_**OP**_   **8.** Pay close attention to <u>what I do</u>.

_**OP**_   **9.** Is Lieutenant Blaine the person with <u>whom I'll be speaking</u>?

**subj.** **10.** <u>How wars are lost</u> is the subject of the book.

_**DO**_ **11.** Doctors can explain <u>why proper nutrition is so important</u>.

**subj.** **12.** <u>That politicians differ in their opinions</u> is obvious.

_**DO**_ **13.** Isaac Newton proved <u>that comets and planets are subject to the laws of gravity</u>.

_**DO**_ **14.** A computer will process <u>whatever is entered into it</u>.

**subj.** **15.** <u>Who sent the yellow roses</u> is a mystery to me.

_**OP**_ **16.** The city council will be presenting awards to <u>whoever has made important

contributions to the community</u>.

Unit 7 **Review**

▶ **Exercise 1** Underline each subordinate clause. Write in the blank *adj.* for adjective clause, *adv.* for adverb clause, or *N* for noun clause.

| adj. | This magazine has pictures of hair styles <u>that you can do yourself</u>. |

| adv. | **1.** <u>Before you leave</u>, fill in all the answers. |

| adj. | **2.** Dogs <u>that undergo extensive training</u> assist people with special needs. |

| adv. | **3.** Airplanes fly above storm clouds <u>whenever they can</u>. |

| N | **4.** <u>Whoever arrives first</u> will win the door prize. |

| adv. | **5.** <u>If it rains</u>, the game will be canceled. |

| N | **6.** Ricky knew <u>that the library book was due</u>. |

| adj. | **7.** The tickets <u>that have come back from the printer</u> are now on sale. |

| adv. | **8.** Alligators and crocodiles live in tropical regions <u>because they are cold-blooded</u>. |

| N | **9.** England is <u>where the Wimbledon tennis tournament takes place</u>. |

| adj. | **10.** Police officers <u>who visit the schools</u> teach classes on safety and crime prevention. |

| adj. | **11.** Pineapples, <u>which grow on bushes</u>, weigh several ounces and have a spiny covering. |

| adv. | **12.** <u>Whenever the referee calls a foul</u>, the clock stops. |

| N | **13.** <u>Whoever owns a vintage 78 r.p.m. recording</u> must handle it very carefully. |

| adj. | **14.** The sound <u>that you heard</u> was made by a stringed instrument. |

| adj. | **15.** Farmers <u>whose land is not eroded</u> can grow many crops. |

| adv. | **16.** Movies portray dinosaurs as vicious creatures <u>although many were really gentle plant-eaters</u>. |

| adv. | **17.** Cactus plants survive in very dry regions <u>because they retain moisture</u>. |

| N | **18.** Architects must know <u>what the purpose of a building is</u>. |

| adj. | **19.** The library subscribes to magazines <u>that are published all over the world</u>. |

| adv. | **20.** Derek breathed a sigh of relief <u>after he won the election</u>. |

Unit 7, Clauses and Complex Sentences **163**

Cumulative Review: Units 1–7

▶ **Exercise 1** Write *adj.* or *adv.* in the blank to indicate whether the italicized word is an adjective or adverb.

__adv.__   Be sure to cook the meat *slowly.*

__adj.__   **1.** The weather service is predicting a *harsh* winter.

__adv.__   **2.** Our math test was *extremely* difficult.

__adv.__   **3.** Musicians must practice *diligently* before concerts.

__adj.__   **4.** Many operas are sung in *foreign* languages.

__adv.__   **5.** This music is *too* loud!

__adj.__   **6.** Have you read *this* book?

__adj.__   **7.** Johann Sebastian Bach wrote music in the *Baroque* style.

__adv.__   **8.** I worked *hard* to finish my English paper on time.

__adj.__   **9.** The puzzle was *hard* so I asked for help.

__adj.__   **10.** Be sure to lock the *inner* gate before you leave.

__adj.__   **11.** This building is *taller* than the one we visited yesterday.

__adv.__   **12.** Because Houston is a large city, I have always wanted to travel *there.*

__adv.__   **13.** Luis searched *everywhere* for the book.

__adj.__   **14.** The museum is having an exhibit of *Chinese* art.

__adv.__   **15.** Please call him back *immediately.*

__adv.__   **16.** Antonio *almost* scored a goal in Saturday's game.

__adv.__   **17.** Joshua plays the piano very *well.*

__adv.__   **18.** The mechanics worked *quickly* to fix the race car.

__adv.__   **19.** Janna waited *patiently* while her teacher graded her paper.

__adj.__   **20.** Only the *fastest* horses run in the Kentucky Derby.

▶ **Exercise 2** Underline each preposition and circle each conjunction. Identify the kind of conjunction by writing *coord.* (coordinating) or *subord.* (subordinating).

_____coord._____   This game of mine has new batteries, (but) it still doesn't work.

_____coord._____   1. Movie cameras use film, (but) video cameras record their images on magnetic tape.

_____coord._____   2. The weather forecaster predicted wind (and) snow during the coming week.

_____coord._____   3. The lights don't work, (and) the switch for the fuse is broken.

_____subord._____   4. Tim won't be able to attend summer school (unless) there is another vacancy in the class.

_____coord._____   5. Connecticut is a small state, (but) it has many places of interest.

_____coord._____   6. The number zero has no numerical value, (nor) can it be a denominator in a fraction.

_____coord._____   7. Compasses point north, (but) they do not point to the true northernmost spot on Earth.

_____subord._____   8. (Because) the weather was good, my brother played basketball outside the house.

_____coord._____   9. Does this computer work (or) should I call the repair department?

_____subord._____   10. I haven't had food this good (since) I left New York in the spring.

_____subord._____   11. Don't touch the computer by the window (if) it is still printing.

_____coord._____   12. Football requires a great deal of stamina, (but) so does soccer.

_____subord._____   13. Hydrofoil watercraft move at greater speeds than conventional boats (because) they can glide across the water.

_____coord._____   14. Tim rode his bike behind the house, (and) Fred rode his skateboard along the sidewalk.

_____subord._____   15. Let's lift weights at the gym (before) we go play tennis.

_____subord._____   16. (Although) there are many endangered species in America, there is much we can do to help them.

_____subord._____   17. We'll win this game (if) you make this field goal before the end of the half.

coord.   **18.** Mark Twain visited several foreign countries(and)wrote <u>about</u> the

experience <u>in</u> *Innocents Abroad.*

subord.   **19.** I feel better,(though)I haven't regained all <u>of</u> my strength yet.

coord.   **20.** The mail hasn't come yet,(nor)have the boxes <u>of</u> books arrived.

▶ **Exercise 3 Underline each subordinate clause. In the blank, identify the clause as** *adj.* **(adjective),** *adv.* **(adverb), or** *N* **(noun).**

adv.   Dew forms on grass <u>before the sun comes up.</u>

adv.   **1.** The streetlights automatically turn on <u>when darkness falls.</u>

adj.   **2.** The Irish firefighter is the one <u>who rescued my cat.</u>

adv.   **3.** Louisa May Alcott wrote *Little Women* <u>when she served as a nurse during the</u>

<u>Civil War.</u>

_N_   **4.** <u>What happened during science class</u> surprised everybody.

adj.   **5.** Candles <u>that come in many colors</u> have only a few scents.

_N_   **6.** Championship games are held in <u>whichever stadium can hold the most people.</u>

adj.   **7.** Aesop wrote fables <u>that used animals in the roles of people.</u>

adj.   **8.** The principal gave awards to students <u>whose grade averages were above 3.5.</u>

_N_   **9.** <u>Whichever color you decide to wear</u> will be fine with me.

adv.   **10.** Ancient people drew pictures on cave walls <u>whenever they wanted to record</u>

<u>important events.</u>

adj.   **11.** Tamil wants to go on a vacation <u>where he can learn to ski.</u>

adv.   **12.** Rachel is often tired in school <u>because she goes to sleep too late.</u>

adv.   **13.** <u>Although they perform many calculations per second,</u> computers cannot think

for themselves.

adj.   **14.** Many students <u>who live far from school</u> ride school buses.

adv.   **15.** <u>Since there are more than 800,000 insect species,</u> they outnumber all other

animals.

_N_   **16.** I know <u>that our television is not working well.</u>

Unit 8: Verbals

Lesson 47
Participles and Participial Phrases

Grammar

A **present participle** is formed by adding *-ing* to a verb. It functions as the main verb in a verb phrase (used with forms of *be*) or as an adjective.

The lion was **roaring.** (present participle as main verb)
The **roaring** lion scared us. (present participle as adjective)

A **past participle** is usually formed by adding *-ed* to a verb. It functions as the main verb in a verb phrase (used with forms of *have*) or as an adjective.

The mystery had **baffled** the police. (past participle as main verb)
The **baffled** police looked for clues. (past participle as adjective)

Do not confuse the past participle with the past form of a verb.

The drummer **joined** the band. (past form)
The drummer had **joined** the band. (past participle)

A **participial phrase** is a group of words that includes a participle and other words that complete its meaning. It is used as an adjective. A participial phrase can appear before or after the word it describes. Place the phrase as close as possible to the modified word to avoid unclear meaning.

Growling furiously, the bear clawed at the bars of its cage.
The insects **mounted in this frame** are part of a much larger collection.

Copyright © by Glencoe/McGraw-Hill

▶ **Exercise 1** Underline each participle. Write *V* (verb) or *adj.* (adjective) in the blank to indicate its use in the sentence.

___adj.___ The young campers had an <u>exciting</u> time.

___V___ **1.** Mark Walker had <u>invited</u> Diego to join him and his parents on a wilderness trip.

___V___ **2.** Diego had never <u>camped</u> before.

___adj.___ **3.** <u>Arriving</u> at the campsite, everyone helped put up the tents.

___adj.___ **4.** Two <u>pitched</u> tents would be their homes for the next week.

___adj.___ **5.** Mr. Walker, <u>inspecting</u> their work, praised the boys for their efforts.

___V___ **6.** While the adults were <u>preparing</u> supper, the boys went for a hike.

___adj.___ **7.** The boys discovered a <u>discarded</u> set of antlers from a deer.

__adj.__ 8. The hikers, <u>beaming</u> with pride, displayed their trophy at the campsite.

__adj.__ 9. Then they all ate a delicious meal <u>prepared</u> by Mrs. Walker.

__adj.__ 10. Mr. Walker made cornbread in a <u>frying</u> pan.

__adj.__ 11. <u>Tasting</u> delicious, the food disappeared in record time.

__adj.__ 12. Diego, <u>feeling</u> content, savored every bite of the meal.

__V__ 13. "Do you know what you young men will be <u>doing</u> after the meal?" asked

Mark's dad.

__adj.__ 14. <u>Looking</u> at his friend, Mark replied, "We have to clean up."

__adj.__ 15. That night, <u>waking</u> with a start, Diego heard a strange sound outside the tent.

__adj.__ 16. <u>Shaking</u>, he fumbled for his flashlight in his backpack.

__adj.__ 17. He heard a <u>crackling</u> noise and then a loud crash.

__adj.__ 18. The <u>startled</u> Diego shone his light in the direction of the noise.

__V__ 19. Two skunks had <u>knocked</u> over the trash cans.

__V__ 20. The boy ran for the tent and told the others what he had <u>seen</u>.

▶ **Exercise 2** **Underline each participle or participial phrase. Circle the noun it modifies.**

<u>Scattering in all directions</u>, the (campers) evaded the skunk.

1. Many campers tell about <u>frightening</u> (encounters) with skunks.

2. This (animal,) <u>scampering along many wooded areas</u>, lives only in the Western

Hemisphere.

3. (Skunks) come in various sizes, <u>depending on the type</u>.

4. The <u>striped</u> (skunk) is the most common type.

5. It is a furry, black animal with white (stripes) <u>radiating down its back</u>.

6. In the daytime, <u>sleeping</u> (skunks) rest in underground dens.

7. <u>Hunting at night</u>, most (skunks) catch their own food.

8. Their diet consists mainly of small rodents, caterpillars, and other insects, but they

also eat <u>limited</u> (amounts) of fruit and grain.

9. While out at night, <u>wandering</u> (skunks) sometimes surprise people.

10. The skunk is notorious for the foul, stinking liquid it sprays.

11. This liquid, called *musk*, comes from glands at the base of the tail.

12. Startled by a skunk, a person must remember to use caution.

13. Any alarmed person who sees a skunk should remain calm.

14. Running from the threat, many people scare the skunk.

15. Instinct causes a frightened skunk to spray.

16. The skunk will try to escape, spraying wildly.

17. It is very difficult to remove the stinking substance from clothes.

18. Soaked in tomato juice, clothes may begin to lose the smell.

19. However, the remaining odor usually lasts several days.

20. Experienced campers know to keep their distance from skunks and other wild animals.

Grammar

▶ **Exercise 3** Underline each participle or participial phrase. If it is used as an adjective, draw an arrow to the word it modifies.

Exploring the woods, the students saw many forms of life.

1. Springing from every spot, life fills a forest.

2. Both plants and animals exist in a balancing act of survival.

3. The crawling insects even have a role.

4. A complicated food web connects all the creatures to each other.

5. All the energy in an ecosystem is cycling continuously.

6. The interconnected food chain begins with plants of all sizes.

7. Plants called producers make their own food.

8. All around the world, plants are producing food from sunlight.

9. Called photosynthesis, this process is the main function of leaves.

10. Animals, being hunters, cannot produce food this way.

11. Eating the plants, many animals feed themselves.

12. Plant-eating animals are primary consumers.

13. Other larger animals eat the smaller unprotected ones.

14. Hiking in the woods, we can see all types of creatures.

15. For example, one may see a raccoon living in a tree.

16. Evidence of the amazing diversity of life is everywhere.

17. It is sad to see this diversity threatened by a forest fire.

18. However, some controlled forest fires can be good.

19. Happening naturally, forest fires can be a beneficial part of nature.

20. Forest fires can remove dead trees that are just taking up space.

21. Removing trees, fires can allow new fields of grass to grow.

22. Replenishing the soil, the ashes from a fire provide fresh nutrients.

23. Unfortunately, humans are still starting forest fires.

24. In spite of fires, life is continuing to exist everywhere.

25. Many spirited animals escape the blazes and move to nearby land.

26. Sometimes a changing forest causes some populations to increase.

27. Large families of grazing deer continue to fill the land.

28. Running through the woods, deer are beautiful creatures.

29. When they die, the remaining material decays.

30. Helping break down the remains of plants and animals, decomposers complete the
food cycle.

31. These microscopic organisms constantly remove rotting material from the ecosystem.

32. These tiny organisms are serving a purpose in the forest.

Lesson 48
Gerunds and Gerund Phrases

A **gerund** is a verb form that ends in *-ing* and is used as a noun.

Traveling can be pleasant or tedious. (gerund as subject)
Prilly dreaded **moving**. (gerund as direct object)

A **gerund phrase** is a group of words that includes a gerund and other words that complete its meaning.

Assigning the chores took longer than expected. (gerund phrase as subject)
The family enjoyed **fishing in the bayou**. (gerund phrase as direct object)

Do not confuse gerunds with participles, which also end in *-ing*. They are distinguished by their function in a sentence.

Freddy is **coloring**. (participle as main verb)
Maria thrived on the **loving** attention. (participle as adjective)
Crying is not always a sign of sadness. (gerund as subject)

▶ **Exercise 1** Underline each gerund or gerund phrase.

Giggling uncontrollably is her way to show that she is nervous.

1. Gregor tremendously enjoyed showing his dogs.

2. Taking a long drive calms many people.

3. To buy the new bike, Ava began saving her money.

4. Cleaning the bathroom is a chore that almost no one enjoys.

5. Many people cannot stand waiting in long lines.

6. Hoping for the best is a healthy practice.

7. Walking is good exercise.

8. The state championships involved competing for the grand prize.

9. Donating money to charity was the purpose of the car wash.

10. Mina's father always liked encouraging the team.

11. Including others in games shows good sportsmanship.

12. Joining the navy has been Kofi's dream since childhood.

13. Adding and subtracting are necessary in division problems.

14. Mark began <u>updating his existing computer file</u>.

15. Rayna finished <u>reading the book</u>.

16. <u>Leading the group</u> is a harder job than I first thought.

17. <u>Finding a bone in my fish sandwich</u> caused me to lose my appetite.

18. Kareem studied <u>fencing at the local gym</u>.

19. <u>Stimulating the frog's leg</u> was the first step in the biology lab procedure.

20. <u>Shedding tears</u> can be a sign of both joy and sorrow.

21. Dana went to the studio to learn <u>dancing</u>.

22. <u>Drinking</u> and <u>driving</u> is a dangerous activity.

23. <u>Eating</u> is allowed only in the lobby.

24. <u>Threading a needle</u> takes steady hands.

25. <u>Trading baseball cards</u> is Elena's favorite hobby.

26. <u>Coming home before ten</u> is a house rule that Kenji never broke.

27. The mosquitoes finally stopped <u>biting</u>.

28. <u>Wearing the itchy sweater</u> bothered Maria.

29. The team started <u>playing</u>.

30. Uncle Howard enjoyed <u>catching that large fish</u>.

31. <u>Winning the game</u> was taking precedence.

32. <u>Flying jets</u> is a career I am considering.

33. The chopped tree began <u>falling</u>.

34. <u>Carving the Thanksgiving turkey</u> has been Grandpa's job for years.

35. I like <u>learning about endangered species</u>.

36. <u>Shrinking the company's debt</u> has been on the president's mind.

37. <u>Creeping across the backyard</u> is how my cat is sneaking up on birds.

38. <u>Swimming the backstroke</u> was the specialty of the athlete.

39. I enjoyed <u>seeing my old friend</u>.

40. I accept <u>cleaning the garage</u> as my weekend chore.

▶ **Exercise 2** Underline each gerund or gerund phrase. Write in the blank its use in the sentence: *S* for subject or *DO* for direct object.

_____S_____   <u>Eating large amounts of fudge</u> is fattening.

___S___ **1.** <u>Caring for the various plants in the garden</u> requires a large amount of Oko's time.

___DO___ **2.** I am enjoying <u>going to the movies every weekend</u>.

___DO___ **3.** Maria loves <u>riding the roller coaster at the amusement park</u>.

___S___ **4.** <u>Collecting stamps from Africa</u> was one of Mr. Kanduja's hobbies.

___S___ **5.** <u>Raking the leaves</u> became a daily chore throughout the autumn season.

___DO___ **6.** My mother is organizing <u>the recycling in the community</u>.

___S___ **7.** <u>Filling all those balloons</u> was an extremely difficult task.

___DO___ **8.** Does table tennis at the recreation center require <u>bringing your own ball</u>?

___DO___ **9.** Jennifer began <u>singing</u> when she was three years old.

___S___ **10.** <u>Bowling in a league</u> is an excellent way to meet people.

___S___ **11.** <u>Succeeding in sales</u> requires self-confidence.

___S___ **12.** <u>Wrestling</u>, <u>swimming</u>, and <u>running</u> keep Matt busy.

___DO___ **13.** Did Jerry remember <u>dropping his notebook</u>?

___S___ **14.** <u>Flying kites</u> is a popular activity at the park.

___S___ **15.** <u>Frying meat too quickly</u> will cause the outside to burn and the inside to be undercooked.

___S___ **16.** <u>Peeling onions</u> makes many people cry.

___DO___ **17.** The orchestra began <u>playing the national anthem</u>.

___S___ **18.** <u>Acting silly</u> comes easily for Marvin.

___S___ **19.** <u>Raising crops on this land</u> will require a lot of hard work.

___S___ **20.** <u>Removing prejudice</u> is a worthy national goal.

___S___ **21.** <u>Sledding down the snow-covered hill</u> became a regular winter activity.

___DO___ **22.** Braking hard, the car avoided <u>hitting the deer</u>.

___S___ **23.** <u>Skating</u> is a terrific way to develop good balance.

___S___ **24.** <u>Swimming in the stream</u> is forbidden by the police.

Grammar

DO 25. Miette enjoys <u>taking long walks in the country</u>.

S 26. <u>Reading</u> improves your vocabulary.

DO 27. My dog finally stopped <u>howling</u>.

S 28. <u>Digesting dairy products</u> is a problem for some people.

S 29. <u>Following the rules in any sport</u> is the responsibility of the players.

S 30. <u>Sleeping on the cold, hard ground</u> was never Li Cheng's idea of fun.

DO 31. Do you know that your job will require <u>driving a car</u>?

S 32. <u>Pushing or shoving in the lunch line</u> will not be tolerated.

S 33. <u>Hauling logs from the river to the sawmill</u> was Ellen's part-time job.

DO 34. The staff enjoyed <u>meeting in the kitchen with Chef Albert</u>.

S 35. <u>Calling long distance</u> is much more economical these days than in our grandparents' era.

S 36. <u>Whistling a tune</u> is a sign of both happiness and nervousness.

DO 37. The whistling valve brought us <u>a warning</u>.

S 38. <u>Drumming</u> is an old term for selling goods.

S 39. <u>Speaking clearly</u> was the teacher's best quality.

S 40. <u>The squeaking of the chairs</u> bothered everyone in the class.

▶ **Writing Link Write a paragraph about learning to ride a bicycle. Use at least five gerunds in your description.**

_____

_____

_____

_____

_____

_____

_____

_____

_____

Lesson 49
Infinitives and Infinitive Phrases

An **infinitive** is a verb form that uses the word *to* followed by the base form of a verb. It often functions as a noun, as either a subject or a direct object. An infinitive can also function as an adjective or adverb. When *to* is used as part of an infinitive, it is not a preposition.

To fly has been a dream of humans since ancient times. (infinitive as subject)
Most people like **to sing**. (infinitive as direct object)
We rode the bus **to the mall**. (prepositional phrase)

An **infinitive phrase** is a group of words that includes an infinitive and other words that complete its meaning.

To keep one's promise is a sign of good character. (infinitive phrase)

▶ **Exercise 1** Underline each infinitive or infinitive phrase.

I prefer to listen to music in my room.

1. Gary is practicing to become the best player ever.

2. The coach wants us to achieve good results.

3. We need to train our dog systematically.

4. The instructor asked me to stop the car.

5. To chew gum can be fun.

6. To keep the lead is difficult.

7. Who wants to go to the zoo?

8. The restaurant wants to satisfy its customers.

9. Ever since childhood, to train dolphins was her goal.

10. Harry wanted to begin the game on a good footing.

11. To ring the bell was her job.

12. His aunt wanted to buy him the book.

13. To feed a pet can lift one's spirits.

14. To sing in a rock band was Ann's goal.

Grammar

15. To help Ben prepare the meal involves giving the cookbook to him.

16. My dog loves to ride in the car.

17. To think of the best way to the stadium was difficult.

18. Who wants to sit beside Grandma?

19. Before dinner, my father likes to ride his exercise bike.

20. To win the game would be a sweet victory.

21. On his way to school, Beka needs to make a left-hand turn.

22. To teach a class can be both difficult and fun.

23. To cook dinner will not take long.

24. To swing is a child's delight.

25. Sonia wants to pay for the ice cream.

26. Pedro loves to pop popcorn after school.

27. The lions hoped to spring at the hyenas.

28. To leave before the end of the show was rude.

29. To run in the Olympics was Jesu's dream.

30. To grow older is a natural part of life.

31. We all need to eat nutritious food.

32. The president proposed to cut taxes.

33. To do that math problem was our homework.

34. To know the secret is the key.

35. Who volunteers to drive to the movie?

36. The officer told the students to be careful crossing the intersection.

37. Stuart learned to write poetry from his English teacher.

38. Feng Ying likes to grow geraniums in the window box.

39. To rise to the top is an energetic goal.

40. Barbie's goal is to win a gold medal at the Special Olympics.

Grammar

Name _____ Class _____ Date _____

▶ **Exercise 2** Underline each infinitive or infinitive phrase. Write in the blank its use in the sentence: *S* for subject or *DO* for direct object.

DO   I need <u>to finish my homework</u>.

DO   **1.** I love <u>to hug my collie</u>.

S   **2.** <u>To act on a Broadway stage</u> is one of Jenny's fondest dreams.

S   **3.** <u>To become a concert pianist</u> requires hours of practice every day.

S   **4.** <u>To bake the perfect raspberry pie</u> was one of Grandpa's talents.

DO   **5.** José needed <u>to get his car at the gas station</u>.

DO   **6.** Athletes must learn <u>to lose gracefully</u>.

S   **7.** <u>To reach the highest level in the video game</u> is the purpose of finding the hidden passage.

S   **8.** <u>To write the article for the school paper</u> took talent.

S   **9.** <u>To win the game</u> is a real challenge.

DO   **10.** Abdul hoped <u>to find pictures of his great-grandparents</u>.

DO   **11.** We need <u>to arrive at least two hours early</u>.

DO   **12.** Dawit and Carmen wanted <u>to raise the flag at the opening ceremonies</u>.

S   **13.** <u>To leave before the storm</u> would be a smart idea.

DO   **14.** The coaches planned <u>to test the team's endurance</u>.

S   **15.** <u>To eat more than one piece of pie</u> is greedy.

DO   **16.** Micah and Jamal have learned <u>to finish their homework before bedtime</u>.

DO   **17.** Wanting only a laugh, Enrique never intended <u>to insult anyone</u>.

DO   **18.** The constant dripping of the faucet threatened <u>to drive him insane</u>.

S   **19.** <u>To own real estate</u> requires saving much money.

S   **20.** <u>To run all the way to the edge of the park</u> is exhausting.

DO   **21.** All the boys wanted <u>to join the choir</u>.

DO   **22.** I am trying <u>to find photos of whales</u>.

S   **23.** <u>To win a soccer match</u> takes teamwork.

S   **24.** <u>To teach a large class</u> requires much patience.

Grammar

  DO   **25.** Would Carlos like <u>to visit his uncle in Oregon</u>?

  DO   **26.** The referee told the booth <u>to restart the game clock</u>.

  S   **27.** <u>To be sure before proceeding</u> may lessen problems later.

  S   **28.** <u>To change schools</u> can be a scary experience.

  DO   **29.** Growing a good crop of tomatoes proves <u>to be time consuming</u>.

  DO   **30.** The poet likes <u>to read his poems at the neighborhood bookstore</u>.

  S   **31.** <u>To organize a family reunion</u> demands a great amount of planning.

  DO   **32.** Ever since she can remember, Marilyn has wanted <u>to become a country-western singer</u>.

DO, DO **33.** While no one liked <u>to cook</u>, everyone liked <u>to eat</u>.

  S, S   **34.** <u>To serve</u> and <u>to lead</u> were the president's wishes.

  DO   **35.** In response to public opinion, the council decided <u>to hire seven new police officers</u>.

  S   **36.** <u>To find the correct answer</u> is not always easy.

  DO   **37.** Because she was so hungry, Suchin wanted <u>to get a sandwich</u>.

  DO   **38.** Brushing your teeth with baking soda helps <u>to clean them</u>.

  DO   **39.** Robin wanted <u>to mail the package</u>, but she needed more postage.

  S   **40.** <u>To match Dan's ability</u> is certainly an accomplishment.

▶ **Writing Link Write a paragraph about learning to swim. Include at least six infinitives.**

_____

_____

_____

_____

_____

_____

_____

_____

Grammar

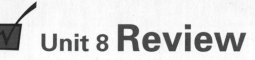

Unit 8 **Review**

▶ **Exercise 1** Write in the blank *part.* (participle), *ger.* (gerund), or *inf.* (infinitive) to
identify the italicized word or words.

__part.__   The *unfinished* pizza remained on the table.

__part.__ **1.** *Gazing* at the sky, Emil imagined he could fly.

__part.__ **2.** For her birthday, Will is *giving* his sister a new tape player.

__ger.__ **3.** *Riding* was the most popular activity at camp except for swimming.

__inf.__ **4.** *To make* the team requires both coordination and speed.

__ger.__ **5.** The entire family enjoys *playing* tennis.

__part.__ **6.** Their new recording is *selling* very well.

__part.__ **7.** Marion had *prepared* for the piano recital.

__part.__ **8.** The *worried* parents finally found the boy.

__inf.__ **9.** The cousins all agreed *to write* to each other.

__ger.__ **10.** We enjoy *singing* folk songs.

__inf.__ **11.** They planned *to make* the variety show an annual event.

__part.__ **12.** We couldn't get out because of the car *parked* behind us.

__inf.__ **13.** Where did you learn *to repair* your bicycle?

__part.__ **14.** *Bounding* down the stairway, the dog greeted its master.

__ger.__ **15.** *Feeding* the cats is Meg's daily chore.

__part.__ **16.** The carriage *bouncing* along the street was a collector's item.

__ger.__ **17.** I began *jogging* around the track every day.

__inf.__ **18.** *To err* is human.

__ger.__ **19.** *Reading* between the lines is a hidden talent.

__part.__ **20.** Arthur found the cow *grazing* in the neighbor's vegetable garden.

Grammar

Cumulative Review: Units 1–8

▶ **Exercise 1** Underline each prepositional phrase. Write *adj.* (adjective) or *adv.* (adverb) in the blank to identify the kind of phrase. Circle each coordinating, correlative, and subordinating conjunction.

adj.   The key to the neighbor's house was missing, (but) Derek had a spare.

adv.   **1.** In the morning she was tired (and) cranky.

adj.   **2.** I (not only) can remember the name of that substitute teacher, (but also) can remember what he wore that day.

adv.   **3.** The realtor would not wait inside the house (because) it was spooky.

adj.   **4.** The hat on the elderly lady's head was (both) bizarre (and) charming.

adv.   **5.** Our swingset (and) birdbath were damaged in yesterday's storm.

adv.   **6.** The shark swam around the coral reef (when) the fishing boat appeared.

adv.   **7.** (Both) strawberries (and) bananas are used in the fruit salad.

adj.   **8.** The first room on the left is yours.

adv.   **9.** The people became quiet (before) the golfer putted on the green.

adj.   **10.** All of the construction workers wore yellow hard hats (and) heavy work boots.

adj.   **11.** The sign in the front yard was (neither) correct (nor) legible.

adv.   **12.** My new CD player will be ready by Monday (or) Tuesday.

adv.   **13.** I looked into the classroom (but) saw nobody I knew.

adj.   **14.** Ryan never drinks iced tea without lemon (and) sugar.

adv.   **15.** They went fishing during the early morning hours (since) the weather was calmer.

adj.   **16.** The wooden fence between these houses needs nails (and) paint.

adj.   **17.** (Although) Mr. Wang coached the soccer team, most of his time was spent teaching health (and) physical education.

adv.   **18.** Elizabeth was brave during the crisis, (but) she panicked later.

adv.   **19.** Under the bed were a worn slipper (and) a giant dust ball.

adj.   **20.** The lanky man with the black hair (and) the bushy beard is our math teacher.

Grammar

▶ **Exercise 2** Write *con.* (concrete), *abst.* (abstract), *col.* (collective), or *comp.* (compound) in the blank to identify the type of noun in italics. Some nouns will fit more than one category.

con., col. The *team* from Wilson Junior High won the debate.

con. 1. Checkers is one of the world's oldest board *games.*

abst. 2. Lianna Black had the original *idea* for the project.

con., comp. 3. Our Siamese cat won a *blue ribbon* at last month's show.

abst. 4. Many people are interested in learning about their *past.*

con., col. 5. The *crowd* at the State Theater anxiously awaited the opening performance.

abst. 6. Cole knew it was *time* to clean his room when he could no longer see his carpet.

con., comp. 7. My best friend, Jen, hates *peanut butter.*

con., col. 8. In the 1960s *audiences* were out of control at the Beatles' concerts.

con., comp. 9. Our school library sold *bookmarks* to raise money for improvements.

abst. 10. Alissa used her mechanical *skill* to fix her sister's bike.

con., col. 11. The *committee* announced its decision to fire the district manager.

abst. *or* con., comp. 12. The jury listened carefully to the *cross-examination* of the witness.

abst. 13. Ben's *hope* is that he will be able to visit Washington, D.C.

abst. 14. Ms. Walker always stressed *creativity* for our journal assignments.

con., comp. 15. Clam chowder is a popular soup in *New England.*

con., comp. 16. The class voted on which *videotape* to watch.

con. 17. Stan called the *electrician* to connect the wiring in the basement.

con. 18. As the sky began to darken, the *parade* proceeded down Main Street.

abst. 19. We saw that the little boy was in *danger,* so we called the police.

abst. *or* con., comp. 20. During the peaceful protest, the courthouse steps were bathed in *candlelight.*

Grammar

► **Exercise 3 Underline the verbal or verbal phrase. In the blank, write *ger.* (gerund), *part.* (participle), or *inf.* (infinitive).**

___ger.___   <u>Moving to Williamsburg</u> sparked Nicole's interest in history.

___ger.___ **1.** Will <u>writing to the publisher</u> have any effect?

___inf.___ **2.** Patches prefers <u>to eat his dog food at room temperature</u>.

___part.___ **3.** The Hiking Club discovered the remains of a log cabin <u>destroyed by fire</u>.

___inf.___ **4.** Lindsay needed the counselor <u>to advise her on the best courses</u>.

___ger.___ **5.** My grandmother enjoys <u>golfing</u> on the weekends.

___ger.___ **6.** <u>Cleaning the roadsides</u> not only helps the environment but also saves money

             for the highway department.

___part.___ **7.** <u>Catered by professionals</u>, the banquet was a flawless success.

___part.___ **8.** <u>Applauding enthusiastically</u>, the audience prompted another curtain call.

___part.___ **9.** Pedro, <u>trying to be brave</u>, opened the door to the shed and went inside.

___inf.___ **10.** Obedience schools help <u>to train owners as well as their dogs</u>.

___ger.___ **11.** John tried <u>painting a mural on the wall</u>.

___ger.___ **12.** <u>Leading the race for student council</u> made Tommy Han happy.

___ger.___ **13.** A worthwhile use of free time is <u>volunteering at the community's soup</u>

             <u>kitchen</u>.

___part.___ **14.** <u>Inching its way through the driving snow</u>, the taxi delivered my grandparents

             from the airport.

___ger.___ **15.** <u>Scuba diving</u> is a favorite sport in Bermuda.

___inf.___ **16.** Marlin plans <u>to study marine biology in college</u>.

___part.___ **17.** The campers <u>staying in the Will-o'-the-Wisp Cabins</u> will wash the dishes

             tonight.

___inf.___ **18.** I like <u>to compose silly song lyrics</u>.

___part.___ **19.** <u>Typing 65 wpm</u>, Vicki quickly finished her history paper.

___inf.___ **20.** <u>To win first chair in the flute section</u>, Julia practiced every day after school.

Unit 9: Subject-Verb Agreement

Lesson 50
Making Subjects and Verbs Agree

If the subject of a sentence is singular, then the verb of the sentence must also be singular. If the subject is plural, then the verb must also be plural. When the subject and the verb are both singular or both plural, they are said to **agree in number**.

That **tree loses** its leaves early in the fall. (both singular)
Those **trees lose** their leaves late in the fall. (both plural)

The irregular verbs *be, do,* and *have* can be main verbs or helping verbs. In either case, they must agree with the subject.

Singular: **She is** painting a portrait. **He does** well. **It has** a good plot.
Plural: **They are** artists. The **students do** try. **They have** completed the lesson.

▶ **Exercise 1** Draw two lines under the verb in parentheses that best completes each sentence.

Astronomers (studies, <u>study</u>) the galaxies.

1. Our galaxy's name (<u>is</u>, are) the Milky Way.

2. The Milky Way (<u>consists</u>, consist) of the sun and other stars, the nine planets, gas, and dust.

3. The combined light from all the stars (<u>spreads</u>, spread) out to form a band of light across the sky.

4. In the night sky the Milky Way (<u>resembles</u>, resemble) spilled milk.

5. Throughout history there (has, <u>have</u>) been many legends about the Milky Way.

6. We now (knows, <u>know</u>) that Galileo, with his improved telescope, first confirmed that the light source was the stars.

7. This is not surprising because there (is, <u>are</u>) about 100 billion stars in our galaxy.

8. The Milky Way is flat like a disk, but it (<u>bulges</u>, bulge) at the center.

9. The spiral arms of the Milky Way (radiates, <u>radiate</u>) from this center.

Grammar

10. Our solar system (<u>exists</u>, exist) 30,000 light years from the center, or two thirds of the

way out on an arm.

11. The stars (rotates, <u>rotate</u>) around the central bulge.

12. The sun (<u>completes</u>, complete) one orbit of the galaxy every 225 million years, which

is one cosmic year.

13. While our galaxy has billions of stars, other larger galaxies (contains, <u>contain</u>) even

more stars.

14. Two dozen galaxies (makes, <u>make</u>) up the "Local Group."

15. Amazingly, scientists (believes, <u>believe</u>) there are billions of other galaxies in the

universe!

▶ **Exercise 2** **Underline the subject of each sentence. Fill in each blank with the verb in
parentheses that best completes the sentence.**

A <u>meteor</u> _____**looks**_____ like a star falling from the sky. (looks, look)

1. <u>Meteors</u> _____**are**_____ often called shooting stars. (is, are)

2. A <u>meteor</u> _____**is**_____ a streak of light that occurs when interplanetary particles

vaporize. (is, are)

3. Many <u>meteors</u> occurring together _____**create**_____ a meteor shower. (creates, create)

4. Comets' <u>debris</u> _____**produces**_____ most meteor showers. (produces, produce)

5. The <u>particles</u> then _____**enter**_____ Earth's atmosphere. (enters, enter)

6. A very large <u>meteor</u> _____**does**_____ not completely vaporize. (does, do)

7. The <u>particles</u> _____**are**_____ known as meteorites when they hit the Earth. (is, are)

8. <u>Meteorites</u> sometimes _____**form**_____ meteorite craters when they hit the moon, Earth,

or other planets. (forms, form)

9. <u>Meteorites</u> _____**are**_____ classified by their composition. (is, are)

10. <u>They</u> _____**contain**_____ different combinations of minerals, such as iron and nickel.

(contains, contain)

Lesson 51
Locating the Subject

The verb must agree with the subject even when the subject and verb are separated. Sometimes a prepositional phrase separates the subject and verb.

The **goal** of those charities **is** to provide shelter for homeless people. (The prepositional phrase *of those charities* separates the subject *goal* and the verb *is.*)

Sometimes the subject comes after the verb, as in sentences that begin with *here* or *there.*

Here **is** the **book** you looked for yesterday. (*Book* is the subject; *is* is the verb.)

In an interrogative sentence, a helping verb may come before the subject.

Does your **dog** really **eat** grapes? (*Dog* is the subject; *Does* is the helping verb; *eat* is the main verb.)

▶ **Exercise 1** Draw one line under the subject and two lines under the verb in each sentence.

Does he have your new phone number?

1. There are more cookies in the kitchen.

2. The night sky, in all its splendor, amazes us.

3. Here are the papers from the storeroom.

4. Has your mother called you?

5. The door with the broken lock has caused us much trouble.

6. There are eight boys in our class.

7. Here is the answer to your problem.

8. The grandmother of the Vasquez children drops them off at school.

9. The kittens on the windowsill watch the birds.

10. There is a bug in your hair.

11. Do the little girls know their address?

12. Here is my favorite picture in the museum.

13. Cars with air bags appear safer than those without them.

14. The <u>boy</u> with the red hair <u><u>is buying</u></u> his ticket first.

15. The <u>director</u> of both bands <u><u>was leading</u></u> the march.

16. Here <u><u>is</u></u> the best <u>recipe</u> for chocolate chip cookies.

17. <u>People</u> from all corners of the world <u><u>come</u></u> for the artist's exhibit.

18. <u><u>Was</u></u> <u>Kelly</u> happy with her final performance?

19. The <u>teacher</u>, with a nod of his head, <u><u>indicates</u></u> his approval.

20. The <u>story</u> about heroic animals <u><u>was</u></u> Arturo's favorite.

▶ **Exercise 2 Draw two lines under the verb in parentheses that best completes each sentence.**

The windows in the family room (was, <u><u>were</u></u>) very dirty.

1. The cheerleaders from the other team (does, <u><u>do</u></u>) a cheer for us before each game.

2. There (is, <u><u>are</u></u>) many boys trying out for the soccer team.

3. Sabine's years in Europe (appears, <u><u>appear</u></u>) to be happy ones.

4. They (waits, <u><u>wait</u></u>) in line for the choir tryouts.

5. (Does, <u><u>Do</u></u>) the boys have a snack after school?

6. Here (is, <u><u>are</u></u>) the ingredients for the salad.

7. There (<u><u>is</u></u>, are) nothing that Jane won't do for a laugh.

8. Our friends from youth group (visits, <u><u>visit</u></u>) us regularly.

9. The members of our team (wears, <u><u>wear</u></u>) blue and white uniforms.

10. The principal of the school (<u><u>changes</u></u>, change) the school's dress code every year.

11. Here (comes, <u><u>come</u></u>) the trumpet players.

12. The temperature in the cabins (<u><u>rises</u></u>, rise) rapidly.

13. On the table (sits, <u><u>sit</u></u>) the trophies we won.

14. Derek with his friends from school (<u><u>climbs</u></u>, climb) the tree in his backyard.

15. The chairs in the corner (is, <u><u>are</u></u>) antiques.

16. Here (<u><u>is</u></u>, are) the article that I told you about.

17. (<u><u>Does</u></u>, Do) this subject interest you?

18. The tables in the cafeteria (needs, <u><u>need</u></u>) wiping.

Lesson 52
Collective Nouns and Other Special Subjects

A **collective noun** names a group. It has a singular meaning when it describes a group that acts as a unit. It has a plural meaning when it describes members of the group acting as individuals.

The **class reads** every day.   The **class read** from their textbooks.

Some nouns that end in -*s* take a singular verb.

Mathematics is my best subject.   **Mumps is** a childhood disease.
The **news is** good.

Some nouns that end in -*s* but name just one thing take a plural verb.

Here **are** the **binoculars.**   **Are** my **clothes** ready?   Where **are** the **pliers?**
The **scissors are** on the desk.   These **jeans are** mine.

A title of a book or work of art is always singular.

Little Women **is** a book by Louisa May Alcott.

If an amount is treated as a single unit, it is singular. If it is treated as many individual units, it is plural.

Twenty dollars is the price of the radio I want.
Twenty dollars are scattered on the floor.

▶ **Exercise 1** Draw two lines under the verb in parentheses that best completes each sentence.

Her clothes (was, <u>were</u>) destroyed in the fire.

1. *Where the Red Fern Grows* (<u>is</u>, are) the book our teacher assigned us.

2. The news (<u>is</u>, are) the only program that my father watches.

3. Five dollars (was, <u>were</u>) lying on the ground, so I turned them in at the office.

4. The binoculars (helps, <u>help</u>) us see the stage from our balcony seats.

5. The group (talks, <u>talk</u>) about the issues that concern each of them.

6. Mathematics (<u>was</u>, were) my favorite subject until I took government.

7. *A Tale of Two Cities* (<u>becomes</u>, become) very exciting toward the end.

8. Your jeans (is, <u>are</u>) still in the dryer.

9. Three dollars (is, are) the price we charge for a car wash.

10. *Guys and Dolls* (starts, start) at eight o'clock this evening.

11. My clothes (gets, get) dirty when I wash the car.

12. *The Water Lilies* (is, are) a painting by the French impressionist Claude Monet.

13. Mumps (makes, make) the face swell up.

14. Millions of dollars (was, were) lost in the bank robbery.

15. The team (was, were) defeated last Saturday.

16. Fifty-five dollars (is, are) too much to pay for that dress.

17. Those scissors (cuts, cut) through anything.

18. After the meeting, the group (goes, go) their separate ways.

19. The class (takes, take) field trips every Friday.

20. Pliers (works, work) well in loosening bolts.

21. The team (accepts, accept) its award at the assembly today.

22. *The Grapes of Wrath* (was, were) written by John Steinbeck.

23. The good news (is, are) that I did well on my science test.

24. Four hours (seems, seem) like a long time to wait in line for tickets.

25. The scissors (is, are) too big for the little girl to hold.

26. The faculty (holds, hold) sessions with each of their students' parents.

27. Twenty minutes (lasts, last) forever when you're waiting for a phone call.

28. Your glasses (breaks, break) every time you sit on them.

29. Twelve days (is, are) a long time to wait for my birthday.

30. Evan's family (has, have) just moved into that house.

▶ **Writing Link** **Write three sentences about clubs you can join at your school. Include collective nouns and other special subjects.**

_____

_____

_____

_____

Lesson 53
Indefinite Pronouns as Subjects

An **indefinite pronoun** does not refer to a specific person, place, or thing. Many indefinite pronouns take a **singular** verb:

another, anybody, anyone, anything, each, either, everybody, everyone, everything, much, neither, nobody, no one, nothing, one, somebody, someone, something

Everybody wants to sign the petition. (singular)

Some indefinite pronouns take a **plural** verb:

both   few   many   others   several
Many of the students **arrive** early. (plural)

Other indefinite pronouns may take a **singular or plural** verb, depending on what follows them:

all   any   most   none   some
All of the parents agree with Mr. Jackson's opinion. (plural)
Not **all of the work is** lost. (singular)

▶ **Exercise 1** Draw two lines under the verb in parentheses that best completes each sentence.

Several of his antique toys (was, <u><u>were</u></u>) very valuable.

1. Another in my collection of books (<u><u>arrives</u></u>, arrive) today.

2. Everybody in my class (<u><u>wants</u></u>, want) to win the candy sale prize.

3. Both of the boys (attends, <u><u>attend</u></u>) science club regularly.

4. (<u><u>Is</u></u>, Are) anybody going to the band concert?

5. Everyone (<u><u>chooses</u></u>, choose) a different animal to imitate.

6. Few (makes, <u><u>make</u></u>) apple pie like my aunt does.

7. Everyone in that show (<u><u>makes</u></u>, make) me laugh.

8. Everything in that store (<u><u>is</u></u>, are) made from chocolate.

9. No one (<u><u>makes</u></u>, make) a noise in the library.

10. Many of the ideas (was, <u><u>were</u></u>) good ones.

11. Nothing (is, are) as difficult as it seems.

12. One (is, are) never sure if Rhonda is being serious.

13. Few of the parents (was, were) as proud as my stepfather.

14. Somebody (helps, help) Dad make dinner every night.

15. Several of the songs (was, were) cut from the choir program.

16. Much (was, were) done to protect the endangered species.

17. Both of the scientists (has, have) made important discoveries.

18. Each of the vegetables (was, were) important for our diet.

19. Many (has, have) tried to change Randy's mind.

20. Everybody (volunteers, volunteer) to help the teacher pass out the papers.

▶ **Exercise 2** **Fill in the blank with the verb in parentheses that best completes the sentence.**

Few _____undertake_____ the training schedule of a marathon runner. (undertakes, undertake)

1. Anything _____is_____ an improvement on the current color of the room. (is, are)

2. Several of the artifacts _____were_____ found among the ancient ruins. (was, were)

3. Few _____understand_____ the message of that movie. (understands, understand)

4. Someone _____takes_____ out the trash every Tuesday. (takes, take)

5. All of the soldiers _____stand_____ at attention when the flag is raised. (stands, stand)

6. Many of the books _____discuss_____ the space program. (discusses, discuss)

7. No one _____minds_____ standing in line for tickets to that concert. (minds, mind)

8. Most of the table _____was_____ covered with plates of food. (was, were)

9. Others _____take_____ the bus, but Michael likes to walk. (takes, take)

10. Something _____bothers_____ Anita when she sits by the window. (bothers, bother)

11. All of us _____are_____ ready for summer vacation. (is, are)

12. When Tony eats spaghetti, none _____remains_____ on the plate. (remains, remain)

13. Either of the ties _____goes_____ well with this striped shirt. (goes, go)

14. Many _____try_____, but few succeed in changing the dress code. (tries, try)

Grammar

Lesson 54
Agreement with Compound Subjects

A **compound subject** consists of two or more subjects that share the same verb.

Micah and **Rosa** cheered at the basketball game.

Two or more subjects joined by *and* or by *both...and* take a plural verb.

Skiing **and** ice skating **are** my favorite winter sports.
Both Liz **and** Jessica **do** well in math class.

However, if *and* joins words that refer to a single person or thing, the subject is singular and takes a singular verb.

A singer **and** songwriter from Missouri **is** here today.

When a compound subject is joined by *or, nor, either...or,* or *neither...nor,* the verb agrees with the subject closer to it.

Neither Bob **nor** his parents **are** at the barbecue.

▶ **Exercise 1** Draw two lines under the verb in parentheses that best completes each sentence.

Nachos and peanuts (is, <u>are</u>) his favorite snacks.

1. English and art (is, <u>are</u>) the subjects I like most.

2. Neither the coach nor the players (looks, <u>look</u>) forward to Friday's game.

3. Both Shari and Nigel (brings, <u>bring</u>) yogurt in their lunches.

4. Max or Jerod (<u>does</u>, do) the washing, and Sarah does the waxing.

5. Hamburgers, hot dogs, and french fries (is, <u>are</u>) on the menu.

6. Either magazines or newspapers (was, <u>were</u>) acceptable at the paper drive.

7. Both singers and dancers (performs, <u>perform</u>) in the parade.

8. Neither bowling nor tennis (<u>interests</u>, interest) Cody.

9. Mario's piano teacher and mentor (<u>is</u>, are) an outgoing person.

10. Two nickels or a dime (<u>works</u>, work) in that vending machine.

11. Either the blue blouse or the pink shirt (<u>looks</u>, look) good with those pants.

12. Sad songs or movies (makes, <u>make</u>) Yvonne cry.

Copyright © by Glencoe/McGraw-Hill

13. Rock or country music (appeals, appeal) to Russ.

14. Boy Scouts and Girl Scouts (earns, earn) badges for their efforts.

15. Blankets and sleeping bags (is, are) necessary for camping.

16. Both Melinda and Trey (works, work) in the cafeteria.

17. Neither drinks nor food (is, are) permitted in the library.

18. Girls or boys can (joins, join) the debate team.

19. Saturday, Sunday, and Monday (is, are) the days Paula helps at the retirement home.

20. Reading, drawing, and painting (amuses, amuse) Ethan in his free time.

▶ **Exercise 2** Write *A* in the blank if the subject and verb agree or *D* if they do not agree.

___A___ Both Mrs. Copeland and her students were at the museum.

___D___ 1. Neither Tammy nor Seth look worried.

___D___ 2. Ordinarily Mitch or Rachel join me for lunch.

___A___ 3. Choir and band are activities that I enjoy.

___D___ 4. Maybe Janet or Sasha remember me.

___A___ 5. The ventriloquist and his puppet were the hit of the talent show.

___A___ 6. Neither my mom nor my dad was able to come to the show.

___D___ 7. Both Joel and Marty plans to go to the party.

___D___ 8. The boy and his puppy runs together every morning.

___A___ 9. Talking and chewing gum are forbidden in study hall.

___D___ 10. Daisies, roses, and a carnation was in the bouquet.

___D___ 11. Vicksburg and Gettysburg is Civil War battle sites.

___A___ 12. My favorite lunch is soup and a sandwich.

___A___ 13. Either a spoon or a fork is appropriate to use.

___A___ 14. The skater and her parents were waiting for her scores.

___D___ 15. Neither Jason nor Samantha like pizza.

___A___ 16. Doctors and nurses watch the sick boy closely.

☑ Unit 9 **Review**

▶ **Exercise 1** Draw two lines under the verb in parentheses that best completes each sentence.

Here (<u>is</u>, are) the recipe for my triple chocolate brownies.

1. The pep club (<u>cheers</u>, cheer) at every football game.

2. Many of my friends (is, <u>are</u>) going to the bonfire tonight.

3. Dave or his brothers (plays, <u>play</u>) in every baseball game.

4. Lacrosse (<u>is</u>, are) a challenging sport.

5. The banks of the river (floods, <u>flood</u>) during the heavy rains.

6. Four dollars an hour (<u>is</u>, are) what the Bennetts pay their baby-sitters.

7. Each (<u>has</u>, have) his or her own way of doing things.

8. Most of Mark Twain's books (contains, <u>contain</u>) humor.

9. Few (appreciates, <u>appreciate</u>) his strange sense of fashion.

10. Mr. Harding (<u>teaches</u>, teach) English in a creative way.

11. The boss (<u>wants</u>, want) to hire a new staff for the project.

12. Mumps (<u>is</u>, are) a contagious disease.

13. Both of the students (scores, <u>score</u>) high on their tests.

14. Abbott and Costello (was, <u>were</u>) famous comedians.

15. The coach's wife (<u>sits</u>, sit) on the bench.

16. Both Joe DiMaggio and Ty Cobb (was, <u>were</u>) great baseball players.

17. Gisele's coach and teacher (<u>is</u>, are) Mrs. Monahan.

18. Neither music nor clowns (cheers, <u>cheer</u>) up the sad little boy.

19. The class (<u>works</u>, work) on the assignment as a group.

20. Everyone (<u>wants</u>, want) to go to the play-off game.

Cumulative Review: Units 1–9

▶ **Exercise 1** Draw one line under the complete subject and two lines under the complete predicate. Circle the item if it is a fragment.

The pig waddled across the pen and sat in the mud.

1. The maraca player kept Jake's attention.

2. We rode the bus.

3. The mayor, the governor, and the president attended the banquet.

4. The guest on the talk show recommended his new film.

5. The audience at the rock concert danced and sang along with the musicians.

6. (Won't even last another day with that problem.)

7. Isaac constantly reminded people how to spell his name.

8. (Visited a college the other day.)

9. We rode all the way to the top of the Eiffel Tower on our tour of France.

10. The elephants, the bears, and the large cats were my favorite attractions at the zoo.

11. The roller coaster threw Jon and Afi against the side of the car.

12. (A large door to the cathedral.)

13. The local cable company sponsored a charity event.

14. Our backpacking trip was cancelled because of bad weather.

15. My grandmother jogs five miles every day.

16. A trip to Canada was one of Jaelyn's dreams.

17. (Never again in a million years!)

18. Chika must pay taxes on her wages.

19. <u>My uncle</u> <u>puts</u> ketchup on everything he eats.

20. <u>Nightcrawler worms</u> <u>make</u> great bait.

▶ **Exercise 2** **Fill in the blank with the form of the verb in parentheses that best completes the sentence.**

Last night, my father _____ **drank** _____ three glasses of soda. (drink)

1. If we had _____ **won** _____ the game, we would have been state champions. (win)

2. Who _____ **chose** _____ that place to eat last weekend? (choose)

3. My mom _____ **brought** _____ me the TV remote control when I was sick in bed. (bring)

4. Because I _____ **cut** _____ the grass, I missed the football game. (cut)

5. That performer once _____ **sang** _____ in the school choir. (sing)

6. We were relieved when my aunt _____ **came** _____ home from the hospital. (come)

7. If you had _____ **laid** _____ the tickets right there, they would not be lost. (lay)

8. At the gourmet restaurant, my father has _____ **eaten** _____ calf brains! (eat)

9. According to legend, King Arthur _____ **sought** _____ the Holy Grail. (seek)

10. I can't believe that you _____ **went** _____ to that concert a year ago! (go)

11. Li Cheng's family cheered when she _____ **swam** _____ in the meet. (swim)

12. Nancy had _____ **blown** _____ up all the balloons herself. (blow)

13. Tomorrow I _____ **will buy** _____ my sister the latest exercise videocassette. (buy)

14. My cousins had _____ **grown** _____ their own vegetable garden. (grow)

15. Sandi _____ **felt** _____ the door for heat before she opened it. (feel)

16. Max had _____ **ridden** _____ away from the stables when he realized he had left the stable door open. (ride)

17. Because his credit was good, the bank _____ **lent** _____ Haloke $10,000. (lend)

18. The principal had _____ **spoken** _____ at many assemblies in the past. (speak)

Grammar

19. My little brother giggled as the monkey _____**swung**_____ from the vine. (swing)

20. It's a good thing I _____**took**_____ your advice and stayed home. (take)

▶ **Exercise 3** Draw one line under the subject in parentheses that best completes each sentence.

The (student, students) watch the movie silently.

1. (Gary, Gary and Camille) eats a hot-fudge sundae.

2. Before the show, the (performer, performers) practice lines.

3. When my (dog, dogs) eat, I also have a snack.

4. Hearing the lifeguard's whistle, the (swimmer, swimmers) exit the pool.

5. The lost (bill, bills) are in my coat pocket.

6. Why (don't, doesn't) the crowd leave?

7. (Those, That) is my reason for leaving.

8. (A field, Fields) of corn stretch for miles along the road.

9. The (sweater, sweaters) with the fancy buttons costs fifty dollars.

10. The art (gallery, galleries) downtown display the paintings made by my mother.

11. At the street festival, (Brad, Brad and Alma) buys some cotton candy.

12. The new (puppy, puppies) chew on anything they can reach.

13. (This map, These maps) show the way to the caves.

14. (She, They) watches the children next door every Saturday.

15. Zach's favorite (book, books) is a mystery.

16. When I have headaches, (Mother, Mother and Father) give me aspirin.

17. Right now, the (network, networks) are airing the State of the Union Address.

18. The (day, days) before the big game is filled with excitement and confusion.

19. The (soldier, soldiers) enters battle.

20. The (child, children) wear heavy coats in the winter.

Unit 10: Diagraming Sentences

Lesson 55
Diagraming Simple Subjects and Simple Predicates

Diagram simple subjects and simple predicates by drawing a horizontal line separated by a vertical line.

Write the simple subject to the left of the vertical line and the simple predicate to the right of the vertical line. Be sure to write only the simple subject and the simple predicate in this part of the diagram. Capitalize any words that are capitalized in the sentence.

A simple predicate may also include helping verbs.

Kittens play.   Dogs are barking.

Kittens	play

Dogs	are barking

▶ **Exercise 1** Diagram each simple subject and simple predicate.

1. Snow falls.

Snow	falls

2. Leaves change color.

Leaves	change

3. My bicycle broke.

bicycle	broke

4. The donkey brays.

donkey	brays

5. The flowers bloom.

flowers	bloom

6. Clouds float.

Clouds	float

7. The bells are ringing.

bells	are ringing

8. The breezes blow.

breezes	blow

9. The fence is breaking.

fence	is breaking

10. Takeo is speaking.

Takeo	is speaking

11. The rabbits hop.

rabbits	hop

12. The glasses broke.

glasses	broke

13. Jamal laughs.

Jamal	laughs

14. Yuri sings.

Yuri	sings

15. The television makes noise.

television	makes

16. She will ask permission.

She	will ask

17. Juan has bought a pen.

Juan	has bought

18. Henry writes a story.

Henry	writes

19. Mr. Reyes said it.

Mr. Reyes	said

20. I called Steven.

I	called

21. We will attend the concert.

We	will attend

22. Peter was playing the guitar.

Peter	was playing

23. He threw the ball.

He	threw

24. I had seen the musical.

I	had seen

Lesson 56
Diagraming the Four Kinds of Sentences

Study the diagrams below of the simple subject and simple predicate of the four basic kinds of sentences. Regardless of the word order in the sentence, the location of the simple subject and simple predicate in a sentence diagram is always the same. In an imperative sentence, the subject is often understood and written in parentheses.

DECLARATIVE
People ride bikes.

| People | ride |

INTERROGATIVE
Is it raining?

| it | Is raining |

IMPERATIVE
Clean the dishes.

| (you) | Clean |

EXCLAMATORY
I forgot my books!

| I | forgot |

▶ **Exercise 1** Diagram each simple subject and simple predicate.

1. The sheep are bleating.

| sheep | are bleating |

2. Are you writing poetry?

| you | Are writing |

3. Do purchase that CD.

| (you) | Do purchase |

4. Our cat is meowing.

| cat | is meowing |

5. When did you meet him?

| you | did meet |

6. I lost my club badge.

| I | lost |

7. Candida is singing.

| Candida | is singing |

8. Give me my tape.

| (you) | Give |

9. Hold the net!

| (you) | Hold |

10. You must study.

| You | must study |

<table>
<tr><td>

11. Do you have the phone number?

you	Do have

12. The show is starting!

show	is starting

13. Wash your face.

(you)	Wash

14. Kelly is here.

Kelly	is

15. Where are the horses?

horses	are

16. Mow the lawn.

(you)	Mow

17. I laughed out loud.

I	laughed

</td><td>

18. The pond froze last week.

pond	froze

19. The parakeet is escaping!

parakeet	is escaping

20. Was that thunder?

that	Was

21. The balloons are drifting away.

balloons	are drifting

22. Wait a minute!

(you)	Wait

23. Did Josh find his sneakers?

Josh	Did find

24. The cake is gone!

cake	is

</td></tr>
</table>

Lesson 57

Diagraming Direct and Indirect Objects and Predicate Words

Place the direct object to the right of the verb when diagraming. Set it off from the verb by a vertical line that does not extend below the horizontal line.

Predicate nouns and predicate adjectives are also written on the horizontal line after the verb, but they are separated from a linking verb by a slanted line. Locate indirect objects on a line below and to the right of the verb with a slanted line touching the verb.

Diana offered her sister the CD.

| Diana | offered | CD |

sister

Sparrows are noisy.

| Sparrows | are \ noisy |

▶ **Exercise 1** Diagram each simple subject, simple predicate, direct object, indirect object, predicate noun, and predicate adjective.

1. Benito called his father.

| Benito | called | father |

2. My bike is new.

| bike | is \ new |

3. Lorena ate the pear.

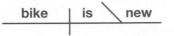

| Lorena | ate | pear |

4. Francis rode the pony.

| Francis | rode | pony |

5. Hakeem sold Charlie the bike.

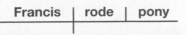

| Hakeem | sold | bike |

Charlie

6. Beth lost her watch.

| Beth | lost | watch |

7. Hazel sent me the letter.

| Hazel | sent | letter |

me

8. Carl heard the song.

| Carl | heard | song |

9. Jerome gave the horse an apple.

| Jerome | gave | apple |

horse

10. Ted plays chess.

| Ted | plays | chess |

Grammar

11. Mali threw Terry the ball.

```
Mali | threw | ball
         \  Terry
```

12. Bill mowed the lawn.

```
Bill | mowed | lawn
```

13. The dog fetched me the paper.

```
dog | fetched | paper
         \  me
```

14. The game was great.

```
game | was \ great
```

15. The day grew warm.

```
day | grew \ warm
```

16. Pat is the center on the team.

```
Pat | is \ center
```

17. Sally became happy.

```
Sally | became \ happy
```

18. That bush seems dead.

```
bush | seems \ dead
```

19. Mr. Cardona signed the note.

```
Mr. Cardona | signed | note
```

20. Tiffany guaranteed us a change.

```
Tiffany | guaranteed | change
              \  us
```

21. The cat chased the mouse.

```
cat | chased | mouse
```

22. My dad is a teacher.

```
dad | is \ teacher
```

23. His answer seems correct.

```
answer | seems \ correct
```

24. My aunt will give me a videotape.

```
aunt | will give | videotape
           \  me
```

Grammar

Lesson 58
Diagraming Adjectives and Adverbs

Place adjectives, including articles, on slanted lines beneath the nouns or pronouns that they modify. Place adverbs on slanted lines beneath the verbs, adjectives, or other adverbs that they modify.

Thick grass must be mowed regularly.

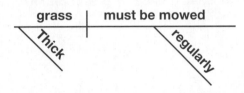

The heavy rain came very swiftly.

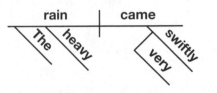

▶ **Exercise 1 Diagram the following sentences.**

1. The bright snow sparkles.

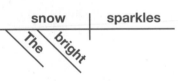

5. Red-breasted robins wake early.

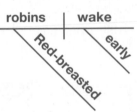

2. Janis runs very fast.

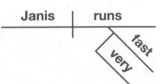

6. Andy regularly throws great pitches.

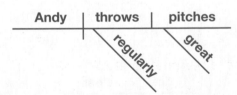

3. Emily speaks well.

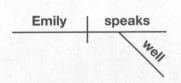

7. Good chess matches take a long time.

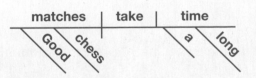

4. Mark Twain wrote great stories.

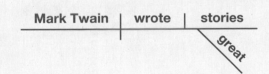

8. Hairstyles change often.

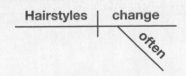

9. My dog barks fiercely.

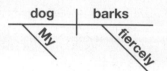

10. I love foreign languages.

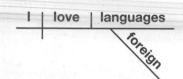

11. Yellow canaries sing sweetly.

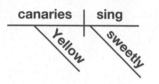

12. The Chinese poet wrote beautiful poetry.

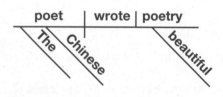

13. The white cat sleeps quietly.

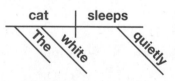

14. Teenagers usually prefer fashionable clothes.

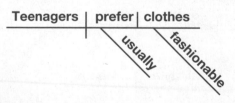

15. Jennifer gave her mom a new watch.

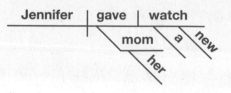

16. Old books need careful preservation.

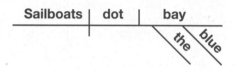

17. Sailboats dot the blue bay.

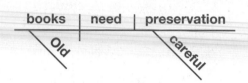

18. Brown sparrows chirp their songs loudly.

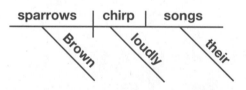

19. The young salesclerk refunded the nice man his money.

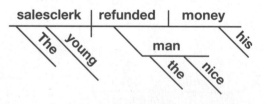

20. Tall, thick trees completely cover those distant hills.

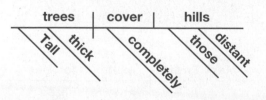

Lesson 59
Diagraming Prepositional Phrases

Connect a prepositional phrase to the noun or verb it modifies. Put the preposition on a slanted line and the object of the preposition on a horizontal line.

The leaves on those trees are bright yellow.

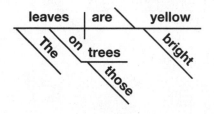

The sound of music echoed throughout the building.

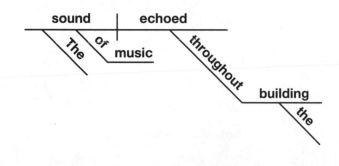

▶ **Exercise 1   Diagram the following sentences.**

1. The color of the sky is red.

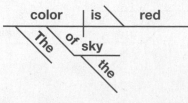

2. Our track team runs across the golf course.

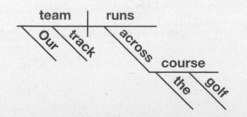

3. My dog went into Mr. Jones's yard.

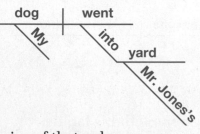

4. Puppies of that color are rare.

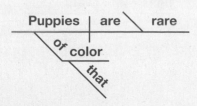

5. We listen to that CD often.

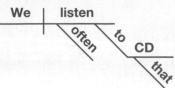

6. Rudy stands within earshot.

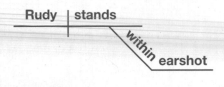

7. You should not handle kittens of a very young age.

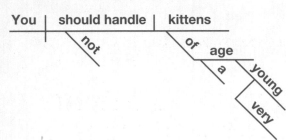

8. My skill with a bow is improving.

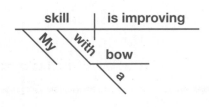

9. Olympus Mons is the largest volcano on Mars.

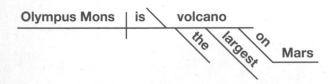

10. Sam went with his family.

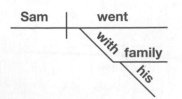

11. Our squad of runners finished behind their squad.

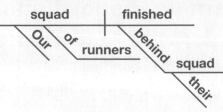

12. Carlos lost everything in his satchel.

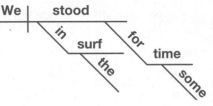

13. We stood in the surf for some time.

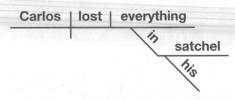

14. The flowers of early spring sprouted under the leaves.

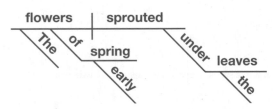

15. My cat sleeps in the sun on the windowsill.

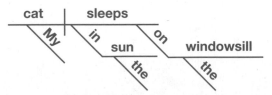

16. The news of the win spread quickly throughout the school.

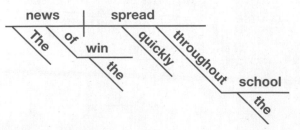

Grammar

Lesson 60
Diagraming Compound Sentence Parts

Coordinating conjunctions such as *and*, *but*, and *or* join words, phrases, or sentences. Diagram these compound parts of a sentence by placing the second part below the first. Write the coordinating conjunction on a dotted line connecting the two parts.

Birds perch and sing.   Water nourishes plants and animals.

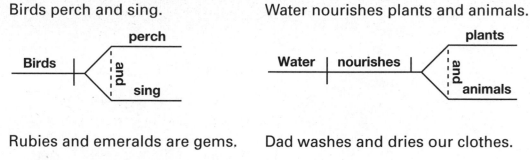

Rubies and emeralds are gems.   Dad washes and dries our clothes.

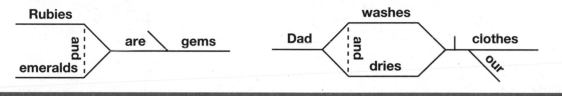

▶ **Exercise 1 Diagram the following sentences.**

1. Emilio and Fred read comics.   **3.** Marcos or Jim will eat the leftovers.

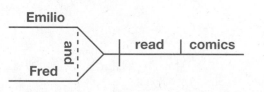

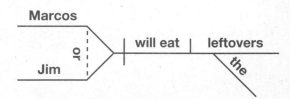

2. Sarah prefers ice cream and cola.   **4.** Alta sits and studies.

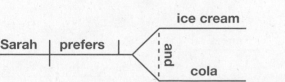

5. Mrs. Welch coaches and plays tennis.

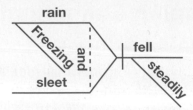

6. Tin whistles and bagpipes make lively music.

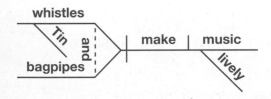

7. Apaches and Navahos inhabited the Southwest.

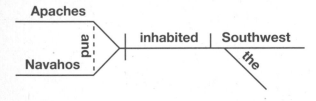

8. Buy or borrow a recorder for class.

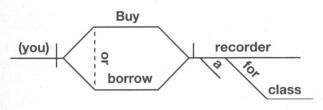

9. A thesaurus and a dictionary are necessary school resources.

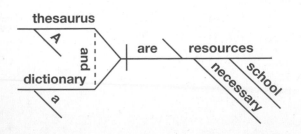

10. Freezing rain and sleet fell steadily.

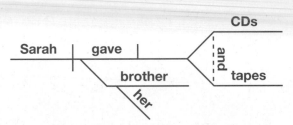

11. Sarah gave her brother CDs and tapes.

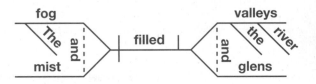

12. The fog and mist filled the river valleys and glens.

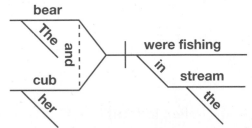

13. The bear and her cub were fishing in the stream.

14. Eagles and hawks are extremely sharp-eyed hunters.

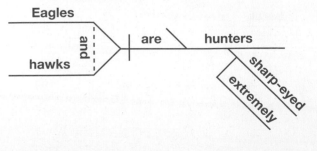

Grammar

Lesson 61
Diagraming Compound Sentences

Diagram each main clause of a compound sentence separately. Use a vertical dotted line to connect the verbs of each clause if the main clauses are connected by a semicolon. If the main clauses are connected by a conjunction such as *and,* *but,* or *or,* place the conjunction on a solid horizontal line connected to the verb of each clause by a vertical dotted line.

Robins sing in the morning, but you can hear owls at night.

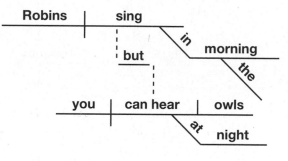

Dolphins leaped along the bow of the ship; seagulls circled overhead.

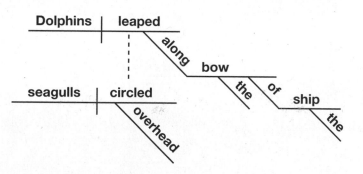

▶ **Exercise 1 Diagram the following sentences.**

1. The horses pulled the plow, and the farmer followed the horses.

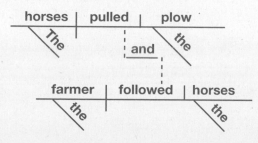

2. We crossed the bridge, and then we entered the city.

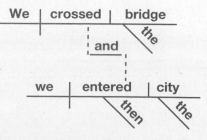

Grammar

3. You must find the papers; then take them to the teacher.

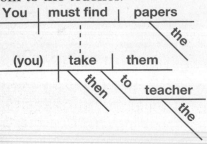

7. Ramon enjoys the city, but he lives in the country.

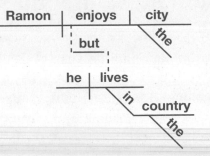

4. I would rather eat pizza for lunch, or maybe we can eat hamburgers.

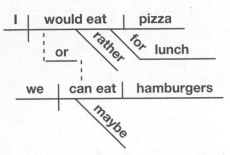

8. Hiroshi is the drummer, and Sandy is the guitarist.

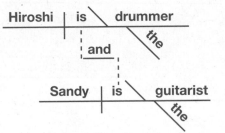

5. Elizabeth painted the picture, but she did not frame it.

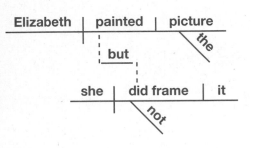

9. Did you watch television last night, or did you read?

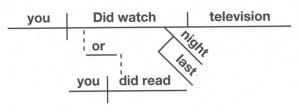

6. Wild European rabbits live in large warrens; other rabbits live individually.

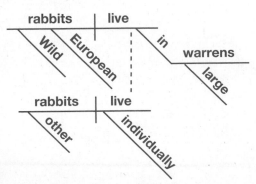

10. Listen to the rain; it falls steadily.

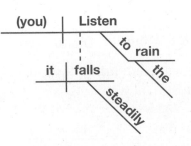

Lesson 62
Diagraming Complex Sentences with Adjective and Adverb Clauses

Diagram a complex sentence with an adjective or adverb clause by placing the adjective or adverb clause below the main clause.

Draw a dotted line between the relative pronoun that introduces the adjective clause and the noun or pronoun it modifies in the main clause. Then diagram the relative pronoun according to its function in its own clause.

Draw a dotted line between the verb in the adverb clause and the verb, adjective, or adverb it modifies in the main clause. Write the subordinating conjunction on the dotted line connecting the verb to the word it modifies.

You can find people everywhere who are interested in soccer.

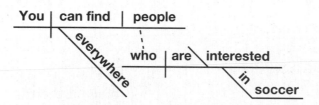

Because she worked quickly, Paula finished first.

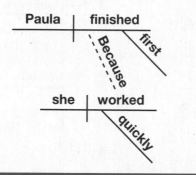

▶ **Exercise 1 Diagram the following sentences.**

1. He recognized the grizzly bear that stood upright.

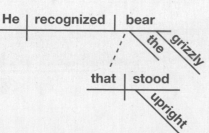

2. She sneezed when she had a cold.

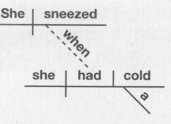

Grammar

3. The soldiers uncovered a cargo plane that had huge propellers.

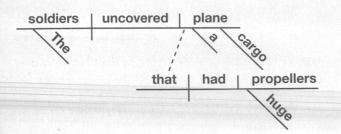

4. It was the Pooles who lost their canary.

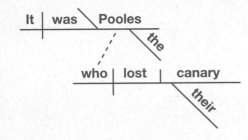

5. The town, which has a fine history museum, is picturesque.

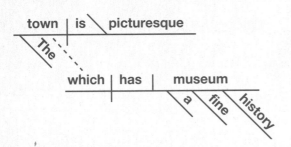

6. Wherever they searched in the woods, mushrooms were common.

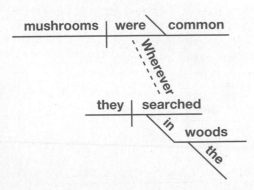

7. While other predators have lived on Earth, the Tyrannosaurus rex outranks all of them.

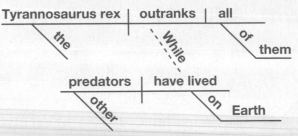

8. King Kong had forearms that were eight feet in length.

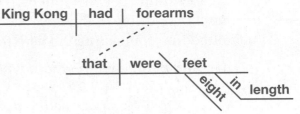

9. The Pima were powerful warriors who protected their farms from Apache raiders.

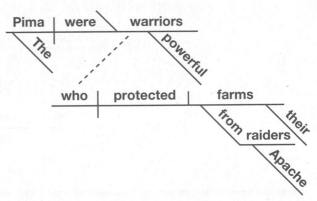

10. Though Susan had many bracelets, one with her initials was her favorite.

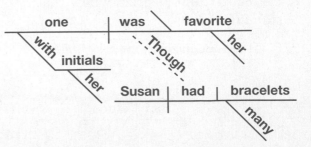

✓ Unit 10 **Review**

▶ **Exercise 1 Diagram the following sentences.**

1. The white blood cells in your blood fight infection.

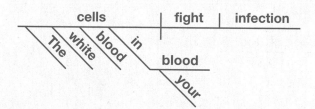

2. The Notre Dame sports teams are called the Fighting Irish.

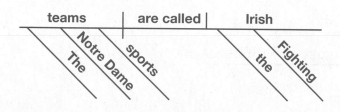

3. Mini caught the baseball.

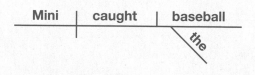

4. The infant cried because he was hungry.

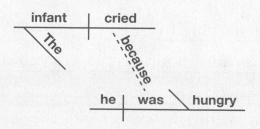

5. Vito accidentally ate some bad meat, but he did not become ill.

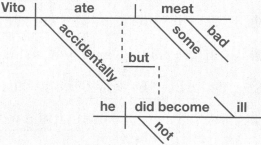

6. I had a backache and stomach cramps yesterday.

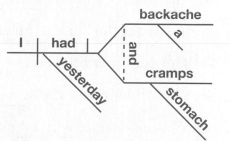

7. That actor has played the noble hero and the evil villain.

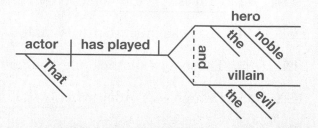

8. The movie that we saw received great reviews.

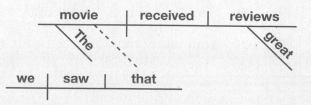

Grammar

Cumulative Review Units 1–10

▶ **Exercise 1** Underline each adverb and adjective clause in the following sentences. Write *adj.* (adjective) or *adv.* (adverb) in the blank to identify the clause.

adj.   Are these the baseball cards that you bought?

adj. 1. Samantha tells stories that astound us.

adj. 2. The book that is on the table is not mine.

adj. 3. We called Kevin, whose bike had been stolen.

adv. 4. After I buy the CD, I will call you.

adj. 5. This coat is one that she will like.

adv. 6. Cal was sad when he heard the news.

adj. 7. The teacher who knew the subject gave the lecture.

adj. 8. It was not the job that I had wanted.

adv. 9. The dog buried the bone where no one could find it.

adv. 10. We will help you if you will let us.

adj. 11. Your model car, which I put on your desk, needs polishing.

adv. 12. Juan wore the jacket, although he didn't like it.

adv. 13. Unless it is too late, we will call her.

adj. 14. The lilac bush that we planted is blooming already.

adj. 15. Those new clothes that you bought are fantastic.

adv. 16. I watch this video whenever I have time.

adj. 17. This is the teacher whom you requested.

adv. 18. Wherever they are, they are late.

adv. 19. She did not believe me until you told her the story, too.

adv. 20. Your show remains on the air while my favorite program has been cancelled.

▶ **Exercise 2** Underline each participle or participial phrase, gerund or gerund phrase, and infinitive or infinitive phrase. Then write the type of word or phrase in the blank.

_____gerund_____	Sherry loves painting.
_____participle_____	1. Our team is a winning team.
_____gerund phrase_____	2. Holding a grudge does one no good.
_____gerund_____	3. Running is Carla's favorite sport.
_____gerund phrase_____	4. Mr. Smith says he dreads public speaking.
_____gerund phrase_____	5. Learning a foreign language is hard work.
_____infinitive_____	6. Our team must practice more often if they want to win.
_____gerund phrase_____	7. I like eating hamburgers and salad.
_____infinitive phrase_____	8. We hope to have a better team next year.
_____gerund phrase_____	9. I prefer walking home from school.
_____participial phrase_____	10. Recognizing the importance of the test, we studied hard.
_____gerund phrase_____	11. Having all these household chores keeps me busy.
_____infinitive phrase_____	12. When is the best time to call them?
_____participial phrase_____	13. Laughing loudly, he walked into the class.
_____gerund phrase_____	14. I think cleaning the patio is an easy job.
_____gerund phrase_____	15. Your story has a new beginning.
_____gerund phrase_____	16. Discovering the solution to a problem is great fun.
_____participle_____	17. My dog is a trusted pet.
_____participle_____	18. Is that a real wishing well?
_____participial phrase_____	19. The radio, tuned to my favorite station, was bothering my mother.
_____infinitive phrases_____	20. You have to work hard to succeed.

Grammar

► **Exercise 3** Underline each preposition or prepositional phrase, and circle each conjunction.

The ball is <u>in the drawer</u> (or) <u>on the desk</u>.

1. Jerry (and) Hector like to go <u>to town</u>.

2. Why did the Bears try <u>for two points</u>?

3. They listened <u>to the advice</u>.

4. Did you hear <u>about the accident</u>?

5. The cat came <u>from the door</u> (and) <u>into the kitchen</u>.

6. You left the lawn mower <u>under the tree</u>.

7. Thunder comes <u>before rain</u> (and) <u>after lightning</u>.

8. I like boats (and) ships.

9. (Until) she comes, let's go <u>into the arcade</u>.

10. <u>For your dessert</u>, would you prefer ice cream (or) sherbet?

11. The puppy ran <u>into the living room</u>.

12. We were tired (but) happy.

13. <u>After the game</u>, we went <u>to the restaurant</u> (and) mall.

14. Class ended, (but) I was not finished.

15. They feared the threat <u>of rain</u>.

16. It happened <u>around noon</u>.

17. Maria came home <u>with a new coat</u> (and) a book bag.

18. The wind beat heavily <u>against the window</u>.

19. I like that movie <u>with the fast action</u> (and) car chases.

20. Yolanda dives gracefully <u>off the high board</u>.

*U*sage

Unit 11: Usage Glossary

Lesson 63
Usage: *accept* to *a lot*

Words that are similar are sometimes misused.

accept, **except** *Accept* means "to receive." *Except* means "other than."

I **accept** your apology.   Everyone is here **except** Lisa.

all ready, **already** *All read*y means "completely prepared." *Already* means "before" or "by this time."

I am **all ready** for the exam.   They had **already** eaten.

all together, **altogether** *All together* means "in a group." *Altogether* means "completely" or "entirely."

The puppies sleep **all together** in the box.   You are **altogether** too modest.

a lot *A lot* means "very much." It is always two words. Because its meaning is vague, it is more acceptable to use *many* or *much* or to give a specific amount.

Our library has **a lot** of books. (vague)
Our library has more than five thousand books. (clear)

▶ **Exercise 1** **Underline the word or words in parentheses that best complete each sentence.**

I met everyone (accept, <u>except</u>) Suki at the game.

1. I (all ready, <u>already</u>) saw this movie.

2. Mother did not (<u>accept</u>, except) my explanation for being late.

3. Can we travel (<u>all together</u>, altogether) in one car?

4. The noisy television was (all together, <u>altogether</u>) too distracting.

5. I like all vegetables (accept, <u>except</u>) cabbage.

6. Cory completed all the items on the test (accept, <u>except</u>) the last one.

7. The mail carrier asked if we would (<u>accept</u>, except) the package.

8. The radios are piled (<u>all together</u>, altogether) in the storeroom.

Usage

9. (A lot of, Many) people came to the memorial service.

10. I don't (all together, altogether) trust this skateboard!

11. She can carry everything (accept, except) the tent.

12. The lead runner has (all ready, already) completed the race.

13. There was no sound (accept, except) the twitter of a bird.

14. Did she (accept, except) his invitation to the party?

15. Call me when everyone is (all ready, already) to go.

▶ **Exercise 2** Write in the blank the correct form of the italicized word or words. If the italicized word or words are correct, write *C* in the blank.

already	Has her brother *all ready* passed the math exam?
altogether	**1.** This test is *all together* too hard.
except	**2.** I have written thank-you notes to everyone *accept* Grandma.
already	**3.** You should have received an answer *all ready*.
_C_	**4.** We will jump out *all together* and yell "Surprise!"
all ready	**5.** The house is *already* for them to move in.
many	**6.** We have *a lot of* flowers in our yard.
altogether	**7.** I am *all together* exhausted!
except	**8.** He has cleaned all the rooms *accept* his bedroom.
_C_	**9.** After our pranks, Uncle Max was *altogether* disgusted with us.
much	**10.** I have *a lot of* confidence in you.
all together	**11.** The mother wolf tried to keep her pups *altogether* for safety.
already	**12.** I thought you had visited Mammoth Cave *all ready*.
_C_	**13.** I can find all the constellations *except* Cassiopeia.
_C_	**14.** The astronaut will *accept* the keys to the city.
all ready	**15.** The class is *already* for winter vacation.
accept	**16.** Will they *except* a check at that store?
_C_	**17.** Keep the children *all together* until they have crossed the street.
except	**18.** All the Smiths can swim *accept* Jean.

Lesson 64
Usage: *beside* to *chose*

---

beside, besides *Beside* means "next to." *Besides* means "in addition to."

My shoes are **beside** my bed.   **Besides** music, I love astronomy.

between, among Use *between* for two things or people. Use *among* for three or more things or people.

The treaty was made **between** the United States and France.
The six new students discussed the schedule **among** themselves.

bring, take *Bring* means "to carry from a distant place to a closer one." *Take* means "to carry from a nearby place to a more distant one."

Please **bring** me the paper.   Ivan **takes** his suits to the cleaners.

choose, chose *Choose* means "to select." *Chose* is the past tense of *choose.*

I usually **choose** mystery novels.   Yesterday I **chose** a biography.

▶ **Exercise 1** **Underline the word in parentheses that best completes each sentence.**

Please (bring, <u>take</u>) this briefcase to your mother.

1. There is no difference in price (between, <u>among</u>) these four jackets.

2. This suitcase is too heavy, so I will not (bring, <u>take</u>) it on the trip.

3. Our dog sleeps (<u>beside</u>, besides) the radiator after its bath.

4. Can you (bring, <u>take</u>) me to school if I miss the bus?

5. This will be a secret (<u>between</u>, among) you and me.

6. The paper (choose, <u>chose</u>) to run a front-page story about yesterday's fire.

7. She speaks many languages (beside, <u>besides</u>) English.

8. I will (<u>bring</u>, take) my gym clothes when I come home from school today.

9. The championship game is (<u>between</u>, among) the Falcons and the Tigers.

10. He doesn't want to (<u>choose</u>, chose) between pizza and fried chicken.

11. We plant our vegetables in rows (<u>beside</u>, besides) the garage.

12. Will you (<u>bring</u>, take) me a souvenir from your trip?

13. I have to (<u>choose</u>, chose) an outfit to wear to the party.

14. (Beside, <u>Besides</u>) the orchestra, Ms. Roberts also conducts the band.

15. (Bring, <u>Take</u>) the dog for a walk before you study.

▶ **Exercise 2 Write in the blank the correct form of each italicized word. If the italicized word is correct, write *C* in the blank.**

besides	Many birds *beside* cardinals visit my bird feeder.
C	**1.** Did you *take* the lawn mower back to the Thayers?
chose	**2.** I *choose* to take an art course at the museum last summer.
between	**3.** Kenji doesn't see the difference *among* the two computers.
among	**4.** Distribute these questionnaires *between* audience members.
C	**5.** Where is the dictionary that belongs *beside* the chair?
bring	**6.** We should *take* the geraniums inside before the first frost.
choose	**7.** I must *chose* a topic for my report.
among	**8.** There was much movement *between* the many horses in the corral.
Besides	**9.** *Beside* Hans, whom else did you see at the game?
between	**10.** Just *among* you and me, who do you think will win tonight?
beside	**11.** Is the library the building *besides* the arcade?
take	**12.** Will you come with me to *bring* the cat to the vet?
among	**13.** There was constant singing *between* all the birds in our yard.
chose	**14.** Last night Sal *choose* to study at the library instead of at home.
C	**15.** Let's *take* our recent photographs when we visit Grandpa.

▶ **Writing Link Write two or three sentences about a choice you've made. Use *choose* and *chose* at least once.**

_____

_____

_____

_____

Lesson 65
Usage: *in* to *teach*

in, into *In* means "inside." *Into* indicates an action toward the inside.

Bears live **in** a den.   He chased the calves **into** the barn.

its, it's *Its* is the possessive form of *it*. *It's* is the contraction of *it is*.

The cat licked **its** fur.   **It's** time to watch the news.

lay, lie *Lay* means "to put" or "to place." *Lie* means "to recline" or "to be positioned."

Lay the tomatoes in the sun to ripen.   My dog likes to **lie** in the sun.

learn, teach *Learn* means "to receive knowledge." *Teach* means "to give knowledge."

Tricia **learns** about astronomy.   Mr. Bonilla **teaches** English to foreign students.

▶ **Exercise 1** Underline the word in parentheses that best completes each sentence.

Don't (lay, <u>lie</u>) on the grass in your good clothes.

1. Can you (learn, <u>teach</u>) me how to program the VCR?

2. I will (<u>lay</u>, lie) newspapers on the floor before I paint.

3. Rex is (<u>in</u>, into) his doghouse.

4. The squirrel is burying many of (<u>its</u>, it's) nuts.

5. Does your town (lay, <u>lie</u>) north or south of the river?

6. I hope (its, <u>it's</u>) not too late for supper.

7. Reiko has difficulty getting (in, <u>into</u>) the car because of the cast on her leg.

8. Frank hopes to (<u>learn</u>, teach) Spanish before he visits Mexico.

9. The builder (<u>lays</u>, lies) down a foundation of concrete blocks.

10. If there is not enough helium (<u>in</u>, into) the balloon, it will sink.

11. Diego hopes to (learn, <u>teach</u>) his brother to swim.

12. (Its, <u>It's</u>) hard to watch the game from the top rows of the stadium.

13. The valley (lays, <u>lies</u>) between two mountain ranges.

Usage

14. Will the sandbags keep the river water from rushing (in, <u>into</u>) the houses?

15. Irene is trying to (learn, <u>teach</u>) her baby sister to tie her shoes.

16. The magazine changed (<u>its</u>, it's) cover logo.

17. (<u>Lay</u>, Lie) your pencils down when you have finished the test.

18. Did you (<u>learn</u>, teach) your lines for the play yet?

19. The colt stuck (<u>its</u>, it's) head into the bucket of oats.

20. The tent is rolled up (<u>in</u>, into) your backpack.

▶ **Exercise 2** Write in the blank the correct form of each italicized word. If the italicized word is correct, write *C* in the blank.

_____learn_____	The student likes to *teach* about marine life.
_____into_____	**1.** When they saw the tornado, the family rushed *in* the storm cellar.
_____lies_____	**2.** My bedroom *lays* just above the living room.
_____C_____	**3.** Dimas wants to *teach* me how to take pictures.
_____its_____	**4.** The oak tree shed *it's* leaves early this year.
_____in_____	**5.** The cat stayed *into* the closet until the thunder stopped.
_____C_____	**6.** I don't think I'll ever *learn* how to ski!
_____C_____	**7.** Where did you *lay* that report?
_____lie_____	**8.** I think I'll *lay* on the couch for a while.
_____It's_____	**9.** *Its* too bad he can't come to the game.
_____lie_____	**10.** The X-ray technician helped my uncle *lay* down on the table.
_____teach_____	**11.** Where did Mr. Leal *learn* students before he came to our school?
_____in_____	**12.** Stay *into* the house until your fever is gone.
_____C_____	**13.** The quilt lost all *its* color in the sun.
lie *or* lay	**14.** Several strawberry beds *lay* in the back garden.
_____C_____	**15.** I didn't *learn* about World War II until last year.
_____lays_____	**16.** The artist *lies* her paints and brushes on the table.
_____It's_____	**17.** *Its* too late to call them now.
_____C_____	**18.** The car lost two of *its* hubcaps on the long trip.

Copyright © by Glencoe/McGraw-Hill

Usage

Lesson 66
Usage: *leave* to *sit*

---

leave, let *Leave* means "to go away." *Let* means "to allow."

We will **leave** for the game soon.   **Let** me carry that package for you.

loose, lose *Loose* means "not firmly attached." *Lose* means "to misplace" or "to fail to win."

The shutters are **loose**. Do not **lose** the house key.   I hope we don't **lose** the game.

raise, rise *Raise* means "to cause to move upward." *Rise* means "to move upward."

Raise the painting a little higher.   The hot-air balloon began to **rise**.

set, sit *Set* means "to place" or "to put." *Sit* means "to place oneself in a seated position."

Please **set** that package on the floor.   Don't **sit** on the wet paint!

▶ **Exercise 1** Underline the word in parentheses that best completes each sentence.

The director, Mrs. Kwan, (<u>sets</u>, sits) her chair at the front of the stage.

1. "Everyone (set, <u>sit</u>) down so we can read the play," she said.

2. Alma said, "I didn't mean to (loose, <u>lose</u>) my script, but I did."

3. She asked me to (leave, <u>let</u>) her read from my copy.

4. Mrs. Kwan did not (set, <u>sit</u>) quietly as we read.

5. She liked to (raise, <u>rise</u>) often and show us where a piece of furniture would be placed onstage.

6. "Wear old, (<u>loose</u>, lose) clothing for rehearsal, because the stage will be very dusty," she warned us.

7. My character was a young girl who wanted to (<u>leave</u>, let) her small hometown and go to work in a factory.

8. She wanted to (raise, <u>rise</u>) from the position of worker to supervisor of the factory.

9. One of the other characters tried not to (leave, <u>let</u>) her get ahead.

10. The stagehands began to (<u>raise</u>, rise) and lower the various curtains.

11. We laughed to see them (leave, <u>let</u>) one curtain come down right in front of Mrs. Kwan.

12. As opening night approached, Mrs. Kwan told us, "I want you all to work hard on this play, but I don't want you to (loose, <u>lose</u>) sleep over it."

13. I could hardly (set, <u>sit</u>) through dinner on the day our play opened.

14. However, mother would not (leave, <u>let</u>) me go without a good meal.

15. "I didn't (<u>raise</u>, rise) my daughter to be a skinny actress," she joked.

16. Finally she turned me (<u>loose</u>, lose) to hurry to school.

17. When I got to the dressing room, I (<u>set</u>, sat) my makeup on the long table.

18. "I hope my parents didn't (loose, <u>lose</u>) their tickets because of their excitement," said my friend Alma.

19. The intercom in the dressing room was to (leave, <u>let</u>) us hear the sounds from the auditorium.

20. The noise increased as more and more people came in to (set, <u>sit</u>) down.

21. With the noise and excitement, I needed fresh air, so I asked someone to (<u>raise</u>, rise) the window a little.

22. Then, my heart pounded as I watched the huge velvet curtain slowly (raise, <u>rise</u>) for the beginning of the play.

23. The leading character walked onstage to (<u>set</u>, sit) a suitcase on the living room floor.

24. As I waited for my cue, I felt as if there were butterflies (<u>loose</u>, lose) in my stomach.

25. Soon it was time to (<u>raise</u>, rise) the home set and replace it with the factory scenery.

26. As I made my entrance, I did not (leave, <u>let</u>) my nerves distract me.

27. I calmly crossed the stage to (<u>set</u>, sit) down my factory tools and to deliver my first lines.

28. I hoped I would not (loose, <u>lose</u>) my memory and forget what to say.

29. Then I could feel my voice (raise, <u>rise</u>) up clearly into the rafters.

30. The applause at the end of the scene did (leave, <u>let</u>) me know I had done my job well.

Usage

Lesson 67
Usage: *than* to *whose*

than, then *Than* introduces the second part of a comparison. *Then* means "at that time."

I am taller **than** my friend.   We'll see you **then**.

their, they're *Their* is the possessive form of *they*. *They're* is the contraction of *they are*.

This is **their** home.   **They're** leaving on vacation.

whose, who's *Whose* is the possessive form of *who*. *Who's* is the contraction of *who is*.

Whose striped sock is this?   **Who's** knocking on the door?

▶ **Exercise 1 Underline the word in parentheses that best completes each sentence.**

I introduced myself to the twins, and (than, <u>then</u>) we became friends.

1. Jamil and Kwasi are twins (who's, <u>whose</u>) family emigrated from Nigeria.

2. (Their, <u>They're</u>) both in my class, although I know Jamil better than Kwasi.

3. Jamil likes to joke that he's older (<u>than</u>, then) Kwasi by three minutes.

4. When they play "(<u>Who's</u>, Whose) Who?" we have to be really quick to guess.

5. Although (<u>their</u>, they're) looks seem identical, there are small differences.

6. Jamil has slightly larger ears (<u>than</u>, then) his brother has.

7. Kwasi is the one (who's, <u>whose</u>) arms are longer.

8. If they look so much alike, (than, <u>then</u>) what are we supposed to do?

9. The boys agreed to wear (<u>their</u>, they're) hair in different styles.

10. On some days (their, <u>they're</u>) also dressed differently.

11. Both boys play sports, and sometimes (<u>their</u>, they're) coaches can't tell them apart.

12. Kwasi plays soccer, while Jamil is the one (<u>who's</u>, whose) a terrific runner.

13. Jamil runs faster (<u>than</u>, then) anyone else in our school.

14. You will never guess (who's, <u>whose</u>) record he broke when he ran the 200-meter dash.

15. Even though he's faster (<u>than</u>, then) I am, we are still good friends.

▶ **Exercise 2** Write in the blank the correct form of each italicized word. If the italicized word is correct, write *C* in the blank.

_____**Who's**_____ *Whose* from a family that has twins?

_____**C**_____ **1.** Twins *whose* genes are the same are called identical twins.

_____**They're**_____ **2.** *Their* so much alike that it is hard to tell them apart.

_____**than**_____ **3.** Fraternal twins, as far as genes are concerned, are no more alike *then* siblings.

_____**C**_____ **4.** With fraternal twins, a mother can give birth to a boy and *then* three minutes later give birth to a girl.

_____**than**_____ **5.** Twins—especially identical twins—tend to share a much closer bond *then* other siblings do.

_____**C**_____ **6.** Often when twins are very young, they invent *their* own language to use with each other.

_____**they're**_____ **7.** Since no one else can understand what *their* saying, this adds to feelings of closeness.

_____**whose**_____ **8.** Researchers study twins *who's* lives have been very different due to separation at birth.

_____**than**_____ **9.** Similarities between identical twins raised apart are more *then* amazing.

_____**Their**_____ **10.** *They're* personalities, intelligence, habits, hobbies, tastes, likes, and dislikes are often the same despite different upbringings.

_____**who's**_____ **11.** Twins across the country feel a special bond and form clubs to keep in touch with *whose* doing what.

_____**C**_____ **12.** *Then,* every year they get together in Twinsburg, Ohio, for the annual Twins Day Festival.

✓ Unit 11 **Review**

▶ **Exercise 1** Underline the word or words in parentheses that best complete each sentence.

Let's go out and (lay, <u>lie</u>) in the sun.

1. Will you (bring, <u>take</u>) the life preserver over to the other side of the boat?

2. I like to sing (<u>in</u>, into) the shower.

3. (Beside, <u>Besides</u>) the championship, which other games have you attended?

4. The principal and the teacher spoke quietly (<u>between</u>, among) themselves outside the classroom door.

5. Joker pulled (<u>loose</u>, lose) from his leash, but I caught him when he stopped to pick up a stick.

6. There is a shopping mall so large that (its, <u>it's</u>) spread out over several acres.

7. The children watched as the huge, brightly colored balloon began to (raise, <u>rise</u>) into the air.

8. I doubt that anyone can (learn, <u>teach</u>) me to roller skate!

9. It's time to (leave, <u>let</u>) Joshua cross the street by himself.

10. I need some room to (<u>lay</u>, lie) out my science project.

11. Those people think (their, <u>they're</u>) the only citizens who have concerns.

12. Mother and Father will (set, <u>sit</u>) at the head of the table.

13. I thought the Sammons were coming (<u>all together</u>, altogether) in the same car.

14. I'm glad that yesterday I (choose, <u>chose</u>) Sal as my reading partner.

15. We can carry all the suitcases (accept, <u>except</u>) that large blue one.

16. The black car has more rust (<u>than</u>, then) the green one.

17. (<u>Who's</u>, Whose) the captain of this team?

18. The dog chased the cat (in, <u>into</u>) the shed.

19. Please feel free to (<u>bring</u>, take) your grandmother to our gathering.

20. I have (all ready, <u>already</u>) seen that movie.

Usage

Cumulative Review: Units 1–11

▶ **Exercise 1** Draw a line under each prepositional phrase. Draw a second line under each preposition. Then, circle each object of a preposition.

Take the pie from the (oven) and set it on the pie (rack).

1. The river flowed beneath the (bridge) and then into a (reservoir).

2. In front of that famous (painting) stood people in huge (groups).

3. The dog ran among the (sheep) to force them inside the (enclosure).

4. Aside from (Marcy), no one wants any of the (pie).

5. Our car slid on the (ice) and bounced off the (curb).

6. You have been a good friend throughout this long (crisis).

7. Write to the (publisher) and ask for more (information).

8. The birds quickly flew away from the (cat).

9. All of (us) will help the senior citizens with their grocery (carts).

10. The emergency van drove around (town) warning people of the (hurricane).

11. Stand in front of (me) and you will see better.

12. Jackie's cat sleeps on that (rug).

13. The wildebeests plunged into the (river) and swam across (it).

14. I can't imagine our school without (you).

15. There is a stack of old (papers) on top of the (refrigerator).

16. I think the couch will look better across from the (fireplace).

17. Julene carefully climbed up that (ladder).

18. The ice chunks slid off the (roof).

19. The captain of the tennis (team) practiced for the upcoming (match) against the best (team) in the (league).

20. The *Voyager* spacecraft will eventually travel beyond the solar (system).

Usage

▶ **Exercise 2** **Draw one line under each noun or pronoun and two lines under each verb.**

Sedimentary <u>rock</u> usually <u><u>contains</u></u> many <u>fossils</u>.

1. <u>We</u> <u><u>will have exercised</u></u> for two <u>hours</u> by the <u>time</u> the <u>class</u> <u><u>ends</u></u>.

2. <u>Mother</u> <u><u>says</u></u> <u>Rex</u> <u><u>is</u></u> a pure <u>collie</u>, but <u>I</u> <u><u>am</u></u> sure <u>he</u> <u><u>is</u></u> just a <u>mutt</u>.

3. <u><u>Do</u></u> <u>you</u> <u><u>think</u></u> a <u>pair</u> of <u>earmuffs</u> <u><u>will make</u></u> a good <u>gift</u> for <u>her</u>?

4. The <u>detective</u> <u><u>questioned</u></u> the <u>suspect</u> but <u><u>did</u></u> not <u><u>get</u></u> a <u>confession</u>.

5. This <u>food</u> <u><u>is</u></u> too spicy for <u>me</u>.

6. <u>George</u>, <u>John</u>, and <u>Helen</u> <u><u>gave</u></u> <u>their</u> <u>mother</u> a <u>ride</u> on the <u>tractor</u>.

7. The <u>weeds</u> <u><u>fill</u></u> more <u>space</u> in <u>my</u> <u>garden</u> than the <u>flowers</u>.

8. Please, <u><u>do</u></u> not <u><u>set</u></u> <u>those</u> on the <u>stereo</u>.

9. The <u>kite</u> <u><u>has</u></u> red <u>stripes</u> and <u><u>is</u></u> visible for <u>miles</u>.

10. <u>We</u> <u><u>sat</u></u> for <u>hours</u> in the traffic <u>jam</u>.

11. <u>I</u> <u><u>prefer</u></u> orange <u>juice</u> to that <u>kind</u> of <u>soda</u>.

12. The two <u>teams</u> <u><u>ran</u></u> out on the <u>field</u> while <u>their</u> respective <u>fans</u> <u><u>cheered</u></u> <u>them</u>.

13. <u>They</u> <u><u>will conduct</u></u> <u>tours</u> through that old <u>steamship</u> down at the <u>riverfront</u>.

14. The <u>runner</u> <u><u>took</u></u> a wrong <u>turn</u>, but <u>she</u> <u><u>won</u></u> the <u>race</u> anyway.

15. The <u>colt</u> <u><u>pranced</u></u> across the <u>field</u> to <u>his</u> <u>mother</u>.

16. When the <u>lights</u> <u><u>flickered</u></u>, <u>we</u> <u><u>lit</u></u> the <u>candles</u>.

17. A loud <u>sound</u> <u><u>signaled</u></u> that <u>we</u> <u><u>were nearing</u></u> the <u>ocean</u>.

18. When the <u>plane</u> <u><u>landed</u></u> safely, <u>everyone</u> <u><u>breathed</u></u> easily again.

19. When the <u>ice</u> <u><u>broke</u></u> on the <u>river</u>, <u>it</u> <u><u>sounded</u></u> like a <u>gunshot</u>.

20. <u>Leroy</u> <u><u>will present</u></u> <u>his</u> comedy <u>act</u> at the <u>club</u> tonight.

21. <u>We</u> <u><u>had</u></u> already <u><u>sung</u></u> that <u>song</u> when <u>our</u> <u>director</u> <u><u>arrived</u></u>.

22. <u>That</u> <u><u>is</u></u> <u>mine</u>, but <u>you</u> <u><u>may borrow</u></u> <u>it</u> if <u>you</u> <u><u>wish</u></u>.

23. <u><u>Do</u></u> <u>you</u> <u><u>know</u></u> <u>who</u> <u><u>is entering</u></u> the writing <u>contest</u>?

24. To <u>whom</u> <u><u>are</u></u> <u>you</u> <u><u>giving</u></u> <u>your</u> <u>CD</u>?

▶ **Exercise 3** Underline the word or words in parentheses that best complete each sentence.

I keep my telescope (<u>beside</u>, besides) my bed.

1. Tomorrow we will (<u>choose</u>, chose) players for our team.

2. I thought the mayor's response was (all together, <u>altogether</u>) appropriate.

3. Can you (bring, <u>take</u>) Reiko to school before you go to work?

4. The police did not (<u>accept</u>, except) the suspect's alibi.

5. The majorettes waited (<u>beside</u>, besides) the grandstand.

6. Mario put the boxes (in, <u>into</u>) the car trunk.

7. Those dogs seem to think (their, <u>they're</u>) the kings of the neighborhood!

8. Should I (leave, <u>let</u>) Lenny have a snack before supper?

9. Don't (<u>set</u>, sit) that dish on the newly polished surface!

10. This poor bicycle is on (<u>its</u>, it's) last legs.

11. Guess (<u>who's</u>, whose) the new basketball coach at school!

12. I want to (<u>learn</u>, teach) about alligators and crocodiles on our trip to Florida.

13. Ted tried to (<u>raise</u>, rise) the blind slowly so the sun would not hurt his eyes.

14. If we (loose, <u>lose</u>) the game tonight, everyone will be very disappointed.

15. If you'll be around after the dance, we'll see you (than, <u>then</u>).

16. When I (lay, <u>lie</u>) flat on a rock, I feel like a desert snake.

17. The license plate has come (<u>loose</u>, lose) from the car.

18. This act will (<u>bring</u>, take) the show to a close.

19. The teacher gathered us (<u>all together</u>, altogether) to tell us about the award.

20. (Beside, <u>Besides</u>) collecting newspapers, our class recycles plastic and cans.

Mechanics

Unit 12: Capitalization

Lesson 68

Capitalization of Sentences, Quotations, and Salutations

Capitalize the first word of a sentence, including the first word of a direct quotation that is a complete sentence.

An apple a day keeps the doctor away.
Ricardo said, "**H**istory is my favorite subject."

Do not capitalize an indirect quotation. An **indirect quotation** does not repeat the speaker's exact words, nor does it appear in quotation marks. Often, the word *that* introduces an indirect quotation.

Ricardo said that **h**istory is his favorite subject.

When a quoted sentence is interrupted by an explanatory phrase such as *he said*, do not capitalize the second part of the sentence. Always capitalize the pronoun *I*.

"This music," said Diana, "**i**s wonderful."
"If the phone rings," he said, "**I**'ll answer it."

If a new sentence begins the second part of a quotation, put a period after the explanatory phrase and capitalize the second part.

"I like this show," said Marcus. "**I**t's funny."

Capitalize the first word in the salutation of a letter and the title and name of the person being addressed. Capitalize a title used in place of a name.

Dear Mr. Trinh: **T**o whom this may concern: **D**earest **C**arolyn,   **D**ear **S**ir:

Capitalize the first word in the closing of a letter.

Sincerely yours,   **Y**ours truly,

▶ **Exercise 1 Underline the correct letter in parentheses.**

(J̲, j)amaal said, "(T̲, t)his is my favorite food."

1. (M̲, m)om wanted me to tell you that (Y, y̲)ou should be home before dinner.

2. Keshia said, "(I̲, i)'ll call you later."

3. (C̲, c)ordially (Y, y̲)ours,

4. "(T̲, t)oday," said our teacher, "(I, i̲)s the first day of the science fair."

Mechanics

5. "(R, r)ead this," said Rafi. "(I, i)t's very funny."

6. (V, v)ery (T, t)ruly (Y, y)ours,

7. "(M, m)ost of the time I just read," said Jim.

8. (T, t)he principal asked, "(W, w)here were you yesterday?"

9. (M, m)y computer does not work correctly.

10. (D, d)ear (M, m)adame:

11. Carlos said that (H, h)e was expecting a good grade on the test.

12. Sunee said, "(I, i) wish I could have seen the play."

13. "(T, t)his is the right answer," said Dan.

14. (W, w)ith (B, b)est (W, w)ishes,

15. "(C, c)het," said Mali, "(I, i)s going to tutor me in math."

16. "Nina wrote this," said the teacher. "(S, s)he wants to read it to the class."

17. "(I, i)f you understand division," said Poloma, "(F, f)ractions won't be very hard."

18. Catalina said that (T, t)his was the last bag of cookies.

19. (D, d)ear (C, c)ustomer:

20. (H, h)e told me that (H, h)e ran all the way home.

21. "(D, d)id she see it?" asked Alicia. "(I, i) know she likes comedies."

22. "Honolulu," said Kenji, "(I, i)s a beautiful city."

23. "(W, w)ell," exclaimed Alicia, "(T, t)hat should do it!"

24. (D, d)ear (M, m)iss Sharvy:

25. Geoff said that (T, t)he water was too cold for swimming.

26. "(I, i) can't wait," said Nguyen. "(I, i)'m hungry now."

27. Cecilia said, "(D, d)on't wait for me. I'll join you later."

28. (M, m)ost of the students said they (F, f)inished their reports in less than a week.

29. "(C, c)all me," she said, "(W, w)hen you're ready to leave."

30. (Y, y)our (F, f)riend,

31. Luis said that (T, t)he other team had a better record.

32. Bonita asked, "(H, h)as anyone seen my book?"

Lesson 69

Capitalization of Names and Titles of Persons

Capitalize a person's name and initials.

Paul **R**evere   **S**usan **S**t. James   John **F**. **K**ennedy   **F.D.R.**

Capitalize a title or an abbreviation of a title that comes before a person's name or that is used in direct address.

Sen. Mike Gravel   **M**r. Schmidt   **S**gt. York   **D**r. Gibson   **G**overnor Brown
Then **C**orporal Salazar said, "Here's the report, **C**olonel."

Do not capitalize a title that follows a person's name.

Dukakis, the former **g**overnor of Massachusetts, ran with Bentsen, the former **s**enator from Texas.

Capitalize names and abbreviations of academic degrees that follow a person's name. Also capitalize *Jr.* or *Sr.* when it follows a name.

Mary Pulaski, **M.D.**   Jacques Burton, **A**ttorney at **L**aw   Alan Karlin, **Ph.D.**
Ramon Delgado **Jr.**

Capitalize words that show family relationships when they are used as titles or substitutes for a person's name.

Is **A**unt Winona visiting this week?   Next month, **F**ather will install a dishwasher.

Do not capitalize words that show family relationships when they follow a possessive noun, a possessive pronoun, or an article.

My **u**ncle is a veterinarian.   She became an **a**unt when her **s**ister had a baby.

Always capitalize the pronoun I.

This is one class **I** think **I** am going to like.

▶ **Exercise 1 Underline the correct letter in parentheses.**

Please come bowling with me and my (U, <u>u</u>)ncle.

1. (<u>M</u>, m)r. and (<u>M</u>, m)rs. (<u>N</u>, n)elson (<u>B</u>, b)urton enjoy the sport of (B, <u>b</u>)owling.

2. Bowling is popular with the entire (<u>B</u>, b)urton (F, <u>f</u>)amily.

3. Nelson (<u>B</u>, b)urton (<u>S</u>, s)r. was a champion during the sport's "golden age."

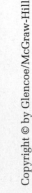

4. His (S, s)on, (N, n)elson (J, j)r., has an instructional segment on a network sports show.

5. The (W, w)ebers of St. Louis are also famous bowlers.

6. (P, p)ete (W, w)eber (S, s)r. is a champion bowler and author.

7. (M, m)r. (W, w)eber wrote a book about bowling that featured his (S, s)on and (D, d)aughter.

8. The bowler's (S, s)on, (P, p)ete (W, w)eber (J, j)r., is also a champion bowler.

9. Sometimes (C, c)ousin (B, b)ob, who is an excellent bowler, considers becoming a professional bowler.

10. His (M, m)other and (F, f)ather do not encourage him, however.

11. Although bowling can be fun, (I, i) prefer to watch football.

12. (W, w)alter (C, c)amp, a football player for Yale University, helped to modernize football.

13. In 1905 (P, p)resident (T, t)heodore (R, r)oosevelt called for changes in the rules of football to make the game safer.

14. Football was a popular sport with (J, j)ohn (F, f). (K, k)ennedy.

15. On the White House lawn, (P, p)resident (K, k)ennedy would play touch football with his (F, f)amily.

16. Another political figure, (J, j)ack (K, k)emp, has a connection with football.

17. Before being elected to the House of Representatives, (C, c)ongressman (K, k)emp was a professional football player.

18. Another sport (I, i) watch and study is basketball.

19. (J, j)ames (N, n)aismith, (M, m).(D, d)., invented basketball in December 1891.

20. Before (M, m)r. (N, n)aismith became a doctor, he was an instructor at the YMCA Training School in Springfield, Massachusetts.

21. (B, b)ill (B, b)radley, a (S, s)enator from New Jersey, played basketball at Princeton University.

Mechanics

22. Later, (<u>S</u>, s)enator (<u>B</u>, b)radley played professional basketball for the New York Knickerbockers.

23. (<u>J</u>, j)ulius (<u>E</u>, e)rving, one of the most exciting players of the National Basketball Association, was nicknamed (<u>D</u>, d)r. (<u>J</u>, j).

24. (<u>U</u>, u)ncle Brady, my (A, <u>a</u>)unt, and my (F, <u>f</u>)ather once saw him play in Philadelphia.

25. Neither my (B, <u>b</u>)rother nor (<u>I</u>, i) ever saw (<u>D</u>, d)r. (<u>J</u>, j) play.

26. Although (<u>I</u>, i) find football and basketball fun, my (F, <u>f</u>)ather prefers the game of tennis.

27. In 1873 (<u>M</u>, m)ajor (<u>W</u>, w)alter (<u>C</u>, c)lopton (<u>W</u>, w)ingfield modified indoor court tennis and invented a new game.

28. The game (<u>M</u>, m)ajor (<u>W</u>, w)ingfield came up with was called lawn tennis.

29. Some people argue that (<u>M</u>, m)ajor (<u>H</u>, h)arry (<u>G</u>, g)em of England, who played a form of tennis in the 1860s, should share the credit for founding the sport with (<u>W</u>, w)ingfield.

30. (<u>M</u>, m)ary (<u>E</u>, e)wing (<u>O</u>, o)uterbridge introduced lawn tennis to the United States in 1874.

▶ **Exercise 2 Draw three lines under each letter that should be capitalized.**

A few years ago uncle claudio played baseball for the Detroit Tigers.

1. Another Tiger player was the legendary ty cobb.

2. One good baseball movie starred geena davis and tom hanks.

3. Another baseball movie, *The Natural*, starred robert redford.

4. ernest lawrence thayer wrote a poem about baseball in 1901 called "Casey at the Bat."

5. In 1908, jack norworth wrote the words to the popular song called "Take Me Out to the Ball Game."

6. When aryn's uncle took us to a major league game, I can remember hearing the familiar organ music.

7. uncle scott and his friend, dr. keller, bought us hot dogs and peanuts for a snack.

8. In 1839 abner doubleday established ground rules for the game.

Mechanics

9. Various forms of baseball were played before mr. doubleday's efforts.

10. In 1876 william a. hulbert headed a committee that founded the National League of Professional Baseball Clubs.

11. Baseball's first commissioner was kenesaw mountain landis.

12. Mr. landis, who was also a judge, was appointed to this position in 1921.

13. To ensure an honest sport, landis enforced a strict ethical code for baseball players.

14. In 1944 judge landis passed away.

15. He was succeeded by albert chandler.

16. In 1965 william eckert became the commissioner.

17. Commissioner eckert was a retired general.

18. Bowie kuhn replaced general eckert in 1969.

19. One of baseball's most famous players is george herman "Babe" ruth.

20. Babe ruth hit 714 home runs during his career.

21. ruth's record was broken on April 8, 1974, by henry louis "Hank" Aaron.

22. hank aaron hit 755 home runs during his career.

23. Another famous player was jack roosevelt "Jackie" robinson.

24. In 1947 mr. robinson became the first African American to play in the big leagues.

25. My grandfather remembers watching mickey mantle.

26. In 1985 mickey charles mantle published his autobiography, *The Mick*.

27. I asked grandma Joyce about the time she met willie mays.

28. He hit 660 home runs, grandma told me, and was one of the most exciting baseball players in history.

29. Another great baseball player was roberto walker clemente from Puerto Rico.

30. In 1995 cal ripken jr. broke lou gehrig's record for consecutive games played.

Mechanics

Lesson 70
Capitalization of Names of Places

Capitalize the names of specific places because they are proper nouns. However, do not capitalize articles and prepositions that are part of these places. Capitalize the names of cities, counties, states, countries, regions, and continents.

Australia   **Ethiopia**   **Orange County**   the **United States of America**

Capitalize the names of geographical features and bodies of water.

Pacific Ocean   the **Sahara**   **Cape Horn**   **Mt. Everest**   **Strait of Hormuz**

Capitalize the names of sections of the country, but do not capitalize compass points when they indicate direction. Do not capitalize adjectives derived from words indicating direction.

New England   the **South**   the **Pacific Northwest**   **southern California**
northern wind   **eastern Indiana**   **Texas is south of Oklahoma.**

Capitalize the names of streets and highways.

High Street   **Interstate 10**

Capitalize the names of buildings, bridges, and monuments.

World Trade Center   **Bay Bridge**   **Vietnam Veterans Memorial**

Capitalize the names of celestial bodies and constellations.

Andromeda   **Saturn**   **Orion**   Exceptions: the moon   the sun

▶ **Exercise 1 Underline the correct letter in parentheses.**

Have you ever been to (<u>M</u>, m)inneapolis, (<u>M</u>, m)innesota?

1. The (<u>U</u>, u)nited (<u>S</u>, s)tates (O, <u>o</u>)f (<u>A</u>, a)merica has many scenic attractions.

2. To the (N, <u>n</u>)orth lies (<u>A</u>, a)laska, the last (F, <u>f</u>)rontier.

3. Alaska's (S, <u>s</u>)tate flag features the (<u>B</u>, b)ig (<u>D</u>, d)ipper.

4. The (<u>W</u>, w)est (<u>C</u>, c)oast is more than just beaches and sunshine.

5. The (<u>I</u>, i)mperial (<u>V</u>, v)alley in (S, <u>s</u>)outhern (<u>C</u>, c)alifornia produces excellent crops when irrigated.

6. The (<u>G</u>, g)olden (<u>G</u>, g)ate (<u>B</u>, b)ridge at the entrance of (<u>S</u>, s)an (<u>F</u>, f)rancisco (<u>B</u>, b)ay is one of the (W, <u>w</u>)orld's longest suspension bridges.

7. Our nation's highest temperature ever, 134°F, was recorded in (<u>D</u>, d)eath (<u>V</u>, v)alley in (S, <u>s</u>)outhwest (<u>C</u>, c)alifornia.

8. Our lowest temperature ever recorded was -80°F in (<u>P</u>, p)rospect (<u>C</u>, c)reek, (<u>A</u>, a)laska.

9. (<u>D</u>, d)eath (<u>V</u>, v)alley is also our (C, <u>c</u>)ountry's driest place, receiving less than two inches of precipitation annually.

10. Precipitation varies greatly, however, as (<u>M</u>, m)ount (<u>W</u>, w)aialeale in (<u>H</u>, h)awaii receives about 460 inches of rain each year.

11. Much of (<u>C</u>, c)alifornia's cultural influence comes from (<u>M</u>, m)exico and (E, <u>e</u>)astern (<u>A</u>, a)sia.

12. (<u>C</u>, c)alifornia's neighbors, (<u>A</u>, a)rizona and (<u>N</u>, n)evada, are extremely dry.

13. A ski resort, (<u>C</u>, c)loudcroft, is 4,000 feet above the (D, <u>d</u>)eserts of (<u>N</u>, n)ew (<u>M</u>, m)exico.

14. Further (N, <u>n</u>)orth, (<u>W</u>, w)ashington and (<u>O</u>, o)regon have vast forests.

15. The (<u>C</u>, c)ascade (<u>M</u>, m)ountains include the (V, <u>v</u>)olcanoes (<u>L</u>, l)assen (<u>P</u>, p)eak in (<u>C</u>, c)alifornia and (<u>M</u>, m)ount (<u>S</u>, s)aint (<u>H</u>, h)elens in (<u>W</u>, w)ashington (S, <u>s</u>)tate.

16. The (<u>R</u>, r)ocky (<u>M</u>, m)ountains are the largest mountain system in (<u>N</u>, n)orth (<u>A</u>, a)merica, and they extend from (N, <u>n</u>)orthern (<u>A</u>, a)laska all the way (S, <u>s</u>)outh to (N, <u>n</u>)orthern (<u>N</u>, n)ew (<u>M</u>, m)exico.

17. The largest of the lower forty-eight states is (<u>T</u>, t)exas.

18. Two of (<u>A</u>, a)merica's largest cities, (<u>H</u>, h)ouston and (<u>D</u>, d)allas, are in (<u>T</u>, t)exas, but they seem small on a map of such a large state!

19. The (<u>A</u>, a)lamo, located in (<u>S</u>, s)an (<u>A</u>, a)ntonio, is the site of a famous battle.

20. (<u>T</u>, t)exas's (S, <u>s</u>)outhern border is a (R, <u>r</u>)iver called the (<u>R</u>, r)io (<u>G</u>, g)rande.

21. (<u>M</u>, m)esa (<u>V</u>, v)erde (<u>N</u>, n)ational (<u>P</u>, p)ark is also found in the (<u>S</u>, s)outhwest.

22. Another well-known (R, <u>r</u>)iver, (T, <u>t</u>)he (<u>M</u>, m)ississippi (<u>R</u>, r)iver, is 2,350 miles long.

23. It is an important part of the lore of (<u>L</u>, l)ouisiana.

24. The (<u>G</u>, g)ulf (O, <u>o</u>)f (<u>M</u>, m)exico, from (<u>F</u>, f)lorida to (S, <u>s</u>)outhern (<u>T</u>, t)exas, is bordered by the (<u>G</u>, g)ulf (<u>C</u>, c)oastal (<u>P</u>, p)lain.

Mechanics

25. The (A, a)labama, (M, m)ississippi, (R, r)io (G, g)rande, and (T, t)rinity are (R, r)ivers that flow into the (G, g)ulf (O, o)f (M, m)exico.

26. Jazz, a unique (A, a)merican style of music, was born in (N, n)ew (O, o)rleans, (L, l)ouisiana.

27. Like many cities in the (S, s)outh, New Orleans enjoys warm weather while the (N, n)orth endures cold winters.

28. Farther to the (E, e)ast and (S, s)outh of (L, l)ouisiana, (F, f)lorida is especially popular during the winter months.

29. Historic (G, g)eorgia, (N, n)orth of (F, f)lorida, is an industrial giant in the (S, s)outh.

30. A sand dune at (K, k)itty (H, h)awk, (N, n)orth (C, c)arolina, is the site of the Wright Brothers' first flight in 1903.

▶ **Exercise 2 Draw three lines under each letter that should be capitalized.**

Many people like to vacation in the mountains of the eastern united states.

1. The Great Smoky mountains are located in tennessee.

2. The appalachian mountains run parallel to the atlantic ocean.

3. This mountain range extends from Quebec, canada, to northern Alabama.

4. The highest peak in the Appalachians is mount mitchell at 6,684 feet.

5. The appalachian trail is a 2,020-mile footpath that runs from Maine to georgia.

6. Extending from southeastern maine across the eastern and southern states to eastern texas are the Coastal Lowlands.

7. This region includes virginia, which is just north of north carolina.

8. Thomas Jefferson's home, monticello, is located near charlottesville, virginia.

9. The atlantic Coastal Plain includes several rivers, the delaware, the hudson, and the potomac, as well as Cape Cod bay, Chesapeake bay, and Long island Sound.

10. Our nation's capital, washington, d.c., is near chesapeake bay.

11. George Washington's home, mount vernon, stands near the potomac river.

Mechanics

12. To the north, new england is home to several scenic states, including vermont.

13. The green mountains in central Vermont supply much of our country's maple syrup.

14. The empire state, new york, has many famous attractions.

15. The nation's busiest financial district is on wall street.

16. The statue of Liberty, a gift from france, has greeted immigrants from many nations.

17. For many years, the Empire State building was the tallest skyscraper in the world.

18. New york city has tremendous ethnic diversity.

19. Near buffalo, New york, niagara Falls borders canada.

20. A northern state, minnesota is usually the first to feel the cold, icy air of winter.

21. The midwest is called "America's Heartland."

22. The largest city in this area is chicago, illinois.

23. The sears tower in chicago is taller than the empire state building.

24. Rivers of the midwest include the mississippi, the missouri, and the ohio.

25. The great lakes are five lakes that provide a resource for both industry and recreation.

26. In southern Michigan, detroit is famous for manufacturing automobiles.

27. The National road runs east and west through the middle of Ohio.

28. It was first known as the Great National pike.

29. Work began on the road in 1811, and it went from cumberland, maryland, to vandalia, illinois.

30. It is now paved from washington, d.c., to st. louis, missouri, and is known as the National old trail road.

Lesson 71
Capitalization of Other Proper Nouns and Adjectives

Capitalize the names of clubs, organizations, businesses, institutions, religions, and political parties.

Joe's **D**iner   **T**oronto **B**lue **J**ays   **S**outhern **B**aptist   **L**ibertarian party

Capitalize brand names but not the nouns following them.

Olivet macaroni   **S**parkle shampoo   **R**eflections metal polish

Capitalize the names of important historical events, periods of time, and documents.

the **B**attle of the **B**ulge   the **F**irst **A**mendment   the **M**iddle **A**ges

Capitalize the days of the week, months of the year, and holidays. Do not capitalize the seasons.

Wednesday   **J**uly   **B**astille **D**ay   winter

Capitalize the first, last, and all other important words in the titles of books, plays, songs, articles, movies, television shows, magazines, newspapers, and book chapters.

Toledo Dispatch   "**C**oming **T**hrough the **R**ye"   *Old Yeller*   **P**astoral **S**ymphony

Capitalize the names of ethnic groups, nationalities, and languages.

Mexican   **H**ebrew   **C**hinese   **T**hai

Capitalize proper adjectives formed from the names of ethnic groups and nationalities.

Arabic language   **I**rish music   **G**erman author

▶ **Exercise 1** Rewrite the word or words in italics, adding the appropriate capitalization. If the sentence is correct, write *C* in the blank.

On Sunday, we will celebrate *mother's day*. __Mother's Day__

1. My father used to watch *the jack benny show*. __The Jack Benny Show__

2. We bought our car from the *ford motor company*. __Ford Motor Company__

3. The football team played *mayfield high school*. __Mayfield High School__

4. Abeque decided to take *french*. __French__

Mechanics

5. The *battle of gettysburg* was a violent incident. __Battle of Gettysburg__

6. I heard a musician playing in *central park*. __Central Park__

7. The article in the *phoenix gazette* was very well researched. __Phoenix Gazette__

8. My favorite breakfast food is *krispy krunch cereal*.
   __Krispy Krunch cereal__

9. The dinosaurs lived in the *mesozoic era*. __Mesozoic Era__

10. Many *world war* II pilots flew over the Pacific Ocean. __World War__

11. Alfonso's family hosted a big picnic on the *fourth of july*. __Fourth of July__

12. Do you have to work this *saturday*? __Saturday__

13. Let's plant a tree in honor of *arbor day*. __Arbor Day__

14. I was moved to tears reading *the diary of anne frank*. __The Diary of Anne Frank__

15. Sometimes the temperature drops below zero in *the winter months.* __C__

16. Many people sent money and supplies to *ethiopian families* during the great famine.
   __Ethiopian families__

17. My history class watched the film detailing the life of *the apache geronimo.*
   __the Apache Geronimo__

18. Every year my family gives money to *the march of dimes.* __the March of Dimes__

19. I have sometimes looked at the magazine *u.s. news & world Report.* __U.S. News & World Report__

20. Akili programmed her universal remote to operate her *Zenith television.*
   __C__

21. My mother attended summer school at the *university of wisconsin.*
   __University of Wisconsin__

22. Jake protected his car with the latest product, *ultra-sheen car wax.*
   __Ultra-Sheen car wax__

23. The *battle of wounded knee* took place in 1890. __Battle of Wounded Knee__

24. The government offices were closed on Monday in recognition of *Presidents' Day.*
   __C__

Mechanics

25. Modern housing is found on *navajo reservations*. __**Navajo reservations**__

26. After graduation from college, Lindsay wanted to be a reporter for the *dallas morning*

news. __**Dallas Morning News**__

27. Bach's work *the art of the fugue* was left unfinished. __**The Art of the Fugue**__

28. We enjoyed seeing a display of *african art* over the weekend. __**African art**__

29. On a bright *winter day in january*, the family decided to go skiing.

__**winter day in January**__

30. On Saturday we saw *the chicago cubs of the national league* play baseball in Wrigley

Field. __**the Chicago Cubs of the National League**__

▶ **Exercise 2** **Draw three lines under each letter that should be capitalized.**

We visited a jewish synagogue.

1. My cousin joined the democratic party.

2. Many people eat turkey on thanksgiving day.

3. On wednesdays I have piano lessons.

4. The *boston globe* is an excellent newspaper.

5. World war I was also called the Great War.

6. The watson heating and cooling company employs practically the entire town.

7. I have never been to the pontiac silverdome.

8. Garry tried to play the english horn.

9. Uncle James belongs to the vietnam veterans of america.

10. For Christmas I bought my cousin a subscription to *popular mechanics*.

11. The Stamp act was passed in 1765.

12. My sister joined the Girl scouts of america.

13. Several films have been made of Steinbeck's novel *of mice and men*.

14. Have you eaten at that new restaurant, hamburger heaven?

15. Do you know the beatles' song "I want to hold your hand"?

Mechanics

16. Europe fell into the dark ages for about 500 years.

17. I was able to buy boardwalk and Park place the last time I played Monopoly.

18. In the autumn I like to listen to the song "autumn leaves."

19. My favorite kind of food is chinese food.

20. Have you ever been to yellowstone national park?

21. Both Franz and Donna had ball games on tuesday, wednesday, or friday through the

month of july.

22. Parts of Mark Twain's book *life on the mississippi* were published in the *atlantic*

monthly as "old times on the mississippi."

23. The tokyo national museum has a valuable collection of asian art.

24. The symphony performs at the palace theater.

25. The spanish, french, and mexican flags once flew over Texas.

26. Every saturday Ben and his friends treated themselves to pizarro's pizza.

27. The U.S. constitution and the declaration of independence are two important

american documents.

28. The period of human culture during which stone tools were first used is known as the

stone age.

29. Many people with a norwegian background settled in Minnesota.

30. The cousins sat on the porch swing and sang "my old kentucky home" and "suwannee

river."

▶ **Writing Link** Write four sentences in which you demonstrate the correct use of at least
four of the capitalization rules in this lesson.

_____

_____

_____

_____

_____

_____

Mechanics

✓ Unit 12 **Review**

► **Exercise 1** Draw three lines under each letter that should be capitalized. Draw a slash (/) through each letter that should be lowercase.

Our country's thirty-third President was a democrat from Missouri.

harry truman, the thirty-third President of the United states, served his Terms from 1945 to 1953. born in lamar, Missouri, Truman became a Lieutenant in the National guard. After a brief Military career, truman entered politics and eventually became vice President under Franklin d. roosevelt. Truman became President when F. d. r. died on april 12, 1945, only eighty-three days after the beginning of the term. among president Truman's accomplishments was overseeing the Victory in europe after World WAR II. Later in his Career, he led the western nations against communism in the korean war. Harry Truman, a southern democrat, is known for creating The Truman doctrine and NATO (the North Atlantic treaty organization).

Some lighter aspects of Truman's Life include his 1948 victory over Thomas e. dewey. Early polling data suggested that dewey would Win. Newspapers were even printed with the quote, "dewey defeats truman." Truman's defeat of republican Thomas Dewey was considered an upset.

Truman did not seek Reelection in 1952. "i have served my Country long," He said, "And i think efficiently and honestly. i do not think it is my duty to spend another Four Years in the White House."

After leaving the white house on january 20, 1953, Truman returned to his home in independence, missouri. The Former President continued to be active in Politics and in the democratic party. Soon his friends began raising funds to build the Harry Truman library in independence. The Library opened in 1957 and holds Truman's Papers and Souvenirs.

Truman died on december 26, 1972, and was buried in the Truman library courtyard.

Mechanics

Cumulative Review: Units 1–12

▶ **Exercise 1** Circle each pronoun and underline each noun. If the noun is a proper noun, write *prop.* above it.

                                               prop.
(Who) wants to drive to Lincoln Junior High School?

1. The holidays were coming, and (I) could not wait for Thanksgiving. **prop.**

2. **prop.** Jeff read the cartoon and laughed at (it)

3. (I) would like a solid oak desk for (my) birthday.

4. The costume Hussein **prop.** wore, King Arthur **prop.**, was the best (one) there.

5. (It) bothered (me) when Jim **prop.** screamed in the car.

6. The U.S. Congress **prop.** is out of session.

7. The car drove over the hill and into the night.

8. (We) love to shop for (them) at Bloomingdale's **prop.**.

9. **prop.** Clint bought (himself) a brand new pair of skis.

10. **prop.** **prop.** **prop.** (I) saw Chan drive (his) Ford into the town of Burbank.

11. **prop.** Pazi sold (her) first short story to a magazine.

12. **prop.** James answered the telephone for (his) friend.

13. **prop.** **prop.** Tony had a friend take a picture of (him) shaking the hand of Don Mattingly.

14. The deer leaped through the underbrush of the forest.

15. **prop.** **prop.** Clay, (my) younger brother, likes to pretend that (he) is John Wayne.

16. (Everyone) agreed that the telephone given to Gene **prop.** was very nice.

17. (My) family has traveled to France **prop.**, Belgium **prop.**, and the English countryside.

18. (You) had better water (your) Christmas poinsettia.

19. Whose is this cherry-flavored soda?

20. In history class, we are studying the involvement of Germany in World War II.

prop.   prop.

▶ **Exercise 2** Underline the verbal phrase. Write in the blank *participial*, *gerund*, or *infinitive* to identify the type of phrase.

_____gerund_____   I have always enjoyed eating bacon and eggs.

_____infinitive_____ **1.** Diego has always wanted to learn a foreign language.

_____gerund_____ **2.** Printing out a long document takes much time.

_____infinitive_____ **3.** To wait in line for movie tickets may be dull, but it is often worthwhile.

_____participial_____ **4.** My mother relaxed, drinking a warm cup of coffee.

_____participial_____ **5.** The science teacher, believing in her theory, demonstrated the concept.

_____gerund_____ **6.** Solving logic puzzles is one of my hobbies.

_____infinitive_____ **7.** For his part-time job, Obike decided to work at the supermarket.

_____participial_____ **8.** Strumming the guitar, Rayna sang a folk song.

_____infinitive_____ **9.** The school board planned to meet next Wednesday.

_____gerund_____ **10.** Who does not enjoy playing a fun game?

_____gerund_____ **11.** Fighting between nations broke out again this weekend.

_____participial_____ **12.** Feeling nauseated, Debbie left the amusement park.

_____infinitive_____ **13.** His dream was to be an action hero in the movies.

_____infinitive_____ **14.** In the 1960s our goal was to reach the moon.

_____participial_____ **15.** The track star, defeated in a close race, congratulated the winner.

_____gerund_____ **16.** Beating the clock was the object of the game.

_____gerund_____ **17.** Daneene enjoys dancing to fast music.

_____participial_____ **18.** Playing the tuba, he marched across the field.

_____infinitive_____ **19.** To write a kind letter can really raise someone's spirits.

_____participial_____ **20.** Beautifully displayed here, this sculpture is very expensive.

Mechanics

▶ **Exercise 3** Draw three lines under each letter that should be capitalized. Draw a slash (/) through each letter that should be lowercase.

my Family loves to watch old tarzan Movies.

1. "wait here," He said. "i'll only be a minute."

2. Father, mother, uncle Jake, and my sister have all joined me to celebrate.

3. The Coach told me That i need to practice more.

4. "My favorite TV show," Ina said disappointedly, "Is not on tonight."

5. dear Mr. jameson:

6. My report concerned general george s. patton, a famous World War II General.

7. After practice, coach seckel handed us october's schedule.

8. Douglas fairbanks jr. starred in many Movies.

9. Why would i ever want to leave, dad?

10. After attaining his degree, he could now sign letters as domingo pena, ph.d.

11. i observed the big dipper in the winter sky.

12. Deep in the gobi, the chinese found Dinosaur bones.

13. When i start a career, I want to work on Madison avenue.

14. The strait Of Gibraltar lies between spain and Morocco.

15. Why would mother want to move to northern california?

16. This summer, my mother read *the Scarlet letter* By Nathaniel hawthorne.

17. My background includes language studies in french, Irish, And welsh.

18. The atlantic ocean borders the east coast.

19. Andy warhol is famous for his Paintings of campbell's soup cans.

20. In 1823, president Monroe issued the monroe doctrine.

Mechanics

Unit 13: Punctuation

Lesson 72

Using the Period and Other End Marks

Use a **period** at the end of a declarative sentence or an imperative sentence. A declarative sentence makes a statement. An imperative sentence gives a command or makes a request.

Kahlil went to the convenience store. (statement)
Don't forget the vegetables. (command)
Please tell us all about your good fortune. (request)

Use a **question mark** at the end of an interrogative sentence. An interrogative sentence asks a question.

Is Matt in the seventh grade?

Use an **exclamation point** at the end of an exclamatory sentence or after an interjection. An exclamatory sentence expresses strong feeling. An interjection is a word or group of words that expresses strong emotion.

What a wonderful surprise this is! Hooray! You have finally arrived!

▶ **Exercise 1** **Place a *C* in the blank next to each sentence that has correct end punctuation. Correct the end punctuation in the other sentences.**

__C__   Why do all these tomatoes look so different?

_____ **1.** Many varieties of tomatoes are available that suit different purposes*!*.

__C__ **2.** Is the tomato a fruit or a vegetable?

__C__ **3.** The tomato is considered a fruit.

_____ **4.** That simply cannot be true*?* **!** *or* **.**

__C__ **5.** Our family usually plants four kinds of tomatoes.

_____ **6.** The Rutgers variety is best suited for producing lots of juice*!* .

_____ **7.** Are these yellow ones good*!* **?**

__C__ **8.** Yes, they are very low in acid content.

_____ **9.** Beefsteak tomatoes grow very large and have lots of firm flesh*?* .

__C__ **10.** They are wonderful for slicing and serving as a side dish.

Mechanics

_C_ **11.** Don't eat that one without washing it.

_____ **12.** When he first saw these, all Mark could say was, "Wow/" !

_____ **13.** May I take one of these home/ ?

_C_ **14.** My mother will be astounded!

_C_ **15.** What are these tiny little ones?

_____ **16.** They are called cherry tomatoes/ .

_____ **17.** Aren't they perfect for salads and snacking/ ?

_____ **18.** This pear-shaped variety is called Roma? .

_C_ **19.** What on Earth are they for?

_C_ **20.** Because they are very solid, they make wonderful paste for use in sauces.

▶ **Exercise 2 Add the best end mark to each sentence.**

Do you enjoy working with plants?

1. Last week, our class took a tour of a large greenhouse.

2. The business is named Green with Ivy.

3. I can't believe the huge size of the place! *or* .

4. Is this the largest in our area?

5. Mr. Tappan specifically said, "Don't touch anything." *or* !

6. Be quiet, look, and listen.

7. How much of the space was filled with starts of vegetable plants?

8. The owner, Nadia Pavlik, cultivates fourteen varieties of tomatoes.

9. I never dreamed that there were so many kinds of cabbage! *or* .

10. The plants are started from seed grown in peat moss.

11. Do you know why a constant mist of water is sprayed over the plants?

12. Fertilizer is dissolved in the water for maximum growth of the plants.

13. The acres of annual flowers were a fantastic sight! *or* .

14. Did you see the many colors of petunias?

15. Wow! I counted seventeen colors of impatiens! *or* .

Mechanics

Lesson 73
Using Commas to Signal Pause or Separation

Use a **comma** to show a pause after an introductory word. Also use commas to separate three or more items in a series.

No, I won't be attending the meeting. (introductory word)
The cat jumped off the counter, landed on a throw rug, and skidded across the floor. (series)

Use a comma after two or more introductory prepositional phrases, an introductory adverb clause, an introductory participle, or an introductory participial phrase.

In the middle of winter, a flower is an encouraging sight. (two prepositional phrases)
Although we were cold, we still had a good time. (adverb clause)
Remembering the open window, Josh ran upstairs. (participial phrase)

Use commas to set off appositives that are not essential to the meaning of the sentence or to set off words that interrupt the flow of thought in a sentence.

Uncle Doug, Dad's youngest brother, works for an insurance company. (non-essential appositive)
Ice hockey, to be sure, can be a violent sport. (interruption)

Use commas to set off names in direct address.

Charlene, you may begin.

▶ **Exercise 1** Add commas where necessary. Use the delete symbol (⌆) to eliminate commas used incorrectly. If the sentence is correct, write *C* in the blank.

_____ To many people in the United States, autumn brings to mind one kind of tree.

_____ 1. From the Atlantic to the Mississippi,this beloved tree paints forests scarlet.

_____ 2. Leaf watchers come by car,bus,and bicycle to experience this tree's beauty.

_____ 3. Attracted by the breathtaking reds,yellows,and oranges of this tree,tourists

begin taking in the sights around the middle of October.

___C___ 4. Yes, other trees also turn color in the fall.

_____ 5. Ash,black cherry,oak,and sweet bun trees put on quite a show.

Copyright © by Glencoe/McGraw-Hill

Mechanics

_____ 6. However, only one tree,you understand,can wear so many different beautiful costumes.

_____ 7. Starting in September or October,this tree signals the beginning of autumn.

_____ 8. Of course,this tree is the sugar maple.

_____ 9. The sugar maple is a favorite,because of its colorful leaves; furthermore, it has many other uses.

_____ 10. All maples,but especially the sugar maple,are important woods in furniture making.

_____ 11. Sugar maple wood is used to make chairs,tables,beds,and dressers.

_____ 12. Sugar maple,also known as rock or hard maple,is used in the manufacture of floors,boxes,and crates.

__C__ 13. The wood of the sugar maple can also be made into veneer.

_____ 14. Veneer,a thin sheet of wood,is sliced from a tree trunk.

_____ 15. After the veneer is removed from the trunk, it can be glued,onto inexpensive wood.

__C__ 16. Therefore, inexpensive wood can be made to look like expensive wood.

_____ 17. The round,and dense,crown of the sugar maple keeps buildings cool in hot weather.

__C__ 18. Finally, the sugar maple is a favorite tree for yet another reason.

_____ 19. Pancake and waffle eaters,please tell us why the sugar maple is your favorite tree!

__C__ 20. The sugar maple is, of course, the source of maple syrup.

_____ 21. Made from boiled-down sap,real maple syrup is a rare and delicious treat.

_____ 22. The sugar maple,known as *acer saccharum*,is one of several types of maples.

__C__ 23. Others include the red maple and the silver maple.

_____ 24. The red maple turns red,yellow,and orange in the autumn.

Mechanics

Lesson 74
Using Commas in Clauses and Compound Sentences

Use a **comma** before a coordinating conjunction such as *and, or,* or *but* when it joins main clauses in a compound sentence.

My grandparents came to visit, **and** they brought me a present.
Ali may choose football, **or** he may prefer to play soccer.

Use a comma to set off an adverb clause that comes at the beginning of a complex sentence. Adverb clauses begin with subordinating conjunctions such as *after, although, as, because, before, considering (that), if, since, so that, though, unless, until, when, where, whether,* and *while.*

Unless a miracle happens, the Raiders will lose the game.

Do not use a comma with an adverb clause that comes at the end of a sentence.

Peter was late **because he stopped to help Kurt**.

▶ **Exercise 1** Add commas where necessary. Write *C* in the blank if the sentence is correct.

_____ Diamonds are a beautiful gemstone, and they are the hardest natural substance on earth.

_____ **1.** Since time began, diamonds have been highly prized gemstones.

_____ **2.** Gem diamonds are a lasting investment, and they grow more valuable with age.

_____ **3.** Because they are very hard, diamonds are used as tools as well as ornaments.

__C___ **4.** Most industrial diamonds are used as cutting tools.

_____ **5.** Impurities give a diamond off-color spots, or they cause a cloudy appearance.

__C___ **6.** These impurities lessen a diamond's brilliance.

_____ **7.** Diamonds with flaws are used in industry, but the more perfect ones become gems.

_____ **8.** Though artificial diamonds have been produced synthetically, diamonds are rare natural stones.

__C___ **9.** The General Electric Company was the first to make synthetic diamonds and to use such stones commercially.

_____ **10.** Whether they are natural or synthetic, diamonds are formed of pure carbon.

_____ 11. Diamonds are formed deep in the earth, or synthetic ones are made in laboratories.

___C___ 12. Both kinds of diamonds are measured in metric units called *carats* because they are rather small.

___C___ 13. One metric carat equals one fifth of a gram.

___C___ 14. Gems are cut into various shapes with many sides.

_____ 15. These sides are called *facets*, and they enhance the gem's brilliance.

▶ **Exercise 2** **Add commas where necessary. Use the delete (⌁) symbol to eliminate commas used incorrectly.**

Although some exceptions exist, most gemstones are minerals⌁that can be polished to become items of beauty.

1. Amethysts range from violet to purple in color, and these beautiful stones were used in both Greek and Roman jewelry.

2. Although aquamarine is of the same family as the emerald, the abundance of aquamarine makes it less valuable.

3. Copper carbonate is deep blue⌁and is found in most copper mines.

4. Bloodstone is a dark green quartz spotted with red jasper, and it is often used in rings.

5. Although it was once applied to any red stone, the name *carbuncle* refers to a garnet cut in a special way.

6. Cat's-eye is found in a great range of colors, but its distinctive mark is the streak or line **(optional comma)** through the middle,like a cat's eye.

7. Whether it is used for earrings or pendants, the clear yellow citrine is very popular.

8. The pearl is not a true gemstone⌁because it comes from an oyster.

9. Both pearl⌁and coral are by-products of sea animals.

10. A brilliant deep-green emerald is very valuable⌁because it is very rare.

11. Although they are usually deep red, garnets can be found in almost any color except blue.

12. The Chinese have used jade for centuries, and Asian works of art often include huge jade carvings.

Mechanics

Lesson 75
Using Commas with Titles, Addresses, and Dates

Use **commas** before and after the year when it is used with both the month and the day. Do not use a comma if only the month and the year are given.

Beethoven was born on December 4, 1770, and died in March 1827.

Use commas before and after the name of a state or country when it is used with the name of a city. Do not use a comma after the state if it is used with a ZIP code.

The Jacksons moved here from Tupelo, Mississippi, last fall.
Write to me at 12 Sarandon Circle, Bainbridge Island, WA 98110.

Use a comma or a pair of commas to set off an abbreviated title or degree following a person's name.

The letter was signed Hilda Greenberg, Ph.D., and dated last week.

▶ **Exercise 1** **Place a *C* in the blank beside each sentence that is punctuated correctly.**

___C___   Jake moved to Portland, Oregon, on July 3, 1994.

___C___   **1.** Anne and Charles were married on September 13, 1827.

_____   **2.** Is Kansas City, Missouri, the site of the Truman Library?

_____   **3.** Upon returning home, we found that Nyoko Hayashi L.L.D., was the interim chairperson.

___C___   **4.** Maria would never forget the flood of April 1990.

___C___   **5.** Every year, Chris Meyer, R.N., donated money to his alma mater.

_____   **6.** The diary began on May 27 1942 and continued for eighteen years.

___C___   **7.** The information plate on the back reveals that the TV was made in Korea.

___C___   **8.** His name, Orville Montoya, L.P.A., was well known in the area.

___C___   **9.** We will have Elaine Warner, Ph.D., as our guest speaker.

_____   **10.** Their family doctor, Ramos Hernandez D.O., was located in Tulsa.

_____   **11.** Our choir will sing in Tokyo Japan this summer.

_____   **12.** Is November 11, 1944 the correct date of the D-Day Invasion?

_____   **13.** The company's address is 4967 Alder Avenue, Louisville, KY, 40299.

Mechanics

___C___ **14.** New York, New York, has been nicknamed "The Big Apple."

_____ **15.** December 12, 1913 marked the beginning of our business, Mom's Apple Pies.

_____ **16.** Mr. Salazar accepted a position with a software company in Toronto Ontario.

___C___ **17.** There was a postmark on the envelope which read Ada, OK 74820.

_____ **18.** Kevin Applegate M.A. was hired as the new English teacher.

___C___ **19.** Gary, Indiana, is a large industrial port on Lake Michigan.

___C___ **20.** Do you know what's special about July 4, 1776?

▶ **Exercise 2** **Add commas where necessary. Use the delete symbol (⌘) to eliminate commas used incorrectly.**

Gary became Gerald Hopkins, Ph.D., in February, 1946.

1. The first-aid training was administered by Juanita Oliver, L.P.N.

2. July, 1976, marked two hundred years of independence for the United States.

3. The ZIP code for, Pine Beach, New Jersey, is 08741.

4. Have you read the book *Time Is Money* by Anita Moore, C.P.A.?

5. Chicago, Illinois, was the site of a World's Fair.

6. Send your order to P.O. Box 777, Forney, TX, 75126.

7. Does Cosby, Tennessee, have a shopping mall?

8. When did Alma get her M.A., degree?

9. Confederate forces attacked Fort Sumter on April 12, 1861.

10. People came from as far away as Fort Wayne, Indiana, to see the light show.

11. My baby brother was born on the seventeenth of August, 1991.

12. Why is the address 10 Downing Street, London, England, famous?

13. The city of Pisa, Italy, is famous for its Leaning Tower.

14. Your entry must be in the mail before October 15, 1996.

15. U.S. Grant was elected president in November, 1868 and took office in January, 1869.

16. While Quentin is recuperating, you may send cards to General Hospital, 1438

Recovery Drive, Indianapolis, IN 46206.

Mechanics

Lesson 76
Using Commas with Direct Quotes, in Letters, and for Clarity

Use a comma or pair of commas to set off a direct quotation.

"My cousin," Marla said, "will be thirteen next week."

Use a comma after the salutation of a friendly letter and after the closing of both a friendly and a business letter.

Dear Melanie,   Your friend,   Sincerely yours,

Use a comma to prevent misreading.

Compared to Maine, Maryland is a southern state.

▶ **Exercise 1 For each item, add commas where necessary.**

Tina said, "I like anchovies."

1. Yours truly,

2. As she rang the little bell, Mom announced, "Dinner is served."

3. While eating, the chicken pecks at the ground to get its food.

4. Dear Aunt Mary,

5. We expected that, because Kelvin had warned us.

6. "The rabbit," cried Teresa, "has disappeared from its cage!"

7. "You may work on your solar system projects with a partner," explained the science teacher.

8. Because of the rain, fields were too muddy for plowing.

9. Instead of five, seven points was the winning margin.

10. The supervisor said, "I think you will become absorbed in the landscaping project once you get started."

11. "Admission is six dollars," said the attendant.

12. Love always,

13. Unlike horses, cows chew a cud.

Mechanics

14. Jalicia said, "This is a great party!"

15. Anthony said, "I am afraid of the man wearing the scary costume."

16. Prior to the snow, trails in the woods were easily passable.

17. Sincerely yours,

18. Stronger than his brother, Tom lifted the log over the fence.

19. After Jim, Bob will step to the plate.

20. Although the Bears were winning, the game was only in the second quarter.

21. Ms. Wilson declared, "Always be on time if you want to succeed."

22. Since breakfast was late, lunch will be delayed.

23. Better than tapes, compact discs offer extremely accurate reproduction.

24. Good-bye for now,

25. The weather forecaster stated, "Snow is unlikely."

26. Except for Pablo, Lisa had the highest score.

27. In 1985, 497 students graduated from Memorial High School.

28. Dear Rita,

29. "I have a dream," announced Martin Luther King Jr.

30. "Today," remarked Jane, "is the first day of May."

31. "I searched for more of Tolkien's works," Bill said, "after reading *The Hobbit* and the ring trilogy."

32. His opening words were, "I am so afraid to speak in public!"

33. "Once upon a time," Frank read, "there was a buried treasure."

34. The sign said, "Keep off the grass."

35. With best regards,

36. The ad read, "No down payment."

37. Larger than cars, trucks are designed for hauling cargo.

38. "Give me a hand," requested the leader.

39. All the bewildered mayor could say was, "Who was that masked man?"

40. Compared to the railroad, cars are much faster.

Lesson 77
Commas in Review

▶ **Exercise 1** **For each item, add commas where necessary.**

After a long journey on a bus, our trip ended on March 9, 1995.

1. Turning the corner, I saw Benny, Drew, and Cliff climb into a taxi.

2. Undoubtedly, they will arrive before dark.

3. Humming to herself, Dora tried to recall the words to the song.

4. For thousands of years, nomadic peoples have lived in desert areas.

5. Jenny, of course, had to have her own way.

6. The Seminoles, proud Native Americans, are from the southeastern part of the country.

7. Officer Kono, how long have you been on the force?

8. Much of our woodland is disappearing and many of our wetlands are drying up.

9. Because of the lack of natural predators, the deer population is growing rapidly.

10. Miguel received his first remote-controlled car on May 7, 1992.

11. Is Paris, France, where the Eiffel Tower is located?

12. Karina Miller, D.V.M., will speak at the next meeting of the Towerton Humane Society.

13. Before the dinner, guests arrived in white limousines.

14. The quail gets its nickname from its call, "Bob White, Bob White."

15. Your buddy,

16. Unless we find the directions, Georgia won't help with the assembly of the model car.

17. Hoping to find my ring, I continued the search.

18. The factory relocated to Kilgore, Tennessee.

19. The door of the barn in my backyard is white, but the rest of the barn is red.

20. Mr. O'Brien's garden contained carrots, peas, green beans, and corn.

21. Yes, you may go to the volleyball match.

22. Walking on air, Ken could hardly wait to show his report card to his father.

Mechanics

23. In the nick of time, the rabbit darted into its burrow.

24. Ms. Ramirez, the report is on your desk.

25. The grass in the backyard is very tall, but Robert will mow it after school.

26. Mail the disk to Box 323, Topeka, KS 66603.

27. The man's business card read, "Harold Jenkins, C.P.A."

28. Carrying two slickers and an umbrella, Aunt Rose was prepared for the weather.

29. "Please," said the officer, "try to remain calm."

30. Dear Dad,

31. Instead of Eve, Hector presided over the meeting.

32. Julia's favorite sports are basketball, diving, and fencing.

33. Lions are very large, but the smaller cheetah can outrun them.

34. Mercenaries, soldiers for hire, have been used in many conflicts.

35. I warned you, James, that lying would cause you problems.

▶ **Writing Link** **Write a friendly letter to describe your nearest neighbors to a friend in another state. Use direct quotations and commas where necessary.**

_____

_____

_____

_____

_____

_____

_____

_____

_____

_____

_____

Mechanics

Lesson 78
Using Semicolons and Colons

Use a **semicolon** to join parts of a compound sentence when a conjunction such as *and*, *but*, or *or* is not used. Use a semicolon to join parts of a compound sentence when the main clauses are long and are subdivided by commas.

The thunder sounded louder; the downpour was only minutes away.
Mom's bird feeders, all fourteen of them, constantly needed to be refilled; but our yard had more sparrows, chickadees, and robins than any place in town.

Use a **colon** to introduce a list of items that ends a sentence. Use a phrase such as *these*, *the following*, or *as follows* before the list. Do not use a colon immediately after a verb or a preposition.

The jerseys are available in the following colors: red, blue, green, and purple.
Claire bought fabric, thread, and buttons.

Use a colon to separate the hour and the minute when writing the time of day.
Use a colon after the salutation of a business letter.

The mail carrier usually arrives at 3:15 P.M.
Dear Ms. Carley: To whom this may concern:

▶ **Exercise 1 Add colons or semicolons where necessary. Use the delete symbol (૪) to eliminate any colons or semicolons used incorrectly.**

Flying kites is a popular pastime; people all over the world fly creative kites.

1. Murray went straight home; but after he reached his house, he realized that he hadn't brought his homework.

2. I have the following things to trade: four video cartridges, a catcher's mitt, and a set of handlebars.

3. The Kos' new home has ૪ a tennis court, a three-car garage, and a swimming pool.

4. The eclipse will begin at 5:34 A.M.

5. Dear Ms. Esterbrook:

6. Camels are impressive creatures; they are much larger than one might imagine.

7. The weather was very good for gardens this summer; our flowers bloomed more than any time I can remember.

8. Without hesitation, Kevin took the oath; now he is a full-fledged police officer.

9. Mom, I need the following items: a red sweater, my stamp collection, and several extra pairs of socks.

10. The movie begins at 8:30 P.M.

11. The items missing from the first-aid kit were: a tourniquet, adhesive tape, and iodine.

12. His library is filled with many kinds of books; his favorites are the mysteries.

13. Did you mean 6:20 A.M. or P.M.?

14. Dear Mrs. Gallagher:

15. Those persons selected for the dance committee are as follows: Karen, Estella, Harvey, and May-Li.

16. Can you be there by 10:15?

17. Sue and Harry walked home from school; they got caught in the rain when they were halfway home.

18. The Athletic Boosters will meet at 7:30 P.M.

19. By the time the bus got to Akira's stop, the rain had stopped; but as he stepped off the bus, he landed in a deep puddle.

20. Most of the electronics available here were made: in Japan, Korea, or Mexico.

21. This letter is to confirm your order for the following items: a fishing rod, a spinning reel, and a tackle box.

22. Dear Councilman Harper:

23. On our hike, I saw these animals: two deer, a muskrat, a rabbit, and four squirrels.

24. Manuel selected the following electives: art, choir, and band.

25. Kyle sent postcards: to Angie, Martha, and Hiroshi; but Martha's card never arrived.

26. Sarah received these presents: a softball bat, a socket set, and a blow dryer.

27. The nominees for president are: Phil, Caroline, and Soku.

28. Some of the items to be auctioned are: a bedroom suite, a dinette set, and a television.

Lesson 79
Using Quotation Marks I

Use **quotation marks** before and after a direct quotation. Also use quotation marks with a divided quotation.

"Step right up and try your luck," shouted the carnival worker.
"Pasta," remarked Mr. Cortez, "actually originated in China."

Use a **comma** or commas to separate a phrase such as *he said* from the quotation itself. Place the comma outside opening quotation marks, but inside closing quotation marks.

Troy asked, "Where are the baseball bats?"
"Someday," said Gwen, "I hope to live in Hawaii."

▶ **Exercise 1 Add quotation marks and commas where necessary.**

"Competitive rabbit shows," stated Mr. Sanchez, "are becoming very common."

1. Tabitha asked, "What makes one rabbit better than another?"

2. "That depends on what breed of rabbits you are talking about," answered Chuck.

3. "Each breed," said Mr. Sanchez, "is judged according to a written standard."

4. Emily said, "The standards are set by the American Rabbit Breeders Association."

5. "Every part of the rabbit has some value in the standard," said Rick.

6. "Even eye color and toenail color count," added Emily.

7. "My neighbor, Mr. Brown, has some Dutch rabbits," said Tabitha.

8. "What," asked Chuck, "is the most important thing about a Dutch rabbit?"

9. "The Dutch rabbit," answered Rick, "has distinctive markings on its head, feet, and body."

10. "Since the markings vary on every animal," said Emily, "the judge must decide which one is closest to perfection."

11. "The breeds called commercial breeds emphasize meat-producing qualities," said Mr. Sanchez.

12. "All the other breeds," he continued, "are collectively called fancy."

13. "Netherland Dwarfs are very tiny rabbits," he said.

Mechanics

14. Tabitha asked, "Are Flemish giants just the opposite?"

15. Chuck replied, "Yes! I saw one of those at the fair."

16. "How much did it weigh?" asked Rick.

17. "I don't know exactly," Chuck responded, "but it was more than twenty pounds."

18. Tabitha inquired, "Are there a lot of different breeds?"

19. "The American Rabbit Breeders Association," answered Emily, "recognizes forty-four breeds."

20. "The average rabbit show," she said, "has more than one thousand entries."

21. She added, "There are nearly two thousand shows each year."

22. "An elimination is a serious fault that can be corrected," explained Mr. Sanchez.

23. Emily said, "Eliminations include things like colds and broken toenails."

24. "What," asked Chuck, "is a disqualification?"

25. "That is a serious fault that is permanent," said Mr. Sanchez, "and cannot be corrected."

26. He asked, "Who can give examples of a disqualification?"

27. Emily replied, "Two disqualifications I can name are buck teeth and, in a colored rabbit, white spots."

28. Tabitha said, "It sounds as if owners take these shows seriously."

29. "Many exhibitors pay big prices for winning stock," said Rick.

30. "I have sold winning animals for as much as a thousand dollars," added Mr. Sanchez.

31. "A beginner," he said, "can expect to pay about forty dollars for a good rabbit."

32. "Are there any shows near here?" asked Tabitha.

33. "The Metropolitan Rabbit Fanciers holds its annual show at our fairgrounds," said Emily.

34. Chuck added, "It is held on the second weekend of April."

Mechanics

Lesson 80
Using Quotation Marks II

A **period** is always placed inside closing quotation marks.

Ed said, "Let me help you with that heavy carton."

Place a **question mark** or **exclamation point** inside the closing quotation marks when it is part of the quotation. Place a question mark or exclamation point outside the marks when it is part of the entire sentence.

Sam asked, "Is there any more chocolate?" (part of the quotation)
Did I hear you say, "Buy it now, pay for it later"? (part of the entire sentence)

Use **quotation marks** for the title of a short story, essay, poem, song, magazine or newspaper article, or book chapter.

"The Ransom of Red Chief" (short story)
"Invictus" (poem)   "Love Me Tender"(song)

▶ **Exercise 1 Add quotation marks as needed.**

"Be sure," reminded Cara, "that you take a warm sweater."

1. April screamed, "Watch out!"

2. Grandpa said, "Please pass the biscuits."

3. Mark Twain wrote a short story called "Baker's Blue Jay Yarn."

4. How many people replied, "Not me"?

5. Pablo announced, "I am going to Cancun for my vacation next month."

6. Have you ever read a poem called "Old Ironsides"?

7. The title of the article you are looking for is "Ducks, Ducks, and More Ducks."

8. Joe exclaimed, "What a big dog!"

9. "Fame" is the title song from the Broadway show of the same name.

10. A title like "Sonnet XIV" gives no clue to the content of the work.

11. Montel said, "This is a good reason to take a break."

12. Who sang the song "Respect"?

13. The newspaper headline read "Seven Youths Earn Awards."

Mechanics

14. My favorite story in the anthology was "In the Bag."

15. Did Gerald really say, "Money is no object"?

16. "China," said Janice, "is a land of great, proud heritage."

17. "The Gift of the Magi" was written by O. Henry.

18. Which story is shorter, "Sisterhood" or "Golden Feet"?

19. "I Know That My Redeemer Liveth" is an example of an aria from an oratorio.

20. "Puff, the Magic Dragon" is a folksong.

21. "Dave Calls Me for Advice" appeared in the magazine *Ask Miss Sarah.*

22. Did Andrew Lloyd Webber compose "I Don't Know How to Love Him"?

23. Can you imagine the cheers when our coach said, "You played flawlessly"?

24. Our librarian put an article in the school paper called "New for You."

25. "Music of the Night" is from *The Phantom of the Opera.*

26. "Because you have worked hard," Coach Andretti announced, "practice will be over early."

27. "When you were young," asked Amy, "were there electric lights?"

28. Harold won the contest with his essay entitled "I Choose the Trumpet."

29. "Ah!" shrieked Rivka, "A mouse!"

30. "Fanfare for the Common Man" was composed by Aaron Copeland.

▶ **Writing Link** **Write a short conversation among three people.**

_____

_____

_____

_____

_____

_____

_____

_____

Mechanics

Lesson 81
Using Italics (Underlining)

Use italics (underlining) to identify the title of a book, play, film, television series, magazine, or newspaper.

Inherit the Wind (play)   *Newsweek* (magazine)   *Animal Farm* (book)

▶ **Exercise 1 Underline any words that should be in italics.**

Judy Blume wrote the humorous book <u>Freckle Juice</u>.

1. <u>The Red Badge of Courage</u>, by Stephen Crane, is one of the shortest novels in literature.

2. Archibald MacLeish's <u>J.B.</u> is a play that tells the story of the biblical Job in a modern setting.

3. One of the most spectacular movies ever produced is <u>Ben Hur</u>.

4. <u>Roots</u>, tracing author Alex Haley's ancestors, impressed television viewers.

5. Would you say that <u>Time</u> is the leading news magazine?

6. Other newspapers picked up this article from the <u>Cleveland Plain Dealer</u>.

7. We argued over who wrote <u>The Hound of the Baskervilles</u>.

8. If you like fiction that is based on history, you should read <u>A Tale of Two Cities</u>.

9. How many movies entitled <u>Frankenstein</u> have been released?

10. His article on raising rabbits was published in <u>Country Living</u>.

11. One of John Philip Sousa's most famous marches is named for a newspaper, the <u>Washington Post</u>.

12. For her birthday, Kimiko's mother gave her a subscription to <u>Writer's Digest</u>.

13. Hailed as one of the greatest novels ever, <u>Gone with the Wind</u> is an epic drama of the Civil War.

14. My first dramatic role was in a play called <u>The Lottery</u>.

15. The musical <u>My Fair Lady</u> is based on the play <u>Pygmalion</u>.

16. For good fantasy tales, buy a copy of <u>Amazing Stories</u>.

17. Before coming to the <u>Daily News</u>, Frances was a staff reporter for the <u>Clarion</u>.

18. He plans to call his novel <u>My Own Man Again</u>.

19. Mark Twain's <u>The Prince and the Pauper</u> is an excellent work based on a case of mistaken identity.

20. Mary Martin starred in both the stage and the movie versions of <u>Peter Pan</u>.

21. Saluting the dedication of the underdog, the film <u>Rocky</u> and its several sequels have drawn huge crowds.

22. How many times have you seen this episode of <u>Little House on the Prairie</u>?

23. My sister eagerly awaits every issue of <u>American Girl</u>.

24. I follow the market reports in <u>U.S.A. Today</u>.

25. My aunt's favorite movie is Alfred Hitchcock's <u>Rear Window</u>.

26. Edith Wharton wrote an insightful novel entitled <u>Ethan Frome</u>.

27. <u>Annie</u> and <u>Annie Get Your Gun</u> are totally different musical plays.

28. Marlon Brando became famous for his role in <u>On the Waterfront</u>.

29. Do you remember the television series <u>The Cosby Show</u>?

30. Mother's subscription to <u>Good Housekeeping</u> has expired.

31. Did you know that Benjamin Franklin was the founder of <u>The Saturday Evening Post</u>?

32. <u>Twenty Thousand Leagues Under the Sea</u> is an early masterpiece in the science fiction realm.

▶ **Writing Link** **Write a paragraph about your favorite television series.**

_____

_____

_____

_____

_____

_____

_____

_____

_____

Mechanics

Lesson 82
Using Apostrophes

Use an **apostrophe** and an s (*'s*) to form the possessive of a singular noun or of a plural noun not ending in s.

dog + *'s* = dog's   Charles + *'s* = Charles's   women + *'s* = women's
geese + *'s* = geese's

Use an apostrophe alone to form the possessive of a plural noun that ends in *s*.

engineers + *'* = engineers'   Smiths + *'* = Smiths'   songs + *'* = songs'

Use an apostrophe and an s (*'s*) to form the possessive of an indefinite pronoun.

anyone + *'s* = anyone's   somebody + *'s* = somebody's

Do not use an apostrophe in a possessive pronoun.

The dog wagged its tail.   **This coat is hers.**

Use an apostrophe to replace letters that have been omitted in a contraction.

can + not = can't   it + is = it's   they + are = they're   we + will = we'll

Use an apostrophe to form the plurals of letters, figures, and words when they refer to themselves.

four *g*'s   seven 6's   *and*'s, *but*'s, and *or*'s

▶ **Exercise 1** Underline the correct form of the word in parentheses.

(<u>Sheila's</u>, Sheilas') jacket is hanging on the back of the door.

1. Have you met (Carlos', <u>Carlos's</u>) brother?

2. I am looking for the (<u>children's</u>, childrens') coats.

3. I am feeding the (Joneses', <u>Jones'</u>) cat while they are on vacation.

4. Marcie found (<u>someone's</u>, someones) purse on the floor of the classroom.

5. Alan (couldnt, <u>couldn't</u>) understand our lack of enthusiasm.

6. Donna was awakened by the two (<u>movers'</u>, mover's) shouts.

7. The baby robin flapped (<u>its</u>, it's) wings in vain.

8. Linda was fascinated by the (cars, <u>car's</u>) unique horn.

9. Please direct Carl to the (boy's, <u>boys'</u>) locker room.

10. (It's, Its) about time for the meeting to start.

11. If Patty gets a hit, (we're, were) sure to win the game.

12. Mr. Ulrich didn't receive (anyones, anyone's) homework on time.

13. The six (Americans', American's) tour bus left an hour ago.

14. Johann tried to join the (women's, womens') discussion.

15. Lemon pie is (Margarets, Margaret's) specialty.

16. The (house's, houses) exterior was painted white.

17. Adequate housing became the two (cities', citie's) most urgent problem.

18. Your decision (isnt, isn't) very popular.

19. The results of the (mens', men's) downhill were just posted.

20. Joan said that the soccer ball was (her's, hers).

21. No (buts, but's), Raji; just do it!

22. The bald eagle is one of our (nation's, nations) symbols.

23. (Manufacturers, Manufacturers') warranties do not cover that part.

24. (Everyone's, Everyones') lunches were placed on the third shelf.

25. If (you'll, youll) hold my place, I will get punch for both of us.

26. My phone number ends with three (3s, 3's).

27. The first team to compete is (our's, ours).

28. (Carmen's, Carmens') phone number is unlisted.

29. The accident was (nobodys', nobody's) fault.

30. All of the (drivers, drivers') cargoes were perishable.

31. Have you seen (Thomas', Thomas's) skateboard?

32. Is the (Jenkins's, Jenkinses') dog named Hoover?

33. Shingles were missing from the (sheds, shed's) roof.

34. The (musicians's, musicians') lively performance made the audience cheer loudly.

35. The (conductor's, conductors) stand has been misplaced.

Lesson 83
Using Hyphens, Dashes, and Parentheses

Use a **hyphen** to show the division of a word at the end of a line. Always divide the word between its syllables.

Will and Cindy decided to enroll in the table tennis tournament sponsored by the Athletic Club.

Use a hyphen in compound numbers from twenty-one through ninety-nine. Use a hyphen in a fraction that is used as a modifier. Do not use a hyphen in a fraction used as a noun.

The new restaurant served seventy-eight dinners last night.
James awoke one-half hour before Harry. (modifier)
One third of the money raised will be spent on research. (noun)

Use a hyphen or hyphens in certain compound nouns. Check the dictionary to see which ones need hyphens. Use a hyphen in a compound modifier only when it precedes the word it modifies.

My great-aunt loves to knit. Sid is Lou's brother-in-law.
A well-rehearsed band played first. Our band was well rehearsed.

Use a **dash** to show a sudden break or change in thought. If the sentence continues, use a second dash to mark the end of the interruption.

Mary—she just turned twelve—is my neighbor.

Use **parentheses** to set off material that is not part of the main statement but that is, nevertheless, important to include.

The yo-yo (a spinning top on a string) has been popular for years.

▶ **Exercise 1** Insert hyphens, dashes, or parentheses as needed. Write *C* in the blank if the sentence is correct. **For some sentences accept either dashes or parentheses.**

_____ There were thirty-six books on the selective reading list.

_____ 1. Rolanda's dad is thirty-seven years old.

_____ 2. The *streusel* (a German dessert) made by Hans's mother was the hit of the picnic.

__C__ 3. The audience was thrilled by the long-awaited performance.

__C__ 4. The scoreboard donated by Christy's Grocery needs to be replaced.

_____ 5. Mr. Jones (the man who owns the Palace Theater) gave us free passes.

Mechanics

_____C_____ 6. Does a light-year measure distance or time?

_____ 7. Bingo was a well-trained dog.

_____ 8. Dr. Khanduja he's from India is my family doctor.

_____ 9. Of all the sports available to the class, basketball drew the largest num

ber of participants.

_____ 10. Saint Bernards (huge, hardy dogs) are popular in the Alps.

_____ 11. Don't you just love French-fried onion rings?

_____ 12. The clock on my desk a present from Mom is shaped like a computer.

_____C_____ 13. That book has twenty-two chapters.

_____ 14. The Lions (members of the Monroe High School soccer team) thwarted our

entire offense.

_____ 15. After dinner, we visited with my great-grandmother.

_____ 16. Despite its shop-worn appearance, George purchased the magazine.

_____C_____ 17. The brown gelding—we now have four horses—proved to be a terrific pleasure

horse.

_____ 18. Especially in summer, the woods behind Aunt Meredith's barn were fas-

cinating to every member of the family.

_____ 19. The basketball team scored eighty-eight points.

_____C_____ 20. Three fourths of our class had the flu last week.

_____ 21. Rance is our first-string tackle.

_____ 22. My cousin Phil he turned thirteen last month is staying with me for the

weekend.

_____ 23. With great relish, Akira looked forward to his monthly relaxing week-

end at the cabin.

_____ 24. The kiwi (a small flightless bird native to Australia) lays a large egg in

proportion to its body size.

_____C_____ 25. The middle-aged man longed to return to his youth.

_____ 26. The marching band boasted ninety-five members.

Mechanics

Lesson 84
Using Abbreviations

Abbreviate titles and professional or academic degrees that follow names.

Mr. Albert Huang **Jr.** (Junior)   Kim Birchfield, **Ph.D.** (Doctor of Philosophy)
Arlene Johnson, **M.D.** (Medical Doctor)   **Dr.** Stephen Zwilling

Use all capital letters and no periods for abbreviations that are pronounced letter by letter or as words. Exceptions are U.S. and Washington, D.C., which do use periods.

NCAA (National Collegiate Athletic Association)
RAM (random-access memory)   PBS (Public Broadcasting System)

Use the abbreviations A.M. (*ante meridiem,* "before noon") and P.M. (*post meridiem,* "after noon") for exact times. For dates use B.C. (before Christ) and, sometimes, A.D. (*anno Domini,* "in the year of the Lord," after Christ.)

Abbreviate calendar items only in charts, lists, and graphs.

Mon.   Wed.   Sun.   Mar.   Oct.   Dec.

Abbreviate units of measure in scientific writing, such as charts, lists, and graphs.

inch(es) **in.**   foot(feet) **ft.**   gram(s) **g**   liter(s) **l**   cubic centimeter(s) **cc**

Abbreviate street names on envelopes.

Street **St.**   Road **Rd.**   Avenue **Ave.**   Court **Ct.**   Boulevard **Blvd.**

Use the Postal Service abbreviations for the names of states on envelopes.

Maryland **MD**   Texas **TX**   Utah **UT**   North Carolina **NC**

▶ **Exercise 1 Look at each item in parentheses. If it can be abbreviated in that sentence, write the abbreviation. If the sentence is correct as it is, write *C.***

__WPA__   The (Works Projects Administration) provided jobs during the Depression.

__Dr.__   1. (Doctor) Louis Pasteur invented a way to make milk safer for drinking.

__C__   2. Beacon Station (Road) is where the old mill is located.

__M.D.__   3. Linda Gomez, (Medical Doctor), has an office near here.

__P.M.__   4. Remind Sarah to take her medicine at 8:00 *(post meridian).*

__CIA__   5. Darnell's father works for the (Central Intelligence Agency).

Mechanics

_____C_____ 6. The pitcher holds two (liters) of lemonade.

_____C_____ 7. Valerie's birthday is (September) 14.

_____Jr.____ 8. Neil Allen (Junior) will follow in his father's footsteps.

____Ph.D.___ 9. Emil Green, (Doctor of Philosophy), was the speaker at my cousin's commencement.

_____C_____ 10. The young tree in our yard is seventy-two (inches) high.

_____C_____ 11. She will return to class on (Monday).

____NATO____ 12. (North Atlantic Treaty Organization) began as a defense group.

_____C_____ 13. Jeannie moved to Sycamore (Street) last week.

____C.P.A.___ 14. Miriam sent the letter to Teresa Kazuo, (Certified Public Accountant), on April 13.

_____C_____ 15. The mall on Fillmore (Boulevard) is the closest mall.

____A.M.____ 16. At 6:18 (*ante meridiem*) our plane takes off.

_____C_____ 17. Send the flowers to 378 Shropshire (Court) in Boca Raton.

__cc *or* C__ 18. That tiny vial holds one (cubic centimeter) of the solution.

_____C_____ 19. The alligator was twelve (feet) longer than the ferret.

____NASA____ 20. We toured the (National Aeronautics and Space Administration) headquarters for two hours.

▶ **Exercise 2** **Rewrite each phrase, using the correct abbreviation.**

37 kilometers _____37 km_____

1. 76 Avondale Court _____
   76 Avondale Ct.

2. October 8, 1865 __Oct. 8, 1865__

3. Thornton, Idaho __Thornton, ID__

4. Topeka, Kansas __Topeka, KS__

5. 300 yards __300 yd.__

6. *anno Domini* 375 __A.D. 375__

7. United Nations __UN__

8. Hansberger Avenue _____
   Hansberger Ave.

9. Tonawanda, New York _____
   Tonawanda, NY

10. 2:00 in the afternoon __2:00 P.M.__

11. 10 Downing Street _____
    10 Downing St.

12. Lansing, Michigan __Lansing, MI__

Lesson 85
Writing Numbers

Always spell out ordinal numbers. Also spell out numbers that you can write in one or two words. For numbers of more than two words, use numerals.

Maureen placed **second** in the spelling bee. (ordinal number)
My father is **thirty-four** years old. (one word)
Yasser's house is **214** miles from the border. (more than two words)

Spell out any number that begins a sentence, or reword the sentence so that the number appears later.

One hundred seven days remain until Christmas.

Write a very large number as a numeral followed by the appropriate word, for example, *million* or *billion.*

Relief is needed for **14 million** flood victims.

If one number in a sentence is in numerals, related numbers must be in numerals.

I picked 109 bushels of apples while Joyce picked 95 bushels.

Use words for amounts of money that can be written in one or two words, for the approximate time of day, and for the time of day when A.M. or P.M is not used.

four cents   a quarter past **four**   half past **two**   **two** o'clock

Use numerals for dates; for decimals; for house, apartment, and room numbers; for street or avenue numbers; for telephone numbers; for page numbers; for percentages; for amounts of money involving both dollars and cents; to emphasize the exact time of day; or when A.M. or P.M. is used.

April **10, 1874**   **13** percent   **$50.60**   **4:07** P.M.

▶ **Exercise 1** Write in the blank the correct form for each number. Write *C* if the number is written correctly.

__thirty-seven__   For his science project, Bela collected 37 different insects.

__C__   1. We have 246 seventh graders at our school.

__Four hundred__   2. 400 is an enviable batting average.

__C__   3. Did the NFL draw more than 30 million fans this year?

__first__   4. The Adamsville Blue Angels finished 1st in their soccer league.

__five o'clock__   5. Be at my house around 5:00.

Mechanics

_____555-0411_____ 6. Whose phone number is five five five zero four one one?

_____nineteen_____ 7. There are 19 trees in the picnic area.

_____512_____ 8. The old computer had only five hundred twelve kilobytes of RAM.

_____C_____ 9. One hundred four people brought their vehicles to our car wash.

_____9_____ 10. Some of the night sky's visible stars are more than nine billion miles

away.

_____second_____ 11. "Today is the 2nd time you have not completed your homework," said

Mr. Ortega.

_____C_____ 12. The bus will leave at 6:10 A.M.

_____$7.56_____ 13. With tax, that will be seven dollars and fifty-six cents.

_____C_____ 14. Marcie has twenty-four comic books.

_____940_____ 15. The paper reported that fewer than nine hundred forty persons voted in

our precinct.

_____C_____ 16. Two hundred eleven cards graced Tamaka's hospital room.

_____C_____ 17. The population of Sweden is just over 8 million.

_____ninety_____ 18. Besides having 90 sheep, the rancher owned fourteen horses.

_____C_____ 19. By the tenth day, Mi-Young had fully recuperated.

_____9:05_____ 20. On Thursday, the movie will run at five after nine P.M. on ABC.

_____38_____ 21. Driver, take me to thirty-eight Mountain View Boulevard.

_____twenty-five_____ 22. Can you believe this costs only 25 dollars?

_____C_____ 23. The local deer population is estimated at 650.

_____Thirty-eight_____ 24. 38 members attended the meeting.

_____93_____ 25. Earth is ninety-three million miles from the sun.

_____seventh_____ 26. Mieko lost her purse on the 7th day of her tour.

_____9:57_____ 27. The bell for third period rings at nine fifty-seven A.M.

_____July 1, 1983_____ 28. An-Li was born on July first, nineteen eighty-three.

_____C_____ 29. After paying tax, the customer received only nine cents in change.

_____8 percent_____ 30. Our profit margin was less than eight %.

Mechanics

☑ Unit 13 **Review**

▶ **Exercise 1** Write the correct word, phrase, number, or abbreviation in the blank. Write *C* in the blank if the sentence or phrase is correct. Use italics (underlining) or quotation marks as needed.

_____ C _____	Micah won the lottery in August 1990.
_____ C _____	**1.** Yours truly,
_____ Dr. _____	**2.** Doctor Amma Yamaguchi
_____ 25 _____	**3.** Twenty-five million
_____ twenty-three _____	**4.** Alvin read 23 books.
_____ C _____	**5.** I can barely remember my great-grandmother.
_____ C _____	**6.** Kelly—she's on vacation now—is my best friend.
The Old Man and the Sea	**7.** Did Ernest Hemingway write the novel The Old Man and the Sea?
_____ Dear Sir: _____	**8.** Dear Sir,
_____ "Trees" _____	**9.** Dad's favorite poem is Trees.
_____ James's _____	**10.** James' last name is Guerrero.

▶ **Exercise 2** Edit the following sentences. Add any punctuation that is needed and use the delete symbol (⅄) to mark any punctuation that should be removed.

Daydreaming, Jorge leaned his head⅄against the wall.

1. Ms. Jefferson asked⸴"What were the *Nina* and the *Santa Maria?*"

2. After weeks of concern, Dr. Martin was glad to see the rain; it came in time to save his rose garden.

3. Yes, I heard the assignment; we are to read pages⅄93–97.

4. Yawning, I looked out the window to see the Joneses' dog⅄chasing our cat.

5. Marla said⸴"The hand, as you know, is quicker than the eye."

6. The batter, a lanky left-hander, swung at the first three pitches.

7. Mrs. Thiele, may Margaret come to my house?   **(Quotation marks may be used to enclose item 7 but are not required.)**

Mechanics

Cumulative Review: Units 1–13

▶ **Exercise 1** Draw three lines under each letter that should be capitalized. Add any needed punctuation.

While we were on the plane, we met dr. henry kissinger.

1. During our stay in paris, we visited the louvre and notre dame cathedral.

2. Grandma's house is an example of victorian architecture, but it has been remodeled.

3. The pirates are making a strong bid to win the pennant, and all of pittsburgh is

   supporting them.

4. The british monarchy has its seat at buckingham palace in london.

5. "Somewhere over the rainbow" was first sung by judy garland, one of Hollywood's

   former leading ladies.

6. Are the washington redskins i never followed that team in the american football

   conference?

7. Can you tell me who wrote the book *dr. jekyll and mr. hyde?*

8. We went to visit aunt rita, who lives in tyler, and my two uncles in galveston.

9. Oko's afternoon classes are as follows: math, English, and biology.

10. The band played concerts in england, france, and all european countries bordering the

    mediterranean.

11. The panel included pastor ferrera, professor jenkins, and doctor adkins.

12. My favorite vacation was our trip to grand canyon national park, and it seems like only

    yesterday.

13. Because she wants to become a professional musician, inez invested in the *larousse*

    dictionary of music.

14. Durrell's new horse, a registered tennessee walker, is very well trained.

15. Myron's favorite instruments are the trombone, the french horn, and the tuba.

16. Donna and Felipe went to new orleans on the *delta queen*, a sternwheeler, and

    returned by railroad.

Mechanics

17. Alta enjoys both italian and greek cuisine.

18. Millie's family is renowned for fine-quality hampshire hogs.

19. Before Jonas came to school, he dropped off dad's dry cleaning.

20. Roxie, the girl next door, likes canadian bacon on her pizza.

▶ **Exercise 2** Write *M* in the blank if the group of words in italics is a main clause, *S* if it is a subordinate clause, or *N* if it is not a clause.

_____M_____ My alarm goes off at seven, but *I seldom get up at that time.*

_____S_____ **1.** *Unless I fall asleep before ten,* I am going to watch the news special.

_____M_____ **2.** Juan likes tacos, but *his sister can't eat them.*

_____S_____ **3.** *Since Guillaume made the first-string team,* his confidence has blossomed.

_____M_____ **4.** Candace has a paper route, and *she always has plenty of pocket money.*

_____N_____ **5.** Erik went home *before the end of the game.*

_____S_____ **6.** Ian caught seven fish *before he ran out of bait.*

_____M_____ **7.** Elvis has a skateboard; *Sharon has two skateboards.*

_____M_____ **8.** Otters are aquatic mammals, and *they are among the most playful creatures on earth.*

_____S_____ **9.** *Whenever Paloma runs the meeting,* the business session progresses smoothly.

_____N_____ **10.** *Walking down the street,* Osvaldo whistled happily.

_____M_____ **11.** *Growing up has many pitfalls,* and Abeque experienced many of them.

_____S_____ **12.** Mary ran the vacuum *while Jimmy did the dusting.*

_____M_____ **13.** I ordered ice cream, but *Dad had a milkshake.*

_____N_____ **14.** We purchased all new furniture *since last month's flood.*

_____S_____ **15.** *When Dad sleeps late,* we all pitch in and do his chores.

_____N_____ **16.** The potatoes and carrots are from the garden *down by the creek.*

_____M_____ **17.** The Soap Box Derby is a lot of fun, but *I have become too busy to participate.*

_____S_____ **18.** *Because my sister is a paramedic,* she has taught CPR to all of us.

_____N_____ **19.** *Because of my high grades,* my name appeared on the honor roll.

_____M_____ **20.** Hatsu kissed Aunt Koto good-bye, but *I was too shy to kiss her.*

Mechanics

▶ **Exercise 3** Write *G* in the blank if the word in italics is a gerund, *P* if it is a participle, or *V* if it is part of a verb phrase.

___V___   The movie star was *waving* to her many fans.

___V___ **1.** The kids were *sliding* down the banister.

___G___ **2.** *Making* the baseball team was a great achievement for Takashi.

___P___ **3.** Isaac, *feeling* very contented, stretched out on the sofa.

___P___ **4.** *Swaying* in the breeze, the branches scratched against the side of the house.

___V___ **5.** Each member is *making* a valuable contribution to the success of the team.

___G___ **6.** *Killing* time is a wasteful activity.

___P___ **7.** *Exploring* the old barn, the girls found a huge cowbell.

___V___ **8.** The twins were *looking* at the catalog.

___G___ **9.** Jason loved *hiking* more than any other activity.

___P___ **10.** Ralph, *sleeping* till noon, missed breakfast and lunch.

___G___ **11.** *Encouraging* her younger sister is fun for Nell.

___P___ **12.** The *galloping* horse skidded to a stop.

___G___ **13.** The Millers are all experts at *fishing.*

___V___ **14.** Kosey had *prepared* a terrific presentation.

___P___ **15.** *Glowing* with pride, Marc displayed the empty space where a tooth used to be.

___G___ **16.** The Scouts liked *camping* in Keller's Hollow.

___G___ **17.** Mom always enjoys *reading.*

___P___ **18.** *Looking* into the refrigerator, Alfonso asked, "When do we eat?"

___G___ **19.** *Leading* the burro proved to be a monumental task.

___V___ **20.** Hans was *eating* some strawberries.

Mechanics

Vocabulary and Spelling

Unit 14: Vocabulary and Spelling

Lesson 86
Building Vocabulary: Learning from Context

You can often figure out the meaning of an unfamiliar word through context. The **context** of a word is the words and sentences that surround it. The chart below lists different kinds of context clues.

TYPE OF CONTEXT CLUE	CLUE WORDS	EXAMPLES
Definition The meaning of the unfamiliar word is stated in the sentence.	*that is* *in other words* *or* *which means*	The soldiers tried to camouflage, *or* disguise, the tanks.
Example The unfamiliar word is explained through examples.	*like* *such as* *for example* *for instance* *including*	Wild animals use many forms of habitation, *such as* dens, burrows, and nests.
Comparison The unfamiliar word is shown to be similar to a familiar word.	*too* *also* *likewise* *similarly*	The lead driver accelerated; those behind him sped up, *too.*
Contrast The unfamiliar word is shown to be different from a familiar word.	*but* *on the other hand* *unlike* *however*	The suspect evaded the police for several days, *but* they finally caught him.

Copyright © by Glencoe/McGraw-Hill

Vocabulary and Spelling

▶ **Exercise 1** Draw a line under the word or words that help you understand the italicized word in each sentence. Circle the clue words. Write the meaning of the italicized word in the blank.

I always avoid *toxic* plants (such as) poison ivy.   **poisonous** _____

1. Alicia did not like the *curfew* in her town. (For example) if she had to be home by 8:00 P.M., she could not study late in the public library. **rule for being home by a certain time**

2. (Unlike) Kenji, who *fidgets* constantly, Chiyo sits calmly at her desk during class. **moves around constantly; is restless**

3. The *foraging* raccoons (also) searched for food in the campgrounds. **searching for food**

4. The dodo bird is *extinct;* the passenger pigeon, (too) is no longer in existence. **no longer in existence**

5. The papers were scattered *haphazardly,* (which means) they were thrown every which way. **thrown every which way**

6. The desks were *cumbersome;* (on the other hand) the chairs were easy to manage. **hard to manage**

7. Some *placards* called for the mayor's recall; other posters called for his impeachment, (too) **posters**

8. The cabin at the lake is *rudimentary;* (in other words) we cook in the fireplace and sleep in sleeping bags on the floor. **basic**

9. Some of Esperanza's exercises were *strenuous.* (However) others were much easier to do. **difficult to do**

10. The motel sign read "*Vacancy,*" (that is) rooms were still available. **an empty space**

11. The county helped with the national *census;* the city (also) assisted with the population count. **population count**

12. Our *cistern* was overflowing, (unlike) the other wells in the community. **well**

13. Penny was *aloof* at first, (but) she became more friendly after a few days at her new school. **unfriendly**

14. Haloke is *resourceful;* (for instance) he can find a solution to any problem. **capable of finding solutions to problems**

15. *Conifers,* (such as) pines and firs, stay green all through the winter. **trees such as pines and firs**

16. The robbers' *cache,* (or) hiding place, was discovered by hikers. **hiding place**

Name _____ Class _____ Date _____

Lesson 87
Building Vocabulary: Word Roots

A **root** is the main part of a word, and it carries the main meaning of the word. By knowing the meanings of common word roots, you can usually figure out the meanings of unfamiliar words. Study the word roots and their meanings on the chart. When a word root is a complete word, it is called a **base word**

ROOT	WORD	MEANING
script means "writing"	inscription	something written
spec means "see" or "look"	spectacles	devices that improve eyesight
aud means "hear"	audible	can be heard
duct or *duce* means "lead"	conductor	leader of an orchestra
pel or *pul* means "push"	repellant	substance that pushes insects away
ject means "throw"	reject	throw back
port means "carry"	portable	can be carried
dict means "tell" or "say"	dictator	sole ruler

▶ **Exercise 1** Draw a line under the root of each word. Using a dictionary when needed, write a short definition of each word.

spectacle   _something seen that is unusual or entertaining_____

1. reporter _person who gathers news_____

2. auditorium _large gathering room with seats, such as in a school or theater_____

3. projector _machine that shows films_____

4. prescription _an order written by a doctor_____

5. spectators _people who look at something_____

6. dictate _command or order_____

Vocabulary and Spelling

7. introduction _speech or writing that leads to something else_____

8. export _product carried out of a country_____

9. propulsion _process of driving forward_____

10. contradict _to say the opposite of_____

11. prospector _person who searches for something, usually riches or treasure_____

12. description _detailed account that is often written down_____

13. porter _person who carries luggage_____

14. audience _people gathered to hear or see an event_____

15. propellers _devices that push a plane or boat forward_____

16. conduct _lead_____

17. eject _throw out_____

18. rejection _refusal_____

19. audition _a tryout, usually for an acting or singing role_____

20. suspect _someone under watch_____

▶ **Exercise 2** **Draw a line under the word that best fits the definition in parentheses.**

I cannot <u>compel</u> you to study. (force)

1. The <u>speculators</u> filled the stock exchange. (people looking for business opportunities)

2. I <u>object</u> to your tone of voice. (am opposed)

3. The new drapes <u>reduced</u> the noise in the large room. (made smaller)

4. The silly clown made a <u>spectacle</u> of himself. (something viewed that is amusing or unusual)

5. The boss gave <u>dictation</u> to her secretary. (spoken words)

6. The public <u>transportation</u> situation in the city has grown worse. (the carrying of people and goods)

7. I found that strange word in the <u>dictionary</u>. (book of words in the language)

8. Will you <u>subscribe</u> to that new magazine? (order or sign up for)

Lesson 88
Building Vocabulary: Prefixes and Suffixes

A **prefix** can be added to the beginning of a word and a **suffix** can be added to the end of a word. Prefixes and suffixes change the meanings of root words. The spelling of a word can change when a suffix is added.

PREFIXES

Prefixes	Examples	Meanings
un-, dis-, non-, im-, and *il-* usually mean "not" or "the opposite of"	unwrapped dishonest nonprofit immortal illogical	not wrapped not honest not for profit not mortal not logical
re- means "again" or "back"	reheat	heat again
super- means "above" or "beyond"	supersonic	above the speed of sound
sub- means "below" or "under"	subzero	below zero
fore- means "front" or "before"	forenoon	before noon
post- means "after"	postwar	after the war
uni- means "one"	unicycle	one-wheeled vehicle
bi- means "two"	biweekly	every two weeks
tri- means "three"	triangle	with three angles

▶ **Exercise 1** Using a prefix and a base word, write a new word in the blank that matches the definition.

One-wheeled bicycle <u>unicycle</u>

1. not legal <u>illegal</u>

2. not true <u>untrue</u>

3. the opposite of comfort
<u>discomfort</u>

4. undersea vehicle <u>submarine</u>

5. apply again <u>reapply</u>

6. every three months <u>trimonthly</u>

7. beyond the natural <u>supernatural</u>

8. the opposite of sense <u>nonsense</u>

9. soil under the surface <u>subsoil</u>

10. the front of the head <u>forehead</u>

11. not expensive <u>inexpensive</u>

Vocabulary and Spelling

12. not approve <u>disapprove</u>

13. to date after today <u>postdate</u>

14. state again <u>restate</u>

15. two-winged airplane <u>biplane</u>

16. the opposite of practical

<u>impractical</u>

17. front paws <u>forepaws</u>

18. over heated <u>superheated</u>

SUFFIXES

Suffixes	Examples	Meanings
-ship and -hood mean "state of" or "condition of"	neighborhood friendship	state of being neighbors state of being friends
-ment means "act of" or "state of"	management	act of managing
-ward means "in the direction of" or "toward"	homeward	toward home
-ist means "one who"	archaeologist	one who studies archaeology
-ish means "like"	childish	like a child
-ous means "full of" or "like"	courageous	full of courage
-al means "like" or "having to do with"	alphabetical	having to do with the alphabet

▶ **Exercise 2** **Use a base word and a suffix to form a new word that matches the definition.**

1. one who studies science

<u>scientist</u>

2. toward the sky <u>skyward</u>

3. act of being excited <u>excitement</u>

4. state of being a leader <u>leadership</u>

5. one who writes novels <u>novelist</u>

6. having to do with tradition

<u>traditional</u>

7. full of humor <u>humorous</u>

8. act of improving <u>improvement</u>

9. full of peril <u>perilous</u>

10. state of being false <u>falsehood</u>

11. having to do with logic <u>logical</u>

12. one who studies geology <u>geologist</u>

13. one who plays the violin <u>violinist</u>

14. full of thunder <u>thunderous</u>

15. like a boy <u>boyish</u>

16. toward the sea <u>seaward</u>

Vocabulary and Spelling

Lesson 89
Synonyms and Antonyms

Synonyms are words that mean the same or about the same as each other.
Antonyms are words that mean the opposite of each other.

Binte **raced** through her test and **hurried** out to soccer practice. (synonyms)
Kikuyu **raced** through the first part of the course and then **crawled** over the
finish line. (antonyms)

Sometimes you can form an antonym by adding a prefix meaning "not."

I thought my report was **complete,** but my teacher told me it was **incomplete.**

▶ **Exercise 1** Draw a line under the synonym in parentheses that means the same or
about the same as the italicized word in the sentence.

Dinosaurs were *astonishing* animals. (fierce, well-polished, <u>surprising</u>)

1. Many species of animals and plants are no longer on earth; they have become *extinct.*
   (mature, <u>nonexistent</u>, hidden)

2. Some *species* died out because of natural causes. (<u>kinds</u>, special, scientists)

3. *Meteorological* factors, such as periods of drought or severe cold, caused many
   animals to become extinct. (disease, <u>climate</u>, war)

4. Plant-eating dinosaurs were often eaten by *carnivores.* (<u>meat eaters</u>, gorillas,
   vegetables)

5. Today, many species of animals are *endangered.* (<u>imperiled</u>, migrating, adapting)

6. Human activities often destroy the *habitats* of animals. (food, <u>homes</u>, health)

7. If a single oak tree is cut down, 280 species may be affected because they are *linked*
   with that tree in a food chain. (<u>connected</u>, familiar, hostile)

8. Many food chains have a *delicate* balance and can be easily destroyed. (strong, filmy,
   <u>fragile</u>)

9. If owls die out because trees are cut down, the animals on which owls *prey* grow more
   numerous and become pests. (<u>feed</u>, sit, nest)

10. Rain forests *harbor* millions of animal and plant species. (endanger, <u>shelter</u>, number)

11. Scientists fear that continual destruction of rain forest plants will deprive humans of
    remedies for many diseases. (germs, descriptions, <u>cures</u>)

Vocabulary and Spelling

12. Other human behavior also makes it difficult for plants and animals to *survive*. (hide, live, hunt)

13. Chemicals *pollute* the environment, poisoning many species. (color, extend, dirty)

14. When these poisons get into animals' bodies, the adults cannot *reproduce*. (eat, breed, sleep)

15. The pesticide DDT is so dangerous that authorities *banned* it in many areas. (encouraged, sold, prohibited)

16. People also *poach* animals for their skins, tusks, and fur. (hunt, raise, protect)

17. Although such activities are *illicit* in many places, the trade in endangered animal products continues. (encouraged, profitable, illegal)

18. When *alien* species are brought to a new area, they often crowd out native species who are already there. (colorful, foreign, adaptable)

19. When rabbits were brought to Australia, their numbers *increased* until they killed off crops. (shrank, stabilized, grew)

20. Today many people who are concerned about the environment *strive* to protect endangered species around the world. (refuse, try, agree)

▶ **Exercise 2 In order for the sentence to make sense, underline the word in parentheses that is the antonym of the italicized word in the sentence.**

Zoos often house many *common* animals so that they may breed in safety. (normal, rare, sleepy)

1. Some endangered species are being put into *unprotected* areas. (safe, special, illegal)

2. The *tiny* Serengeti National Park in Tanzania, Africa, is home to more than two million rhinos, leopards, zebras, and giraffes. (enormous, overdeveloped, rare)

3. The government of India set up Operation Tiger to help people *hunt* the tigers. (see, raise, protect)

4. Wildlife refuges often have problems because they are *overfunded*. (anti-animal, substandard, underfunded)

5. Manatees are water mammals that have become *numerous* because many are killed or injured by boat propellers. (injured, rare, independent)

6. Environmentalists have created *desert* reserves in order to protect the manatees. (forest, mountain, marine)

Vocabulary and Spelling

Lesson 90
Homonyms

Homonyms are words that sound alike or are spelled alike but have different meanings. The word *homonym* comes from Greek words that mean *same names*. There are two kinds of homonyms. The first type, **homographs** are spelled alike but have different meanings and often have different pronunciations.

The **sow** watched the farmer **sow** his crops. (homographs)

The second type of homonym, **homophones**, are words that sound alike but have different spellings and different meanings.

I **know** you want to stay up late, but I still say **no**. (homophones)

▶ **Exercise 1** Write *N* above the italicized homograph if it is a noun, *V* if it is a verb, and *adj.* if it is an adjective.

                V
The teacher will *record* our scores.

         N
1. I have a *record* of my grades.

               N
2. Terri has taken the *lead*.

            adj.
3. Carla is our *lead* cheerleader.

          N
4. A strong *wind* knocked over our antenna last night.

           V
5. Sook will *wind* the tape.

          V
6. Jamal *read* about it in the school paper.

                  N
7. Nancy Drew mysteries are a good *read*.

            N
8. That is a strange *object*.

           V
9. How can you *object* to this video?

      N
10. The *fleet* sailed into the harbor.

       adj.
11. The *fleet* deer sailed over the thorny hedge.

           N
12. I won't shed a *tear* over spilled milk.

          N
13. Charles saw a *tear* in my new jacket.

               V
14. Listen to those motorcycles *tear* down the street.

           adj.
15. Yoshi must learn to tie a *bow* tie.

Vocabulary and Spelling

16. A viking ship had a high *bow*.   **N**

17. The fans are really *wound* up for the game.   **adj.**

18. I thought you *wound* the old clock yesterday.   **V**

19. A white *dove* landed on the park bench.   **N**

20. Sheila *dove* off the high board.   **V**

▶ **Exercise 2 Draw a line under the words that are homophones. A sentence may contain several homophones.**

    My dad bought a small <u>sailboat</u> at the boat <u>sale</u>.

1. The baby <u>threw</u> the toy <u>through</u> the bars of his crib.

2. It has been a <u>week</u> since my operation, but I still feel <u>weak</u>.

3. <u>Their</u> packages were sitting out <u>there</u> all day, so I suppose <u>they're</u> soaked with rain by now.

4. I simply will <u>not</u> tie this silly <u>knot</u>!

5. <u>It's</u> not <u>fair</u> for the bus company to raise <u>its</u> <u>fare</u> again!

6. Are you <u>two</u> going <u>to</u> the game, <u>too</u>?

7. I <u>hear</u> a finch over <u>here</u> in the trees.

8. The wind <u>blew</u> so hard that the ocean's <u>blue</u> water turned to grey.

9. If you give me another <u>pear</u> to <u>pare</u>, then I will have a <u>pair</u>.

10. The expert sailor sailed <u>straight</u> through the narrow <u>strait</u>.

11. The <u>presence</u> of my grandmother usually means there are <u>presents</u> for us.

12. I can't <u>wait</u> any longer to lose the <u>weight</u> I put on.

13. We had to <u>brake</u> quickly to avoid the water that was spilling out of the <u>break</u> in the levee.

14. Will you give me some <u>peace</u> if I give you another <u>piece</u> of pie?

15. Solada got the <u>one</u> thing she really wanted when the Tigers <u>won</u> the championship game.

16. It gave Molly great <u>pain</u> to tell her father she had broken the window <u>pane</u>.

17. Ouch, <u>I</u> poked a finger in my <u>eye</u>!

18. While I had the <u>flu</u>, a bird <u>flew</u> down the chimney <u>flue</u> and into the house.

Vocabulary and Spelling

Lesson 91
Basic Spelling Rules I

SPELLING *IE* AND *EI*

The *i* comes before *e*, except when both letters follow *c* or when both letters are pronounced together as an *ā* sound, as in *neighbor* and *weigh*.

ach**ie**ve   gr**ie**ve   dec**ei**ve   c**ei**ling   w**ei**ght

There are some exceptions to this rule, so you should memorize their spellings. Exceptions include *species, weird, either, seize, leisure,* and *protein*.

SPELLING UNSTRESSED VOWELS

An unstressed vowel sound is a sound that is not emphasized when the word is spoken. For example, the second syllable *(i)* in *sim-i-lar* is an unstressed vowel sound. If you are not sure which vowel to use when spelling an unstressed syllable, think of a similar word. In the word *rel__tive*, is the missing letter *a, e, i, o,* or *u?* Think of the word *relation,* which uses the vowel *a,* to spell the word *relative.*

▶ **Exercise 1** Write in the blank the correct spelling for each word. If a word is already correct, write *correct.* Use a dictionary if necessary.

releif _____relief_____

1. retreive	retrieve	13. viel	veil
2. cieling	ceiling	14. defanition	definition
3. compitition	competition	15. seizure	correct
4. neither	correct	16. decieve	deceive
5. neice	niece	17. oppisite	opposite
6. imaganary	imaginary	18. hygeine	hygiene
7. height	correct	19. conceit	correct
8. weird	correct	20. eighth	correct
9. reciept	receipt	21. wiegh	weigh
10. createve	creative	22. informitive	informative
11. diet	correct	23. photagraph	photograph
12. observent	observant	24. special	correct

Vocabulary and Spelling

SUFFIXES AND SILENT *E*

For most words that end with silent *e*, keep the *e* when adding a suffix. When you add the suffix *-ly* to a word that ends in *l* plus silent *e*, drop the *-le*. Also drop the silent *e* when you add a suffix beginning with a vowel or a *-y*.

safe + *-ly* = safely   drizzle + *-ly* = drizzly   bubble + *-ing* = bubbling

SUFFIXES AND FINAL *Y*

For words ending with a vowel + *y*, keep the *y* when adding a suffix. For words ending with a consonant + *y*, change the *y* to *i*. The exception is when the suffix begins with an *i*. To avoid having two *i's* together, keep the *y*.

joy + *-ful* = joyful   silly + *-ness* = silliness   cry + *-ing* = crying

ADDING PREFIXES

When you add a prefix to a word, do not change the spelling of the word.

il- + legal = illegal   *re-* + cook = recook   *un-* + tie = untie

▶ **Exercise 2** Use the spelling rules in this lesson to spell the words indicated.

copy + *-ing* = __copying__

1. bite + *-ing* = __biting__
2. migrate + *-ion* = __migration__
3. sleepy + *-ly* __sleepily__
4. *pre-* + heat = __preheat__
5. tune + *-ful* = __tuneful__
6. nerve + *-ous* = __nervous__
7. imagine + *-able* = __imaginable__
8. *un-* + truthful = __untruthful__
9. waste + *-ful* = __wasteful__
10. fly + *-er* = __flier__
11. spray + *-ing* = __spraying__
12. advise + *-able* = __advisable__

13. rely + *-ed* = __relied__
14. peppy + *-est* = __peppiest__
15. sprinkle + *-ed* = __sprinkled__
16. trouble + *-ing* = __troubling__
17. ice + *-y* = __icy__
18. peace + *-ful* = __peaceful__
19. startle + *-ed* = __startled__
20. *sub-* + atomic = __subatomic__
21. *dis-* + respect = __disrespect__
22. froth + *-y* = __frothy__
23. babble + *-ing* = __babbling__
24. cry + *-er* = __crier__

Vocabulary and Spelling

Lesson 92
Basic Spelling Rules II

DOUBLING THE FINAL CONSONANT

Double the final consonant when a word ends with a single consonant following one vowel and the word is one syllable or the last syllable is accented both before and after adding the suffix.

jog + -*er* = jogger   omit + -*ed* = omitted

Do not double the final consonant if the accent is not on the last syllable or if the accent moves when a suffix is added.

enter + -*ed* = entered   refer + -*ence* = reference

Also do not double the final consonant if the word already ends in two consonants or if the suffix begins with a consonant.

sing + -*er* = singer   equip + -*ment* = equipment

When adding the suffix -*ly* to a word ending in -*ll*, drop one *l*.

hill + -*ly* = hilly   bull + -*ly* = bully

FORMING PLURALS

Form the plural of most nouns ending in -*s*, -*sh*, -*ch*, -*x*, or -*z* by adding -*es*. If the noun ends with a consonant + -*y*, change the *y* to *i* and then add -*es*.

patch + -*es* = patches   fox + -*es* = foxes   fly + -*es* = flies

Add -*s* to nouns ending with a vowel + -*y* or *o* as well as to nouns ending with a consonant + *o*.

toy + -*s* = toys   patio + -*s* = patios   solo + -*s* = solos

Some common exceptions are *cargo-cargoes*, *hero-heroes*, and *tomato-tomatoes*.

If a noun ends with a vowel + -*f* or -*lf*, change the *f* to a *v* and add -*es*. If a noun ends with -*fe*, change the *f* to a *v* and add -*s*. Just add an -*s* for nouns ending with -*ff* and for some nouns ending with a vowel + -*f*.

loaf + -*es* = loaves   half + -*es* = halves   wife + -*s* = wives
knife + -*s* = knives   roof + -*s* = roofs   sniff + -*s* = sniffs

Irregular plurals include *man-men*, *mouse-mice*, *goose-geese*, *foot-feet*, *woman-women*, *child-children*, and *tooth-teeth*.

Vocabulary and Spelling

FORMING COMPOUND WORDS

Keep the complete spelling of the original words in the compound.

snow + storm = snowstorm   broad + cast = broadcast   gear + shift = gearshift

▶ **Exercise 1** Use the rules from this lesson to write the plural form of each word.

child _____children_____

1.	wolf	wolves	11. hobby	hobbies
2.	piano	pianos	12. injury	injuries
3.	glass	glasses	13. leaf	leaves
4.	tax	taxes	14. kangaroo	kangaroos
5.	igloo	igloos	15. chimney	chimneys
6.	self	selves	16. mouse	mice
7.	calf	calves	17. scarf	scarves *or* scarfs
8.	staff	staffs	18. whiff	whiffs
9.	tomato	tomatoes	19. photo	photos
10.	buzz	buzzes	20. marsh	marshes

▶ **Exercise 2** Write in the blank the correct spelling for each word.

donkies _____donkeys_____

1.	grabing	grabbing	11. housboat	houseboat
2.	tooths	teeth	12. waltzs	waltzes
3.	forgetable	forgettable	13. womans	women
4.	skiscraper	skyscraper	14. potatos	potatoes
5.	shoping	shopping	15. cuffves	cuffs
6.	ladys	ladies	16. wooly	woolly
7.	spys	spies	17. baskeball	basketball
8.	singging	singing	18. gooses	geese
9.	bushs	bushes	19. ferrys	ferries
10.	melodys	melodies	20. preferrence	preference

Vocabulary and Spelling

✓ Unit 14 Review: Building Vocabulary

▶ **Exercise 1** Underline the word or words in parentheses that best complete each sentence. Use a dictionary if necessary.

(Their, They're) planning to attend the Computer Club meeting.

1. After his heart surgery, the patient was wheeled to the (preoperative, postoperative) ward.

2. The wild (boar, bore) is a fierce animal native to the forests of Asia and North Africa.

3. Because the angry man's tone was so vengeful, I decided to (open the door, call the police).

4. When the flexion returned to the woman's wrist after the operation, she was able to (wash, bend) it again.

5. The lawyer carried the important legal papers in a leather (scolex, portfolio).

6. The fisherman from Nova Scotia spoke a (dialect, semaphore) so unusual that we had a hard time understanding him.

7. The prince vouchsafed the traveler passage through his territory; as a result, the traveler (succeeded, failed) in reaching the distant castle.

8. In preindustrial society, most people earned their living by working (in factories, on farms).

9. A metronome beside the piano helped the students (play the correct notes, count the correct rhythm).

10. Since she began (telecommuting, collating) in her job, my mother is able to spend much more time at home.

11. Pollution from burning fossil fuels can damage the (stratosphere, biosphere), the part of the earth's atmosphere where we live.

12. The photographer asked us to (<u>wait</u>, weight) in her studio.

13. The impecunious students had to go without coal to heat their room; likewise, the family across the hall had little (intelligence, <u>money</u>).

14. Because they coproduced the award-winning film, (one, <u>both</u>) of them will receive the prize.

15. I could tell the patient's (<u>gustatory</u>, visual) abilities were damaged because he couldn't taste anything.

16. The way he taps his pencil during tests is beginning to (great, <u>grate</u>) on my nerves.

17. My little sister went to an audiologist to have her (vision, <u>hearing</u>) tested.

18. My grandmother's (library card, <u>antique diamond pin</u>) was irreplaceable.

19. Because my mom saw no color in my (<u>pallid</u>, glowing) face, she put me to bed.

20. The king's message was benedictory, and his subjects (<u>rejoiced</u>, grew fearful).

▶ **Exercise 2** Write a synonym and an antonym for each word. Use your dictionary or thesaurus as needed. **Answers may vary**

WORD	SYNONYM	ANTONYM
sad	glum	happy
1. feeble	weak	strong
2. excited	enthusiastic	unexcited
3. optional	voluntary	required
4. rapid	swift	slow
5. stay	remain	leave
6. liberal	generous	stingy
7. sunset	dusk	dawn
8. criticize	blame	praise
9. smart	intelligent	dumb
10. saunter	stroll	run
11. careful	cautious	careless
12. childish	juvenile	mature

✓ Unit 14 Review: Basic Spelling Rules

▶ **Exercise 1** Underline the word or phrase that is spelled correctly.

The two presidents announced they were completely (commited, <u>committed</u>) to seeking peace.

1. The first thing Mom did when we moved into our new apartment was to assemble the (<u>bookshelves</u>, bookshelfs).

2. A (<u>bookkeeper</u>, bookeeper) for a company needs to know how to use a computer.

3. There must be six or seven (partys, <u>parties</u>) planned for our eighth-grade graduation.

4. Kristin was (<u>totally</u>, totaly) surprised when she received the package.

5. Three former (secretary of the interiors, <u>secretaries of the interior</u>) were present for the hearings.

6. The (remainning, <u>remaining</u>) test questions don't look too difficult.

7. Our family and the (Ramirezs, <u>Ramirezes</u>) often do things together.

8. The clown was wearing a goofy checked jacket with ugly (<u>striped</u>, stripped) pants.

9. Many different (<u>species</u>, specieses) are considered endangered.

10. (Shoing, <u>Shoeing</u>) a thousand-pound workhorse can't be an easy job!

11. Almost every music group today makes (<u>videos</u>, videoes).

12. Telephoning everyone doesn't seem like a (practicel, <u>practical</u>) solution to the problem.

13. Both teams played (<u>their</u>, thier) best game of the season.

14. Miranda doesn't get nervous at all when the (<u>spotlight</u>, spottlight) is on her.

15. The weather in April is so (<u>changeable</u>, changable)!

16. When the singer asked if the crowd was ready to rock and roll, the crowd (shoutted, <u>shouted</u>) back "Yes!"

Vocabulary and Spelling

17. The governor will make a (statment, <u>statement</u>) at 3:30 this afternoon about the

hurricane damage.

18. She would have (<u>applied</u>, applyed) for the program by now if she were really

interested.

19. The scoreboard showed nothing but (<u>zeros</u>, zeroes) for the Milton batters through eight

innings.

20. Uncle Roy got a (<u>fishhook</u>, fishook) in his finger and had to take it out carefully.

▶ **Exercise 2** Write the new word formed by combining two words or by combining the
word with the prefix or suffix indicated. Use a dictionary if necessary.

plant + -*ing* __planting__

1. broken + -*ness* __brokenness__	**11.** play + book __playbook__
2. incredible + -*ly* __incredibly__	**12.** sincere + -*ly* __sincerely__
3. hill + -*ly* __hilly__	**13.** stop + -*ed* __stopped__
4. *mis*- + spelling __misspelling__	**14.** flee + -*ing* __fleeing__
5. suit + case __suitcase__	**15.** escape + -*ing* __escaping__
6. propel + -*ed* __propelled__	**16.** develop + -*ment* __development__
7. blue + berry __blueberry__	**17.** open + -*ness* __openness__
8. use + -*able* __usable__	**18.** *un*- + natural __unnatural__
9. curl + -*y* __curly__	**19.** state + -*ed* __stated__
10. fame + -*ous* __famous__	**20.** *re*- + alignment __realignment__

▶ **Exercise 3** Write the plural form of each word in the blank.

fox __foxes__

1. mouse __mice__	**5.** essay __essays__
2. disc jockey __disc jockeys__	**6.** photo __photos__
3. ax __axes__	**7.** folly __follies__
4. leaf __leaves__	**8.** Jones __Joneses__

Vocabulary and Spelling

Composition

Unit 15: Composition

Lesson 93
The Writing Process: Prewriting

Before you begin writing, you must decide what to write about. There are a number of **prewriting** exercises that will help you decide on a topic. The **topic** is the subject you are going to write about. *Freewriting* is a prewriting method by which you build on a thought. A writer freewrites by not lifting the pen from the paper, thereby writing out a continuous series of thoughts. Other prewriting methods include *collecting information* on different subjects and *compiling lists.* Yet another prewriting exercise might be *asking* general questions. Once you have decided on a topic, make a cluster diagram to further develop your ideas. Consider your purpose in writing. Some purposes are to tell a story, to persuade, to inform, to describe, or to amuse. Finally, think about your audience. The people for whom you write will determine your choice of words and the writing style you use. Keep in mind how much your audience already knows about the topic.

▶ **Exercise 1 Try a freewriting exercise in which you write about the first thought that occurs to you. Compile any ideas or images related to this thought in one continuous piece of writing.**

_____

_____

_____

_____

_____

_____

_____

_____

_____

_____

Composition

▶ **Exercise 2** List five things about three different topics that interest you. Feel free to list things that you may have written down in the previous freewriting exercise.

Bicycles: racing bikes, dirt bikes, ten-speeds, bike races, bike trails.

_____

_____

_____

_____

_____

▶ **Exercise 3** Choose three items or ideas from Exercise 2, and write a topic sentence about each one.

I wish we had a bike trail near my house.

_____

_____

_____

▶ **Exercise 4** Identify the topic of each sentence. Tell whether the purpose is to persuade, to inform, to describe, to tell a story, or to amuse.

The recent lack of rain has hurt the gardens and lawns. **Topic:** _lack of rain_____

Purpose: _to inform (Other answers are possible.)_____

1. Motor scooters are very noisy. **Topic:** _motor scooters_____

   Purpose: _to persuade (Other answers are possible.)_____

2. We should have canceled the picnic when we saw the storm clouds. **Topic:** _the picnic_

   Purpose: _to persuade_____

3. I spent the summer at my aunt's home on the coast. **Topic:** _spending summer at aunt's_

   _home_____

   Purpose: _to describe (Other answers are possible.)_____

4. The first time I was ever in a canoe was my last! **Topic:** _first time in canoe_____

   Purpose: _to amuse (Other answers are possible.)_____

Composition

5. Watching birds in the nearby park is relaxing. **Topic:** _bird watching_

Purpose: _to describe (Other answers are possible.)_

6. You should not ride your bikes on a busy street. **Topic:** _riding bikes on a busy street_

Purpose: _to persuade_

7. My special method of studying works really well. **Topic:** _special method of studying_

Purpose: _to inform (Other answers are possible.)_

8. Every day, on the way to school, I see an old horse all alone in a field.

Topic: _old horse in a field (Other answers are possible.)_

Purpose: _to tell a story_

9. There are ten reasons our class should help keep the school grounds clean.

Topic: _reasons our class should keep school grounds clean_

Purpose: _to persuade (Other answers are possible.)_

10. My favorite author is Mark Twain. **Topic:** _favorite author_

Purpose: _to inform_

▶ **Exercise 5** Write a sentence that conveys both the stated topic and purpose.

Topic: stories **Purpose:** to persuade your friend that making up stories is a good way to pass the time _Making up stories is a great way to pass the time because it's fun and creative._

1. Topic: class car wash **Purpose:** to persuade the class to organize a car wash
Our class should organize a car wash because the money could help buy new gym equipment.

2. Topic: a favorite magazine **Purpose:** to inform friends about a magazine that you like very much _Sports Illustrated covers all the sports and has super pictures!_

3. Topic: ant farm **Purpose:** to describe an ant farm that you once had _I once had a large ant farm filled with dirt and lots of ants._

4. Topic: giving your dog a bath **Purpose:** to amuse your classmates
The last time we tried to give my dog a bath, he started shaking and everyone got drenched!

5. Topic: a sports car **Purpose:** to describe it _It was a bright red convertible with gray leather seats._

Composition

6. **Topic:** the recycling program in your community **Purpose:** to inform friends about what they can do to help. To make our recycling program a success, you must save all your newspapers, cans, and bottles.

7. **Topic:** toad in the house **Purpose:** to amuse your friends I will never forget the time I started up the stairs, and suddenly, I saw a big, fat, lumpy toad!

8. **Topic:** favorite television show **Purpose:** to persuade everyone to watch the show I guarantee that if you watch this show, you won't stop laughing!

9. **Topic:** first time you went to a play **Purpose:** to tell a story about the experience The first time I went to a play I was amazed by the fancy scenery and costumes.

10. **Topic:** your weekend activities **Purpose:** to describe what you did over the weekend I had a very busy, yet rewarding, weekend cleaning out the garage.

▶ **Exercise 6** For each audience listed below, write a brief paragraph about the following topic:

Topic: Should the biology class take a group trip to Sea World?

1. **Audience:** students

_____
_____
_____

2. **Audience:** principal and school board

_____
_____
_____

3. **Audience:** parents

_____
_____
_____

Composition

Lesson 94
The Writing Process: Drafting

Drafting is the next stage of the writing process. It involves putting your ideas into sentence and paragraph form. Use your prewriting notes, lists, or clusters to guide your writing. The combined topic and purpose for writing is called the **theme**. Clearly state your theme in a **thesis statement** in the first paragraph. Each following paragraph consists of a topic sentence that states a main idea, followed by sentences that support or tell more about that idea. Every paragraph should relate to the theme that is stated in the first paragraph. How you write depends on your audience. Think about your readers, and carefully choose the **style**, or **voice**, that you want to use. The voice can be formal and businesslike or informal and friendly.

▶ **Exercise 1** **Write a thesis statement that goes with each topic and purpose.**

Topic: black cats **Purpose:** to inform a friend about silly superstitions __Black cats are__

__objects of silly superstitious beliefs.__

1. **Topic:** pets **Purpose:** to inform friends about pet ownership __When you have a pet, you__

__experience love, companionship, and a great deal of fun.__

2. **Topic:** William Shakespeare **Purpose:** to inform your classmates about the playwright

__William Shakespeare was an English playwright who wrote comedies and tragedies.__

3. **Topic:** baseball **Purpose:** to describe the game __Baseball is a popular outdoor__

__sport.__

4. **Topic:** sports clubs **Purpose:** to persuade friends to start a sports club __Sports clubs are a__

__great way to make new friends and to get into shape through exercise.__

5. **Topic:** Garfield, the cat **Purpose:** to amuse readers __Let's follow Garfield through some of his__

__adventures, and you will see why he is so funny!__

6. **Topic:** summer jobs **Purpose:** to persuade the reader to look for a summer job

__Summer jobs keep you busy and give you extra spending money.__

7. **Topic:** family picnic **Purpose:** to tell a story __Our family had a very__

__eventful picnic last July fourth.__

Composition

8. **Topic:** saving money **Purpose:** to persuade a friend to save money

   It is very important to save money for emergencies.

9. **Topic:** flying buffaloes **Purpose:** to amuse friends Yes, indeed, I remember the day when I

   first saw a flying buffalo!

10. **Topic:** honey **Purpose:** to describe honey Honey is a sweet, sticky substance made by bees

   from the nectar of flowers.

11. **Topic:** a sunset **Purpose:** to describe its beauty A sunset, with its reds, oranges, and

   purples, can be breathtaking.

12. **Topic:** a day at an amusement park **Purpose:** to describe what you did My friend and I

   spent the whole day going on rides, seeing shows, and trying to win prizes.

13. **Topic:** civic issues **Purpose:** to persuade students to be concerned about their

   community If you want our town to be a safe and attractive place to live, you must get involved.

14. **Topic:** student meetings **Purpose:** to inform students about methods of running a

   student meeting There are a number of methods we can use to run our student meetings.

15. **Topic:** Thomas Edison **Purpose:** to inform your classmates about his inventions

   Thomas Edison is responsible for many inventions, including the lightbulb and motion picture

   equipment.

16. **Topic:** the joys of playing the guitar **Purpose:** to persuade the reader to learn how to

   play the guitar Playing the guitar is fun and relaxing, and you can take it with you almost

   anywhere!

17. **Topic:** honor society **Purpose:** to describe the honor of being asked to join It is a great

   honor to be asked to join a student honor society.

18. **Topic:** a favorite musical group **Purpose:** to inform friends about the songs on a new

   CD that you like There is a new CD out that has all of our favorite group's greatest hits plus

   some new ones.

Composition

▶ **Exercise 2** Write a thesis statement for each theme.

Theme: the tragedy of the American Civil War __The Civil War was a great tragedy for America.__

1. **Theme:** the fun of shopping for clothes __Shopping for clothes can be great fun!__

2. **Theme:** the importance of remembering names and faces __One secret to success is to remember names and faces.__

3. **Theme:** the value of knowing about computers __You must know about computers if you want to succeed.__

4. **Theme:** bicycling is fun and a good form of exercise __Not only is bicycling fun, but it is also a good form of exercise.__

5. **Theme:** learning about useful study tips __If you follow certain study tips, your grades are sure to improve.__

6. **Theme:** Eleanor Roosevelt, wife of President Franklin D. Roosevelt __Eleanor Roosevelt was one of the most respected first ladies the United States has ever had.__

7. **Theme:** the fascinating planet Mars __Mars is a mysterious and absolutely fascinating planet.__

8. **Theme:** painting in watercolor __Watercolor is a fun and beautiful way to express yourself.__

9. **Theme:** those odd porcupines __Porcupines are fascinating animals, but don't get too close!__

10. **Theme:** knowing about fats in foods __For your own health, it is important to know about fats in foods.__

11. **Theme:** Tyrannosaurus rex __The most ferocious dinosaur was the Tyrannosaurus rex.__

12. **Theme:** the great Sioux leader Red Cloud __The great Sioux leader Red Cloud was an important figure in the West.__

13. **Theme:** a visit to a park __A visit to a park can be a fun and educational experience.__

14. **Theme:** the dolphin __The dolphin is a highly intelligent mammal.__

15. **Theme:** reading the novels of Cynthia Voigt __Cynthia Voigt wrote novels about people we can all identify with.__

Composition

► **Exercise 3** Write three related sentences that provide details to support each topic sentence.

A good dictionary is a student's best friend.

Not only does a dictionary provide definitions for words, but it also gives their pronunciations. It can give you the part of speech and origin for a word you have selected. This can be very helpful when you are trying to write a good paper.

1. Mathematics is a very important subject to study. _____

_____

_____

2. Summertime is the best time of the year. _____

_____

_____

3. I would like to visit an archaeological museum. _____

_____

_____

► **Exercise 4** Write one brief paragraph related to each theme. Use the voice indicated.

1. **Theme:** a story to amuse your friends **Voice:** talkative and friendly.

_____

_____

_____

_____

2. **Theme:** a letter of complaint to your town's newspaper **Voice:** formal and firm, yet respectful.

_____

_____

_____

_____

Composition

Lesson 95
The Writing Process: Revising

Revising what you have already written helps you improve the first draft. Look for three things as you revise: *meaning, unity,* and *coherence.* Meaning refers to your theme. Did you stick to your topic? Unity refers to organization. Is the organization of your sentences logical? Do the details support the topics? Coherence refers to flow. Is your writing clear, natural, and interesting? Did you accomplish your purpose? Did you keep your audience in mind?

▶ **Exercise 1 Revise and rewrite each paragraph for meaning, unity, and coherence.**

1. Just as important as being a speaker is being an active listener. When you speak, look at the person. Don't interrupt. Having good conversation skills is important in relating to people. You also need to read a lot. Show interest in what the other is saying. Keep eye contact. Keep to the subject.

Having good conversation skills is important in relating to people. It is just as important to be an

active listener as it is to be a good speaker. Show interest in what the other person is saying by

keeping eye contact. Respond to what is being said, but do not interrupt. When you speak, look at

the person to whom you are speaking, and stick to the subject.

_____

_____

2. A most unloved plant has been garlic. Not allowed to eat it in India were Brahmins, and Hsuan Ch'uang made a law two thousand years ago that if somebody wanted to eat garlic, they had to eat outside of town. The English ate it for hundreds of years, but by the nineteenth century gave it up because they thought it the food of foreigners. It produces bad breath. It is tasty. It has health benefits.

Garlic is a most unloved plant. Brahmins in India were not allowed to eat it. In China, the ruler Hsuan

Ch'uang made it a law that whoever wanted to eat garlic had to eat it outside the town. The English,

on the other hand, ate it for hundreds of years. They gave it up by the nineteenth century, however,

because they considered it the food of foreigners. Unfortunately for garlic and garlic lovers, it

produces bad breath. On the other hand, it is very tasty and does have health benefits.

_____

Composition

3. Wigs were popular during Revolutionary War America. Men and women in town wore powdered wigs all the time. The wigs itched. The American militia from the countryside and the frontier wore their long hair without wigs, and townspeople were afraid of them at first. Some people powdered their hair as if they were wigs. The powdering process always raised dense clouds and made everyone cough. That is why they had special "powder rooms."

During the Revolutionary War, wigs were very popular in America. Although wigs itched, city dwellers

wore wigs all the time. These wigs were powdered. Some people even powdered their natural hair.

The powdering process always raised dense clouds and made everyone cough. That is why they had

special "powder rooms," to actually powder their hair or wigs. The townspeople were afraid of the

country people because they wore their hair long and without wigs.

_____

_____

4. Earth's twin planet is Venus. It is so named because of its similar size and density. Its clouds made its surface a complete mystery because they obscured it so heavily. Radar data have eventually been provided by space probes from Russia and America. Now we know that the surface temperature is almost 900 degrees fahrenheit and that carbon dioxide makes up 94 percent of the planet's atmosphere. Its clouds are made up of sulfuric acid. One picture each of the surface was beamed back to Earth by two Russian probes that landed in 1975 and 1982. Then they melted.

Venus is called the twin planet of Earth because they are similar in size and density. The surface of

Venus has long been a mystery because it is obscured by clouds made up of sulfuric acid. We have

now been able to learn more about Venus, thanks to the radar data provided by Russian and

American space probes. Two Russian probes, landing on Venus in 1975 and 1982, sent back to Earth

pictures of the surface. Now, we know that the surface temperature of Venus is almost 900 degrees

Fahrenheit and that carbon dioxide makes up 94 percent of the atmosphere.

_____

_____

_____

Composition

Lesson 96
The Writing Process: Editing

Edit your revised writing by checking various elements of grammar, such as correct word usage, subject-verb agreement, verb tenses, and clear pronoun references. Look again at your sentences. Are there any awkward run-on sentences or sentence fragments? **Proofread** your paper to check for spelling, punctuation, and capitalization. These are common proofreading symbols:

MARK	MEANING	EXAMPLE
∧ (caret)	insert	w∧ng
(dele)	delete	birdϒ
#	insert space	new#bicycle
⌒	close up space	semi⌒colon
≡	capitalize	≡mary
/	make lowercase	⫽Their
⟨ ⟩ sp	check spelling	(writting) sp
∼	switch order	⟨out watch⟩
		spaek
⊙	insert period	Look at this⊙
∧̦	insert comma	Joey,∧Ray, and Robert...
¶	new paragraph	...how I felt. ¶ Just then....

▶ **Exercise 1 Edit and proofread each sentence. Some answers may vary.**

my sister stacy bought a Note⌒book, and/hse filled it∧with home⌒work assi#nments.
(≡ my, ≡ stacy)

1. Have you call∧ed her yetϒ ?

2. Tanya will∧ speak to me about it tomorrow.

3. The choir has∧ sung that alϒready.
or sang

4. Hakeem brought ⟨yesterday the project⟩.

5. I will∧ go to the ≡mall after school.

6. The team is∧ are ready for the game.

Composition

7. George washington was our first one. ^president^

8. The game is exciting of hockey.

9. Snow, a sled, and a hill side makes for great ~~summer~~ fun. ^winter^

10. Scandinavians say is a good day, Friday for marriage. ^r^

11. Aunt hazel not live in boston. ^does^

12. I loves learning French.

13. Was born Abraham Lincoln in a log cabin. ^#^

14. I heard that Amanda ~~and~~ Charles ain't comming. ^aren't^

15. I learned to tie knots there in the Girl Scouts. ^when I was^ ^#^

16. can we skate on the pond ~~and~~ if it is frozen enough?

17. ~~Them~~ big amusement parks are packed with fun activities.

18. The best food ever invented ~~has been~~ pizza! ^was *or* is^

19. Geology, my best subject, I think. ^is^

20. Sally loves calligraphy to do all the time.

21. Cal lost his homework when the wind blwe it a way. ^#^

22. The byrds sang beautifully outside the windwo. ^i^

23. I hoped you werent late to the Rock concert. ^#^ ^for^

24. My new bycicle isn't broken; it just needs oilling. ^i^ ^y^

25. Sheila thought so, too, didmt she.? ^n^

26. juan went too the movies with out me.

27. Carla will you come her? ^e^

28. She don't know if they are coming?. ^es^

29. Puncuation are important, good grammar too. ^t^ ^is^ ^and so is^

30. The thundar clap startled Me. ^e^

31. why dont you come over, sue?

32. Does Sheila know where are my glasses?

33. Dhe moon shone brighty on the heath. ^T^ ^l^

34. Mercury is My favorite planet.

35. I luv my school Books. ^ove^

Composition

Lesson 97
The Writing Process: Presenting

After completing a piece of writing, you may want to **present**, or share, your writing with others. As early as the prewriting stage, you should have your audience in mind. Knowing the audience often defines the final format for your work. Possible audiences include a school or local newspaper, a class, a community, a magazine, or a contest. If the presentation is oral, *visual aids* such as pictures or photographs can add flavor to your presentation. For more information about magazines that publish the work of young writers, check your school or local library.

▶ **Exercise 1** Suggest an audience for each writing described below.

An opinion about a local issue _school newspaper, local newspaper, city council_

_____

1. a story about your school _a school newspaper, a local newspaper_

_____

2. a book review _your class, school newspaper, local newspaper, youth magazine_

_____

3. an essay on pets _your class, youth magazine, pet magazine_

_____

4. a review of school activities over the past year _school yearbook_

_____

5. a story about your childhood _youth magazine_

_____

6. a science paper describing an experiment _class project, school newspaper_

_____

7. a romance story _teen magazine, romance magazine_

_____

8. a biography of a music star _school newspaper, teen magazine_

_____

Composition

9. a complaint about street repair ___community newspaper, letter to city council___

_____

10. a story about your favorite hobby ___your class, hobby magazine___

_____

▶ **Exercise 2** **Suggest a visual aid to help you present a piece of writing.**

a story about a birthday party ___a party hat, a favor, or photo or illustration of a birthday cake___

1. a story about a family pet ___photo or illustration of pet or the pet itself, pet's toys___

_____

2. a research paper on rain and storms ___photos of storms, rain gauge/barometer___

_____

3. a poem about flowers ___live flowers, pictures of flowers___

_____

4. a review of a book that you liked ___a copy of the book, a special passage put on posterboard, a___ book jacket ___

5. a story about the family home ___photo or illustration of family home, special items from the___ home ___

6. an explanation of the rules of football ___a diagram of football field, a football, uniform,___ protective equipment ___

7. a speech to fellow students about civic responsibility ___photo of trash found in___ neighborhood areas and in local waterways ___

8. a story about pirates ___model boat, pictures, costume___

_____

9. a call for students to clean up the environment ___trash bag, rake or hoe, recycling bin___

_____

10. the outline of an amusing play that you like ___photo of actors, an amusing dialogue put on___ posterboard ___

Composition

Lesson 98
Outlining

Writing the first draft is easier if you organize the material created by your prewriting work. One way to organize data is **outlining**. In this way, you can organize your writing, mapping out each paragraph. Always work from the general to the specific and follow a logical sequence. Putting all your prewriting information on index cards is very helpful. Show your main topics by using Roman numerals, and show your supporting information with capital letters. Then organize the supporting information with regular numbers.

I. Deciding to buy a bicycle
  A. Preparing to shop for the bike
    1. happy and excited
    2. looked in phone book for bike shops
    3. made a list of shops nearby
  B. Going into the first shop
    1. told the salesperson what I was interested in
    2. looked at several bicycles
    3. found three that I really liked
II. Trying to make a choice

▶ **Exercise 1** **Rewrite the following outline so that it has a logical sequence.**
I. Our two dogs
  A. Fido
    1. the family cat, Tiger, striped
    2. Fido, our big dog, likes to play in the yard
    3. Fluffy, our little dog
    4. Fluffy sleeps all day
    5. Fido's tricks
  B. Fluffy likes riding in the car
    1. Willy, the parakeet, likes to sing and is bright yellow
II. Tiger sleeps on a windowsill
  A. Tiger has a toy mouse
    1. Our parakeet is named Willy

I. **Our two dogs** _____

  A. **Fido** _____

    1. **Big** _____

    2. **Plays in yard** _____

    3. **Does tricks** _____

  B. **Fluffy** _____

    1. **Little** _____

    2. **Sleeps all day** _____

    3. **Likes riding in car** _____

II. **Other pets** _____

  A. **Tiger, cat** _____

    1. **Striped** _____

Composition

2. Sleeps on windowsill	B. Willy, parakeet
3. Has toy mouse	1. Bright yellow
	2. Likes to sing

▶ **Exercise 2** **Organize the following topics and details into an outline on penguins.**

They are excellent swimmers; have short, stocky bodies; wings that function as flippers; have webbed feet, they raise their young on land; although they are birds, they cannot fly; feathers are waterproof; white front; they live in the Southern Hemisphere, Australia, New Zealand, Antarctica; they live mainly on fish and krill; they lay their eggs on land; krill is a small crustacean; live in colonies called rookeries; fat keeps them warm in icy water; short, thick feathers; black in back

Penguins

I. **Birds that swim instead of fly**

    A. **Wings function as flippers**

    B. **Excellent swimmers**

        1. **Flippers**

        2. **Webbed feet**

        3. **Fat keeps them warm in icy water**

II. **Appearance**

    A. **Stocky bodies with short legs**

    B. **Thick, waterproof feathers**

    C. **White bellies**

    D. **Black backs**

III. **Habits**

    A. **Eat fish and krill, small crustaceans**

    B. **Make nests on land**

        1. **Lay eggs on land**

        2. **Raise young on land**

        3. **Live in colonies called rookeries**

IV. **Where they live**

    A. **Antarctica**

    B. **New Zealand**

    C. **Australia**

Composition

Lesson 99
Writing Effective Sentences

Sentences are the building blocks of writing. The writer uses them just as a builder uses bricks, mortar, and wood. All sentences do not need to follow the same pattern. Varying your sentences makes your writing more interesting and enjoyable to read. You can vary the length of the sentences. You can vary the structure by using a combination of simple, compound, and complex sentences. A change in sentence pattern can help emphasize a particular point. In verbs, avoid **passive voice** and use **active voice** wherever possible. In active-voice sentences, the subject performs the action. In passive-voice sentences the action is performed on the subject. Use the passive voice only if you really do not want to say who or what is performing the action.

▶ **Exercise 1** **Combine the four sentences of each group into one interesting topic** sentence. **Answers may vary.**

  a. Louis Agassiz was a geologist.
  b. He lived during the nineteenth century.
  c. He thought that ice once covered North America.
  d. No one believed him.

When the nineteenth-century geologist Louis Agassiz thought that ice once covered North America,

no one believed him.

1. **a.** Bicycling is fun.
    b. It is a healthy form of exercise.
    c. You also get to see the countryside.
    d. You can travel with friends.

Bicycling is an enjoyable and healthy form of exercise in which you get to travel with friends and see

the countryside.

2. **a.** Kyle paints portraits.
    b. Kyle is my cousin.
    c. He has many portraits in his studio.
    d. His work is well known and respected.

My cousin Kyle, a well-known and respected portrait painter, has many portraits in his studio.

3. **a.** Polar bears are huge.
    b. They are the largest land animals in their domain.

Composition

    c. Sometimes they are called the "Lords of the Arctic."
    d. Seals are their main source of food.

Eating mainly seals, polar bears, sometimes called "Lords of the Arctic," are the largest land animals

in their domain.

4. a. Ludwig van Beethoven was born in 1770.
    b. His talent was soon recognized.
    c. He lost his hearing completely by the time he was 40 years old.
    d. The famous composer never heard his greatest work.

Born in 1770 and completely without hearing by the time he was 40 years old, the famous composer

Ludwig Van Beethoven never got to hear his greatest work.

5. a. Chichén Itzá is an important archaeological site.
    b. It is located on the Yucatan peninsula in Mexico.
    c. The Maya people built it.
    d. It has an astronomical observatory.

The important Mayan archaeological site of Chichén Itzá, known for its astronomical observatory, is

located on the Yucatan peninsula in Mexico.

6. a. Teak is an important natural resource.
    b. It is a very hard wood.
    c. It can be found from eastern India to Malaysia.
    d. It is used for various wood products.

The important natural resource teak is a very hard wood that is used for various wood products and

can be found from eastern India to Malaysia.

7. a. Water skiing is very challenging.
    b. It started in the 1920s.
    c. It originated in southern France and the United States.
    d. There are national and international competitions.

The challenging sport of water skiing, which originated in Southern France and the United States in

the 1920s, has national and international competitions.

8. a. Ben Franklin was a writer.
    b. He worked at the printing trade.
    c. He eventually became a diplomat.
    d. He wrote a really entertaining autobiography.

A writer, a printer, and a diplomat, Ben Franklin wrote a very entertaining autobiography.

9. a. Hay fever is a common ailment.
    b. It is actually considered a disease.

Composition

c. It is most commonly exhibited by an allergy to grasses.
d. It happens in the fall.

In the fall, many people suffer from hay fever, a disease that is most commonly exhibited by an

allergy to grasses.

10. **a.** Indian summer occurs in November.
   b. It consists of hazy days and cold, clear nights.
   c. The exact origin of the term *Indian summer* is uncertain.
   d. Interestingly, both the United States and Europe have an Indian summer.

Indian summer occurs in November in both the United States and Europe and consists of hazy days

and cold, clear nights; the exact origin of the term *Indian summer* is uncertain.

▶ **Exercise 2** Write whether each sentence has an active or passive voice verb. Rewrite any sentence you think needs its verb changed. Some answers may vary.

The mail carrier was barked at by the dog. Passive; The dog barked at the mail carrier.

1. The bird was watched by the cat. Passive; The cat watched the bird.

2. Li Cheng called me yesterday. Active; (no rewrite necessary)

3. Sam and Betty were given the lessons by Mr. Cardona. Passive; Mr. Cardona gave Sam and Betty the lessons.

4. We were soaked by the steadily falling rain. Passive; The steadily falling rain soaked us.

5. This shirt was bought for me by my mom. Passive; My mom bought me this shirt.

6. The tropical breezes were loved by them. Passive; They loved the tropical breezes.

7. Those robins were singing in the tree. Active; (no rewrite necessary)

8. The length of the field was run by the rabbit. Passive; The rabbit ran the length of the field.

9. The bicycle tire was deflated by the puncture. Passive; The puncture deflated the bicycle tire.

10. The swimming pool was crowded by our class. Passive; Our class crowded the swimming pool.

Composition

▶ **Exercise 3 Rewrite the following paragraph with effective sentences.**

The Erie Canal was completed by New York State in 1825. It was first proposed by Governor Morris in 1777. Work was begun in 1817. Much of the canal was dug by Irish laborers. A canal was also wanted by Ohio. Work was begun in 1825. Thousands of workers were killed by malaria and cholera. The Ohio canals were officially opened in 1833 after eight years of work.

Completed by New York State, the Erie Canal opened in 1825. Governor Morris first proposed it in

1777, but work didn't begin until 1817. Irish laborers dug much of the canal. Ohio then wanted a canal,

also. Ohioans began work in 1825. Unfortunately, malaria and cholera killed thousands of workers in

Ohio. After eight bitter years of work, the Ohio canals were officially opened in 1833.

_____

_____

_____

_____

Composition

Lesson 100
Building Paragraphs

You can build a paragraph in different ways. **Chronological order** places events in the order in which they happened.

After we entered the zoo, we first went to see the lions, then we saw the alligators, and finally we visited the elephants.

Spatial order describes the way something looks.

The zoo is a very big place. Near the entrance to the left are the lion dens. The alligator pens surrounded by water are in the middle of the zoo. The elephants are located behind the picnic areas on the far side of the zoo.

Compare/contrast order shows similarities and differences. Notice how the compare and contrast order makes a very interesting zoo paragraph:

In our zoo, the lion dens are big and roomy with lots of space for the lions to roam about. The alligator pens are much smaller, however, and contain a lot of water. The area that holds the elephants is the largest of all. It covers many acres.

A good writer learns to use all three orders for effective writing.

▶ **Exercise 1** **Number the following ten sentences in chronological order.**

___6___ I rode to the store.

___9___ After paying the clerk, I left.

___2___ Mother gave me the grocery list.

___1___ My mother asked me to go to the store.

___5___ I put the basket on the handle bars and was ready to go.

___4___ I got out the bicycle.

___3___ She asked for bread and milk.

___10___ I returned home.

___7___ Looking for the bread, I found the milk first.

___8___ Then I got the bread.

Composition

Name _____ Class _____ Date _____

▶ **Exercise 2** **Put the following paragraph into chronological order by numbering the sentences. Then rewrite it.**

I said sure. I rode my bike to Melissa's house that evening. Friday was the big game against Central. By the fourth quarter, the score was tied, seven to seven. I asked Melissa if she wanted to go. When Friday came, I had a headache, but it was gone by the afternoon. She already had a ride and asked me if I wanted to go with her. Her older sister, Tammy, took us to the game. The crowd went wild. She is a senior this year. Alonso threw the ball to Hakeem, who managed to dodge through the tacklers. Central played well, but our team really wanted to win. He ran 20 yards for the winning touchdown.

Friday was the big game against Central. I asked Melissa if she wanted to go. She already had a ride and asked me if I wanted to go with her. I said sure. When Friday came, I had a headache, but it was gone by the afternoon. That evening, I road my bike to Melissa's house. Her older sister, Tammy, took us to the game. She is a senior this year. Central played well, but our team really wanted to win. By the fourth quarter, the score was tied, seven to seven. Alonso threw the ball to Hakim, who managed to dodge through the tacklers. He ran 20 yards for the winning touchdown. The crowd went wild.

Composition

▶ **Exercise 3** **Put the following paragraph into spatial order by numbering the sentences. Then rewrite it.**

To my right was a big hallway. I dreamed that I woke up in a big house. I heard laughter out under the trees. Directly in front of me was a big fireplace. I entered the hallway and to my left was a spiral staircase. I looked to my left and saw a big, curtained window. Warm, golden light streamed through it. I stepped off the porch and saw you there under a tree. It was beautiful. It was a wonderful dream. Looking around, I saw this large door, with glass all around it. I stepped out onto the porch and found myself in a wide, shady yard. I opened the door and beyond was a cool porch.

I dreamed that I woke up in a big house. Directly in front of me was a big fireplace. I looked to my left and saw a big, curtained window. Warm, golden light streamed through it. To my right was a big hallway. I entered the hallway and to my left was a spiral staircase. Looking around, I saw this large door, with glass all around it. I opened the door and beyond was a cool porch. I stepped out onto the porch and found myself in a wide, shady yard. It was beautiful. I heard laughter out under the trees. I stepped off the porch and saw you there under a tree. It was a wonderful dream.

Composition

Name _____ Class _____ Date _____

▶ **Exercise 4 Choose one of the following topics. Write a paragraph about your topic using compare/contrast order.**

a. your favorite class

b. how you do your homework

c. the different kinds of books that you like to read

_____

_____

_____

_____

_____

_____

_____

_____

_____

_____

_____

_____

_____

_____

_____

_____

_____

_____

_____

_____

Composition

Lesson 101
Paragraph Ordering

Make sure you carefully organize your paragraphs with unity and coherence. **Unity** means that your paragraph not only opens with a topic sentence, but that the supporting details are related to that topic. **Coherence** means that your comparisons are clear and logical, and that the chronological details are in a correct understandable order. Be sure that ideas are properly linked by transitions. Transitions are words or phrases that connect thoughts between sentences or between paragraphs.

COMMON TRANSITIONS

after	because	here	later	next to
also	before	how	like	on the other hand
although	finally	however	likewise	then
and	for example	in addition	meanwhile	therefore
as a result	furthermore	in front of	moreover	until then

▶ **Exercise 1** **Rewrite the following paragraphs for unity and coherence.**

    I am a student. My time is important for me. Time is important for all of us students. If we organize our time better, we can do more of the things we want to do.

    The first of the four simple rules for organizing time well is to know what you want to get done. The second rule is to make a list of things you need to do. The third is to put the list in order. Rule number four is work on the most important thing first.

    Decide on the things you want to get done. Write them down. Make a list of what you need to do in order to get them done. If you want to study for a test, write down the amount of time that you need to spend each day studying for it. If you want to buy a bike, note how much it costs and how much you will have to save for it.

    Get a calendar. Write a list of things to do each day. Keep your goals in mind. Do the most important thing on your list first. This is the fourth simple rule. Get it done and then go on to the next. You only get one or two things done a day? That is okay. They would not have gotten done by you in any other system either. I'll bet that if you keep at this for a few weeks, you will notice a big improvement.

Knowing how to organize our time is important for students. If we can organize our time well, we can do more of the things that interest us. There are four simple rules for organizing your time. The first is to know exactly what tasks you want to get done and by when. The second is to make a list of tasks. The third is to put them in order of importance, paying attention to any deadlines. The fourth is to work on the most important tasks first.

Composition

After you decide on the tasks you want to accomplish, write them down. This is the second rule. Next to the tasks, write any additional information you may need. If you want to study for a test, write down the amount of time you need to spend studying each day. Next, get a calendar and write the list of tasks in the order in which they need to be completed. Keep in mind your goals and priorities. Remember to do the most important thing on your list first. This is the fourth simple rule. Get it done, and then go on to the next task. If you only get one or two things done a day, that is okay. Keep at this for a few weeks. You will notice a big improvement.

▶ **Exercise 2 Rewrite each pair of sentences using a transitional word or phrase to link them.**

I love to eat soft pretzels.
I always buy one at basketball games.

I love to eat soft pretzels. Therefore, I always buy one at basketball games.

1. Moira went to the mall.
   She didn't stay long.

   Moira went to the mall, but she didn't stay long.

2. Our cat climbed the tree.
   It jumped down.

   Our cat climbed the tree. Then it jumped down.

3. I worked for several hours on my essay.
   I finished it at 11:00 P.M.

   I worked for several hours on my essay. Finally, I finished it at 11:00 P.M.

4. Cows were grazing in the field.
   Sheep and horses were grazing there.

   Cows were grazing in the field. In addition, sheep and horses were grazing there.

Composition

5. Joey hates tomatoes.
He loves spaghetti sauce.

Joey hates tomatoes. On the other hand, he loves spaghetti sauce. _____

_____

6. Maya Angelou wrote an autobiography.
She is a poet.

Maya Angelou wrote an autobiography, and she is a poet. _____

_____

7. The band marched onto the football field.
The cheerleaders were leading a cheer.

The band marched onto the football field. Meanwhile, the cheerleaders were leading a cheer. ____

_____

8. Early in the day we went to the science museum.
We went to the art museum.

Early in the day we went to the science museum. Later we went to the art museum. _____

_____

9. We did many fun things on our day off from school.
We went to a movie.

We did many fun things on our day off from school. For example, we went to a movie. _____

_____

10. I am waiting for Toshi to return my new CD.
I will listen to my old one.

I am waiting for Toshi to return my new CD. Until then, I will listen to my old one. _____

_____

Composition

▶ **Exercise 3** **Read each paragraph for unity and coherence. Draw a line through any sentence that does not support the main idea.**

1. In much of the country, pioneers preferred oxen to horses. Oxen were better suited to plowing rough and stony ground. While horses were faster, oxen were stronger and steadier. ~~Horses are beautiful and make good pets.~~ Oxen also cost less than horses, both to buy and to feed.

2. Doing jigsaw puzzles is a wonderful way to relax. You stare at those little pieces, looking for the shape and color you need, and the time goes by quickly. ~~Building models is also a fun way to relax.~~ A good puzzle can take many days to complete. When you finally put in that last piece, you get a great feeling of satisfaction and accomplishment.

▶ **Writing Link** **Write a short paragraph about a favorite holiday. Include at least three transitional words or phrases.**

_____

_____

_____

_____

_____

_____

_____

_____

_____

_____

_____

_____

_____

_____

Composition

Lesson 102
Personal Letters: Formal

Personal letters are usually letters to relatives or friends. You write them to keep in touch—to find out what the other person is doing, how he or she is feeling, or to tell something about yourself. **Formal personal letters** may be letters to people you do not know well or to whom you want to show respect, such as older relatives. A personal letter can also be a thank-you note or invitation. All these letters are important and much appreciated by those who receive them.

▶ **Exercise 1** **Answer the following questions about this personal letter.**

123 Oak Avenue
Small Water, Nebraska 60000

June 5, 1996

Dear Uncle Basir,
    I hope that you and Aunt Zina are doing well. Everything is fine here. The school year comes to a close soon. I will miss all the school activities. Perhaps this summer I can work in the library. I think I would enjoy it, and I would always have plenty to read!
    How are my cousins, Calid and Anna? I hope they are well. I will write to them soon. When do you think that you might be able to visit us? We look forward to seeing you.

Sincerely,
Mimi

1. Who is Uncle Basir, and why is Mimi writing to him? __Uncle Basir is Mimi's uncle, an older__

__relative she is writing to in order to find out how he and his family have been, to tell them what she__

__has been doing, and to find out when they are coming for a visit.__

_____

2. Is this a good model of a formal personal letter? Why or why not? __Yes, this is a good__

__model of a formal personal letter. It is polite, conveys the information the writer wishes to share, and__

__asks for the information the writer wishes to receive.__

_____

Composition

3. When Uncle Basir writes back, what might he say? **Uncle Basir will thank Mimi for her**

letter, tell her how his family is doing, and let her know when they will come for a visit.

_____

_____

▶ **Exercise 2** Answer the following questions about this personal letter.

123 Elm Street
Hillsdale, Kansas 51111

July 16, 1996

Dear Aunt Lucy,
   Thank you very much for the birthday gift you sent to me. I always wanted a baseball mitt like that, and I will use it in every game I play. I hope you and Uncle Jim are well. Thanks again.

Sincerely,
Louise

1. Why did Louise write this letter? **Louise wrote this letter to thank Aunt Lucy for the baseball**

mitt she sent her for her birthday.

2. Would you have written this letter the same way? Why or why not? **Students' answers**

will vary. While some students may have suggestions for improvements, all responses should

recognize that this letter is respectful and serves the purpose for which it was written.

▶ **Exercise 3** Write an invitation to a friend for a birthday party that your parents are planning for you. Be creative. Mention the kinds of food that will be served, as well as any games or other activities.

Students' invitations will vary. Invitations should include all pertinent information—date, time,

place—as well as descriptions of the food, games, and any other special activities being planned.

The tone of the invitations should be friendly and polite.

_____

_____

_____

_____

Composition

Copyright © by Glencoe/McGraw-Hill

Lesson 103
Personal Letters: Informal

Another form of personal letter is the informal letter. An informal letter is a letter you write to a close friend. It may be written in much the same way as you talk. You want to be clearly understood, and you want to help encourage your friend to write back to you. Informal letters often include postcards and letters to pen pals.

▶ **Exercise 1** Answer the following questions about this personal letter.

123 Shady Lane
Little Creek, Iowa 34444

June 15, 1996

Dear Sarah,

    Now that school is out for the summer, I have time to write to you. How are you doing? I miss you, Luis, Bill, and Hiroko. How did the tennis team do? Is Mrs. Smith feeling better? Write with the news when you can.

    I like my school here. I have met many people and made some new friends. It is hard, of course, to make new friends after having such nice friends as all of you. But it will be okay.

    My writing teacher is really interesting. She has had a number of stories published, and she encourages me to write my poetry. I feel very good about that.

Your friend,
Jenny

1. Who is Sarah, and why is Jenny writing to her? <u>Sarah is Jenny's friend and Jenny misses</u> <u>her.</u>

2. Is this a good model of an informal personal letter? Why or why not? <u>Yes, this is a good</u> <u>model of an informal personal letter because it is friendly, conversational, and full of details.</u>

3. When Sarah writes back, what might she say? <u>Sarah will probably say she is happy Jenny is</u> <u>making new friends and has such an encouraging writing teacher. She will also say that she misses</u> <u>Jenny and tell Jenny what she and the others have been doing.</u>

Composition

▶ **Exercise 2   Answer the following questions about this personal letter to a pen pal.**

123 Forest Lane
Mount Cedar, Missouri 22225

June 20, 1996

Dear Yoshi,
    Hi! My name is Ben, and I am writing to you from America. I am excited to write to someone in another country because I have never done this before. I hope you and your family are well. I live in Mount Cedar, Missouri, and I have a brother and a sister. Do you have a brother or sister, too? I go to Mount Cedar Middle School. My favorite subjects are writing and social studies.
    Write to me and let me know more about yourself. Someday I would like to go to Japan. It would be great to meet you.

Take care,
Ben

1. Who is Yoshi and why is Ben writing to him?   Yoshi is a student around Ben's age who lives

   in Japan. Ben is writing to him because they are pen pals.

2. If you were Ben, how would you improve this letter?   Students' answers will vary. Since

   this is the first time Ben has written to Yoshi, he might include information about why he wanted a

   pen pal and how he received Yoshi's name and address. He could explain more about the United

   States and the state and city in which he lives. He could also tell more about his family and possibly

   include a picture.

3. Rewrite Ben's letter using the suggestions you made in your answer to question 2.

   Students' letters will vary. Letters should follow the format of the letter provided and include the

   same basic information. Letters should also include whatever information students suggested adding

   in their answers to question 2.

Composition

Lesson 104
Business Letters: Letters of Request or Complaint

A letter of request is a type of business letter you write when you want to inquire about a service or need information from someone. Such letters should be courteous, state clearly what you are inquiring about and why, and include the information necessary to respond.

A letter of complaint must be no less courteous than a letter of request. In a letter of complaint, you should state the problem, explain how it happened, and propose a reasonable solution. Use language that will persuade your readers to take action, not make them angry. A letter of complaint needs to be well-organized and businesslike.

▶ **Exercise 1** **Answer the following questions about this letter of request.**

Dear Mr. Smith:

My name is Carla Jones, and I am a student at Lincoln Middle School. As you know, the school year is coming to a close. I understand that some students work as apprentices at the library during the summer. My teacher, Ms. Sanchez, suggested that I contact you and ask for more information. I would be very interested in any opportunity to help in the library. At your convenience, please let me know if this would be possible. Thank you very much for the information.

Sincerely,
Carla Jones

1. What important information is missing from this letter? Mr. Smith's business address,
Carla's address and/or telephone number, and the date

2. Why is this information so important? This information is important because Mr. Smith needs
to know where to send the information and when Carla wrote the letter.

3. Is this letter well-organized? Yes, Carla has presented her request in a well-organized manner.
She begins by explaining who she is and what information she would like to receive, and then she
explains why she wants the information.

4. Is this letter polite or impolite? Use examples to support your answer. This is a polite
letter. Carla asks that Mr. Smith provide the information at his convenience and thanks him for it.

Composition

▶ **Exercise 2** Think of a situation in which you would need to write to someone for information. Then write a letter of request asking for the information.

Students' letters will vary. Letters should clearly state the information being requested and why it is

needed. Letters should include the address where the information can be sent or a telephone number

where the writer can be reached. The tone of the letters should be courteous.

_____

_____

_____

_____

▶ **Exercise 3** Answer the following questions about this letter of complaint.

Attention: City Park Service
    You people have no idea how to take care of the bike trail in the city park. Do you care at all about it, or do you even know it is there? Maybe you sleep all the time. I try to ride my bike there from time to time, but I find it littered with junk, tree limbs, and big branches! And you never keep the pedestrians off of it? How am I supposed to ride when it is crowded with walkers? Do you people work at all? I am disgusted. If I were old enough to vote, I would vote against any funding for the Park Service.

Sincerely disgusted,
Trent Conrad

1. Is this a good letter of complaint? Why or why not? No, this is not a good letter of complaint. This letter is rude and insulting. The writer seems to be upset about the condition of the trail, but he also complains about pedestrians using it. He does not explain what he wants the Park Service to do nor does he offer any solutions. The writer also did not include an address, telephone number, or date.

2. How would you improve this letter? Students' answers will vary but should include making the letter much more courteous and stating what actions the writer would like the Park Service to take to improve the bike trail. The writer should also include an address or telephone number and the date.

Composition

Lesson 105
Business Letters: Stating Your Opinion

Some business letters are written simply to express an opinion. In an **opinion letter**, your opinion is the main idea. If you want to persuade others to agree with your position, you will probably need to supply evidence that supports your opinion. Examples of opinion letters include letters to the editor of a magazine or newspaper as well as letters to businesses about how they operate.

▶ **Exercise 1** Answer the following questions about this opinion letter.

South Coast Video
333 Mohawk St.
Circleville, OH 12335

December 2, 1996

Dear Manager:

    I often go to your video store to rent movies. But the last few times I have gone I have found very little that interests me. Many of the movies for rent were films I have already seen, but most of them I would not care to watch—ever! They are violent and gruesome. Why must you have so many movies like that on your shelves? Please try to get some good movies. I especially want to see *Miracle on 34th Street, E.T.,* and *Little Women.* I look forward to visiting your video store again soon. Have a nice day.

Sincerely,
Jane Becker

1. What is Jane's opinion of the video store? <u>Though she has often rented movies there, she is</u>
   <u>disappointed with the store's selection of videos.</u>

2. Does she express her opinion well? <u>Yes, she is very direct in stating her opinion, but she is</u>
   <u>also polite.</u>

▶ **Exercise 2** You have just heard that your all-time favorite television show is going to be taken off the air. Write a letter to the network stating your opinion about why the show should be kept on. Be clear and courteous.

<u>Students' letters will vary. Letters should clearly state what program the students want to remain on the</u>

<u>air and why. Letters should include specific reasons for keeping the program and should be written in a</u>

<u>polite tone.</u>

Composition

_____

_____

_____

_____

_____

_____

▶ **Exercise 3** **Answer the following questions about this letter to the editor.**

The Weekly Planet
Comics Editor
556 Vine St.
Hartford, CT 35444

June 25, 1996

Dear Editor:
I see you have just changed your comics page. Why did you do it? You took out the best comics and put in junky, unfunny, and stupid ones. Who would want to read your comics page now? Not me! My parents and sister used to like your comics page. We read it eagerly. But now, yuck! Everyone in my family is sick about it. We are all terribly disappointed. This is just one family's opinion, and you won't pay attention to it anyway. It is too bad.

Sincerely,
Cameron Ford

1. What is Cameron's opinion about the comics page? __He thinks the changes recently made__

__have ruined it. He and his family are very disappointed.__

2. Does he express his opinion well? __No; he is very emotional and angry, and he does not express__

__his opinion well.__

3. How could this letter be improved? __This letter could be improved by making it less emotional,__

__explaining more clearly what is wrong with the new comics page, and being more courteous to the__

__editor.__

Composition

*I*ndex

Index

and collective nouns, 187
and compound subjects, 11, 30, 191
and indefinite pronouns, 11, 29, 189
and intervening prepositional phrases, 11, 28, 185
in inverted sentences, 11
and special subjects, 11, 187
with titles, 11, 187
Subjects
   agreement of verb with, 11, 28–31, 183, 185, 187, 189, 191
   complete, 3, 51
   compound, 3, 30–31, 57, 191
   gerunds and infinitives as, 171, 175
   noun clauses as, 161
   simple, 3, 51
Subordinate (dependent) clauses, 9–10, 155, 157, 159, 161
Subordinating conjunctions, 9, 159, 257
   list, 159, 257
Suffixes, 19, 292, 298
Superlative form, 7–8, 36–37, 121, 123, 131
Synonyms, 293

T

Take, bring, 12, 221
Teach, learn, 13, 223
Tenses, defined, 5, 83
   future, 5, 83
   future perfect, 5
   past, 5, 83
   past perfect, 5, 93
   present, 5, 83
   present perfect, 5, 93
Than, then, 14, 227
Their, they're, 14, 227
Theirs, there's, 14
Theme, writing, 20–21, 311
Then, than, 14, 227
There's, theirs, 14
Thesis statement, writing, 311
They're, their, 14, 227
To, too, two, 14
Topic sentences, 307
Transitive verbs, defined, 4, 75

U

Understood subject *you,* 3, 49, 199
Usage glossary, 12–14, 219–228

V

Verb phrases, defined, 4, 87
Verbals and Verbal phrases, defined, 10
   See also Gerunds, Infinitives, Participles
Verbs, defined, 4, 73
   action verbs, 4, 73, 75, 77
   agreement with subjects, rules, 11, 28–31, 183, 185, 187, 189, 191
   auxiliary (helping), 4, 87
   emphatic, 6
   intransitive, 4, 75
   irregular, regular, 5, 32–33, 95, 97
   linking, 4, 79, 81
   lists, 5, 79, 95, 97
   principal parts of irregular, 5, 95, 97
   principal parts of regular, 4–6, 87
   progressive, 6, 91
   tenses of, 5, 83, 93
      See Tenses
   transitive, 4, 75
   voice of, active and passive, 6, 323
Vocabulary building, 19–20, 287–292
   from context, 19, 287–288
   prefixes and suffixes, 18–19, 291, 298
   word roots, base words, 19, 289
Voice of verbs, defined, 6
   active, 6, 323
   effective use of, 323
   passive, 6, 323

W

Where at, avoiding, 14
Who, whom, 7, 113, 157, 161
Who's, whose, 14, 227
Writing process. *See* specific steps.
Writing letters, 21–22, 335, 337, 339
Writing paragraphs, 20–21, 327, 331

Y

You, as understood subject, 3, 49, 199
Your, you're, 14

Unit 1 Test: Subjects, Predicates, and Sentences

▶ **Subtest 1** Write *dec.* (declarative), *int.* (interrogative), *exc.* (exclamatory), or *imp.* (imperative) to identify the kind of sentence. If the item is a sentence fragment, write *frag.* in the blank.

_____ 1. Wash your hands before dinner.

_____ 2. The most unruly dog in the whole obedience class.

_____ 3. Please don't call after nine o'clock.

_____ 4. Do you know the name of this spice?

_____ 5. The population of Mexico is larger than that of Canada.

_____ 6. A very good movie, by the way.

_____ 7. Our team won the championship game fifty-nine to three!

_____ 8. Who ate my tuna sandwich?

_____ 9. The dog and cat traveled more than four hundred miles across the frozen wilderness to find their family!

_____ 10. She decided not to check out the book on bats.

▶ **Subtest 2** Draw one line under the complete subject and two lines under the complete predicate. In the blank, write each simple subject and each simple predicate.

_____ 1. Many people enjoy country music.

_____ 2. The heroine of the movie leaped from the villain's car.

_____ 3. Elvis and his brother carried their sleds up the hill.

_____ 4. The young man ate his dinner at the restaurant.

_____ 5. The seven children ran and played in the tall grass.

_____ 6. Our science teacher drew a diagram on the chalkboard.

_____ 7. A robin and a chickadee flapped their wings and flew away.

_____ 8. We piled the books and magazines neatly on the table.

_____ 9. Sheep make very nice pets.

_____ 10. Roses are often a challenge for gardeners.

_____ **11.** Russell saw the police car.

_____ **12.** The girl raised her hand.

_____ **13.** A bus is leaving for Dallas tonight.

_____ **14.** Farmers usually work long hours.

_____ **15.** The movie is very different from the book.

_____ **16.** The brown cows and the black pony grazed in the meadow.

_____ **17.** Kay and Dan swing and slide at the playground.

_____ **18.** The boys' mother played the piano and sang songs.

_____ **19.** Several candidates for mayor spoke at the meeting of the town

council.

_____ **20.** The brown and white puppy jumped onto my lap and licked

my face.

▶ **Subtest 3** Write *S* before each simple sentence, *C* before each compound sentence, and *R* before each run-on sentence.

_____ **1.** The player shot the ball with one second left, and the crowd held its breath.

_____ **2.** Dad dropped the pie on the floor, what a mess that made!

_____ **3.** Put your pop can in the recycling bin.

_____ **4.** In which room is the French club meeting?

_____ **5.** Pollution is a serious problem today, I hope we can stop polluting.

_____ **6.** I watered the plant every day, but it died anyway.

_____ **7.** Jeremy went to the movie with us, his father did not go.

_____ **8.** His favorite sport is soccer, but his sister prefers softball.

_____ **9.** I didn't care for the taste of the sauce, I ate it anyway.

_____ **10.** The soldier dropped to his knees and inched his way across the battlefield.

Unit 2 Test: Nouns

▶ **Subtest 1** Write *prop.* if the noun is a proper noun. Write *com.* if the noun is common.

_____ **1.** Vietnam

_____ **2.** superhero

_____ **3.** World War II

_____ **4.** author

_____ **5.** city

_____ **6.** Mount Fuji

_____ **7.** Maryland

_____ **8.** Paul McCartney

_____ **9.** ship

_____ **10.** inventor

_____ **11.** Mr. Osborne

_____ **12.** teacher

_____ **13.** college

_____ **14.** St. Simon's Island

_____ **15.** Puget Sound

_____ **16.** conductor

_____ **17.** soil

_____ **18.** leaves

_____ **19.** General Lee

_____ **20.** lieutenant

▶ **Subtest 2** Write *con.* before each concrete noun. Write *abst.* before each abstract noun.

_____ **1.** desk

_____ **2.** Congress

_____ **3.** loyalty

_____ **4.** rain

_____ **5.** color

_____ **6.** silliness

_____ **7.** bravery

_____ **8.** patriot

_____ **9.** mouse

_____ **10.** sunset

_____ **11.** person

_____ **12.** gymnast

_____ **13.** truth

_____ **14.** darkness

_____ **15.** joy

_____ **16.** Pikes Peak

_____ **17.** rainbow

_____ **18.** humor

_____ **19.** peaches

_____ **20.** hyena

▶ **Subtest 3** Write in the blank *coll.* if the italicized noun is collective and *comp.* if the italicized noun is compound.

_____ **1.** Miriam is the *front-runner* in the election.

_____ **2.** My *family* likes to go on picnics.

_____ **3.** The *choir* sang a selection from a current Broadway musical.

_____ **4.** Soldiers in the *front line* of battle are in the greatest danger.

_____ **5.** My *sister-in-law* grew up in Minneapolis, Minnesota.

_____ **6.** The judge asked the *jury* if it had come to a verdict.

_____ **7.** At sunset we saw a *flock* of geese land by the pond.

_____ **8.** The students formed a *committee* to plan three field trips.

_____ **9.** The *bedroom* was painted in shades of gold and cream.

_____ **10.** We bought twelve rolls of *wallpaper* for the kitchen.

_____ **11.** My little brother, Ben, is a *show-off*.

_____ **12.** I heard a click, and then a *flashbulb* blinded me.

_____ **13.** Juong's *contact lenses* are tinted a soft green.

_____ **14.** A small *army* of red ants marched across the tent floor.

_____ **15.** I can't decide whether to have waffles or *pancakes*.

_____ **16.** Stickers from around the world decorated the tattered *suitcase*.

_____ **17.** The college *faculty* presented a talent show on the last day of classes.

_____ **18.** The *committee* vetoed the motion four to three.

_____ **19.** Do you think the orchestra pit can hold the entire *band*?

_____ **20.** Fluffy, our Persian cat, is fascinated by *sunbeams*.

▶ **Subtest 4** Write the plural, possessive, or contraction of the word in parentheses to best complete each sentence.

1. _____ going to have a part in the play. (Aiko)

2. This _____ much too big to fit in the trunk of the car. (drum)

3. You can find new computer _____ on the top shelf. (disk)

4. We saw twenty different _____ at the antique store. (music box)

5. _____ nickname is the Windy City. (Chicago)

6. Both _____ eyes are green. (brother)

7. This _____ title doesn't make any sense to me. (book)

8. The bride had three _____ all dressed in blue. (maid of honor)

9. This _____ flavor is called tutti-frutti. (ice cream)

10. All of the _____ teams will be playing on Saturday. (boy)

11. My mother plays in a _____ volleyball league. (women)

12. The _____ shell is smooth, shiny, and dark brown. (nut)

13. The three _____ findings are published in this journal. (scientist)

14. This is one of _____ notebooks. (James)

15. How many _____ have the Muppets made? (motion picture)

16. The _____ string section contains violins, violas, cellos, and basses. (orchestra)

17. Leo and Tasha were the _____ in the writing contest. (runner-up)

18. This book's two _____ are for names and subjects. (index)

19. Our _____ are only thirty miles apart. (hometown)

20. _____ lunch consisted of a tuna sandwich, carrots, and an apple. (Rex)

21. The lead _____ only costume was an unusual color. (actor)

22. _____ dog barked furiously at the hissing cat. (Celia)

23. Walking along the riverbank is _____ favorite pastime. (Trish)

24. _____ heading straight for the barn! (Trigger)

25. Hand in hand, the _____ glided over the ice. (skater)

▶ **Subtest 5 Underline each appositive or appositive phrase. Add commas where needed. Circle the noun the appositive identifies.**

1. Minerva my sister is three years older than I am.

2. The dugong a large marine mammal is frequently spotted in Florida harbors.

3. Vanilla a common ingredient in cakes and cookies comes from the vanilla bean.

4. My favorite vegetable asparagus is at its peak in the early spring.

5. This steamship an early model had paddles on both sides as well as a full set of sails.

6. The author of this book Jean Fritz has written many historical biographies.

7. Emily Dickinson the New England poet lived a very quiet life.

8. The cardinal the state bird of Ohio is a common sight at bird feeders in winter.

9. Big Bird is a character on *Sesame Street* the popular children's television show.

10. Charles Schulz a very successful cartoonist is the creator of the comic strip "Peanuts."

11. Kevin is training his new dog a lumbering Labrador retriever.

12. The stage version starred Geena Davis my favorite actress.

13. Lucy and Lana my noisy nieces are spending New Year's Eve with us.

14. That walnut tree the tallest tree on our lot provides shade for most of the apartment.

15. Loren has two brothers Mitchell and Kyle.

16. The unkempt prospector showed Julie his bits of silver a precious metal.

17. Edith Head a costume designer in the '50s and '60s won many awards for her

  creations.

18. The oak bookcase a family treasure had graced Linworth Hall for several generations.

19. Do you know Stephen Keeler our president?

20. Our aerobics instructor Teresa sprained her ankle last week.

Unit 3 Test: Verbs

• •

▶ **Subtest 1** Draw two lines under each action verb.

1. The antelope raced across the plain.

2. I know the answer to that riddle!

3. Toshi wanted a dog for a pet.

4. I smelled something in the garage.

5. Hummingbirds eat almost constantly.

6. She tasted everything except the oysters.

7. We really like the science museum.

8. I heard the new song by that group.

9. That child fears loud noises.

10. The Lions defeated the Packers in last night's game.

▶ **Subtest 2** Write *T* above each transitive verb and *I* above each intransitive verb. Underline each direct object. Circle any indirect object.

1. Hakim started his homework early.

2. Grandpa gave me a bicycle helmet for Chanukah.

3. My friend Jamie and I visit there often.

4. Has he sent them the directions to the farm yet?

5. The jeweler showed the bracelet with pride.

6. The troops watched the demonstration in amazement.

7. Stephen Crane, the author, died at an early age.

8. Her sore throat is causing her much pain.

9. Leaves fall from the trees in autumn.

10. The chief greeted the general.

▶ **Subtest 3** Draw two lines under each linking verb. Write *p.n.* above each word that is a predicate noun and *p.a.* above each word that is a predicate adjective. Draw an arrow from the predicate noun or predicate adjective to the subject.

1. Your accident sounds scary.

2. Daniel suddenly grew quiet.

3. It seemed unlikely.

4. Lydia and Erin are the best players on the volleyball team.

5. Sometimes the moon appears almost blue.

6. Her sister turned sixteen yesterday.

7. In spite of the loss, our team remained the best team in the division.

8. Those raspberries taste delicious!

9. Sylvia is the queen of Sweden.

10. I became president of the computer club last month.

▶ **Subtest 4** Circle the correct form of the verb given in parentheses. Write *present, past,* or *future* to indicate its tense.

_____ 1. The candidate (impress, impressed) many voters when she ran for governor last year.

_____ 2. My father still (buy, buys) heating oil from a company in Centerburg.

_____ 3. Janelle (will baby-sit, baby-sit) for them next Saturday night.

_____ 4. When she was younger, my grandmother (work, worked) in a bakery.

_____ 5. The athlete (will train, train) with the college track team next month.

_____ 6. The relative humidity usually (fall, falls) when the temperature goes down.

_____ 7. Next year we (will be, be) in the eighth grade.

_____ 8. Last week we (deliver, delivered) 150 newspapers.

_____ 9. Her best friend now (live, lives) in that apartment building over there.

_____ 10. Yesterday you (said, say) you would like to know how to knit.

▶ **Subtest 5** Underline each helping verb twice. Circle each participle. In the blank write *present* if it is a present participle. Write *past* if it is a past participle.

_____ 1. Have you ever eaten at a Thai restaurant?

_____ 2. The frog had leaped off the lily pad.

_____ 3. She was counting tickets by the door.

_____ 4. Are you expecting a phone call?

_____ 5. Germane has been in the choir for two years.

_____ 6. The weather is definitely turning cooler.

_____ 7. Terri had decided on the red coat.

_____ 8. They were dreading their cousins' visit.

_____ 9. The engine in my mom's car is running hot.

_____ 10. Have you asked Darcie about her computer?

▶ **Subtest 6** Write the correct form or tense of the verb indicated in parentheses.

1. My family _____ Disney World twice. (*visit*, present perfect)

2. The hawk _____ above when the mouse peeped out of its hole.

   (*circle*, past progressive)

3. By the time I got to her house, she _____ for the library. (*leave*, past perfect)

4. I _____ at the bus stop for an hour. (*wait*, past progressive)

5. I _____ all the *Star Trek* movies. (*see*, present perfect)

6. If they _____ the shortcut, they would have beaten us to school.

   (*take*, past perfect)

7. His dad _____ to the hospital today for tests. (*go*, present progressive)

8. J. D. _____ to take geometry next year, but he changed his mind.

   (*plan*, past progressive)

9. My brothers _____ about joining the navy. (*think*, present progressive)

10. Darnell and Philip _____ the best progress this year.

   (*make*, present perfect)

11. You _____ your speech already by the time we arrived. (*give*, past perfect)

12. I _____ you wouldn't be late this time. (*hope*, past progressive)

13. My parents _____ some friends over to watch the parade on television.

(*have*, present progressive)

14. The Knicks _____ a good team for many years. (*be*, past perfect)

15. Dense fog _____ the runway when we landed at the airport.

(*cover*, past progressive)

▶**Subtest 7** **Complete the sentence correctly, using the past tense or past participle of the verb in parentheses.**

1. I think Michelle has _____ the same jeans every day. (wear)

2. Grandma says that Grandpa _____ her heart away many years ago. (steal)

3. She _____ not to run for reelection. (choose)

4. I wish I had _____ about the party earlier. (know)

5. The package you were expecting has _____. (come)

6. I _____ this story was as good as any I've read. (think)

7. Her mother _____ a moped. (win)

8. The team has _____ ten laps this morning. (swim)

9. Our team _____ in the third quarter. (lead)

10. Rey has _____ the team for good, I'm afraid. (leave)

11. Her cat has _____ three mice this week. (catch)

12. Carla _____ for the book. (pay)

13. I _____ my new job last week. (begin)

14. Have you _____ the brownies with you? (bring)

15. We haven't _____ that song in years. (sing)

Unit 4 Test: Pronouns

• •

▶ **Subtest 1** Draw an arrow from the personal pronoun in the second sentence to its antecedent in the first. In the blank, write the number of the antecedent—*singular* or *plural*.

_____ 1. We saw the girls from our class at the rodeo. They seemed to be having a great time.

_____ 2. The cowboy was thrown from the horse. He got up quite slowly.

_____ 3. Margaret Thatcher was prime minister of Great Britain. She was a member of the Conservative party.

_____ 4. Professional football players must be very dedicated. They have to keep in shape year-round.

_____ 5. This car has trouble starting in wet weather. Mom would like to replace it soon.

_____ 6. Alexis and her sisters all take dance lessons. They have gotten very good.

_____ 7. The old tires in the vacant lot look messy. Perhaps the city will take them away.

_____ 8. I try to drink plenty of milk. It is very nutritious.

_____ 9. We just picked these tomatoes. They are very ripe.

_____ 10. Phil Collins is a British singer. He was a member of the band Genesis.

▶ **Subtest 2** Underline the word or words in parentheses that best complete the sentence.

1. The cat tried to clean (it's, its) whiskers after it ate the caramel.

2. Frannie and (they, them) will meet us at the bus stop at two o'clock.

3. The person singing on this tape is (me, I)!

4. Please tell the woman (its, it's) too late to enter the contest.

5. (Hector and she, Hector and her) are running for class president.

6. (Chen and I, Me and Chen) don't want to get involved in their argument.

7. The finished project stood before (us, we).

8. Her mother and (her, she) went shopping for groceries.

9. That blue car over there is (their's, theirs).

10. Should (my brother and I, I and my brother) help with the coats?

▶ **Subtest 3** Label each pronoun by writing *per.* if it is a personal pronoun, *poss.* if it is possessive, or *ind.* if it is indefinite.

1. She is the student council representative from our class.

2. Shall we get something to eat at the snack bar?

3. Their horse has a lame foot.

4. Others will have to do your share of the work if you don't do it.

5. Peering around the corner, she saw nobody.

6. My parents were married in 1982.

7. Both of the tapes are very good for dancing.

8. I am afraid there's nothing anybody can do about it.

9. Much of the nature program was about birds and their habitats.

10. Please tell me everything about your vacation.

▶ **Subtest 4** Write above each pronoun *ref.* if it is a reflexive pronoun, *int.* if it is intensive, or *inter.* if it is interrogative.

1. Which of the coats is Elizabeth's?

2. Rick and DeWayne built the model themselves.

3. Who sent Andres the birthday card?

4. Jennifer saw herself in the mirror and laughed.

5. Sean himself began the community project with only public donations.

Unit 5 Test: Adjectives and Adverbs

▶ **Subtest 1** Draw a line under each adjective. Circle any adjective that is a present or past participle. Do not include articles.

1. The story of the sword of Damocles is a Greek legend.

2. The cat seems restless today.

3. "You must be happy beyond measure," Renaldo said to the man.

4. Mr. Chen looked stern as he asked where we were going.

5. Not a single student failed the difficult test.

6. We saw a bronze plaque on the wall.

7. The peasant gazed at the beautiful statues around the decorated hall.

8. Above me I saw a terrifying sight.

9. A gleaming silver fish jumped out of the water.

10. "Nothing in the handwritten note is true," I protested.

11. Jason could only stare at the surprising sight.

12. The weary traveler laid down the heavy burden and rested.

13. These unusual cookies contain the Indian spice cardamom.

14. I felt relieved when I saw the car.

15. Lovely tulips and daffodils covered the hillside.

▶ **Subtest 2** Underline the word or words in parentheses that best complete the sentence.

1. I don't want (those, them) puppies on the bed.

2. (These, This) fossils are typical of extinct sea animals.

3. (That there, That) book describes Jewish customs and traditions.

4. I'd like to read (that, these) *National Geographic* article about gorillas.

5. Could you give me ten of (those, them there) yellow pencils, please?

6. The first-graders made (these, that) animals out of clay.

7. (Them, Those) houses look alike except for the color of the doors.

8. On Saturday morning I would like to visit (those, that) cathedral.

9. (This, Those) desk is extremely messy.

10. (This, These) windows have old, wavy glass in them.

▶ **Subtest 3** Underline each adverb. Draw an arrow to the word or words it modifies.

1. This iced tea has just enough lemon in it.

2. The twelve snowballs on the back porch are perfectly round.

3. Lonnie sped quickly out of sight on his bicycle.

4. The lid of the wooden box was ornately carved.

5. Ted will now explain the new procedures.

6. We briefly saw the bluebird on its flight through the garden.

7. My dad and brother will dig a hole here for the new spruce tree.

8. Miguel studied hard for the geography bee.

9. Someday you must tell me about your vacation.

10. Very calmly she announced the winners of the writing contest.

11. A lonely pine tree drooped sadly next to the deserted cabin.

12. I'd be very happy to take your package to the post office.

13. The lost dog whimpered woefully at the door.

14. This diamond ring contains an extremely fine stone.

15. The leaves on the trees rustled softly in the wind.

16. Mrs. Lee carefully unpacked the new lamp.

17. I will see you tomorrow.

18. They looked quite surprised by the standing ovation.

Unit 6 Test: Prepositions, Conjunctions, and Interjections

••

▶ **Subtest 1** Underline each prepositional phrase. Draw a second line under each preposition. Then, circle the object of each preposition.

1. My dad is the one standing in front of the large statue.

2. Peter's family lives in an apartment building near the park.

3. If you stand behind me, the snowball won't hit you.

4. Do you know the song "On Top of Old Smoky"?

5. We found his wristwatch among the reeds by the stream.

6. Who's that boy sitting across from you in the cafeteria?

7. Another song I like is the Welsh tune "All Through the Night."

8. Your hands stay warmer with mittens than with gloves.

9. The kitten turned its head toward its mother.

10. Where will they stay during their visit to Chicago?

11. My great-grandmother's favorite song is "By the Light of the Silvery Moon."

12. After dinner we walked around the block.

13. The dog scampered out the door.

14. My sister always eats ketchup on her scrambled eggs.

15. It got dark quickly when the sun dropped below the horizon.

16. *Far from the Madding Crowd* is one of Thomas Hardy's early novels.

17. Inside the church on the left side is the painting I like.

18. Between you and me, I don't like ice cream.

19. I saw the squirrel climb into the barrel.

20. Will is going to the meeting instead of Alicia.

▶ **Subtest 2** Underline the word in parentheses that best completes each sentence.

1. Thank you very much from both Reggie and (I, me).

2. For (who, whom) did they buy that book?

3. Matt offered (her, she) a drink of his soda.

4. According to Alisha and (I, me) our team is definitely number one!

5. We gave (he, him) a ride to school yesterday.

6. The float was finished by (them, they) just in time for the parade.

7. Have you read Hemingway's novel *For (Whom, Who) the Bell Tolls?*

8. You can sit between me and (she, her).

9. Many people write letters to (them, they).

10. To (who, whom) are you writing?

▶ **Subtest 3** Underline each prepositional phrase. Write *adj.* above the phrase if it is an adjective phrase. Write *adv.* above it if it is an adverb phrase. Draw an arrow from the prepositional phrase to the word or words it modifies.

1. At the museum we saw paintings by many artists.

2. The cat was hiding beside the chair.

3. That blue scarf really looks great on her.

4. The Purple Raiders are the best team in our league.

5. Laura did very well in the contest.

6. The sunglasses on the sofa are mine.

7. My grandparents bought me a silver bracelet in Mexico.

8. The train sped through the dark tunnel in the mountain.

9. The screen above the stage was deep blue velvet.

10. Jacie's mom works at night.

▶ **Subtest 4** Write *coord.* (coordinating) or *correl.* (correlative) to identify each italicized conjunction.

_____ **1.** *Both* her mother *and* her grandmother follow the local ice hockey team.

_____ **2.** They *or* she will probably win first place.

_____ **3.** *Not only* the Austrians *but also* the Swiss speak German.

_____ **4.** The two men *and* the woman hope to meet us at the bus station.

_____ **5.** *Neither* Carter *nor* Bush was reelected president.

_____ **6.** *Either* English *or* science is the most difficult class for Brad.

_____ **7.** Crocuses *and* hyacinths are signs of spring.

_____ **8.** Cats make wonderful pets, *but* gerbils are less trouble.

_____ **9.** *Neither* Rhonda *nor* the Montez sisters do well on pop quizzes.

_____ **10.** She doesn't know whether Pittsburgh *or* Cleveland is closer.

▶ **Subtest 5** Circle each interjection.

1. Oops. I'm sorry about that, Mr. Alexander.

2. Gee, that's a shame.

3. Well, I'm glad that's done!

4. We left our report in the cafeteria. Oh, no!

5. Ha! That's a good one.

▶ **Subtest 6** Complete each sentence by writing a word in the blank that is the part of speech indicated in parentheses.

1. _____ coffee _____ tea are popular in many parts of the world. (conjunction)

2. _____! You're not trying hard enough! (interjection)

3. That was the _____ game I've ever seen! (adjective)

4. Purple _____ blue is probably my favorite color. (conjunction)

5. We see _____ at our birdfeeder all winter long. (common noun)

2. _____! You're not trying hard enough! (interjection)

3. That was the _____ game I've ever seen! (adjective)

4. Purple _____ blue is probably my favorite color. (conjunction)

5. We see _____ at our birdfeeder all winter long. (common noun)

6. The sportscaster from the local television station comes into my parents' restaurant _____. (adverb)

7. There's something black and fuzzy growing _____ the refrigerator. (preposition)

8. She gave the answer _____ when the teacher called on her. (adverb)

9. Stand _____ your sister. (preposition)

10. _____, it certainly is hot today! (interjection)

11. They took their cats with _____ on the camping trip. (pronoun)

12. The cake Dad is baking _____ delicious. (linking verb)

13. Their group gave the report _____ blimps and airships. (preposition)

14. Stir the soup _____. (adverb)

15. We have never _____ such an unusual performance. (action verb)

16. That's a fairly _____ color for a fire engine, isn't it? (adjective)

17. _____ the seniors _____ the sophomores entered a float in the parade. (conjunction)

18. Thomas and _____ are building a soapbox derby racer. (pronoun)

19. _____! The wheel fell off! (interjection)

20. The tiger _____ through the trees. (action verb)

21. The happiest day of my mom's life was when she _____ a police officer. (linking verb)

22. Would you like one of these delicious chocolates from _____? (proper noun)

23. The band played their hit song _____. (adverb)

24. The letter was addressed to Roberto and _____. (pronoun)

25. Max looked very _____ in that costume. (adjective)

Unit 7 Test: Clauses and Complex Sentences

▶ **Subtest 1** Write *S* if the sentence is a simple sentence or *C* if it is a compound sentence. Underline each main clause.

_____ 1. Many people enjoy tennis.

_____ 2. Birds fly, but some squirrels glide through the air.

_____ 3. Dogs and cats are the most popular pets.

_____ 4. The firefighters jumped off the truck and quickly unrolled their hoses.

_____ 5. Brick houses have many advantages; however, they also have some

important disadvantages.

_____ 6. General Motors makes both cars and trucks.

_____ 7. Perry will play the guitar, and Della will play the piano.

_____ 8. Propeller planes were used as airliners in the 1950s, but jets are more

common today.

_____ 9. My mother and father washed and dried the dishes.

_____ 10. Thomas threw the ball, and Rachel caught it.

▶ **Subtest 2** Write *complex* before each complex sentence. Underline the main clause and circle each subordinate clause. If the sentence is not complex, write *S* (simple) or *C* (compound).

_____ 1. I must eat something soon because I'm starving.

_____ 2. Did Darren say that his pen pal lives in Singapore?

_____ 3. His pushy tactics may make him unpopular.

_____ 4. When you plant a tree, dig a hole big enough for all the roots.

_____ 5. Pablo won first prize in the art show at school.

_____ 6. He won't get better grades unless he studies more.

_____ 7. My cousins live in Circleville, which is in central Ohio.

_____ 8. The airplane came to a stop, and the passengers got off.

_____ 9. Mindy and Robert are waiting for Dawn and me in the auditorium.

_____ **10.** The mayor is welcome wherever he goes.

_____ **11.** A Jeep Cherokee is the vehicle that my dad wants to buy.

_____ **12.** My sister is interested in running and biking.

▶ **Subtest 3** Underline each subordinate clause. Write *adj.* if it is an adjective clause, *adv.* if it is an adverb clause, or *N* if it is a noun clause.

_____ **1.** The duke and duchess, who are very rich, donated a building to the school.

_____ **2.** Raoul was early because his mom dropped him off on the way to work.

_____ **3.** My brother, who is sixteen, just got his driver's license.

_____ **4.** Whoever has the lowest score wins in cross-country racing.

_____ **5.** The knight did not know how he would get out of the maze.

_____ **6.** Although the temperature is very high in the desert, it doesn't feel
            uncomfortable.

_____ **7.** Do you remember when she is leaving?

_____ **8.** If people burn old tires, the air can become polluted.

_____ **9.** Young children must understand that matches are dangerous.

_____ **10.** The telephone, which was invented by Alexander Graham Bell, is an
            important communication tool today.

_____ **11.** What really bothers me is his constant humming.

_____ **12.** Amie won't finish her science project unless she works on it tonight.

_____ **13.** The pocket knife that I own has three blades.

_____ **14.** The judges will award first prize to whoever is most deserving.

_____ **15.** Dad was really happy when I joined the computer club.

_____ **16.** The coach smiled broadly as the players lifted her on their shoulders.

_____ **17.** My aunt, whom you've never met, is a detective.

_____ **18.** Why they didn't reserve a place is a puzzle to me.

_____ **19.** Can you tell us whose books these are?

_____ **20.** I haven't eaten a thing since I ate breakfast.

Unit 8 Test: Verbals

▶ **Subtest 1** Underline each participle twice. Write *V* in the blank if it is used as part of a verb phrase or *adj.* if it is used an adjective.

_____ 1. The acrobats' performance was amazing.

_____ 2. Michael felt tired after the long bike ride.

_____ 3. I saw a flashing light across the bay.

_____ 4. The class identified ten different flying insects.

_____ 5. Sarah is raking leaves for Mrs. Wu.

_____ 6. We heard the sound of galloping hooves in the distance.

_____ 7. Todd picked up the scattered pieces of newspaper.

_____ 8. Gina is planning a surprise party for her best friend.

_____ 9. The students had practiced their lines all week.

_____ 10. The howling wind rattled the windows of the old house.

▶ **Subtest 2** Underline each participial phrase twice. Draw one line under the word that the phrase describes.

1. Dad, holding the baby in one arm, waved with the other.

2. Curling up in front of the fire, the dog sighed and closed its eyes.

3. The girl wearing the red sweatshirt and a big grin is my sister.

4. Attracted by the warm climate, many people have moved to Florida.

5. That movie lasting over three hours was about the French and Indian War.

6. The president, wearing a heavy winter coat, addressed the crowd at the rally.

7. Encouraged by the cheering fans, the marathon runner finished the race.

8. Jumping to her feet, Melanie yelled, "Wait for me."

9. We saw two baby birds sleeping in the nest.

10. Smoke billowing from the chimneys darkened the sky.

Name _____ Class _____ Date _____

▶ **Subtest 3** **Circle each gerund. Underline each gerund phrase.**

1. Finding a name for my pet snake wasn't difficult.

2. Running in a marathon is one of Tyler's goals.

3. I think I would like playing the clarinet.

4. Traveling across the country by train sounds like fun.

5. I don't enjoy bicycling on busy streets.

6. Having a costume party is a great idea!

7. The Hyatt family demonstrated making ice cream.

8. Long ago trains began transporting automobiles and coal.

9. Eating sauerkraut on New Year's Day is a tradition in our family.

10. Winning the game is not our only goal.

▶ **Subtest 4** **Write *inf.* in the blank if the sentence contains an infinitive. Write *prep.* if it contains a prepositional phrase.**

_____ 1. To win first prize was Hernando's goal.

_____ 2. Do you like to work alone?

_____ 3. It looks to me as if you have your hands full.

_____ 4. Quentin forgot to leave a message.

_____ 5. Go to the front of the castle and cross the bridge over the moat.

_____ 6. Enrico likes to challenge himself.

_____ 7. The teacher read to the children.

_____ 8. Charlie wants to buy the colored pencils.

_____ 9. Bridget needs to discuss her research.

_____ 10. Hernando is planning to enter the poetry contest.

_____ 11. This train runs from Boston to New York City.

_____ 12. How did you travel from Atlanta to Chicago?

_____ 13. Ken hoped to reach the finish line.

_____ 14. Larry wants to be an astronaut when he is older.

_____ 15. He gave the apple to his sister.

Copyright © by Glencoe/McGraw-Hill

Unit 9 Test: Subject-Verb Agreement

▶ **Subtest 1** Draw one line under the simple subject in each sentence and two lines under the simple predicate. If the subject requires a singular verb, write *S*. If it requires a plural verb, write *pl*.

_____ 1. There is a really large insect on the sidewalk.

_____ 2. The walk from my house to yours takes ten minutes.

_____ 3. The heroes of that novel are two doctors.

_____ 4. The team of three girls and two boys does very well in tournaments.

_____ 5. Here are the directions to my house.

_____ 6. Is your father coming to the track meet?

_____ 7. Does David want to help us on Saturday?

_____ 8. The movie, with all its strange twists, was hard to follow.

_____ 9. When are your grandparents arriving from El Salvador?

_____ 10. Two boys in the chess club live in this apartment building.

_____ 11. Dr. Robarts taps out the message in Morse code.

_____ 12. Here is a challenging puzzle!

_____ 13. The loose shutter bangs against the side of the house.

_____ 14. The members of this group are certainly pleasant people.

_____ 15. This group is certainly pleasant.

_____ 16. Tea splashes over the rim of the cup and into the saucer.

▶ **Subtest 2** Draw two lines under the correct verb form in parentheses. Underline the subject once.

1. The crowd (chant, chants) the player's name.

2. Few of the applicants for the position (was, were) qualified.

3. Dinner for all the club members (was, were) served at seven o'clock.

4. That (seem, seems) like a long time to wait for a refrigerator.

5. The audience at the TV game show (seems, seem) to be in a jolly mood.

6. Either the chimpanzee or the gorillas (was, were) the most interesting.

7. Where (does, do) they buy their sheet music?

8. The news about the earthquake (is, are) on the radio now.

9. Nobody (has, have) returned the survey yet.

10. There (is, are) no people left in the cafeteria.

11. My mom or her sister (need, needs) to take the package to Grandmother.

12. Scissors (works, work) best for cutting that material.

13. Her class (has, have) the most students of any in the sixth grade.

14. The largest mammals in the world (is, are) whales.

15. Much still (need, needs) to be done to get the gym ready for the dance.

16. There (are, is) no more logs in the firewood box.

17. Most of the students (is, are) eager to do the assignment.

18. Six dollars (is, are) lying on the sidewalk.

19. A distance of forty miles (were, was) covered in the bicycle race.

20. Both Danielle and Ashley (says, say) the play was very funny.

21. The two tallest people in our class (are, is) Janine and T.J.

22. The best player and captain of the softball team (is, are) Becky.

23. The audience (takes, take) their seats in the auditorium.

24. (Does, Do) everyone understand the question?

25. What (is, are) the reason for your tardiness?

26. *The Collected Poems of Emily Dickinson* (was, were) my brother's birthday present.

27. Here (is, are) the tickets to the game.

28. Of the students in my grade, several (is, are) going to the movie.

29. Neither medications nor rest (seems, seem) to help the patient.

30. A young girl with three dogs on leashes (was, were) walking down the street.

Unit 10 Test: Diagraming Sentences

▶ **Subtest 1** Diagram each simple subject and simple predicate.

1. Nguyen loves chocolate.

2. Hamsters make terrific pets.

3. Darcie will mail the package for me.

4. My mom got a beautiful pair of cowboy boots for her birthday.

5. Sometimes a police officer takes chances.

▶ **Subtest 2** Diagram each simple subject, simple predicate, direct object, and indirect object.

1. Jason collects football cards.

2. Please give me the paintbrush.

3. Did the owl catch the mouse?

4. Lek sent her parents a photograph of herself at camp.

5. We saw a sand shark at the zoo.

6. How often people jaywalk!

7. Could we discuss this later?

8. Please show your sister the scrapbook.

9. Did you bring me anything from San Francisco?

10. The swimmer gave his mom the medal.

▶ **Subtest 3 Diagram each sentence completely.**

   1. Our lazy dog never chases cars.

   2. The young child carefully crossed the busy road.

   3. We did not understand the meaning of the famous painting.

   4. My father sent a nice gift to his brother.

   5. The soprano gave her director a bouquet of flowers.

   6. Renaldo has rarely run a mile in five minutes.

   7. These cherries taste quite sweet.

   8. David Robinson is his favorite basketball player.

   9. Something in the science laboratory smelled horrible.

   10. The leaves on the trees are slowly turning red.

   11. Claire became vice president of the computer society.

   12. The transfer student from Harrison Middle School plays soccer and volleyball.

Unit 11 Test: Usage Glossary

▶ **Subtest 1** Underline the word in parentheses that best completes each sentence.

1. The little girl's mittens were clipped to her coat so she wouldn't (lose, loose) them.

2. I think I know (whose, who's) books these are.

3. Chad gave Mara the signal to (rise, raise) the window blind.

4. We decided to (set, sit) on the edge of the dock and dangle our feet in the water.

5. (It's, Its) important to use oven mitts whenever you take something out of the oven.

6. This pillow is softer (then, than) that one.

7. (Who's, Whose) turn is it to water the plants?

8. (They're, Their) planning a surprise party for Sheryl.

9. Kayla (choose, chose) a book about Harriet Beecher Stowe by Jean Fritz.

10. Please (accept, except) my congratulations.

11. My apartment building is on Sixth Avenue (among, between) Plum Street and Park Street.

12. The sign at the head of the nature trail read "(Leave, Let) only footprints. Take only memories."

13. I will (sit, set) the china cat down next to the catnip mouse.

14. (A lot of, Thousands of) people attended the outdoor concert.

15. When the judge walked into the courtroom, the bailiff announced, "All (raise; rise)."

16. "Let sleeping dogs (lie, lay)" is an old saying that means "Don't stir up someone who is peacefully unaware of what is going on."

17. If I lend you three dollars, (then, than) I won't have enough money for lunch.

18. My neighbor Mr. Wong is going to (learn, teach) me how to tie different kinds of knots.

19. (Their, They're) vegetable garden contains six different kinds of tomatoes.

20. The gate was (loose, lose) on its hinges.

▶ **Subtest 2** Write *C* in the blank if the word in italics is used correctly. If it is used incorrectly, draw a line through the word and write the correct word in the blank.

_____ **1.** The groundhog scurried *in* the hole when the hawk swooped down toward it.

_____ **2.** *Leave* me help you carry that file cabinet.

_____ **3.** At the empty cabin there was no food in the cupboard *except* a box of stale crackers.

_____ **4.** *Beside* winning a red ribbon at the Hartford Fair, Anne's goat won a blue ribbon at the Knox County Fair.

_____ **5.** A cicada is a large insect that sheds *it's* skin.

_____ **6.** The skaters came *into* the shelter and warmed themselves by the fire.

_____ **7.** Margot wants to *learn* how to spin wool into yarn.

_____ **8.** *Their* unhappy about the results of the election.

_____ **9.** Could you help me *lie* the forks, knives, and spoons on the table?

_____ **10.** This gift shop will *accept* Canadian or United States money.

_____ **11.** Today *its* going to be partly cloudy with a 50 percent chance of rain.

_____ **12.** Please *bring* a side dish and a beverage to the potluck dinner at our house.

_____ **13.** Mario has *all ready* selected a name for his new lizard.

_____ **14.** We planted the daffodils *beside* the tulips in the flower garden.

_____ **15.** *Among* family members Elizabeth is called Betsy.

_____ **16.** We can go *altogether* in Mr. Rivera's van.

_____ **17.** Please *take* some of the leftover turkey when you go home.

_____ **18.** I know both twins have parts in the play, but I don't know *whose* who.

_____ **19.** At 4:00 A.M. the streets were *altogether* deserted.

_____ **20.** I would like to go to the dance with you, but I *already* have plans for Saturday night.

_____ **21.** Just *between* you and me I think that hat is hideous!

_____ **22.** *Chose* a topic from the list on the chalkboard.

_____ **23.** I need to *lay* down and take a nap.

_____ **24.** Layered, *lose* clothing helps the body stay warm in frigid weather.

_____ **25.** I must *raise* at 6:00 A.M. tomorrow to go fishing with Uncle Walter.

Unit 12 Test: Capitalization

• •

▶ **Subtest 1** Draw three lines under each letter that should be capitalized.

1. On my twelfth birthday we ate at an italian restaurant.

2. The first chapter of the book was titled "end of the road."

3. In the magazine section of the library, I browsed through the articles in *golf digest* and *sports illustrated.*

4. Some of the soccer players prefer goal-o-matic athletic shoes.

5. This fall, in either september or october, our class will be going on a hayride at a farm in the country.

6. One of the most beautiful poems by John Keats is "ode to a nightingale."

7. In finland some people speak finnish, while others speak swedish.

8. The news reporter quoted the director of the american dental association.

9. On january 16 a well-known german pianist will give a recital at carnegie hall in new york.

10. The middle ages lasted roughly from A.D. 500 to 1500.

11. This computer software is produced by the technoware company.

12. Monique gave a presentation about the battle of gettysburg, the turning point of the civil war.

13. Did you know that easter usually falls in late march or early april?

14. The newspaper stand offered the *chicago tribune* and the *boston globe.*

15. One of Paul Simon's most widely recorded songs is "bridge over troubled water."

16. Last thursday we heard a group of tunisian musicians at memorial auditorium.

17. The declaration of independence was written in 1776 by Thomas Jefferson.

18. My favorite novel is *lad, a dog.*

19. In San Francisco we saw the golden gate bridge and chinatown.

20. The presidential election of 1844 was a contest between the democratic party and the whig party.

Name _____ Class _____ Date _____

▶ **Subtest 2** **Underline the word in parentheses that best completes the sentence.**

1. My (uncle, Uncle) went into the hospital for an operation.

2. Mrs. Shannon is a (colonel, Colonel) in the army.

3. The sign on the door said Hernando Ramirez, (m.d., M.D.)

4. Is (mother, Mother) trying to decide whether to go back to school?

5. Her (aunt, Aunt) lives in Juneau, Alaska.

6. May (i, I) borrow your raincoat?

7. The man on the television show is (general, General) Forrest J. Wayne.

8. Have you read *The Great Gatsby* by (f., F.) Scott Fitzgerald?

9. I would like to introduce Raymont Alexander, (Ph.d., Ph.D.), our speaker for this evening.

10. Let's ask (dad, Dad) if we can go on the camping trip.

11. The student asked (mr., Mr.) Ransom to explain plant photosynthesis.

12. Franklin (D., d.) Roosevelt led the country during World War II.

13. Did you know that (aunt, Aunt) Martha went backpacking for two weeks in the Sierra Mountains?

14. Her sister is Courtney Davis, (d.d.s., D.D.S.)

15. My (cousins, Cousins) are visiting from Richmond, Virginia.

16. DeShayne is the new (president, President) of the student council.

17. Susan (b., B.) Anthony is pictured on a silver dollar.

18. Vlade's (grandmother, Grandmother) was born in Croatia.

19. The disk jockey played a slow song by Harry Connick (jr., Jr.)

20. She plans to send a letter of protest to (governor, Governor) Williams.

21. Then Hector said, "(the, The) Spanish club needs me as its president."

22. My family has visited every part of this coast from New England through (southern, Southern) Florida.

23. Let's go swimming at Dilton's (creek, Creek).

24. Have you ever seen the moons of (jupiter, Jupiter) through a telescope?

Unit 13 Test: Punctuation

• •

▶ **Subtest 1 Add the correct punctuation as needed.**

1. My You certainly are skillful with that yo-yo.

2. What kind of telescope is this

3. Before railroads were built most goods and products were transported on rivers and canals.

4. Bears hibernate in the winter but wild deer remain active.

5. What an incredible stunt the acrobats performed

6. Joshua did you borrow my book about scuba diving

7. This bus travels to Detroit Michigan Columbus Ohio and Louisville Kentucky.

8. Rick announced, My letter was published in *Cricket* magazine!

9. Please hand me those scissors

10. Darlene sometimes visits her cousins in Dubuque Iowa.

11. Did you just say, Dogs make better pets than cats"

12. At the beginning of the story the two main characters don't get along.

13. President Abraham Lincoln was assassinated on April 14 1865.

14. We too would like to go roller-skating.

15. The road through the state park has many scenic overlooks

16. Mr. Bolles our earth science teacher often tells humorous stories.

17. Staring out the window I let my mind wander.

18. Yes my sister and I do look alike.

19. Jim likes to run at the track Megan prefers to run cross-country.

20. My three brothers' names are Alfonso Roberto and Cesar.

21. Eggs are often sold in several sizes medium, large, and extra large.

22. The wooden top as you might guess is a very old toy

Name _____ Class _____ Date _____

▶ **Subtest 2** Underline the word or words in parentheses that best complete the sentence.

1. Skeezix is a (well trained, well-trained) dog.

2. About (sixty, 60) percent of the parents came to the meeting.

3. The (Wangs', Wang's) backyard is fenced.

4. That black car is (ours, ours').

5. Our basketball team is in (6th, sixth) place in the YWCA league.

6. All (68, sixty-eight) students went on the tour of the post office.

7. We ate only (one-third, one third) of the pie.

8. (It's, Its) too bad the softball game was rained out.

9. This small jade jaguar was carved in (A.D., a.d.) 3000.

10. There are (seventy-six, seventy six) trombones in that marching band.

11. The butterfly had bright orange stripes on (it's, its) black wings.

12. My last name is spelled with two (*t*'s, *t*s).

13. I found (someone's, someones) umbrella under the bleachers.

14. My (great grandmother, great-grandmother) fought forest fires as a girl in Wyoming.

15. Jake got up at 5:30 (AM, A.M.) to go fishing with his uncle.

16. (Mrs, Mrs.) Takahashi is my ballet teacher.

17. The large green sign at the corner read "Bleeker (St., Str.)."

18. The zip-code abbreviation for Arizona is (AZ, Ariz.).

19. The distance from here to Green Bay, Wisconsin, is (480, four hundred eighty) miles.

20. (20, Twenty) people were waiting in the checkout line.

Unit 14 Test: Vocabulary and Spelling

• •

▶ **Subtest 1** Write in the blank the letter of the correct word or words using your knowledge of context clues, word roots, prefixes and suffixes, synonyms and antonyms, and homographs and homophones.

_____ 1. Whichever way she turned in the labyrinth, right or left, Becky found herself lost; it was so confusing she began to wonder if she would ever find her way out. (Choose a synonym for *labyrinth*.)
   a. problem　　　**b.** building　　　**c.** danger　　　**d.** maze

_____ 2. The drama club had a surplus of sixty dollars in its treasury; on the other hand, the glee club's treasury was empty. (Choose an antonym for *surplus*.)
   a. shortage　　　**b.** excess　　　**c.** amount　　　**d.** abundance

_____ 3. I'm not trying to say that a deluge is on the way, but it has rained so much lately that my brother is building an ark in the basement. (Choose a synonym for *deluge*.)
   a. thunderstorm　　**b.** danger　　　**c.** river　　　**d.** flood

_____ 4. The army commander posted sentinels at all the gates of the fort to watch for intruders. (What is another place where sentinels might be posted?)
   a. a prison　　　**b.** a picnic　　　**c.** a church　　　**d.** a street corner

_____ 5. The spy's stubbornness seemed to infuriate the general, who threatened to have the spy imprisoned. (Choose an antonym for *infuriate*.)
   a. inflame　　　**b.** amuse　　　**c.** anger　　　**d.** enrage

_____ 6. The director had just completed a new film about the decade of the 1960s. (What does the prefix in *decade* mean?)
   a. year　　　**b.** before　　　**c.** ten　　　**d.** time

_____ 7. Her humorous letter brightened Peggy's day. (What does the suffix in *humorous* mean?)
   a. full of　　　**b.** state of　　　**c.** related to　　　**d.** in favor of

_____ 8. The judge asked for a transcript of the witness's testimony. (Choose the meaning of the root of *transcript*.)
   a. sound　　　**b.** written　　　**c.** distant　　　**d.** light

_____ 9. Chad was saving his money to buy a microscope. (Choose a homophone for *buy*.)
   a. boy　　　**b.** receive for free　　**c.** purchase　　　**d.** by

_____ 10. The stallion will never desert his herd. (What does *desert* mean in this sentence?)
   a. arid land　　**b.** something sweet　**c.** abandon　　　**d.** deserve

▶ **Subtest 2** In each sentence circle the word that is misspelled. Write the correct spelling in the blank. If no word in the sentence is misspelled, write *C*.

_____ 1. When I want to do one thing, she always wants to do the oppasite.

_____ 2. The skaters were ziping around the rink at a dizzying speed.

_____ 3. I ordered fryed shrimp at the seafood restaurant.

_____ 4. It was so quiet in the woods that it was almost unnatural.

_____ 5. The atmosphere of the short story was suspenseful and wierd.

_____ 6. Children must learn to cross the street safly.

_____ 7. My best friend, Kelli, likes weird music.

_____ 8. Our teacher showed us a photo of her newest grandaughter.

_____ 9. We gently turned the turtle on its back to see its painted underside.

_____ 10. The class changed buses twice to get to the science museum.

_____ 11. My sister Angela was married in a biege gown.

_____ 12. The first-prize winner looked extremly proud.

_____ 13. Marlon read a book called *Modern American Heros.*

_____ 14. Our family would have prefered to stay in the other campground.

_____ 15. My mom and I raked leafs all afternoon.

_____ 16. Reggie was disappointed to lose the first game.

_____ 17. Jan hurryed to the gym to meet her teammates.

_____ 18. My buddys and I hope to watch the Super Bowl at Leo's house.

_____ 19. It's ilegal to ride a moped in this state without a safety helmet.

_____ 20. My dad and I went to the mall to look at new stereos.

_____ 21. We had our choice of topings at the pizza parlor.

_____ 22. Foxs rarely travel in packs; unlike wolves, they are usually seen alone.

_____ 23. I noticed the boy had ink on the cuffs of his sleeves.

_____ 24. Aunt Cleo is my favorite reletive.

Unit 15 Test: Composition

• •

▶ **Subtest 1 Edit the following paragraphs and rewrite them based on your editing marks.**

      Yesterday Justine and me visit the planetarium at the local space museum. What an interesting place? We watched 2 fascinating shows. the first show demonstrated how the sun looks on Earth from the beginning of a day to the end, Imagine being able to show a sunset inside a theater. It was amasing to see the glorious, colors of a fiery sunset projected on the domed ceiling.

      The 2nd show was equally spectacular it demonstrated the entire solar system. From where we were sitting. Us had a star's view of the sun and planets. Looking at Earth as one planet in an entire system. made us think about all the possibilitys in space. Whose knows what else is out there! Justine and i, both, wants to become astronauts and find out for themsleves.

_____

_____

_____

_____

_____

_____

_____

_____

_____

_____

_____

_____

_____

_____

_____

_____

_____

▶ **Subtest 2** **Rewrite each topic sentence to attract a reader's attention better. Add supporting details.**

1. Many sights awaited them. _____

   _____

2. Caitlin is an interesting person. _____

   _____

3. I will never forget last winter. _____

   _____

4. The book was on top of the television set. _____

   _____

   _____

5. The room was empty. _____

   _____

6. Jason bought a parrot. _____

   _____

7. A plant in the back of the garden grew tall. _____

   _____

   _____

8. The Cochrans had an unusual dinner party. _____

   _____

   _____

9. A challenge was issued by Mark. _____

   _____

   _____

10. Our vacation plans went wrong. _____

    _____

    _____

► **Subtest 3** Edit the following paragraphs for unity, clarity, and organization. Then rewrite the paragraphs based on your changes.

Brad is an excellent figure skater. I have known Brad since second grade. He practices for four hours every day. He practices for two hours before school and two hours after school. Sometimes Brad skates in competitions.

He is very dedicated. His routine was quite lively. Last week he won first place in a statewide contest. He wore a pirate costume. He skated to music from *The Pirates of Penzance.* He prepared to jump. I was too scared to watch. I could tell he had landed safely. The audience applauded. Everyone in the arena learned that Brad had won.

I was sure Brad would win until I saw the last skater perform. His name was Steve. He skated to music from *Cats.* He jumped well, too. However, once the judges submitted their scores, I was very proud of him.

_____

_____

_____

_____

_____

_____

_____

_____

_____

_____

_____

_____

_____

_____

_____

_____

_____

_____

▶ **Subtest 4** Use the outline below to write a letter thanking a friend or relative for a birthday gift.

Heading: _____

_____

_____

Salutation:

_____

Body: _____

_____

_____

_____

_____

_____

Complimentary Close: _____

Signature: _____

▶ **Subtest 5** Write a letter to a local city council member that brings attention to the problem of litter in your community.

_____

_____

_____

_____

_____

_____

_____

_____

_____

_____

Answer Key to Testing Program

UNIT 1 TEST: SUBJECTS, PREDICATES, AND SENTENCES

Subtest 1
1. imp.
2. frag.
3. imp.
4. int.
5. dec.
6. frag.
7. exc.
8. int.
9. exc.
10. dec.

Subtest 2 (simple subject | *simple predicate*)
1. Many **people** | *enjoy* country music.
2. The **heroine** of the movie | *leaped* from the villain's car.
3. **Elvis** and his **brother** | *carried* their sleds up the hill.
4. The young **man** | *ate* his dinner at the restaurant.
5. The seven **children** | *ran* and *played* in the tall grass.
6. Our science **teacher** | *drew* a diagram on the chalkboard.
7. A **robin** and a **chickadee** | *flapped* their wings and *flew* away.
8. **We** | *piled* the book and magazines neatly on the table.
9. **Sheep** | *make* very nice pets.
10. **Roses** | *are* often a challenge for gardeners.
11. **Russell** | *saw* the police car.
12. The **girl** | *raised* her hand.
13. A **bus** | *is leaving* for Dallas tonight.
14. **Farmers** | usually *work* long hours.
15. The **movie** | *is* very different from the book.
16. The brown **cows** and the black **pony** | *grazed* in the meadow.
17. **Kay** and **Dan** | *swing* and *slide* at the playground.
18. The boys' **mother** | *played* the piano and *sang* songs.
19. Several **candidates** for mayor | *spoke* at the meeting of the town council.
20. The brown and white **puppy** | *jumped* onto my lap and *licked* my face.

Subtest 3
1. C
2. R
3. S
4. S
5. R
6. C
7. R
8. C
9. R
10. S

UNIT 2 TEST: NOUNS

Subtest 1
1. prop.
2. com.
3. prop.
4. com.
5. com.
6. prop.
7. prop.
8. prop.
9. com.
10. com.
11. prop.
12. com.
13. com.
14. prop.
15. prop.
16. com.
17. com.
18. com.
19. prop.
20. com.

Subtest 2
1. con.
2. con.
3. abst.
4. con.
5. con.
6. abst.
7. abst.
8. con.
9. con.
10. con.
11. con.
12. con.
13. abst.
14. con.
15. abst.
16. con.
17. con.
18. abst.
19. con.
20. con.

Subtest 3
1. comp.
2. coll.
3. coll.
4. comp.
5. comp.
6. coll.
7. coll.
8. coll.
9. comp.
10. comp.
11. comp.
12. comp.
13. comp.
14. coll.
15. comp.
16. comp.
17. coll.
18. coll.
19. coll.
20. comp.

Subtest 4
1. Aiko's
2. drum's
3. disks
4. music boxes
5. Chicago's
6. brothers'
7. book's
8. maids of honor
9. ice cream's
10. boys'
11. women's
12. nut's
13. scientists'
14. James's
15. motion pictures
16. orchestra's
17. runners-up
18. indexes
19. hometowns
20. Rex's
21. actor's
22. Celia's
23. Trish's
24. Trigger's
25. skaters

Subtest 5 (*noun identified*; **appositive**)
1. *Minerva,* **my sister,**
2. *dugong,* **a large marine mammal,**
3. *Vanilla,* **a common ingredient in cakes and cookies,**
4. *vegetable,* **asparagus,**
5. *steamship,* **an early model,**
6. *author,* **Jean Fritz,**
7. *Emily Dickinson,* **the New England poet,**
8. *cardinal,* **the state bird of Ohio,**
9. *Sesame Street,* **the popular children's television show**
10. *Charles Schulz,* **a very successful cartoonist,**
11. *dog,* **a lumbering Labrador retriever**
12. *Geena Davis,* **my favorite actress**
13. *Lucy and Lana,* **my noisy nieces,**
14. *tree,* **the tallest tree on our lot,**
15. *brothers,* **Mitchell and Kyle**
16. *silver,* **a precious metal**
17. *Edith Head,* **a costume designer in the '50s and '60s,**
18. *bookcase,* **a family treasure,**
19. *Stephen Keeler,* **our president**
20. *instructor,* **Teresa,**

UNIT 3 TEST: VERBS

Subtest 1
1. raced
2. know
3. wanted
4. smelled
5. eat
6. tasted
7. like
8. heard
9. fears
10. defeated

Subtest 2 (verb or verb phrase; **indirect object,** *direct object*; type of verb)
1. started; *homework*; T
2. gave; **me**; *helmet*; T
3. visit; I
4. Has sent; **them**; *directions*; T
5. showed; *bracelet*; T
6. watched; *demonstration*; T
7. died; I
8. is causing; **her**; *pain*; T
9. fall; I
10. greeted; *general*; T

Subtest 3 (verb; *predicate noun,* **predicate adjective**; subject)
1. sounds; **scary**; accident
2. grew; **quiet**; Daniel
3. seemed; **unlikely**; It
4. are; *players*; Lydia, Erin
5. appears; **blue**; moon
6. turned; **sixteen**; sister
7. remained; *team*; team

8. taste; **delicious;** raspberries
9. is; *queen;* Sylvia
10. became; *president;* I

Subtest 4 (*correct verb;* tense)
1. *impressed;* past
2. *buys;* present
3. *will baby-sit;* future
4. *worked;* past
5. *will train;* future
6. *falls;* present
7. *will be;* future
8. *delivered;* past
9. *lives;* present
10. *said;* past

Subtest 5 (*helping verb;* **participle,** verb form)
1. *Have;* **eaten;** past
2. *had;* **leaped;** past
3. *was;* **counting;** present
4. *Are;* **expecting;** present
5. *has;* **been;** past
6. *is;* **turning;** present
7. *had;* **decided;** past
8. *were;* **dreading;** present
9. *is;* **running;** present
10. *have;* **asked;** past

Subtest 6
1. has visited
2. was circling
3. had left
4. was waiting
5. have seen
6. had taken
7. is going
8. was planning
9. are thinking
10. have made
11. had given
12. was hoping
13. are having
14. had been
15. was covering

Subtest 7
1. worn
2. stole
3. chose
4. known
5. come
6. thought
7. won
8. swum
9. led
10. left
11. caught
12. paid
13. began
14. brought
15. sung

UNIT 4 TEST: PRONOUNS

Subtest 1 (*pronoun;* **antecedent;** number)
1. *They;* **girls;** plural
2. *He;* **cowboy;** singular
3. *She;* **Margaret Thatcher;** singular
4. *They;* **players;** plural
5. *it;* **car;** singular
6. *They;* **Alexis and her sisters;** plural
7. *them;* **tires;** plural
8. *It;* **milk;** singular
9. *They;* **tomatoes;** plural
10. *He;* **Phil Collins;** singular

Subtest 2
1. its
2. they
3. I
4. it's
5. Hector and she
6. Chen and I
7. us
8. she
9. theirs
10. my brother and I

Subtest 3
1. She (personal), our (possessive)
2. we (personal), something (indefinite)
3. Their (possessive)
4. Others (indefinite), your (possessive), you (personal), it (personal)
5. she (personal), nobody (indefinite)
6. My (possessive)
7. Both (indefinite)
8. I (personal), nothing (indefinite), anybody (indefinite), it (personal)
9. Much (indefinite), their (possessive)
10. me (personal), everything (indefinite), your (possessive)

Subtest 4
1. Which (inter.)
2. themselves (int.)
3. Who (inter.)
4. herself (ref.)
5. himself (int.)

UNIT 5 TEST: ADJECTIVES AND ADVERBS

Subtest 1 (adjective, *participle*)
1. Greek
2. restless
3. happy
4. stern
5. single, difficult
6. bronze
7. beautiful, *decorated*
8. *terrifying*
9. *gleaming,* silver
10. *handwritten,* true
11. *surprising*
12. weary, heavy
13. These, unusual, Indian
14. *relieved*
15. Lovely

Subtest 2
1. those
2. These
3. That
4. that
5. those
6. these
7. Those
8. that
9. This
10. These

Subtest 3 (adverb; word modified)
1. just; enough
2. perfectly; round
3. quickly; sped
4. ornately; carved
5. now; will explain
6. briefly; saw
7. here; will dig
8. hard; studied
9. Someday; must tell
10. Very; calmly/calmly; announced
11. sadly; drooped
12. very; happy
13. woefully; whimpered
14. extremely; fine
15. softly; rustled
16. carefully; unpacked
17. tomorrow; will see
18. quite; surprised

UNIT 6 TEST: PREPOSITIONS, CONJUNCTIONS, AND INTERJECTIONS

Subtest 1 (preposition, *object of the preposition*)
1. **in front of** the large *statue*
2. **in** an apartment *building,* **near** the *park*
3. **behind** *me*
4. **On Top of** *Old Smoky*
5. **among** the *reeds,* **by** the *stream*
6. **across from** *you,* **in** the *cafeteria*
7. **Through** the *Night*
8. **with** *mittens,* **with** *gloves*
9. **toward** its *mother*
10. **during** their *visit,* **to** *Chicago*
11. **By** the *Light,* **of** the Silvery *Moon*
12. **After** *dinner,* **around** the *block*
13. **out** the *door*
14. **on** her scrambled *eggs*
15. **below** the *horizon*
16. **from** the Madding *Crowd,* **of** Thomas Hardy's early *novels*
17. **Inside** the *church,* **on** the left *side*

18. **Between** *you* and *me*
19. **into** the *barrel*
20. **to** the *meeting,* **instead of** *Alicia*

Subtest 2
1. me	4. me	7. *Whom*	10. whom
2. whom	5. him	8. her	
3. her	6. them	9. them	

Subtest 3 (adjective phrase, *adverb phrase,* word modified)
1. *At the museum,* saw; **by many artists,** paintings
2. *beside the chair,* was hiding
3. **on her,** great
4. **in our league,** team
5. *in the contest,* did
6. **on the sofa,** sunglasses
7. *in Mexico,* bought
8. *through the dark tunnel,* sped; **in the mountain,** tunnel
9. **above the stage,** screen
10. *at night,* works

Subtest 4
1. correl.		6. correl.	
2. coord.		7. coord.	
3. correl.		8. coord.	
4. coord.		9. correl.	
5. correl.		10. coord.	

Subtest 5
1. Oops	3. Well	5. Ha
2. Gee	4. Oh, no	

Subtest 6 (Answers will vary.)
1. Both, and	10. Wow	18. I
2. Hey	11. them	19. Oh, no
3. wildest	12. smells	20. crashed
4. or	13. about	21. became
5. cardinals	14. often	22. Belgium
6. frequently	15. seen	23. last
7. inside	16. unusual	24. me
8. quickly	17. Neither, nor	25. foolish
9. beside		

UNIT 7 TEST: CLAUSES AND COMPLEX SENTENCES

Subtest 1 (first main clause; **second main clause**)
1. S; *Many people enjoy tennis.*
2. C; *Birds fly;* **some squirrels glide through the air.**
3. S; *Dogs and cats are the most popular pets.*
4. S; *The firefighters jumped off the truck and quickly unrolled their hoses.*
5. C; *Brick houses have many advantages;* **they also have some important disadvantages.**
6. S; *General Motors makes both cars and trucks.*
7. C; *Perry will play the guitar;* **Della will play the piano.**
8. C; *Propeller planes were used as airliners in the 1950s;* **jets are more common today.**
9. S; *My mother and father washed and dried the dishes.*
10. C; *Thomas threw the ball;* **Rachel caught it.**

Subtest 2 (main clause, *subordinate clause*)
1. complex; **I must eat something soon** *because I'm starving.*

2. complex; **Did Darren say** *that his pen pal lives in Singapore?*
3. S; **His pushy tactics may make him unpopular.**
4. complex; *When you plant a tree,* **dig a hole big enough for all the roots.**
5. S; **Pablo won first prize in the art show at school.**
6. complex; **He won't get better grades** *unless he studies more.*
7. complex; **My cousins live in Circleville,** *which is in central Ohio.*
8. C; **The airplane came to a stop, the passengers got off.**
9. S; **Mindy and Robert are waiting for Dawn and me in the auditorium.**
10. complex; **The mayor is welcome** *wherever he goes.*
11. complex; **A Jeep Cherokee is the vehicle** *that my dad wants to buy.*
12. S; **My sister is interested in running and biking.**

Subtest 3
1. who are very rich; adj.
2. because his mom dropped him off on the way to work; adv.
3. who is sixteen; adj.
4. Whoever has the lowest score; N
5. how he would get out of the maze; N
6. Although the temperature is very high in the desert; adv.
7. when she is leaving; N
8. If people burn old tires; adv.
9. that matches are dangerous; N
10. which was invented by Alexander Graham Bell; adj.
11. What really bothers me; N
12. unless she works on it tonight; adv.
13. that I own; adj.
14. whoever is most deserving; N
15. when I joined the computer club; adv.
16. as the players lifted her on their shoulders; adv.
17. whom you've never met; adj.
18. Why they didn't reserve a place; N
19. whose books these are; N
20. since I ate breakfast; adv

UNIT 8 TEST: VERBALS

Subtest 1 (participle; part of speech)
1. amazing; adj.	6. galloping; adj.
2. tired; adj.	7. scattered; adj.
3. flashing; adj.	8. planning; V
4. flying; adj.	9. practiced; V
5. raking; V	10. howling; adj.

Subtest 2 (phrase; word described)
1. holding the baby in one arm; Dad
2. Curling up in front of the fire; dog
3. wearing the red sweatshirt and a big grin; girl
4. Attracted by the warm climate; people
5. lasting over three hours; movie
6. wearing a heavy winter coat; president
7. Encouraged by the cheering fans; runner
8. Jumping to her feet; Melanie

9. sleeping in the nest; birds
10. billowing from the chimneys; Smoke

Subtest 3 (gerund; phrase)
1. **Finding** a name for my pet snake
2. **Running** in a marathon
3. **playing** the clarinet
4. **Traveling** across the country by train
5. **bicycling** on busy streets
6. **Having** a costume party
7. **making** ice cream
8. **transporting** automobiles and coal
9. **Eating** sauerkraut on New Year's Day
10. **Winning** the game

Subtest 4

1. inf.	6. inf.	11. prep.
2. inf.	7. prep.	12. prep.
3. prep.	8. inf.	13. inf.
4. inf.	9. inf.	14. inf.
5. prep.	10. inf.	15. prep.

UNIT 9 TEST: SUBJECT-VERB AGREEMENT

Subtest 1 (simple subject; *simple predicate*; singular or plural)

1. **insect**; *is*; S
2. **walk**; *takes*; S
3. **heroes**; *are*; pl.
4. **team**; *does*; S
5. **directions**; *are*; pl.
6. **father**; *Is coming*; S
7. **David**; *Does want*; S
8. **movie**; *was*; S
9. **grandparents**; *are arriving*; pl.
10. **boys**; *live*; pl.
11. **Dr. Robarts**; *taps*; S
12. **puzzle**; *is*; S
13. **shutter**; *bangs*; S
14. **members**; *are*; pl.
15. **group**; *is*; S
16. **tea**; *splashes*; S

Subtest 2 (subject; verb form)

1. crowd; chants
2. Few; were
3. Dinner; was
4. That; seems
5. audience; seems
6. chimpanzee, gorillas; were
7. they; do
8. news; is
9. Nobody; has
10. people; are
11. mom, sister; needs
12. Scissors; work
13. class; has
14. mammals; are
15. Much; needs
16. logs; are
17. Most; are
18. dollars; are
19. distance; was
20. Danielle, Ashley; say
21. people; are
22. player, captain; is
23. audience; take
24. everyone; Does
25. reason; is
26. *The Collected Poems of Emily Dickinson*; was
27. tickets; are
28. several; are
29. medications, rest; seems
30. girl; was

UNIT 10 TEST: DIAGRAMING SENTENCES

Subtest 1

1. Nguyen | loves

2. Hamsters | make

3. Darcie | will mail

4. mom | got

5. officer | takes

Subtest 2

1. Jason | collects | cards

2. (you) | Give | paintbrush \ me

3. owl | Did catch | mouse

4. Lek | sent | photograph \ parents

5. We | saw | shark

6. people | jaywalk

7. we | could discuss | this

8. (you) | show | scrapbook \ sister

9. you | did bring | anything \ me

10. swimmer | gave | medal \ mom

Subtest 3

1. dog | chases | cars \ Our \ lazy \ never

2. child | crossed | road \ The \ young \ carefully \ the \ busy

3. We | did understand | meaning \ not \ the \ of painting \ the \ famous

4. father | sent | gift \ My \ to brother \ a \ nice \ his

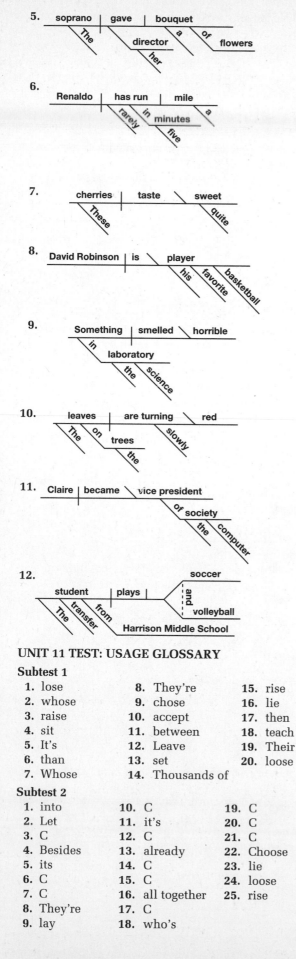

5.

6.

7.

8.

9.

10.

11.

12.

UNIT 11 TEST: USAGE GLOSSARY

Subtest 1

1. lose
2. whose
3. raise
4. sit
5. It's
6. than
7. Whose

8. They're
9. chose
10. accept
11. between
12. Leave
13. set
14. Thousands of

15. rise
16. lie
17. then
18. teach
19. Their
20. loose

Subtest 2

1. into
2. Let
3. C
4. Besides
5. its
6. C
7. C
8. They're
9. lay

10. C
11. it's
12. C
13. already
14. C
15. C
16. all together
17. C
18. who's

19. C
20. C
21. C
22. Choose
23. lie
24. loose
25. rise

UNIT 12 TEST: CAPITALIZATION

Subtest 1

1. Italian
2. End, Road
3. *Golf Digest, Sports Illustrated*
4. Goal-o-Matic *or* Goal-o-matic
5. September, October
6. Ode, Nightingale
7. Finland, Finnish, Swedish
8. American Dental Association
9. January, German, Carnegie Hall, New York
10. Middle Ages
11. Technoware Company
12. Battle of Gettysburg, Civil War
13. Easter, March, April
14. *Chicago Tribune, Boston Globe*
15. Bridge over Troubled Water
16. Thursday, Tunisian, Memorial Auditorium
17. Declaration of Independence
18. *Lad, a Dog*
19. Golden Gate Bridge, Chinatown
20. Democratic, Whig

Subtest 2

1. uncle
2. colonel
3. M.D.
4. Mother
5. aunt
6. I
7. General
8. F.

9. Ph.D.
10. Dad
11. Mr.
12. D.
13. Aunt
14. D.D.S.
15. cousins
16. president

17. B.
18. grandmother
19. Jr.
20. Governor
21. The
22. southern
23. Creek
24. Jupiter

UNIT 13 TEST: PUNCTUATION

Subtest 1

1. My! You certainly are skillful with that yo-yo.
2. What kind of telescope is this?
3. Before railroads were built, most goods and products were transported on rivers and canals.
4. Bears hibernate in the winter, but wild deer remain active.
5. What an incredible stunt the acrobats performed!
6. Joshua, did you borrow my book about scuba diving?
7. This bus travels to Detroit, Michigan; Columbus, Ohio; and Louisville, Kentucky.
8. Rick announced, "My letter was published in *Cricket* magazine!"
9. Please hand me those scissors.
10. Darlene sometimes visits her cousins in Dubuque, Iowa.
11. Did you just say, "Dogs make better pets than cats"?
12. At the beginning of the story, the two main characters don't get along.
13. President Abraham Lincoln was assassinated on April 14, 1865.
14. We, too, would like to go roller-skating.
15. The road through the state park has many scenic overlooks.
16. Mr. Bolles, our earth science teacher, often tells humorous stories.
17. Staring out the window, I let my mind wander.
18. Yes, my sister and I do look alike.

19. Jim likes to run at the track; (*or.*) Megan prefers to run cross-country.
20. My three brothers' names are Alfonso, Roberto, and Cesar.
21. Eggs are often sold in several sizes: medium, large, and extra large.
22. The wooden top, as you might guess, is a very old toy.

Subtest 2

1. well-trained	8. It's	15. A.M.
2. 60	9. A.D.	16. Mrs.
3. Wangs'	10. seventy-six	17. St.
4. ours	11. its	18. AZ
5. sixth	12. *t's*	19. 480
6. sixty-eight	13. someone's	20. Twenty
7. one third	14. great-grandmother	

UNIT 14 TEST: VOCABULARY AND SPELLING

Subtest 1

1. d	4. a	7. a	10. c
2. a	5. b	8. b	
3. d	6. c	9. d	

Subtest 2 (misspelled word; corrected word)

1. oppasite; opposite	13. Heros; Heroes
2. ziping; zipping	14. prefered; preferred
3. fryed; fried	15. leafs; leaves
4. C	16. C
5. wierd; weird	17. hurryed; hurried
6. safly; safely	18. buddys; buddies
7. C	19. ilegal; illegal
8. grandaughter; granddaughter	20. C
9. C	21. topings; toppings
10. C	22. Foxs; Foxes
11. biege; beige	23. C
12. extremly; extremely	24. reletive; relative

UNIT 15 TEST: COMPOSITION

Subtest 1 (Answers will vary.)

Yesterday Justine and I visited the planetarium at the local space museum. What an interesting place! We watched two fascinating shows. The first show demonstrated how the sun looks on Earth from the beginning of a day to the end. Imagine being able to show a sunset inside a theater! It was amazing to see the glorious colors of a fiery sunset projected on the domed ceiling.

The second show was equally spectacular. It demonstrated the entire solar system. From where we were sitting, we had a star's view of the sun and planets. Looking at Earth as one planet in an entire system made us think about all the possibilities in space. Who knows what else is out there? Justine and I both want to become astronauts and find out for ourselves.

Subtest 2 (Answers will vary.)

1. Hundreds of glittering sights awaited them at the amusement park.
2. Caitlin, who has lived in Egypt and Japan, is an interesting person to talk to.
3. I will never forget the frigid temperatures and ice storms we had last winter.
4. The book I searched the entire house for was right where I had left it—on top of the television set.
5. When we reached the spot indicated by the treasure map, the room was empty.
6. Jason entertained his friends by telling them the story of how he bought a parrot.
7. An odd-looking vine in the back of the garden suddenly grew enormous.
8. The Cochrans' dinner party began with an explosion in the kitchen and ended with a wedding on the front lawn.
9. Mark challenged his friends to a winner-take-all skateboarding contest.
10. Our paradise vacation turned into a nightmare before we had even left the travel agency.

Subtest 3 (Answers will vary.)

Brad, whom I have known since second grade, is an excellent figure skater. He practices for four hours every day—two hours before school and two hours after school. He is very dedicated.

Sometimes Brad skates in competitions. Last week he won first place in a statewide contest. His routine was quite lively. He wore a pirate costume and skated to music from *The Pirates of Penzance*. When he prepared to jump, I was too scared to watch, but I could tell from the audience's applause that he had landed safely.

I was sure Brad would win until I saw the last skater perform. His name was Steve and he skated to music from *Cats*. He jumped well, too. However, once the judges submitted their scores, everyone in the arena learned that Brad had won. I was very proud of him.

Subtest 4 (Answers will vary.)

675 Howard Street
Chicago, Illinois 60611
May 27, 1999

Dear Phil,

Thank you for remembering my birthday. I really like the CD you gave me—Scarlet Cardinals is my favorite musical group. I especially like the songs "Create a New World" and "Cold Fusion." Suzanne has already asked me to bring the CD to her party, so everyone will get to hear it. Thanks again.

Your friend,
Bethany

Subtest 5 (Answers will vary.)

Ms. Amy Arnstein
33 Orchard Lane
Sioux Falls, South Dakota 57109
June 2, 1999

Dear Ms. Arnstein:

Would you be interested in starting a campaign against litter? As a member of city council, you could publicize the problem and encourage everyone to help clean up the community. I would be happy to help paint signs or lead a clean-up crew in my neighborhood.

Thank you for allowing me to bring this problem to your attention.

Sincerely,
Stephanie Hunter

CORRELATION CHART

GOALS	WRITER'S CHOICE GRADE 7	WRITER'S CHOICE GRAMMAR WORKBOOK GRADE 7

I. To provide students further practice with grammar usage

GOALS	WRITER'S CHOICE GRADE 7	WRITER'S CHOICE GRAMMAR WORKBOOK GRADE 7
1. subjects, predicates, and sentences	**Unit.Lesson** 7.1 Sentence Fragments 8.2 Sentences and Sentence Fragments 8.1 Kinds of Sentences 8.3 Subjects and Predicates 8.4 Identifying the Subject 8.5 Compound Subjects and Predicates 7.2 Run-on Sentences 8.6 Simple and Compound Sentences Grammar Review 8 Jean Craighead George, from *Water Sky* (model)	**Unit.Lesson** 1.5 Sentence Fragments 1.1 Kinds of Sentences: Declarative and Interrogative 1.2 Kinds of Sentences: Exclamatory and Imperative 1.3 Simple Subjects and Predicates 1.4 Compound Subjects and Predicates 1.6 Simple and Compound Sentences
2. nouns	9.1 Kinds of Nouns 9.5 Collective Nouns 7.8 Incorrect Use of Apostrophes 9.2 Compound Nouns 9.3 Possessive Nouns 9.4 Distinguishing Plurals, Possessives, and Contractions 7.7 Incorrect Use of Commas 9.6 Appositives Grammar Review 9 Anne Morrow Lindbergh, from *Earth Shine* (model)	2.7 Nouns: Proper and Common 2.8 Nouns: Concrete, Abstract, and Collective 2.9 Nouns: Compound and Possessive 2.10 Nouns: Distinguishing Plurals, Possessives, and Contractions 2.11 Appositives
3. verbs	10.1 Action Verbs 10.2 Transitive and Intransitive Verbs 10.3 Verbs with Indirect Objects 10.4 Linking Verbs and Predicate Words 7.4 Incorrect Verb Tense or Form 10.5 Present, Past, and Future Tenses 10.6 Main Verbs and Helping Verbs 10.7 Progressive Forms 10.8 Perfect Tenses 10.9 Irregular Verbs 10.10 More Irregular Verbs Grammar Review 10 Ray Bradbury, from *Dandelion Wine* (model)	3.12 Action Verbs 3.13 Verbs: Transitive and Intransitive 3.14 Verbs with Indirect Objects 3.15 Linking Verbs and Predicate Words 3.16 Verb Tenses: Present, Past, and Future 3.17 Main Verbs and Helping Verbs 3.18 Progressive Forms: Present and Past 3.19 Perfect Tenses: Present and Past 3.20 Irregular Verbs I 3.21 Irregular Verbs II
4. pronouns	11.1 Personal Pronouns 11.2 Pronouns and Antecedents 7.5 Incorrect Use of Pronouns 11.3 Using Pronouns Correctly 11.4 Possessive Pronouns 11.5 Indefinite Pronouns	4.22 Pronouns: Personal 4.23 Pronouns and Antecedents 4.24 Using Pronouns Correctly 4.25 Pronouns: Possessive and Indefinite

GOALS	WRITER'S CHOICE GRADE 7	WRITER'S CHOICE GRAMMAR WORKBOOK GRADE 7
4. pronouns (continued)	**Unit.Lesson** 11.6 Reflexive and Intensive Pronouns 11.7 Interrogative Pronouns Grammar Review 11 Edith Hamilton, from "Phaethon"	**Unit.Lesson** 4.26 Pronouns: Reflexive and Intensive 4.27 Pronouns: Interrogative

5.
adjectives and
adverbs
	12.1 Adjectives
	12.2 Articles and Proper Adjectives
	7.6 Incorrect Use of Adjectives
	12.3 Comparative and Superlative
	        Adjectives
	12.4 More Comparative and Superlative
	        Adjectives
	12.5 Demonstratives
	12.6 Adverbs
	12.7 Intensifiers
	12.8 Comparative and Superlative Adverbs
	12.9 Using Adverbs and Adjectives
	12.10 Avoiding Double Negatives
	Grammar Review 12 Lila Perl, from
	        Mummies, Tombs, and Treasure
	        (model)
		5.28 Adjectives
		5.29 Articles and Proper Adjectives
		5.30 Comparative and Superlative
		        Adjectives
		5.31 More Comparative and Superlative
		        Adjectives
		5.32 Demonstratives
		5.33 Adverbs
		5.34 Intensifiers
		5.35 Adverbs: Comparative and Superlative
		5.36 Using Adverbs and Adjectives
		5.37 Avoiding Double Negatives

6.
prepositions,
conjunctions, and
interjections
	13.1 Prepositions and Prepositional
	        Phrases
	13.2 Pronouns as Objects of Prepositions
	13.3 Prepositional Phrases as Adjectives
	        and Adverbs
	13.4 Conjunctions
	13.5 Interjections
	Grammar Review 13 Laurence Yep, from
	        "The Magical Horse" (model)
		6.38 Prepositions and Prepositional
		        Phrases
		6.39 Pronouns as Objects of Prepositions
		6.40 Prepositional Phrases as Adjectives
		        and Adverbs
		6.41 Conjunctions and Interjections

7.
clauses
	7.1 Sentence Fragment
	7.2 Run-on Sentences
	14.1 Sentences and Clauses
	
	14.2 Complex Sentences
	
	14.3 Adjective Clauses
	14.4 Adverb Clauses
	14.5 Noun Clauses
	Grammar Review 14 John Steinbeck, from
	        The Pearl (model)
		7.42 Simple and Compound Sentences
		        and Main Clauses
		
		7.43 Complex Sentences and Subordinate
		        Clauses
		7.44 Adjective Clauses
		7.45 Adverb Clauses
		7.46 Noun Clauses

8.
verbals
	15.1 Participles and Participial Phrases
	15.2 Gerunds and Gerund Phrases
	15.3 Infinitives and Infinitive Phrases
	Grammar Review 15 Peggy Mann, from
	        Amelia Earhart: First Lady of Flight
	        (model)
		8.47 Participles and Participial Phrases
		8.48 Gerunds and Gerund Phrases
		8.49 Infinitives and Infinitive Phrases

GOALS	WRITER'S CHOICE GRADE 7	WRITER'S CHOICE GRAMMAR WORKBOOK GRADE 7
9. subject-verb agreement	**Unit.Lesson** 7.3 Lack of Subject-Verb Agreement 16.1 Making Subjects and Verbs Agree 16.2 Problems with Locating the Subject 16.3 Collective Nouns and Other Special Subjects 16.4 Indefinite Pronouns as Subjects 16.5 Agreement with Compound Subjects Grammar Review 16 Octavio Paz, from "Robert Frost: Visit to a Poet" (model)	**Unit.Lesson** 9.50 Making Subjects and Verbs Agree 9.51 Locating the Subject 9.52 Collective Nouns and Other Special Subjects 9.53 Indefinite Pronouns as Subjects 9.54 Agreement with Compound Subjects
10. diagraming sentences	18.1 Diagraming Simple Subjects and Simple Predicates 18.2 Diagraming the Four Kinds of Sentences 18.3 Diagraming Direct and Indirect Objects 18.5 Diagraming Predicate Nouns and Predicate Adjectives 18.4 Diagraming Adjectives and Adverbs 18.6 Diagraming Prepositional Phrases 18.7 Diagraming Compound Sentence Parts 18.8 Diagraming Compound Sentences 18.9 Diagraming Complex Sentences with Adjective and Adverb Clauses	10.55 Diagraming Simple Subjects and Predicates 10.56 Diagraming the Four Kinds of Sentences 10.57 Diagraming Direct and Indirect Objects and Predicate Words 10.58 Diagraming Adjectives and Adverbs 10.59 Diagraming Prepositional Phrases 10.60 Diagraming Compound Sentence Parts 10.61 Diagraming Compound Sentences 10.62 Diagraming Complex Sentences with Adjective and Adverb Clauses

II. To provide students further practice with correct usage

11. special usage problems	17.1 Using Troublesome Words I 17.2 Using Troublesome Words II Grammar Review 17 Minfong Ho, from *The Clay Marble* (model)	11.63 Usage: *accept* to *a lot* 11.64 Usage: *beside* to *less* 11.65 Usage: *formally* to *teach* 11.66 Usage: *leave* to *sit* 11.67 Usage: *than* to *you're*

III. To develop in students the ability to use proper punctuation and capitalization

12. capitalization	7.9 Incorrect Use of Capitalization 19.1 Capitalizing Sentences, Quotations, and Letter Parts 19.2 Capitalizing People's Names and Titles 19.3 Capitalizing Place Names 19.4 Capitalizing Other Proper Nouns and Adjectives Grammar Review 19 William Saroyan, from "The Pomegranate Trees" (model)	12.68 Capitalization of Sentences, Quotations, and Salutations 12.69 Capitalization of Names and Titles of Persons 12.70 Capitalization of Names of Places 12.71 Capitalization of Other Proper Nouns and Adjectives
13. punctuation, abbreviations, and numbers	20.1 Using the Period and Other End Marks	13.72 Using the Period and Other End Marks

Correlation Chart **395**

GOALS	WRITER'S CHOICE GRADE 7	WRITER'S CHOICE GRAMMAR WORKBOOK GRADE 7
13. punctuation, abbreviations, and numbers (continued)	**Unit.Lesson** 7.7 Incorrect Use of Commas 20.2 Using Commas I 20.3 Using Commas II 20.4 Using Commas III	**Unit.Lesson** 13.73 Using Commas to Signal Pause or Separation 13.74 Using Commas in Clauses and Compound Sentences 13.75 Using Commas with Titles, Addresses, and Dates 13.76 Using Commas with Direct Quotes, in Letters, and for Clarity 13.77 Commas in Review
	20.5 Using Semicolons and Colons	13.78 Using Semicolons and Colons
	20.6 Using Quotation Marks and Italics	13.79 Using Quotation Marks I 13.80 Using Quotation Marks II 13.81 Italics (Underlining)
	7.8 Incorrect Use of Apostrophes 20.7 Using Apostrophes	13.82 Using Apostrophes
	20.8 Using Hyphens, Dashes, and Parentheses	13.83 Using Hyphens, Dashes, and Parentheses
	20.9 Using Abbreviations	13.84 Using Abbreviations
	20.10 Writing Numbers	13.85 Writing Numbers

IV. To provide further practice in vocabulary and spelling

14. vocabulary and spelling	23.2 Using Context Clues	14.86 Building Vocabulary: Learning from Context
	23.3 Roots, Prefixes, and Suffixes	14.87 Building Vocabulary: Word Roots 14.88 Building Vocabulary: Prefixes and Suffixes Review: Building Vocabulary
	23.4 Synonyms and Antonyms	14.89 Synonyms and Antonyms
	23.5 Homonyms	14.90 Homonyms
	23.6 Spelling Rules I 23.7 Spelling Rules II 23.8 Spelling Problem Words	14.91 Basic Spelling Rules I 14.92 Basic Spelling Rules II Review: Basic Spelling Rules

V. To provide students further practice in the writing process

15. composition Prewriting Drafting Revising Editing Presenting To persuade	2.2 Prewriting: Finding and Exploring a Topic 2.3 Prewriting: Determining Purpose and Audience 2.4 Prewriting: Ordering Ideas 24.6 Taking Notes and Outlining 2.5 Drafting: Getting It in Writing 5.2 Organizing Informative Writing 2.6 Revising: Evaluating a Draft 2.7 Revising: Making Paragraphs Effective 2.8 Revising: Creating Sentence Variety 2.9 Editing: Making Final Adjustments 2.10 Presenting: Sharing Your Writing 1.3 Writing to Celebrate 6.7 Writing a Letter of Complaint 6.2 Forming an Opinion	15.93 The Writing Process: Prewriting 15.98 Outlining 15.94 The Writing Process: Drafting 15.99 Writing Effective Sentences 15.100 Building Paragraphs 15.101 Paragraph Ordering 15.95 The Writing Process: Revising 15.96 The Writing Process: Editing 15.97 The Writing Process: Presenting 15.102 Personal Letters: Formal 15.103 Personal Letters: Informal 15.104 Business Letters: Letters of Request or Complaint 15.105 Business Letters: Stating Your Opinion